# POSTHUMANISM
## IN YOUNG ADULT FICTION

*Children's Literature Association Series*

# POSTHUMANISM IN YOUNG ADULT FICTION
## Finding Humanity in a Posthuman World

Edited by Anita Tarr and Donna R. White

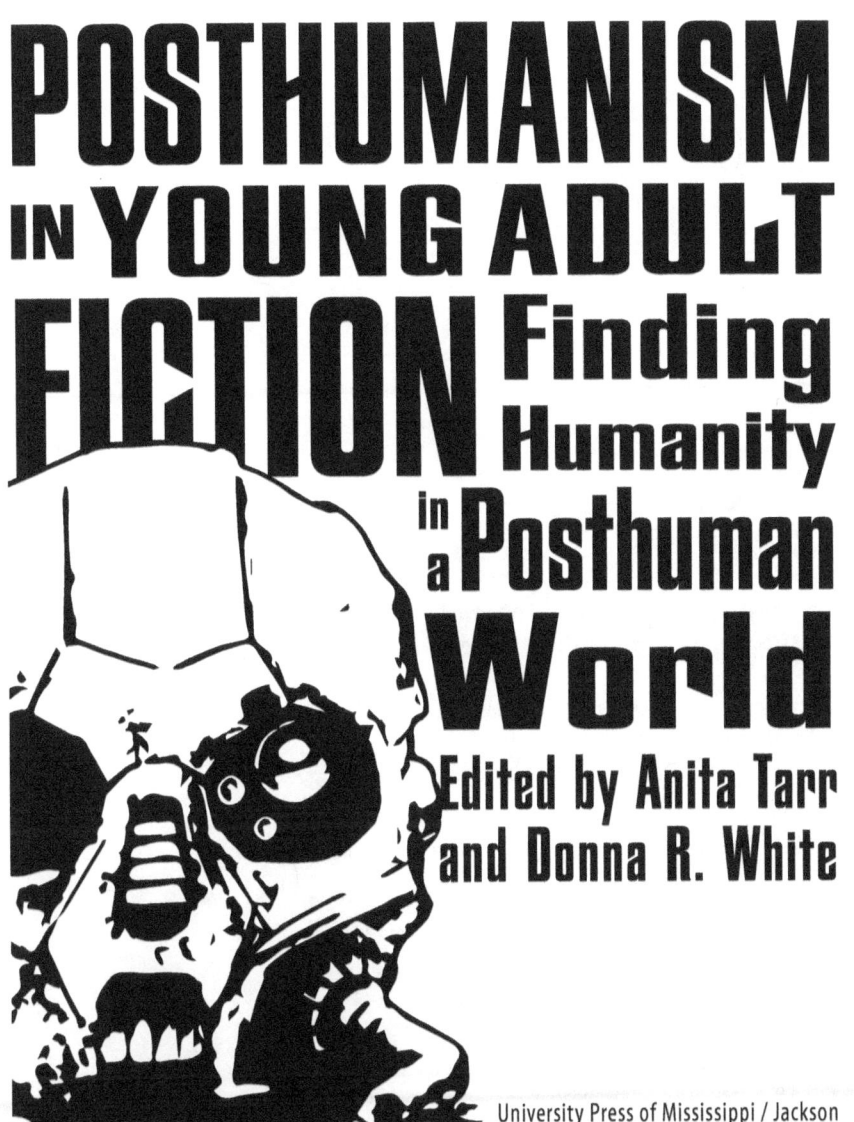

University Press of Mississippi / Jackson

www.upress.state.ms.us

The University Press of Mississippi is a member of
the Association of American University Presses.

Copyright © 2018 by University Press of Mississippi
All rights reserved

First printing 2018
∞

Library of Congress Cataloging-in-Publication Data available

ISBN 978-1-4968-1669-6 (hardcover)
ISBN 978-1-4968-1670-2 (epub single)
ISBN 978-1-4968-1671-9 (epub institutional)
ISBN 978-1-4968-1672-6 (pdf single)
ISBN 978-1-4968-1673-3 (pdf institutional)

British Library Cataloging-in-Publication Data available

# CONTENTS

Acknowledgments . . . . . . . . . . . . . . . . . . . . . . . . . . . . . . . . . . . . . . . . . vii

Introduction . . . . . . . . . . . . . . . . . . . . . . . . . . . . . . . . . . . . . . . . . . . . . . ix

## Part I. Networked Subjectivities

1 **"Open to Me. Maybe I Can Help":** Networked Consciousness and Ethical Subjectivity in Octavia E. Butler's *Mind of My Mind* . . . . . . . . . . . . . . . . . . 3
   *Mathieu Donner*

2 **Information Disembodiment Takeover:** Anxieties of Technological Determinism in Contemporary Coming-of-Age Narratives . . . . . . . . 27
   *Shannon Hervey*

## Part II. The Monstrous Other: Posthuman Bodies

3 **Once upon a Cyborg:** *Cinder* as Posthuman Fairytale . . . . . . . . . . . . . . . . . . . . . . . 55
   *Angela S. Insenga*

4 **The Adolescent Posthuman:** Reimagining Body Image and Identity in Marissa Meyer's *Cinder* and Julianna Baggott's *Pure* . . . . . . . . . . . . . . . . . . . . . . . 75
   *Ferne Merrylees*

5 **"Those Maps Would Have to Change":** Remapping the Borderlines of the Posthuman Body in Leigh Bardugo's Grisha Trilogy . . . . . . . . . . . . . . . . . . . . . 97
   *Maryna Matlock*

6  "Superpowers Don't Always Make You a Superhero": Posthuman Possibilities in Michael Grant's Gone Series .......................................... 117
   *Patricia Kennon*

7  Posthumanism in *The House of the Scorpion* and *The Lord of Opium* ......... 135
   *Donna R. White*

# Part III. Posthumanism in Climate Fiction

8  Coming of Age and the Other: Critical Posthumanism in Paolo Bacigalupi's *Ship Breaker* and *The Drowned Cities* .................... 159
   *Lars Schmeink*

9  Posthuman Potential and Ecological Limit in Future Worlds ............... 179
   *Phoebe Chen*

# Part IV. Accepting/Rejecting Posthumanist Possibilities

10  Negotiating the Human in Ridley Scott's *Prometheus* ..................... 199
    *Torsten Caeners*

11  Posthumanist Magic: Beyond the Boundaries of Humanist Ethics in Lev Grossman's *The Magicians* ........................ 227
    *Tony M. Vinci*

12  China Miéville's Young Adult Novels: Posthumanist Assemblages ........... 247
    *Anita Tarr*

    Notes on Contributors ................................................. 273

    Index ................................................................ 277

# ACKNOWLEDGMENTS

First and foremost, the editors would like to thank our contributors for their patience during the long process of turning this idea into a completed volume. They were always gracious in accepting our comments and timely with their revisions. We are amazed at the wide range of perspectives they have considered to connect posthumanist theories with young adult literature.

Also, many thanks to the Children's Literature Association Publications Committee for their cogent appraisals and acceptance of our work.

We both are grateful to our companion species: Donna for her cats, who liked to type for her when she grew tired; and Anita for her canine Jane Eyre, who slept faithfully next to her desk.

Anita would also like to thank Rodger for his understanding during her long absences in her office.

# INTRODUCTION

> What a piece of work is a man! How noble in reason, how infinite in faculty! In form and moving how express and admirable! In action how like an angel, in apprehension how like a god! The beauty of the world. The paragon of animals. (Hamlet 2.2.303–7)

What does it mean to be human? Is it possible to designate a point in the evolution of *homo sapiens* that marks the first appearance of what we could call a human being, exhibiting human behavior, representing humanity? If there were such a point and such a human, did *homo sapiens* then suddenly stop evolving—never having to adapt to environmental changes or diseases or food availability or agricultural practices? Once this human had acquired the skill of fire-making, would he never see the need to mold a pot or construct a boat or tame a horse or invent Velcro?

Leonardo da Vinci's famous drawing of the perfectly proportioned man (the Vitruvian Man) of the late fifteenth century has helped to crystallize the belief that humankind, in its Western European manifestation, has reached its apogee. The Renaissance and the Enlightenment further propagated the idea that *man* had, physically and mentally, nowhere else to go. (Spiritually, though, was obviously another matter.) Factor in Shakespeare's *Hamlet*, the Rationalists' emphasis on reason over emotion, mind over body, and the value of individual freedom, and what emerges is the liberal humanists' portrait of the human being: rational, independent, autonomous, unified, universal. Mankind reigns supreme over nature and all other species, the center of this world just as the earth was once the center of the universe.

The downfall—but not the extinction, for it is still alive and well in many quarters—of humanism came about as a result of three dramatic steps in philosophy and science, says Neil Badmington: (1) since the acknowledgment that the earth revolves around the sun, and not the other way around, humans must recognize that they are only a small part of the cosmos, not the center of it;

(2) because of Darwin's and others' theories, we are aware that humans were not created to be masters of all creatures but are themselves animals; and (3) Freud's theories of the unconscious testify to the dismantling of humans' belief in themselves as rulers of their own minds (Introduction 6–7). Donna Haraway, who refers to these three steps as "three great historical wounds to the primary narcissism of the self-centered human subject," adds a "fourth wound, the informatics or cyborgian, which infolds organic and technological flesh and so melds that Great Divide [between human and nonhuman] as well" (11–12).

Posthumanism advocates a completely new worldview that contests long-held beliefs based on liberal humanism. The humanists were wrong about human exceptionality. We do not "progress" toward a pinnacle of perfection. Being human has never been a fixed state but always dynamic, still changing, always evolving. Always becoming. Recognizing that *human* is no longer a viable term to describe our multiple manifestations of humanity, theorists have turned to *posthuman* or *posthumanist* as more inclusive designations. The restrictive boundaries are no longer in play. We do not define who we are by what we are not (animal, machine, monster). In general, posthumanism rejects androcentric ideology in order to embrace all forms of beingness. There is no one aspect that makes a being human, not self-awareness or emotion or a sense of justice or artistic creation or problem-solving or having a soul.[1] In recent decades, scientists have proved that every presumably essential human characteristic can be found in other species along with our shared DNA. Pramod K. Nayar explains that symbiosis, our co-evolving with many other species and the environment, makes us what we are. Once-independent bacteria were engulfed by our cells to become the energy pump for mitochondria, for example, and bacteria in our intestines help with digestion. The supposed definitive test for humanity, our DNA, is not unique to us at all; in fact, DNA is only "one of several components with little more than an average role to play" (Nayar 59). It is essential, but it is not sufficient. The Human Genome Project, explains Elaine Graham, was mythologized as "the key to all mysteries of human behavior, both biological and cultural" (119). A primary problem with this conclusion is that a particular DNA code must be chosen to represent all of humanity, which in itself suggests confusion, not only because we share DNA with many other species, but because choosing a representative gene code would essentially disqualify many of us who varied from such an archetype (122). Our DNA code provides statistical possibilities about our particular genes' purpose, but whether these genes are turned on or not is dependent upon the environment. A child might be born with the genes correlating to being a psychopath, but a loving family will likely discount their negative influence. In Graham's words, "the Human Genome Project does not give a definitive account of what it means to be human" (120).

Posthumanists deny the humanist definition of *human* as boundaried, exclusive, unique, exceptional, or naturally dominant. Instead, our intelligence, our bodies, our behavior are all interconnected with other species and the environment. We share the earth with many other creatures and have ourselves created technologies that work organically. There are many animals, of course, that are more humane than some humans, and there are new technologies that not only think better than we do but behave better than we do. Rather than asking what does it mean to be human, we should be asking what does it mean to be posthuman.

## Defining Posthumanism

Neither humanism nor posthumanism is a monolithic concept. Just as there are many types of humanism (e.g. secular, religious, philosophical, cultural), there are also multiple branches of posthumanism, many of which overlap. Andy Miah offers a brief definition: "[P]osthumanism is a philosophical stance about what might be termed a *perpetual becoming*" (98). The type that most people associate with the term posthumanism is often called popular posthumanism and is the perspective we see in popular films like the Matrix and Terminator series[2] and young adult dystopias such as Peter Dickinson's *Eva* or Scott Westerfeld's *Uglies*. Generally speaking, popular posthumanism reflects society's fears of biotechnological changes. Will artificial intelligences replace humans as the dominant species (if we can call AIs a species)? Will medical enhancements or genetic engineering create a stratified society that is even more inflexible than feudalism? Fears of technological change are nothing new, but in the past we feared mostly for our livelihoods: traditional hand-knitters protested against the mechanical stocking frame as far back as the mid-eighteenth century, and the twentieth century saw automobile workers losing jobs to the machines on the assembly lines. We continue to fear for our jobs—robots can replace many jobs that involve physical labor or clerking—but now we are increasingly worried about the effects of technology on our political, social, and family structures and even more afraid for our bodily integrity and the survival of our species.

Whether it is aliens invading Earth from another world or robots rebelling against their human masters, we have always created an Other for us to fear, to demonize, to label as monster, to demarcate boundaries that both protect us and imprison us. Those monsters haunt us, however, demonstrating the leakiness, the permeability of the borders. What posthumanism is trying to do is acknowledge the Other within us: "We [humans] are what/who we are because we are also Other" (Nayar 126). Even more than aliens, though, cyborgs perhaps evoke more fear, primarily because we can see the organic human and mechanical technology working and appearing together. Cyborgs are not alien enough, but not human enough, either. Posthumanists admit that we are all cyborgs, always have been. Cary Wolfe explains that the so-called human "is a fundamentally prosthetic creature that has coevolved with various forms of technicity and materiality, forms that are radically 'not-human' and yet have nevertheless made the human what it is" (xxv). Humans have always used prosthetics and technology—even learning to control fire—to survive (Nayar 20–21): a cane to lean on, glasses to improve vision, a hearing aid, a hook for a missing hand. *Homo sapiens* evolved *because* of interrelationships with other entities, organic and inorganic. Prosthetics are not just replacements or enhancements; they *are* us.

Popular posthumanism is in many ways a response to the branch of posthumanism known as transhumanism. Transhumanists pursue a utopian vision of improving or perfecting the human species via life extension processes (millions of nanobots scouring disease from our bodies and improving our cognitive abilities), genetic enhancement, and biotechnological prostheses. Transhumanism celebrates the notion of a future technological singularity—an idea popularized by Raymond Kurzweil, although he did not come up with it—in which the pace of technological change increases exponentially to the point that it explodes beyond our comprehension and creates a superintelligence that will make humanity redundant unless we have merged with it to become cyborgs. Scholars writing about posthumanism in children's and young adult literature often mistake transhumanism (and the various reactions to it) for the whole of posthumanism, creating a limited and mistaken view of the posthumanist perspective.[3]

Along with popular posthumanism, another reaction to transhumanism is an approach that can be called political posthumanism, practiced by bioconservatives like Francis Fukuyama. In *Our Posthuman Future* (2002), Fukuyama warns about the possibilities of abusing biotechnology and thus creating a radical inequality that endangers liberal democracy and even the nature of the human species. Because of its alarmist views about the disastrous future biotechnology will inevitably lead to, Fukuyama's brand of political posthumanism is sometimes called apocalyptic posthumanism, a term also applied to popular posthumanism. Badmington, for instance, applies the term to both transhumanism and the fear of transhumanism, and Rosi Braidotti refers to "the four horsemen of the posthuman apocalypse: nanotechnology, biotechnology, information technology and cognitive science" (59). Braidotti, however, is one of the political posthumanists who take a more positive view of the future than does Fukuyama. Although she worries about the ways capitalism assigns biovalue to living creatures, commodifying them into so many useful organs and genetic codes, she proposes an "affirmative politics" that transmutes "negative passions into productive and sustainable praxis" (122). In other words, a new kind of posthuman ethics can solve the problems generated by biotechnology.

Braidotti's ideas lead directly to bioethical posthumanism, which converges with the political side in both her works and Fukuyama's. In fact, rather than being a separate branch of posthumanism, the bioethical variety may simply be one aspect of political posthumanism. The bioethical argument rests on the distinction between compensation (or correction) and enhancement (or augmentation). Is it okay to transplant a hand from one newly deceased human to another human who has lost a hand to a shark bite? Then is it also okay to rev up that hand, give it extrasensory touch, steroidize it to become a superhuman hand? What if the hand is entirely mechanical, inorganically operating to produce titanic strength and fantastic dexterity? If enhancement of human abilities becomes more available, the worry is that only the moneyed elite will have access, thus creating a hierarchy not just of possibilities and opportunities, but of actual humanness. Democracy becomes a sham if certain humans can become—or be born as—superior in intellect and physical ability. Fukuyama calls for immediate government regulation of current and future processes that could enhance humans. Envisioning a brave new world of hierarchical positioning, Fukuyama becomes the voice of doom. He and Franco Furger have proposed the creation of a new federal agency to oversee reproductive medicine because the responsibility for regulating biotechnology is currently spread over too many different agencies, making it impossible to deal with the issues ethically.[4]

Another ethical concern of many posthumanists focuses on the civil rights of those who are cyborgs or even completely artificial. Haraway wrote her famous manifesto on cyborgs, and Chris Hables Grey has presented a list of rights for cyborgs. Some of these issues are already in the popular imagination, thanks to *Star Trek: The Next Generation*'s episode in which android Data's right to not be disassembled is debated (see Graham 137–44). Similarly, the question of animal rights has been taken up by Wolfe, Haraway, Peter Singer, and others. This aspect of posthumanism is not just a self-righteous attack against vivisection and breeding animals for meat and clothing, but also indicates a shift in general thinking, reflecting posthumanists' argument that the "barriers between animals and humans have now begun to collapse, identifying the difference between as being one of degree, rather than of kind" (Miah 88). Ending the exclusion of groups of human beings from the demarcation *human* is a large part of posthumanists' political and social agenda. Martha Nussbaum has proposed a "Capabilities Approach" for all beings, marginalized humans as well as animals (Duncan 40–41). Although Nussbaum's main concern is with humans who have disabilities, Janet Duncan points out that animals trained to help the disabled "do not elect to live a life of servitude" (40) and that both animals and the disabled share a history of mistreatment and are still regarded as subhuman or incompetent (46). The mentally or physically ill, children, the poor—and of course, those disenfranchised because of race, religion, sex, or gender—all have been regarded as subhuman or animalistic. Political post-humanism appears to offer a long-awaited adjustment to the unfair attitudes towards the Other that humanism has promoted for so long.

So far we have been discussing the branches of posthumanism that focus primarily on biotechnology. One idea that these varieties of posthumanism share is that, due to advancing technology, the definition of what it means to be human needs to be expanded; nanotechnology, psychopharmacology, genetic engineering, and other fast-developing technologies are altering our bodies and minds in many ways, and information technology is changing the way we think. Internet addiction is a real syndrome, and those afflicted show changes in areas of their brains. Even those of us more casually connected to the Web manifest brain changes: Nicholas Carr laments how we rarely dive into a good novel anymore, which requires our brains to be focused, but instead we skim the surface of the Web, looking for an easy catch of information, which requires speed reading and results in a shorter attention span. However, our brains have always needed to adjust to new technology: noting the various writing instruments we have employed over millennia and how each has contributed to the way our brains work, especially the pen to the typewriter to the keyboard, Carr declares that the brain "is forever a work in progress"—forever *becoming* (38).

The most compelling recent work in posthumanist theory emerges from a cluster of posthumanisms variously labeled philosophical posthumanism, cultural posthumanism, and critical posthumanism. Since it is nearly impossible to parse the differences among these three without a Ph.D. in posthumanism (if such a thing existed), we will lump them together by their shared concerns. All three focus on *post* meaning "after or beyond" and *humanism* referring to the philosophical system of values and beliefs that the Western world has shared for more than six centuries. Most of the best known posthumanist scholars and works fall into one or more of these three types: here we find Haraway's cyborgs and companion species, Wolfe's *Animal Rites*, and Katherine Hayles's embodiment. These posthumanists see themselves as the next generation after the anti-humanists of the 1970s and '80s—thinkers like Derrida and Foucault, who questioned humanist assumptions, and feminists like Hélène Cixous, who specifically challenged humanist ideologies that championed the universal subject as male and marginalized the female as Other. These philosophers set the stage for our current milieu that questions the certainty of the liberal humanist subject—rational, autonomous, and unified—and proposes that we all have multiple subjectivities that are in a constant state of construction. It also suggests that the anthropocentric views of Western humanism are now making way for new views of humanity as part of nature rather than above it, as one of many species that share ecosystems.

These new posthumanisms rotate around three main axes: embodiment, embeddedness, and binaries. Since the publication of Hayles's *How We Became Posthuman* (1999), embodiment has been a centerpiece of critical posthumanism. In humanism, Descartes's *cogito ergo sum* separated the mind from the body and exalted the former over the latter, and early cyberneticists assumed the two could therefore be separated. Hayles took cybernetics and transhumanism to task for their belief that such a separation is possible and that someday we will be able to upload a human consciousness into a machine or free it from physicality completely. No, says Hayles; all knowledge, all information is instantiated in some physical form and cannot exist without it. Human consciousness is tied to the human body, not just in the brain but throughout every micrometer of the physical self. Similarly, that physical self is embedded in a natural environment, not separate from that environment but part of it. "Embodied and embedded" became the catchphrase of these branches of posthumanism. *Binaries* refers to humanism's practice of defining the human by setting it apart from what it is not: if to be human means to be rational, then any being that is not rational is not human. The anti-humanists claimed that the liberal humanist subject set up binaries such as male/female, white/not white, heterosexual/not heterosexual, and colonizer/colonized, and their critiques of humanism's rejection of the Other led to posthumanism's consideration of a different set of Others: animals, monsters, machines, the disabled, cyborgs, clones, and aliens (the kind from other planets). Posthumanists claim that far from being Other, such beings are really part of the posthumanist self. In published works, the main focus has been on challenging the mind/body, human/animal, human/nature, and human/machine binaries.

These newer posthumanist thinkers also caution against throwing the baby out with the bathwater. That is, they warn that posthumanism cannot exist without humanism. David Ross Fryer explains that "humanism has had to reformulate itself, absorb the anti-humanist critique, and emerge in a new form" (7). Stefan Herbrechter defines a critical posthumanism as "postanthropocentric" with "the possibility of a return to some fundamental aspects of humanism" (106), fearing the "dehumanizing tendencies" of posthumanism and the possibility "that the dissolution of a universalist notion of humanity would foster the return of old racisms in a new form" (71). Badmington speaks of "humanism's ghost" ("Theorizing" 15), and Bart Simon writes that "the posthuman is figured not as a radical break from humanism, in the form of neither transcendence nor rejection, but rather as implicated in the ongoing critique of what it means to be human" (8). Posthumanism is not so much anti-humanism as it is a re-envisioning. The barbarians are at the gates; however, the walls of the fortress have never been made of stone but are simply an intersection to allow free-flowing traffic between the body and the environment, between so-called humans and nonhumans.

This brief discussion of the differences among the various branches of posthumanism has necessarily oversimplified the concepts, but it will be useful for readers who are meeting posthumanism for the first time. All of the branches overlap and interact in multiple ways. Posthumanist theory, fittingly enough, is networked and communal, fluid and changeable, always becoming—a mirror image of the posthumanist self.

## The Essays

Investigating how posthumanist theories are being used in young adult literature is important for several reasons. Hayles writes, "Literary texts are not, of course, merely passive conduits. They actively shape what the technologies mean and what the scientific theories signify in cultural contexts" (21). They deal with the moral and cultural repercussions that celebrated leaps in science do not always foresee. Likewise, literature influences scientific theories; there are cross currents between the two, the heart of which is narrative (21). As such, we would suggest that literary texts (and films and games, etc.) serve as the body for scientific theories, each one offering a unique way that the theory or data is articulated. Young adult literature is our focus here because, as Hayles says, communicating theories and ideologies is best done through telling stories. Infants can be and are indoctrinated with specific ideologies through stories told and read to them, but the children are barely aware of these influences and are not cognitively capable of thinking about them until their teenage years. During adolescence, when young adults are beginning to consider consequences, meaning, and purpose, readers can actually reflect on what is being presented to them and decide for themselves how they might change the way they think about the world and their place in it. Furthermore, adolescents are especially concerned with body issues, and embodiment is a crucial aspect of posthumanism. We are not proposing that posthumanist ideas *should* be incorporated into young adult literature; rather, we seek here through our essays to investigate *how* posthumanism is or is not being conveyed.

Stories for young adults are particularly well suited for posthumanist study because, as Badmington suggests, adolescents, as they operate in our socially constructed stage of in-between-ness, are already posthumanist: "To challenge both school and law," as so many adolescents do, "is to challenge the culture of humanism and the humanism of culture. . . . Teenagers, it seems, would not be teenagers if they did not act a little inhuman, a little alien-ated, from time to time" (*Alien Chic* 127).

Posthumanist considerations are relatively new in philosophy, science, and politics, and analyses of posthumanist thought in young adult literature are just beginning to emerge. But the impetus is growing rapidly, as we see from the scholarship of just this decade. Victoria Flanagan's *Technology and Identity in Young Adult Fiction: The Posthuman Subject* (2014) focuses on how biotechnology affects citizenship and surveillance and how focalization and point of view construct posthumanist subjectivity. The following year yielded two more volumes on posthumanism: Amy Ratelle's *Animality in Children's Literature and Film* (2015), which approaches posthumanism via animal studies; and Zoe Jaques's *Children's Literature and the Posthuman: Animal, Environment, Cyborg* (2015), which examines children's fantasy through the lens of posthumanism. These monographs are not the first attempts to apply posthumanism to children's literature. An essay collection published two years earlier entitled *Contemporary Dystopian Fiction for Young Adults: Brave New Teenagers* (edited by Balaka Basu, Katherine R. Broad, and Carrie Hintz, 2013) contains a section that is purportedly about posthumanism, but since only one of the essays discusses the term, this volume does not make a major contribution to the understanding of posthumanism. Kerry Mallan has written two essays on posthumanism and YA literature: the first is included in *New World Orders in Contemporary Children's Literature: Utopian Transformations* (2008); another is included in *Contemporary Children's Literature and Film: Engaging with Theory* (2011). There are also nearly a dozen journal articles that tackle posthumanism in children's and young adult literature.[5] Obviously, applying posthumanist theory to children's and young adult literature is a recent undertaking that still needs a lot of work.

One of the outstanding features of our collection of essays is that all of our contributors are focused exclusively on applying posthumanist theory to recent works for young adult readers. All of the essays uncover the power inequities implicit in the novels, which so often serve as motivations for adolescent characters to question traditional social hierarchies and construct new moral values that reflect their personal experiences. All of them also explore various ideas of posthumanism, but many concentrate on anti-anthropocentrism, democratization of power and body enhancements, hybridity, melting of borders between human and nonhuman, multiplicity and plurality, and the body as networking with the environment.

## Part I. Networked Subjectivities

This section includes two essays that focus on the posthumanist concept of subjectivity as multiplicitous and constantly under construction. In the first essay, Mathieu Donner recovers the late Octavia Butler's novels as posthumanist in "'Open to Me. Maybe I Can Help': Networked Consciousness and Ethical Subjectivity in Octavia E. Butler's *Mind of My Mind*." Donner shows how Butler anticipates postmodernist thinking in her portrayals of characters whose minds are capable of networking with each other, exposing this contradiction: in order to gain a sense of self, one must become vulnerable and join with others. The second essay, by Shannon Hervey, looks at contemporary YA novels set in present time: "Information Disembodiment Takeover: Anxieties of Technological Determinism in Contemporary Coming-of-Age Narratives." Showcasing adolescent characters writing in public forums of social media, the question Hervey poses is whether these characters are writers or are being written, as they realize that there is no individualized self but that which is distributed across the ether. Both of these essays suggest that posthumanist theories are not just anti-androcentric but embrace feminist ideals of connection rather than egotism, of equality rather than dominance, of sharing rather than conquering.

## Part II. The Monstrous Other: Posthuman Bodies

The five essays here all investigate adolescent bodies that, due to scientific or magical causes, are transformed or artificially created. At issue is how these characters cope with and adjust to their transformed bodies. Some of the protagonists of the examined novels display superhuman abilities, some are cyborgs or clones, and some are human/animal hybrids. These essays bring together adolescents' concerns about their changing bodies with posthumanist ideas that dissolve the borders between human and Other, re-envisioning the body as connected to others. Angela Insenga's essay, "Once Upon a Cyborg: *Cinder* as Posthuman Fairytale," details how Marissa Meyer takes the hyper body-conscious fairytale of "Cinderella" and re-envisions it, with all its adolescent anxieties, into a broader story of global concern. Cinder herself is the epicenter of cultural upheaval involving technologically enhanced cyborgs, earth humans, and magically enhanced Lunars. Ferne Merrylees discusses both *Cinder* and Julianna Baggott's Pure trilogy in the second essay, "The Adolescent Posthuman: Reimagining Body Image and Identity in Marissa Meyer's *Cinder* and Julianna Baggott's *Pure*." Both female protagonists suffer discrimination because of their hybridity (Cinder is a cyborg; Pressia's hand is fused with a doll's head), and both eventually accept their hybrid bodies. In the third essay, "'Those Maps Would Have to Change': Remapping the Borderlines of the Posthuman Body in Leigh Bardugo's Grisha Trilogy," Maryna Matlock offers a feminist analysis of the tangled relationship between the all-powerful Darkling and the Sun Summoner, Alina, set in a re-envisioned Tsarist Russia. The superhuman powers gifted to them make them posthuman, but the Darkling is highly anthropocentric, clashing with Alina's growing sense of empowerment as a hybrid being. The fourth essay in this section, Patricia Kennon's "'Superpowers Don't Always Make You a Superhero': Posthuman Possibilities in Michael Grant's Gone Series," exposes the humanist workings underlying the posthumanist veneer of this popular series. Kennon shows how a group of under-fifteen-year-olds who suddenly have superhuman powers and are forced to live on their own under a dome generally perform as expected; that is, some superpowers are used for good, and some are used for evil. In "Posthumanism in *The House of the Scorpion* and *The Lord of Opium*," Donna White analyzes Nancy Farmer's two dystopian novels, which describe the development of Matt, a clone created solely to provide donor organs to El Patrón, ruler of the isolated border country of Opium between Mexico and the United States. As a posthuman, Matt's status changes from object to animal to human ruler, and he struggles to accommodate the many factors of his subjectivity. Every one of these five essays evokes the fears of transhumanism, that if scientific progress is not controlled, human society will be stratified and divided between the haves and have-nots. Enhancement implies responsibility; power and privilege corrupt.

## Part III. Posthumanism in Climate Fiction

Lars Schmeink focuses on the chimeric character Tool in "Coming of Age and the Other: Critical Posthumanism in Paolo Bacigalupi's *Ship Breaker* and *The Drowned Cities*." In spite of a setting of a corporation-dominated, flood-ravaged dystopic world, Bacigalupi's two novels offer a kind of hope as his adolescent characters, including Tool, learn that their subjectivity is determined by the decisions they make, not by their DNA.[6] In "Posthuman Potential and Ecological Limit in Future Worlds," Phoebe Chen compares three novels' resolutions to the question of human subjectivity in a post-ecological crisis-damaged world. The three female protagonists in Janet Edwards's *Earth Girl*, Stacey Jay's *Of Beast and Beauty*, and Sherri L. Smith's *Orleans* fight against biological determinism as they seek to reconnect with nature. Both Schmeink's and Chen's essays are focused on novels that could be considered "cli-fi," that is, climate fiction, concerned with climate change. Even very young children can come home from preschool and lecture their parents on the importance of recycling, but older children and adolescents are cognitively developed enough to empathize with characters who are coping with global flooding and nuclear fallout. Paolo Bacigalupi, whose novels are analyzed by Schmeink, in particular feels the weight of future climate change and writes novels that show us "how to live in and beyond . . . a ruined world" ("Telling"). Preparing for a tsunami or earthquake or asteroid strike or even a zombie apocalypse inspires people to hunker down and consider any means necessary to survive. Fiction, however, says Bacigalupi, has a "superpower," because it "builds empathy" for people whom we don't know but who are struggling to create a "sustainable, global future" ("Telling").

### Part IV. Accepting/Rejecting Posthumanist Possibilities

This last section includes three essays: Torsten Caeners's "Negotiating the Human in Ridley Scott's *Prometheus*"; "Posthumanist Magic: Beyond the Boundaries of Humanist Ethics in Lev Grossman's *The Magicians*," by Tony Vinci; and "China Miéville's Young Adult Novels: Posthumanist Assemblages," by Anita Tarr. Caeners illustrates how, as a precursor to the Alien films, *Prometheus* is particularly suited as an example of YA literature. Although the Alien series obviously foregrounds the humanist human/alien oppositional binary, Caeners argues, through his psychoanalysis of the two main characters, that Elizabeth Scott and the android David each display typical adolescent anxieties—indeed, that posthumanist theories are the ideal method to use to analyze adolescent development. Caeners examines how Elizabeth rejects posthumanist possibilities while David accepts them. The last two essays in our collection focus on how two YA novelists employ posthumanist ideas to overturn the conventions of fantasy narrative. Vinci's essay examines how Quentin, gifted with the potential to be a powerful magician, rejects his posthumanist possibilities—realizing that "becoming a magician means becoming posthuman"—and maintains the humanistic reality/fantasy binary. Quentin will not allow himself to be open to multiple worlds and multiple subjectivities, preferring to view fantasy as adolescent wish-fulfillment. Tarr's essay investigates Miéville's works for younger audiences, which employ his Marxist ideologies to challenge the authority of the book, of adults, of worldviews, of just about everything. Although Miéville will not always allow his characters to accept posthumanist possibilities, at his best he creates a space for posthumanist ideas to carry the characters beyond what they had thought possible.

The essays in this collection reveal how writers for young adults have their typing fingers on the pulse of new thinking; their stories create vibrations that emanate outwards, causing the walls that define humanism to come tumbling down—in fact, we see that the walls were never really there in the first place. Our speciesism, our sense of privilege as (male) humans, our fortressing against the Other have all been performances, socially constructed acts based on fear and dominance. We are all hybrids. We are all networked with others and the environment. We are all posthuman.

## Notes

1. Elephants can paint pictures of flowers, and Koko the gorilla could talk and use sign language; both of the activities were the result of their learning from humans. But chimpanzees using tools and dolphins passing down to subsequent generations how to round up fish and push them up onto a beach are techniques these animals developed themselves.

2. Of course, not all science fiction movies display posthumanist tendencies. Badmington theorizes that science fiction movies of the fifties, such as *Them* (1954) and *Invasion of the Body Snatchers* (1956, 1978), produced paranoia about nuclear energy and otherworld aliens, and *Independence Day* (1996) and the *Alien* series (1979 and still going) reinforce this cultural paranoia. *Close Encounters of the Third Kind* (1977) and *E.T.* (1982), both Steven Spielberg productions, helped change the dynamic, making aliens seem friendlier (*Alien Chic* 50–62). More recently South African director Neil Blomkamp, with both *District 9* (2009) and *Chappie* (2015), has challenged the popular fear of cyborgs and androids, though with *Chappie* he does follow the highly questionable theory that intellect and personality can be downloaded from one entity to another. The television series *Battlestar Galactica* (2004–9), although beginning with the usual animosity toward artificial beings known as Cylons, ended up questioning whether there is really any difference between humans and Cylons, and, furthermore, why should we care? Our point here is that, as evidenced in movies in popular culture, there is already a change in the public imagination.

3. See, for example, Elaine Ostry's much-quoted article "'Is He Still Human? Are You?': Young Adult Science Fiction in the Posthuman Age" and Erin Newcomb's "The Soul of the Clone: Coming of Age as a Posthuman in Nancy Farmer's *The House of the Scorpion*."

4. See Furger and Fukuyama, "Beyond Bioethics: A Proposal for Modernizing the Regulation of Human Biotechnologies."

5. Hilary S. Crew, "Not So Brave a World: The Representation of Human Cloning in Science Fiction for Young Adults" (2004); Elaine Ostry, "'Is He Still Human? Are You?': Young Adult Science Fiction in the Posthuman Age" (2004); John Stephens, "Performativity and the Child Who May Not Be a Child" (2006); Naarah Sawers, "Capitalism's New Handmaiden: The Biotechnical World Negotiated Through Children's Fiction" (2009); Richard Gooding, "*Clockwork*: Philip Pullman's Posthuman Fairy Tale" (2011); Kinga Földváry, "In Search of a Lost Future: The Posthuman Child" (2014); Annette Wannamaker, "A 'Heap of Meaning': Objects, Aesthetics and the Posthuman Child in Janne Teller's Y.A. Novel *Nothing*" (2015); Petros Panaou, "'What Have They Done to You Now, Tally?': Post-posthuman Heroine vs. Transhumanist Scientist in the Young Adult Science Fiction Series Uglies" (2015); Fiona McCulloch, "'No Longer Just Human': The Posthuman Child in Beth Revis's Across the Universe Trilogy" (2016); Dawn Heinecken, "Contact Zones: Humans, Horses, and the Stories of Marguerite Henry" (2017).

6. Bacigalupi has recently published the final book in this trilogy: *Tool of War* (2017). As the title suggests, it focuses on the character of Tool; however, it was not available when Lars Schmeink wrote this article.

## Works Cited

Badmington, Neil. *Alien Chic: Posthumanism and the Other Within*. New York: Routledge, 2004. Print.

———. Introduction. *Posthumanism*. Ed. Neil Badmington. New York: Palgrave Macmillan, 2000. 1–10. Print. Readers in Cultural Criticism.

———. "Theorizing Posthumanism." *Cultural Critique* 53 (2003): 10–27. Project Muse. Web. 4 June 2016.

Basu, Balaka, Katherine R. Broad, and Carrie Hintz, eds. *Contemporary Dystopian Fiction for Young Adults: Brave New Teenagers*. New York: Routledge, 2013. Print. Children's Literature and Culture 93.

Bradford, Clare, Kerry Mallen, John Stephens, and Robyn McCallum. *New World Orders in Contemporary Children's Literature: Utopian Transformations*. New York: Palgrave Macmillan, 2008. Print. Critical Approaches to Children's Literature.

Braidotti, Rosi. *The Posthuman*. Cambridge: Polity, 2013. Print.

Carr, Nicholas. *The Shallows*. New York: Norton, 2010. Print.

Crew, Hilary S. "Not So Brave a World: The Representation of Human Cloning in Science Fiction for Young Adults." *Lion and the Unicorn* 28.2 (2004): 203–21. Project Muse. Web. 4 June 2016.

Duncan, Janet M. "Interdependence, Capability, and Competence as a Framework for Eco-Ability." *Earth, Animal, and Disability Liberation: The Rise of the Eco-Ability Movement*. Ed. Anthony J. Nocell, II, Judy K. C. Bentley, and Janet M. Duncan. New York: Peter Lang, 2012. Print.

Flanagan, Victoria. *Technology and Identity in Young Adult Fiction: The Posthuman Subject*. New York: Palgrave Macmillan, 2014. Print. Critical Approaches to Children's Literature.

Földváry, Kinga. "In Search of a Lost Future: The Posthuman Child." *European Journal of English Studies* 18.2 (2014): 207–20. *Taylor & Francis Online*. Web. 17 Dec. 2014.

Fryer, David Ross. *Thinking Queerly: Race, Sex, Gender, and the Ethics of Identity.* Boulder: Paradigm, 2010. Print.

Fukuyama, Francis. *Our Posthuman Future: Consequences of the Biotechnology Revolution.* New York: Farrar, Straus and Giroux, 2002. Print.

Furger, Franco, and Francis Fukuyama. "Beyond Bioethics: A Proposal for Modernizing the Regulation of Human Biotechnologies." *Innovations: Technology, Governance, Globalization* 2.4 (2007): 117–27. *MIT Press Journals*. Web. 14 June 2016.

Gooding, Richard. "Clockwork: Philip Pullman's Posthuman Fairy Tale." *Children's Literature in Education* 42 (2011): 308–24. *Academic Search Complete*. Web. 4 June 2016.

Graham, Elaine L. *Representations of the Post/Human: Monsters, Aliens and Others in Popular Culture.* New Brunswick: Rutgers UP, 2002. Print.

Grey, Chris Hables. *Cyborg Citizen: Politics in the Posthuman Age.* New York: Routledge, 2001. Print.

Haraway, Donna. *When Species Meet.* Minneapolis: U of Minnesota P, 2008. Print.

Hayles, N. Katherine. *How We Became Posthuman: Virtual Bodies in Cybernetics, Literature, Informatics.* Chicago: U of Chicago P, 1999. Print.

Heinecken, Dawn. "Contact Zones: Humans, Horses, and the Stories of Marguerite Henry." *Children's Literature Association Quarterly* 42.1 (2017): 21–42. *Project Muse*. Web. 16 May 2017.

Herbrechter, Stefan. *Posthumanism: A Critical Analysis.* London: Bloomsbury, 2013. Print.

Jaques, Zoe. *Children's Literature and the Posthuman: Animal, Environment, Cyborg.* New York: Routledge, 2015. Print. Children's Literature and Culture 102.

Mallan, Kerry. "Technoscience, Critical Theory, and Children's Fiction." *Contemporary Children's Literature and Film: Engaging with Theory.* Ed. Kerry Mallan and Clare Bradford. New York: Palgrave Macmillan, 2011. 147–67. Print. Critical Approaches to Children's Literature.

McCulloch, Fiona. "'No Longer Just Human': The Posthuman Child in Beth Revis's Across the Universe Trilogy." *Children's Literature Association Quarterly* 41.1 (2016): 74–92. Print.

Miah, Andy. "A Critical History of Posthumanism." *Medical Enhancement and Posthumanity.* Ed. Bert Gordijn and Ruth Chadwick. Berlin: Springer, 2008. 71–94. *ResearchGate*. Web. 7 May 2016.

Nayar, Pramod K. *Posthumanism.* Cambridge: Polity, 2014.

Newcomb, Erin T. "The Soul of the Clone: Coming of Age as a Posthuman in Nancy Farmer's *The House of the Scorpion*." *Contemporary Dystopian Fiction for Young Adults: Brave New Teenagers.* Ed. Balaka Basu, Katherine R. Broad, and Carrie Hintz. New York: Routledge, 2013. 175–88. Print. Children's Literature and Culture 93.

Ostry, Elaine. "'Is He Still Human? Are You?': Young Adult Science Fiction in the Posthuman Age." *Lion and the Unicorn* 28.2 (2004): 222–46. *Project Muse*. Web. 27 May 2016.

Panaou, Petros. "'What Have They Done to You Now, Tally?': Post-posthuman Heroine vs. Transhumanist Scientist in the Young Adult Science Fiction Series Uglies." *Bookbird* 53.1 (2015): 64–74. *Literature Online*. Web. 16 May 2017.

Ratelle, Amy. *Animality in Children's Literature and Film.* New York: Palgrave Macmillan, 2015. Print. Critical Approaches to Children's Literature.

Sawers, Naarah. "Capitalism's New Handmaiden: The Biotechnical World Negotiated through Children's Fiction." *Children's Literature in Education* 40 (2009): 169–79. Academic Search Complete. Web. 4 June 2016.

Simon, Bart. "Introduction: Toward a Critique of Posthuman Futures." *Cultural Critique* 53 (2003): 1–9. Project Muse. Web. 18 Sept. 2016.

Stephens, John. "Performativity and the Child Who May Not Be a Child." *Papers: Explorations into Children's Literature* 16.1 (2006): 5–13. Papers: Explorations into Children's Literature. Web. 4 June 2016.

"Telling the Story of Climate Change—In Fiction." *Science Friday*. Hosted by John Dankowsky. NPR. 8 April 2016. Web. Accessed 13 Apr. 2016.

Wannamaker, Annette. "A 'Heap of Meaning': Objects, Aesthetics and the Posthuman Child in Janne Teller's Y.A. Novel *Nothing*." *Lion and the Unicorn* 39.1 (2015): 82–99. Project Muse. Web. 16 May 2017.

Wolfe, Cary. *Animal Rites: American Culture, The Discourse of the Species, and Posthumanist Theory*. Chicago: U of Chicago P, 2003.

———. *What is Posthumanism?* Minneapolis: U of Minnesota P, 2010.

# PART I
# NETWORKED SUBJECTIVITIES

# 1

# "OPEN TO ME. MAYBE I CAN HELP"
## Networked Consciousness and Ethical Subjectivity in Octavia E. Butler's *Mind of My Mind*

*Mathieu Donner*

A few pages into *Mind of My Mind* (1977), the second novel in Octavia E. Butler's Patternist series, the narrator informs us that the novel's antagonist, Doro, is a being whose original body died four thousand years ago as a result of his transition, his coming-of-age and coming-to-power. Jumping from body to body in order to survive ever since, he has been "struggling to build a race around himself" (*Mind* 16). *Wild Seed* (1980), Butler's prequel to *Mind of My Mind*, is predominantly concerned with this eugenic program. Focused around the conflict that emerges from Doro's encounter with another powerful being who is able not only to regenerate and transform herself but also to heal others, it explores the problematic ethical dilemma at the heart of Doro's program. A more or less direct continuation of that novel, *Mind of My Mind* proposes to expand this exploration of the ethical obligation we bear toward others and to relocate it within a broader argument about the emergence of the political and social subject in an ever-expanding and interconnected world. As in many of her other novels, Butler's interest lies less in the interaction between humans and technology—here telepathic communication, itself an obvious analogy for the new technologies emerging at the time[1]—than in technology's impact on social relations between human beings (Melzer 94). Through her series, she signals the potential for political engagement that these technologies open up, specifically for younger generations of activists, while at the same time interrogating the limitations presented by the networked form of ethical subjectivities they produce.

Butler's Patternmaster series exposes the benefits presented by the kind of networked model of subjectivity enforced by interconnectivity. Yet as the term itself already suggests, this enforcement is not without problems. Far from

3

introducing a new utopian system of shared humanity, Butler's narrative operates more directly as a "caution against utopian generalizations" (Melzer 93), a critique of the posthumanist dream and the new power relations established by new technologies.[2]

Focusing primarily on *Mind of My Mind*,[3] this essay explores the relation Butler weaves between new technologies, adolescence, and ethical responsibility. Reading the novel alongside critical theories on the limits of the mind and their implication for our understanding of the self and its place in the world, I argue that through the coming-of-age story of her protagonist, Butler invites a reconceptualization of subjectivity understood not as an individual quest for uniqueness but as an ethical awakening to the presence, both outside and at the core of the self, of an irreducible and infinite form of alterity. Exploring the individual and collective impact of communication, Butler exposes the vulnerability at the heart of the subject as well as the performative, fluid, and inherently protean dimension of the human, thus challenging the relevance and necessity of its *post-* incarnation and reframing it instead as yet another source of epistemological violence.

## Adolescence, Liminality, and Vulnerability

According to Butler herself, her fiction has tended to be shaped and informed by a vivid interest in the power dynamics at work in people's relations to others. Her particular predilection for science fiction stems from the opportunity it allows "to imagine new ways of thinking about people and power" (qtd. in Mixon). In her Patternist series, this interest primarily unfolds through the tensions that come to surround the control of the telepathic Pattern implied in the series's title. Opening in Africa in the midst of the colonial age, *Wild Seed* introduces readers to Doro, a four-thousand-year-old patriarch intent on creating a new race by bringing "his people" (57) together, that is, by gathering individuals who, like him, present some sort of supernatural powers. In *Mind of My Mind*, Doro finds himself confronted with one of his own protégées, the young Mary, who, as she awakes to her powers (when she transitions from "latent" to "active"), accidentally triggers the formation of a telepathic pattern of mental connections. Creating precisely the interconnected community of gifted individuals Doro had hoped to achieve through careful and forced interbreeding, Mary quickly becomes a threat to his supremacy.

Mary's emergence as the new and legitimate leader of her community also slowly awakens her to the responsibility and vulnerability that this position inherently entails. Literally tied to her people, their safety, and well-being, Mary finds herself "neatly positioned within a pattern or web structure" (Hampton 50), forced to evolve, transform, and maybe even die within the dangerous social network she inherited. A fundamental part of both Mary's experience and Butler's narrative, this adherence to the network is, however, not a simple fact of life, a product of existence. Instead, transition is shown to occur around puberty and to concern only a select group of people. When Mary unconsciously triggers the transition of the thirty-year-old Clay, Doro's disbelief highlights the chronologically limited dimension of the process: "Clay lost any chance he had for becoming an active over ten years ago" (*Mind* 136). Implicitly linked to adolescence, the shift from latent to active reframes the individual's entrance into adulthood as a dangerous and often fatal, yet necessary, ritual of passage.

Sociological and psychological approaches have both tended to conceptualize adolescence as a period of transition from dependence to independence. Marked by a move away from the child's reliance on adults and toward a form of individually detached and mature mode of positionality, adolescence has traditionally been understood as the entrance into the cleanly separated and distinct realm of the Symbolic. Introducing distance, becoming adult corresponds to a parallel move toward autonomy. It implies "find[ing] and liv[ing] in accordance with one's own law," states Jennifer Nedelsky (10), becoming one's own master. However, and as Nedelsky herself recognizes, this positioning does not necessarily preclude social inscription. As her use of the word "find" suggests, "we do not make or even exactly choose our own law" (10). Instead, the finding of one's own law is a process always already "shaped by the society in which one lives and the relationships that are a part of one's life" (10).

In a similar way, Butler's reframing of adolescence is not simply a transformative process through which latent people are given access to the complex and fully fleshed subjectivity signified by becoming an active. On the contrary, the transitional period unfolds as a threshold between singularity and plurality, a site of passage from exclusion to inclusion, from enclosure to openness. Doro explains that transition operates primarily through the removal of a latent's "childhood shield," the "mental protection that served young actives until they were old enough to stand transition" (*Mind* 52). It involves opening the egocentric and centripetal self to the centrifugal forces surrounding it. In her conceptualization of adolescence as a mode of passage toward plurality, Butler thus introduces a precursor to Nedelsky's understanding of autonomy. Indeed, transition here not only implies conceptualizing youth as a space of liminality, a "cultural realm that has few or none of the attributes of the past or coming state" or a space "neither here nor there . . . betwixt and between the positions assigned and arrayed by law, custom, convention, and ceremonial" (Turner 95); it also entails reframing this passage as a fundamental deterritorialization and reterritorialization whose primary effect is the inscription of the subject within a broad network of relations. In the shift from childhood to adulthood, the subject develops a socially active, majoritarian, and culturally recognized form; she becomes subject, understood here as an autonomous state of existence.[4] However, at the same time, this entrance into subjectivity implies a simultaneous recognition of the wider network from which subjectivity itself derives its meaning and power.

Though this conceptualization of adolescence as a move from dependence to autonomy (understood here as a form of being *with*) may seem rather obvious, its implications are less clear. First, what this approach presupposes is a recapture of adolescence as a necessary and inevitable identity crisis. If we take as foundation of identity theory a certain form of compulsory continuity, a thinking "that holds that 'selfhood is sameness,' that there is such a thing as continuity of identity over time and for all time" (Elliott 15), adolescence can but be perceived and received as a rupture. It involves a violent and forceful shattering of the core foundations and possibility of identity. Best explained by Karl, Mary's husband, transition implies change: "you're changing. I've been watching you change, wondering how far you would go" (*Mind* 188). However, more than a simple ontological shift, transition is also shaped by the system of power relations within which it is enacted. Having once dominated Mary from his position of authority as subject, Karl recognizes that her access to the Pattern has affected her own position within their relationship, confessing that he "can remember when it was easier to intimidate you" (188). Beyond a simple status change, the disruption signaled by adolescence marks the opening up of the self to a powerful form of ambiguity. It suggests a puncturing of the subject's ontological core and the opening up of a bi-directional flow responsible for the evanescence of the same and a simultaneous intrusion of difference. Projected and caught up in a temporary limbic space of indeterminacy, the adolescent subject or subject-to-be finds herself "somehow left out in the patterning of society" (Douglas 96), relegated to a space of cultural nonexistence.

As Mary Douglas argues, "To have been in the margin is to have been in contact with danger, to have been at a source of power" (98). Despite being a source of a tremendous amount of power, however, being outside of culture is also marked by vulnerability. Doro's earlier reference to the lifting up of shields already suggests that adolescence unfolds, for Butler, as a space of violent openness. This potential for harm is highlighted when Mary herself undergoes transition. As Doro explains to Karl, during her transition "she's going to be reaching for the worst possible stuff.... That's what's going to attract her attention. She'll get an avalanche of it—violence, pain, fear, whatever" (*Mind* 53). Having been stripped of the social shields conventionally thought to be protecting children, Mary finds herself subjected to an overpowering and overwhelming bombardment of impressions and emotions, utterly vulnerable to a broad network of influences and forces. The Patternist's transition thus unfolds as a ritual of passage similar to those that have traditionally surrounded the move from childhood to adulthood. Themselves triggered and structured by peer influence, these rituals often imply some very real physical danger to the initiate herself and are part and product of a cultural movement whose objective is to encourage, if not directly force, its new members to conform to social expectations, to enter the dominant framework of society.

Vulnerability and openness to the world come to characterize the liminal period that is adolescence in Butler's series. It signals a transition which, though painful and often dangerous to the individual (Doro himself died in transition before finding himself able to switch from body to body and thus remaining immortal), remains a necessary step in the emergence of a fully formed subject. In other words, transition operates as what Simon Critchley calls "the original trauma" at the core of being ("The Original Traumatism" 237). As Karl slowly realizes when he attempts to shield Mary mid-transition in order to protect her from the world, "He was preventing her from going through the suffering that was normal for a person in transition. And since the suffering was normal, perhaps it was in some way necessary" (*Mind* 58). Terrifying and potentially lethal as it may be, the vulnerability implicit in transition is also what constitutes the foundation of subjectivity itself. Creating the conditions for the intrusion of influence into the ontological fabric of the subject, its openness allows the subject to emerge as a relational project. It creates a framework within which the concepts of personal identity and selfhood can be thought of as a continuous state of "dialogue with society, with language, and with other people" (McCallum 3), a collective enterprise engaging both the subject and her world.

Opening up a rethinking of subjectivity not as a solipsistic event produced by the subject's own action but rather as a collective enterprise through which each and all subjects "*develop into* responsible moral persons through socialization," this reading of adolescence also suggests that each individual "rise[s] to meet the expectations [her] caregivers have for [her]" (Cash, "Extended Cognition" 652); that is, each individual emerges as subject within a structure of demands and obligations. By locating in vulnerability the core foundation of the normal adolescent experience, Butler thus echoes traditional sociological approaches that have tended to perceive in it a moment of crisis between individuality and collectivity. As B. Bradford Brown, Jeremy P. Brakken, Suzanne W. Ameringer, and Shelly D. Mahon suggest, "one of the most prominent concerns that American adults express about adolescence as a life stage [is] the power of peer influence" (17). Contingent on an implicit recognition of the vulnerability of all adolescents, this approach reads in this transitional phase the moment of emergence of the idiosyncratic adult. Yet it also suggests that this development is one that requires external input, perceiving therefore in adolescence a period of struggle in which the subject attempts to achieve or construct her own sense of self while continuously being subjected to concurrent and often violent forms of influence. In traditional readings, adolescence thus unfolds as a paradoxical double movement: an inward-looking "quest to find uniqueness, to stand from the crowd," and a simultaneous outward search for belonging, a "need for a group" or a desire to fit in (Blanton and Burkley 94).

The framing of puberty as the period of emergence of a strong and autonomous self, capable of shielding itself from the bombarding network of forces that strive to remodel while also being part and product of these forces, takes as foundational structure a strict separation between public and private spheres. It reframes the self as a property over which both the collective and the individual simultaneously claim mastery. This conflict between group and individual is at the heart of Butler's work. Informed by a long-lasting interest in the legacy of slavery, her novels tend to narrate the journey of a protagonist toward self-fulfillment and self-ownership. *Wild Seed* describes Doro's strategies to recruit Anyanwu, who has established her own settlement of networked people in colonized Africa. She explains her vision of the world in which "some people [are] masters and some [are] slaves" (9). This initial dichotomic framing sets the tone for the entirety of the Patternist series. Later in the novel, when Doro invites Anyanwu to join his people in a small settlement upriver where, as he tells her, "[o]nly my people live" and "they do not enslave each other," she simply reminds him how redundant this enslaving would be, his people "[a]ll belonging, as they do, to [him]" (95). Similarly, in *Mind of My Mind*, when Mary is introduced to her new house, she defines Karl's relation to his servants as one of absolute ownership: "Karl owned his servants more thoroughly than even Doro usually owned people. Karl owned their minds" (37). As all those examples suggest, within the economy of the series, becoming subject corresponds to a shift in ownership or, as Mary phrases it, to the idea that, by undergoing transition, she would, for once in her life, "be one of the owners instead of one of the owned" (102). As Nedelsky points out, the process of becoming an autonomous adult involves a shift in power relations, a process by way of which one becomes one's own master.

This impression of mastery, however, ultimately unfolds as little but an illusion or a fantasy. Indeed, the transitional process through which it emerges invariably requires passage through a space of opening in which the amount of "mental garbage" (*Mind* 62)—a thinly veiled analogy for peer influence—can, if left unchecked, lead one to madness. As the narrator in *Wild Seed* explains, transition "was the time when the madness of absorbing everyone else's feelings seemed endless—when in desperation, they would do anything to stop the pain" (186). In many ways, this period of vulnerability is defined throughout the series as a temporary and transitional event in the life of the active subject, the presence of first Doro and later Mary herself both suggesting a more permanent form of dispossession. As Mary herself realizes later in *Mind of My Mind*, not even her own position as master of the Pattern leaves her untouched by vulnerability. Indeed, Mary makes clear to Doro her own contempt for dependency: "I never liked depending on other people and their cars, anyway. When I rode the bus, I went when I wanted, where I wanted" (103). Yet Mary exposes the paradoxical nature of the subject's position when, coming back after a long day, she finds herself seeking the bonds she previously rejected: "I didn't want to be alone. I couldn't have put into words how much I suddenly didn't want to be alone, couldn't stand to be alone, how much it scared me" (103). More important, though, is her next realization, that is, that at that precise moment of need, when "Karl came back to my bed without another word[,] . . . he could have really hurt me with just a few words" (103). Revealing what Anthony Elliott calls "the illusions of a purely private world, supposedly unaffected or cut off from the wider social world" (4), Butler invites her readers to challenge and question the solipsistic perspective on the self that has come to define Western philosophy at least since Descartes. In its stead, she promotes an understanding of subjectivity born out of "human interaction and interpersonal relationships" (Elliott 28–29), a vision in which the subject always emerges in an open and bi-directional relation to the world.

However, as Butler's emphasis on the proprietary dimension of the self also suggests, this relation is far from being entirely unproblematic. Indeed, if we take the self to be composed of a set of positions in constant dialogue with the culture that set the conditions for their emergence, we also have to recognize that the different positions available to the subject do not all have the same authoritative weight, that is, to acknowledge that, as Mason Cash argues, "different positions within such relationships shaped individuals in different ways, reinforcing patterns of power and privilege, disadvantage and disempowerment, ability and inability" ("Cognition Without Borders" 69). To inscribe the subject within a network of relation, to challenge the strict delineation between private and public spheres, necessarily entails remaking subjectivity as an object in partial control of powers outside the subject. It implies accepting that all notions of individual control and mastery are but illusions, that, as the narrator suggests when relating how Anyanwu "in her pride . . . had denied that she was a slave" (*Wild Seed* 130), to become subject always already involves a dimension of objectivity. It entails a simultaneous acknowledgment of the subject's own object-ness, of its dependency on, if not enslavement to, the fundamentally normative structures of the collective.

Within the economy of the series, Doro and later the Pattern as a whole can thus be perceived as an analogy for the normative dimension often imputed by peer influence theory to the relation established between an individual and the community she is part of. In its most extreme stance, this approach leads us close to Ludwig Wittgenstein's understanding of thought as a derivate of our common languages. Best exemplified in the question he puts forth in his *Philosophical Investigations* when asking, can one "'have the thought before finding the expression?' what would one have to reply? And what to the question 'What did the thought, as it existed before its expression, consist in?'" (§335), the usefulness of Wittgenstein's conceptualization of language for us here lies in its articulation of the restrictive dimension of all collective structures on the positions available to the subject. It suggests that, as Hubert J. M. Hermans posits, "people do not construct meanings in a free space with equal opportunities to express their views. On the contrary, meanings are organized and colored by the societal positions represented by the collectivities to which they belong" (263).

Already implicit in Anyanwu's binary conception of society—her dichotomic reading of the world is itself a product of the slave/master relation that shaped her early experience—this conceptualization of epistemology as a fundamentally social phenomenon fully materializes in the Patternist society of Butler's next novel, *Patternmaster*. Taking place centuries after the events of *Mind of My Mind*, *Patternmaster* tells the story of a young telepath, Teray, striving to gain authority and power amidst a rigidly hierarchized society ruled by the eponymous Patternmaster and in which "mutes," people without any telepathic ability, act as servants; "outsiders," telepaths who do not properly belong to any clan, are considered "permanent inferior[s]"; and only apprentices may one day become their own masters (*Patternmaster* 15). As this tripartite organization suggests, the social structures of Teray's society set up the conditions for knowledge production and, through this, operate as an organizing principle in the delineation of the subject itself. Defining who qualifies as a person and who does not, the hegemonic system governed by the Patternmaster configures the set of rights and privileges attached to the notion of personhood itself and thus strictly delineates the available set of positions individuals are allowed to occupy and the kinds of thought they are allowed to have. A collective mindset, the pattern becomes here an epistemic muzzle whose role and function is to contain the revolutionary potential of the subject.

Though it has often been approached as such, peer influence and the collective voice it represents are not in and of themselves inherently negative. As

Brown et al. explain, "peer influence is multidirectional; it is capable of encouraging healthy as well as harmful behaviour" (18). One might even argue, as Joseph P. Allen and Jill Antonishak do, that "being influenced to behave in a way that one's peers find most acceptable and attractive is actually very close to being precisely the definition of what it means to be a well-socialized individual" (142). As the notion of "mental institution" suggests, cultural systems are at the core of our thinking process. They "allow us to think in ways that [are] not possible without such institutions" and, in a very literal sense, materialize as epistemological extensions of our minds (Gallagher 6). Originally posited by Andy Clark and David Chalmers, the notion of the extended mind thus proposes to bridge the gap between the solipsistic mind and the world within which it navigates. And though their theory has been largely discussed, implemented, and expanded upon since its publication, the question at its heart—"where does the mind stop and the rest of the world begin?" (7)—continues to resonate within contemporary culture. Promoting a conception of consciousness as an amalgam of internal and external elements, a complex structure supported by "promiscuously opportunistic, soft-assembled, hybrid coalitions of neural, bodily and environmental elements" (Cash, "Cognition Without Borders" 61), their approach proposed a deterritorialization and decentering of the mind whose primary effect is the dissolution of the latter's boundaries and the implementation of a mode of "cognition without borders" (69).

Throughout the Patternist series, Butler exposes some of the problems one quickly encounters when adopting this approach. Indeed, as her narrator explains early in *Mind of My Mind*, entrance into the Pattern comes at a great price: "Doro had never before been able to keep a pair of active telepaths together without killing one of them and taking that one's place. This would be explanation enough for them. Because by the time they had been together for a while they would know how hard it was for two actives to be together without losing themselves, merging into each other uncontrollably" (36). Operating under a constant threat of de-differentiation, active telepaths are forced to continuously protect and reiterate the limits of their own minds against foreign incursions. The intensity of their negative reaction to the absolution of the mind's boundaries is not, in and of itself, surprising. Indeed, autonomy and control have historically occupied a core if not foundational place in Western conceptions of personhood. As Nedelsky reminds us, the concept of self-determination—a concept that obviously relies on a prior delineation of the self—"remains one of the most powerful dimensions of liberal thought" (8). And because self and mind have traditionally been conceived as interchangeable notions, Butler's adoption of the extended mind theory presents a violent challenge to the ability of the subject to pursue what has commonly been understood as one of the core stages of "normal" human development, that is, the "pursuit of a distinct identity" (Blanton and Burkley 96), or the creation of an idiosyncratic and unique narrative of self.

Notwithstanding the strong hold that the notions of autonomy and mastery continue to have on our cultural conception of selfhood, numerous philosophers have argued for a more porous and fluid understanding of the subject. Indeed, from Jean-Jacques Rousseau's notorious theory of social corruption to Sigmund Freud and later Jacques Lacan's conception of ego development as a dialogical process between *Innenwelt* and *Umwelt*, or Jean-Paul Sartre's enquiry into the relation between self and Other, the simple dichotomic model that saw the self as emerging against an Other from which it is completely distanced has been considerably complicated. Supported by recent developments in cognitive sciences and the discovery of mirror neurons in both child and adult brains (Gallese and Goldman 493), these approaches all invite us to reframe, or more accurately to *deframe*, the subject as an entity in constant relation to the world around her. They rearticulate the essence of the schism traditionally established between inner and outer realms, self and others, as a dialogical relation in which "our minds, our bodies and the world are continuous" (Pepperell 20). Making away with the possibility of absolute autonomy, this reframing of the subject as an entity in relation projects the individual into a wide network of similarly connected individuals, a worldwide web of sorts, in which each and every one of us is essentially both part and product of everybody else; or, as Mary herself puts it, where all subjects become "a pattern strand. A slender, fragile-seeming thread . . . a member of the pattern" (*Mind* 132).

## Self, Space, and Ethics

Where this reading of the subject as a mode of being-in-and-with-the-world has been widely adopted by posthumanist theory, it is one thing to argue, as Jean-François Lyotard does, that "no self is an island" (15) and quite another to do away with the notion of self altogether. Assuming the culturally necessary endurance of a form of individuality, subjectivity, or selfhood, we are thus left with a problematic question as to how we can think of the self as an entity distanced and separated from others while simultaneously recognizing the invariably social and plural dimension of this self. Toward the end of Butler's novel, Mary enters into a long fight with Doro. While striking mental blows at each other, Doro inadvertently steps into Mary's own mental space and finds himself trapped by her Pattern. As the narrator explains, "she had used her mental closeness with him to draw him into her web. Her Pattern. He panicked. He was a member of the Pattern. A Patternist. Property. Mary's property" (*Mind* 219). If Mary's emphasis on ownership here highlights again the conflictual dimension of the individual's relation to the collective, it is her next comment that truly allows the possibility of an answer. As she relates, this move to absorb Doro within her Pattern not only results in his inscription within the collective, but also signals the forced absorption by Doro of the collective itself: "the thread was part of him. A mental limb. A limb that he could find no way to sever" (*Mind* 219). Moving away from a framing of the individual as a single, coherent entity, Butler's reading introduces a rethinking of the self as "a matrix of dispersed but interconnected processes" (Pepperell 25), an entity both marked by idiosyncrasy and shaped by her inherent relational nature. In the Pattern, the individual subject not only finds a space of inscription, a way to enter a large, interconnected, and complex matrix of relations but also finds the vulnerability intrinsic to subjectivity itself or that which allows her to move away from Doro's nonhumanity.

Indeed, though it is here directly connected to the suprahuman capacities of Butler's telepaths, the interconnectedness characteristic of the Pattern is nothing but a fundamentally human dimension. Operating along the same lines as the deterritorializing effects Andy Clark assigns to new modes of communication, the Pattern signals the dislocation of the subject away from the unitary and centralized position she so far occupied. As Clark suggests when he invites readers to "look at all the people around you talking on their cell phones" and asks us to consider where they are (89), modes of communication create networks whose primary effect is to deterritorialize the subject, or at least to offer an illusion of dislocation. By opening up the subject to almost continuous contacts with the world, these technologies—whether these are cellphones, the internet, or Butler's Pattern—inscribe her "into a web of personal and business communications, which deliberately disrespects current physical location" (Clark 89) and unbind the subject from the strict geography of her body. Like Doro's ability to transcend bodily boundaries—as he explains, his existence relies not upon a single body but on a "series of bodies" (*Mind* 217)—Mary's Pattern presents a violent challenge to the notion of a localized and localizable subject. Offering a fantasized dream of ubiquity, it "transform[s] our senses of locality and community" (Morley 3) and opens the subject up to a dematerialized reading of space where her own individuation is not bound by the traditional limits of her own self.

This deterritorialization of the subject is not without important and problematic consequences. Indeed, beyond suggesting a possible form of transcendentalism, an escape away from the limits of the flesh, Mary's Pattern and its subsequent expansion in *Patternmaster* also contain a profoundly ethical dimension. In his history of the self, Charles Taylor argues that "To know who I am is a species of knowing where I stand" (27). Outside of the link it draws between identity and space, what Taylor's argument here highlights is the intrinsic relation that space entertains with morality and ethics. The superimposition of space and moral positioning implicit in his mobilization of the verb "to stand" is not, in other words, accidental. Morality is intrinsically tied to proximity, to the point that, as Arne Johan Vetlesen explains, "encountering distance, morality halts" (17). Unable to "transcend whatever distance may have come between ego and alter" (Vetlesen 17), morality expands only to those with whom the subject is in direct contact. In his work on ethics, Emmanuel Levinas similarly defines ethics as a relation to the face of the Other in which "the face is exposed, menaced, as if inviting us to an act of violence" while, at the same time, forbidding us to kill (*Ethics and Infinity* 86). For Levinas, ethics is proximity to "the other human being, whom I cannot evade, comprehend, or kill and before whom I am called to justice, to justify myself" (Critchley, *The Ethics of Deconstruction* 5).

As this already suggests, Levinas's reading of ethics as a mode of address, a proximal relation to the Other to whom and for whom I am responsible, operates on the ground of a subject whose boundaries are clearly delineated. Itself the product of a liberal philosophy that locates as its foundation an autonomous and bounded subject, Levinas's ethics tends to rely for its functioning on an understanding of the individual subject as distinct from other subjects, an autonomous agent whose actions can be weighed against those of others. Confronted with the kind of society portrayed by Butler, we are therefore left asking how such an ethical positioning of the subject can accommodate the Patternist ethereal and boundless subject and how this subject herself may be affected by the expansion of her scope of engagement. Mary realizes, shortly after the establishment of the Pattern, how close she has become to her own Patternist and, more importantly, how this proximity itself has exposed her to danger. Following an altercation with Karl, she relates how the latter's sense of imprisonment, his obligatory relation to Mary, opens her to harm, explaining that "if he couldn't get away from me, he'd hurt me. He shouldn't have been able to hurt me. But he was" (*Mind* 140). If connection thus opens up the subject to harm, it also invariably calls her to responsibility. As Mary herself explains only a few lines later, her new position within the Pattern comes with a new set of responsibilities. First hinted at in her pondering, "if [she] can push one latent toward transition . . . [why] can't [she] push others? "(*Mind* 134), this new sense of obligation really comes to light a page later when she considers her own cousins' situation: "Doro didn't pay any attention to Jamie and Christine, and their parents had given up on them years ago. No transition was supposed to come along and put them back in control of their lives, so, let alone, they'd probably wind up in prison or in the morgue before they were a lot older. But I wasn't going to let them alone" (135).

By allowing Mary to transcend the distance that separates her from her cousins, the Pattern bridges the gap that morality, according to Vetlesen, previously could not. Awakening Mary to her own being-in-and-for-the-world, the Pattern thus exposes the direct relation subjectivity entertains with ethics. Levinas argues, "the very node of the subjective is knotted in ethics understood as responsibility" (*Ethics and Infinity* 95). Understood in these terms, obligation is not an additive element superimposed upon the subject, but "the essential, primary and fundamental structure of subjectivity" itself (*Ethics and Infinity* 95).

Though mostly manifest in Mary's journey from solipsism to interdependence, this interest in vulnerability and obligation operates as a connecting thread throughout Butler's series. As Anyanwu is about to leave her African home to follow Doro back to America in *Wild Seed*, Doro explains that "it would not be hard to make her follow him. She had sons and she cared for them, thus she was vulnerable" (19). Putting his words into action, he then entices her with the prospects of "children [she] will never have to bury" (22), an argument she finds herself unable to resist. Similarly, Teray's journey from apprentice to Patternmaster in Butler's eponymous novel involves understanding that responsibility lies in power. Having been incorporated into an opponent's House, a sub-Pattern of sorts, he is made aware that his telepathic ability could easily kill every mute (non-telepathic person) in the House. Both Doro's enticement to Anyanwu and Teray's realization of power reveal what Judith Butler refers to as "the thrall in which our relations with others hold us," or the ways in which violence necessarily challenges "the very notion of ourselves as autonomous and in control" (23). In other words, violence's primary effect is not to increase distance but to effect rapprochement. And in this rapprochement, it exposes how the relations the subject entertains with the world, those ties she believed hers are not possessions but rather "mode[s] of being dispossessed, a way of being *for* another or *by virtue of* another" (J. Butler 24).

As a condition of her full subjectivity, Mary's entrance into the Pattern also invariably marks the inscription of all its members into her own being. As Jean-Paul Sartre argues, the intrusion of the Other within the subject's agentic field corresponds to "a fixed sliding of the whole universe ... a decentralization of the world" (279). If in this decentralization Sartre reads the first signs of "the solidification and alienation of [the subject's] own possibilities" (286), Octavia Butler perceives in this vulnerability the mark of our common humanity. Indeed, the sense of obligation borne out of vulnerability is what distinguishes Doro, at the most fundamental level, from both Anyanwu and Mary. Doro does not hesitate to take lives to sustain his own: he tells Anyanwu after he kills one of her daughters and takes over her body, "There was no other way she could be of use to me. She had had enough children, and she could not care for them. What did you expect me to do with her?" (*Wild Seed* 270). In contrast, Anyanwu's experience is defined by the collectivity she created around herself. One of her children notes in response to her refusal to leave, "We're your weakness, aren't we? You could outrun him for a hundred more years if not for us" (*Wild Seed* 242). This reading is later confirmed when Anyanwu herself explains to Doro, "These people need me, and I need them," and "All I need is my own kind around me. My family or people who feel like my family" (*Wild Seed* 222). Expressed not in terms of desire but necessity, Anyanwu's confession exposes the fundamental role played by the ethical relation in her conception of what it means to be human.

Throughout the series, Butler thus seems to define humanity as a specific mode of response, a response that Doro lacks. As he explains to Mary early in *Mind of My Mind* when pressed to define what race he belongs to, "I'm not black or white or yellow, because I'm not human" (94). In contrast to Mary, whom he himself assures is "different" though "certainly human," Doro is closer to being "a mutation. A kind of parasite. A god [or a] devil" (*Mind* 94). If he himself does not specify what keeps him outside the realm of the human, the series's emphasis on vulnerability and responsibility suggests that humanity lies precisely in the subject's ability "to respond to the face, to understand its meaning," and to recognize "what is precarious in another life or, rather, the precariousness of life itself" (J. Butler 134). After Doro coldly announces he has murdered one of her children for his own survival, Anwanyu tells him that the growing disregard for life he expresses is resulting in his progressive dehumanization: "Killing gives you too much pleasure. Far too much. . . . The human part of you is dying, Doro. It is almost dead" (*Wild Seed* 270). Anyanwu's emphasis on Doro's pleasure suggests that *in*humanity is not so much the result of a material or physical action, in this case murder; the true horror underlying this passage lies instead in the ontological emptying of life itself, in the framing of death and murder as insignificant, in the sense that it has literally no signification, no meaning. It lies in Doro's incapacity to recall "the last time he had felt pain at killing a man" (*Wild Seed* 21). Pain and shame, which Doro is incapable of experiencing, are here reframed not as the marks of a weakness in the human soul but as the symptoms of a vulnerability that lies at the core of our human subjectivity. Promoting a rearticulation of subjectivity as a mode of being hostage to the Other or, as Jacques Derrida puts it, of being "delivered to the other in the sacred openness of ethics" ("Eating Well" 112), Butler signals the powerful place occupied by responsibility in our understanding of what it means to be human.

Beyond the impact it bears upon the humanity of the individual herself, Butler's portrayal of Mary's awakening to subjectivity is a lesson in responsibility. Mary explains to Doro that the primary thing that differentiates them by the end is his disregard for the pain of others: "You've been watching them die for thousands of years.... You've learned not to care. I've just been saving them for two years, but I've already learned the opposite lesson. I care" (*Mind* 196). Mary's comment introduces a new perspective on the collective of which she is an intrinsic part. Benedict Anderson, in his work on community building, defines the community as the product of a willful and disinterested act of imagination of the collective. Being as it is supra-individual, the community is inherently without interest; and it is precisely this disinterestedness that allows it to request sacrifice from its members (Anderson 144–45). Though Butler's community is similarly founded on the notion of sacrifice—as Mary explains on the eve of her last fight with Doro, "I wouldn't risk the people, the Pattern, even if I were willing to risk myself" (*Mind* 200)—this sacrifice is not the result of disinterestedness but of the dispossession at the heart of the subject. Sacrifice, according to Butler, is always a sacrifice for others. It symbolizes the actualization of the subject's essence, her literal being-for-others at the same time as it simultaneously becomes the possibility of community. Levinas argues that responsibility before the face of the Other acts as the "original fact of fraternity" (*Totality and Infinity* 214), signaling a being-for-others that allows the constitution of a real network of dispossession.

Shortly before Mary enters her final fight against Doro, Jan, one of the other Patternists, mentions that "with the responsibility [Mary]'s taken on for all that she's built here, she belongs to us, the people" (*Mind* 209). By inscribing the subject within a collective network, the ethical relation between self and Other forces the relocalization of the subject's origins outside herself. In this sense, Mary's "proprietary feelings" (*Mind* 64) toward what she quickly comes to call *her* pattern are not the marks of a unidirectional mode of address but rather the signs of a bi-directional relationship in which the individual belongs to the collective as much as the collective itself belongs to the subject. When she questions her own relation to the Pattern, Mary suggests that dominance and necessity are not as distant as one may initially think: "Altruism, ambition—what else was there? Need? Did I need those latents, somehow?" (*Mind* 144). Stemming from the realization of the subject's inherent partialness, this mutual sense of dispossession and intense vulnerability is itself drastically heightened during the transitional period that is adolescence. Victor W. Turner argues that one of the predicates of the liminal stage is an awakening to the shared and "generalized social bond that has ceased to be and has simultaneously yet to be fragmented into a multiplicity of structural ties" (96). A materialization of what he later labels the "communitas" (108–09), a space of ambiguity in which the subject is confronted with the foundational interconnected web that ties her to all humankind and that signals her absolute responsibility, Butler's Pattern marks the communal foundations of all subjects, the space of their communal belonging.

Before her final fight with Doro, Mary seems to awaken to her own responsibility: "God, I've got ethics all of a sudden" (*Mind* 210). However, and because of the collective dimension of the self that transition exposes, this sense of obligation is never simply restricted to the singular Other but always expands to all in a move toward justice. In this way, transition unfolds as the locus of what Critchley refers to as the shift "from the proximity of the one-for-the-other to a relation with all the others whereby I feel myself to be an other like the others and where the question of justice can be raised" (*The Ethics of Deconstruction* 220). This perspectival shift or recalibration of the collective as a force *through* which, as opposed to *against* which, the subject emerges as ethical subject marks a reversal in the traditional approach associated with peer influence or group behavior theory. In traditional readings, the adolescent's entrance into the collective has been largely seen as a process through which the individual loses part of her agency. As Vetlesen argues, the inscription of the individual into large and complex social institutions, be they political, social, or economic groups, has tended to be read as a parallel abandonment of all sense of responsibility in subjection to a communal agentic power (5). Subsumed by a powerful form of collective will, individual agencies until then partially defined by autonomy find themselves replaced by a broader social order.[5]

In contrast to this reading, the approach to adolescence Butler suggests is marked by the awakening of a form of autonomy arising not against but *from* the entrance into the collective. Echoing Nedelsky's vision of autonomy as a process grounded not in isolation but in integration, Butler locates in Mary's adolescent transition the roots of her shift toward a more ethical existence. As she progressively accepts more responsibilities for her own actions, Mary becomes a "symbiont, a being living in partnership with her people" (*Mind* 217). And through this move, she comes to materialize Doro's earlier wish that she would move away from her "total disregard for human life—except for your own, of course" (*Mind* 31) and toward an active form of sociopolitical engagement. Moving away from her original understanding of herself as a parasite, Mary's *becoming-plural* (symbionts are in essence a form of becoming-*with*) signals a rethinking of the relation between individual agency and the network of forces within which it is invariably entangled. As she herself explains, by the end of the novel, she comes to realize that "[s]he was not a parasite, though he had encouraged her to think of herself as one" (*Mind* 217). Her relation to the collective is not a zero-sum game but rather a mutually beneficial one in which "[s]he gave them unity, they fed her, and both thrived" (*Mind* 217). Inviting a reframing of the individual's relation to the community as a symbiotic one, Butler signals a possible escape from the oppressive model that has tended to dominate the Western portrayal of the crowd and toward a model in which the subject's own idiosyncrasy, her own individuality, emerges as part and product of a larger collective she is both responsible for and the responsibility of.

Late in *Wild Seed*, Anyanwu relates how transition quickly becomes for most latents a period of hope, a time when the individual begins "to feel there was a way just beyond their reach—a way of controlling the madness, shutting themselves away from it. A way of finding peace" (186). Therefore, becoming subject, for Butler, is equated with finding agency or, at least, since Anyanwu specifies this control to reside "just beyond their reach," the fantasy of its possibility. Where Sartre therefore perceived in this pull toward the Other "a subtle alienation of all [the subject's] possibilities" (288), a stripping of her transcendental illusion and ultimately a profound and violent loss of control, Butler's series opens up the possibility of an alternative model of subjectivity rooted not in distance and separation, but in openness, symbiosis, and multiplicity. In opposition to Doro (who perceives every single form of attachment as a loss of sovereignty), vulnerability, attachment, and the relation she entertains with the people in her pattern become integral parts of Mary's being. Refusing to portray this openness and dependence as a form of limitation, a restriction of Mary's potentiality, Butler on the contrary presents it as the source of Mary's strength and, more importantly, of her freedom: "the only freedom [she] cared about" was the freedom "to grow again" (*Mind* 221).[6] Breaking away from a notion of subjectivity conceived in isolation, Butler presents subjectivity as a state in continuous centrifugal erosion and prey to a constant flow toward others. She echoes Levinas's understanding of the subject as an openness to multiplicity, "a multiple existing [*un exister multiple*]—a pluralism" (*Totality and Infinity* 220). Thus Butler opens her protagonist up to the alterity of the Other and her inherent infinity, suggesting the possibility of communion, the realization that coupling relations are always already constitutive relations, that *being-with* is always already *being-part-of*.

## The Posthumanist Dream

In this last section, I would like to return to the question of posthumanism and consider what new light Butler's reframing of subjectivity as essentially vulnerable and yet ethically obliged may ultimately shed on current conceptions of the posthuman. Progressive as it may be, Butler's model is ultimately far from being unproblematic. The increasingly hierarchical dimension Mary's Pattern develops throughout the series, culminating in the heavily stratified framework in which Teray is forced to evolve in *Patternmaster*, inevitably leads to numerous forms of violence. Signaling the limitations of any system contingent on notions of centrality, control, and order, this development also allows an interesting foray into what may be called posthumanist territories. Maria Aline Ferreira's reading suggests that Butler's narratives have tended to be approached through the lens of a specific posthumanist framework in which "adapting to new situations [and] forgoing part of their sense of humanity" is the only way for her protagonists to survive (407). Positing a form of rupture between humanity and what comes after it, this approach is not without foundations. Mary's own self-description as "a living creature of fire," a being "[n]o more human than [Doro] was" (*Mind* 217), would tend to promote a reading of the Patternists as suprahuman beings. Presented with the markers of a hierarchical framework in which Patternists and Clayarks are both framed as the results of seemingly posthuman evolution, readers are logically led to ask the same question with which Mary confronts Doro when he confesses his nonhuman status, that is, "If you're not human, what are you?" (*Mind* 94).

Posthumanism and the posthuman figure have been the objects of multiple interpretations over the years. Unfolding alternatively as "re-distributions of difference and identity" (Halberstam and Livingston 10), a "historical moment in which the decentering of the human by its imbrication in technical, medical, informatic, and economic networks is increasingly impossible to ignore" (Wolfe xv), or a questioning of the human "in a time where philosophy has become suspicious of claims about human subjectivity" (MacCormack 1), posthumanist philosophy proposes to challenge and deconstruct the dichotomies and claims of universalism that characterize humanism. As such, it has tended to posit an after-the-human in which the individual is reframed as an open system inscribed within a network of constant information flow (Wolfe xii). However, its emphasis on temporality is where Butler's mobilization of posthumanist thinking departs from traditional readings. Indeed, what her series suggests is not the breaking away from the human promoted earlier by Ferreira. Butler's recourse to posthumanist epistemology is not rooted in the idea that "a significant change has taken place: a shift from 'human' to 'posthuman'" (Rutsky 101), but rather in a rethinking of the human itself as always already interconnected. In this way, Butler's reconfiguration of the human in the Patternist series unfolds not so much as the accomplishment of the posthumanist dream than as its deconstruction.

Midway through *Patternmaster* and after having for the first time been directly addressed by a Clayark, Teray finds himself contemplating his own people's belief. As he explains, "Patternists and Clayarks stared at each other across a gulf of disease and physical difference and comfortably told themselves the same lie about each other. The lie that Teray's Clayark had tried to get away with: 'Not people'" (122). Posthumanist readings of Butler's fiction have tended to focus on the oppositional dynamic animating her interest in power relations. Yet by highlighting the distinction between human and non- or posthuman characters, these studies all seem to miss out on the broader argument underlying her work and instead simply replicate the "lie" at the heart of her Patternist series. Throughout her series, Butler indeed regularly emphasizes how reading the relation between the different groups composing her narrative as one of opposition would be to mistake difference and alterity, the core foundation of the subject, for negation. As the series progresses, the powerful illusion of ontological distinction that animates some of her characters is repeatedly proven to be but the product of a fantasy of difference whose roots are not so much ontological but performative, a reiterative process of crystallization whose initial fantasized dimension dissolves over time.[7] Whether through Teray's own realization or through the inclusive points of view of *Clay's Ark*'s two surviving protagonists, Eli and Kerry, the Patternist series repeatedly signals that understanding evolution as a form of rupture is to mistake appearances for ontology. Instead, what Butler proposes is a reframing of humanity itself as a mode of performance. Evidenced in Mary's comment to Karl that "[a]ll I want us to do is settle down and start acting like human beings again" (*Mind* 122), this epistemic shift challenges the idea of humanity as an ontological category and repositions it instead as a mode of acting. In other words, "being" human, in Butler's Patternist series, is not so much constructed around what one *is* but around what one *does*.

By promoting a reading of the alien, infected, or supernatural subject as a continuation or derivation of the "normal human," Butler proposes to disrupt the notion of a posthuman creation and to expose instead its problematic underlying assumption. Indeed, as she suggests when she equates telepathic linkage with corporeal touch—"She simply took Teray's hand and held it [but] the sensation was much like being linked with her again" (*Patternmaster* 153–54)—the fantasies constitutive of the posthumanist dream are nothing but the reframing, under yet another label, of a condition intrinsic to human subjectivity. A simple technological enhancement of dimensions already present in human experience, the abilities of both Patternists and Clayarks are not signs of a truly differentiated ontology. Whether we decide to label it as human or posthuman, whether the thought that produced it derives from humanist or posthumanist ideologies, the label itself is nothing but a fantasy, a symbolic superimposition or dream of differentiation. Born out of the limitations inherent to an epistemological system forever hostage to its own contingency on language and its need for order, the epistemic process which seeks to ontologically distinguish Clayarks, humans, and Patternists is thus only replicating the humanist desire for the classification it purports to escape.

In contrast, adopting a truly posthumanist or posthuman epistemology would require us to do away with such notions as classification, linearity, order, and difference and to embrace instead "the complex and random processes of mutation, processes which can never be entirely reduced to patterns or standards, codes or information" (Rutsky 111). It would imply abandoning posthumanism altogether, relinquishing any and all possibility of knowledge beyond a continuously mutating and shifting idiosyncratic experience and opening the self to the essential randomness of this experience. Promoting a vision of the human that does not necessarily reject internal contradictions but rather embraces co-presence, fluidity, and mutation as its cores foundations, Butler foregrounds a new epistemological model in which subjectivity itself implies an infinite form of becoming, an openness to the subject's own ethical significance and an embrace of the overwhelming burden of responsibility. It means to be, like Blake in *Clay's Ark*, "so right, so wrong, and so utterly helpless" (*Clay's Ark* 200), haunted by the undecidability lodged at the heart of every decision (Derrida, "Force of Law" 965).

By reformulating adolescence as an open space of ethical potentiality, a liminal period during which the increased vulnerability of the subject opens the self to a becoming multiple, Butler exposes the incredible potential for social and political engagement that emerges from adolescence. By addressing humanity as a form of performance, her work exposes the illusionary dimension of posthumanism. Opening up a new pathway for a rethinking of the human operated not in terms of futurity, a post- or beyond humanism sign of a transcendental escape away from our shared humanity, but in terms of a direct commitment to others and to the mutational power of relationships, she promotes a renewed awareness of the voice(s) and consciousness all subjects come to form together. Foregrounding a human subject appraised not through self-enclosure, coherence, and fixity but through notions of co-presence, fluidity, and mutation, her Patternist series forces upon us, in a mirroring move, the realization that what has traditionally been meant by humanity is naught but the result of a continuous discursive reiterative process which, due precisely to the space of instability it opens up between each iteration and the vulnerability it posits to be at the core of subjectivity, continuously exposes itself to new resisting forces. It is therefore in those resisting forces and their aggregated power, in the space of instability that is adolescence, that Butler locates the most powerful site of reconfiguration. And here may lie the most progressive and politico-social dimension of Butler's series: by re-articulating adolescence as a space of openness and ethical awakening, she challenges and questions the history and legacy of violence upon which our current epistemological model has been built and continues to sustain itself. Butler forces readers to ponder how one might think the Other without reducing this Other to the Same when the sheer act of thinking the Other, and of thinking itself, inherently implies, in Critchley's words, "the reduction of plurality to unity and alterity to sameness" (*The Ethics of Deconstruction* 29). She exposes the inherent process of exclusion that dominates any attempt at classification and labeling, including those intrinsic to posthumanist thought.

## Notes

1. In 1974, three years prior to the publication of *Mind of My Mind*, the American high-technology company Bolt Beranek and Newman opened Telenet, a packet-switched network service and first commercial and public iteration of the ARPANET (Advanced Research Projects Agency Network). Designed to put in contact, through its own network, military, governmental, commercial, and private bodies, Telenet officially marked the entrance into a new era of communications. For more, see Shea and Garson.

2. For the sake of clarity, the notion of the posthuman discussed here refers to the idea developed by R. L. Rutsky that "the posthuman implies that a significant change has taken place: a shift from 'human' to 'posthuman'" (101), suggesting a fundamental difference or departure from traditional notions of humanity, as both a reality and a concept.

3. Though this chapter uses material from both *Wild Seed* and *The Patternmaster* (1976), its primary focus remains the representation of youth offered by *Mind of My Mind*. *Survivor* (1978) and *Clay's Ark* (1984), being not directly concerned with the Patternist society, have been excluded from this discussion.

4. Because Butler's approach to subjectivity tends to differ from the traditional androcentric model offered by Western philosophy, a subject who has been, throughout history defined by traditionally masculine attributes (self-enclosure, control, disembodiment, etc.) and addressed by way of the masculine pronoun, references to the unspecified subject in this chapter shall be restricted to the female pronouns "she" and "her."

5. The paradox here is that childhood is itself often defined as a form of dependent state of being. The entrance into adulthood is therefore marked by a bi-directional and contradictory shift toward both independence and autonomy on the one hand and socialization and a loss of idiosyncrasy on the other.

6. It should be noted that though it is predominantly portrayed as a positive force in Mary's liberation, this vulnerability and openness to harm is not entirely devoid of violence. Violence becomes here simply the price to pay for freedom and subjectivity.

7. This is most clearly manifested in *Clay's Ark* when Eli, one of the Clayarks, tells the non-infected Keira, "'We're not superhuman,' Eli said quietly. 'We're not anything you won't be eventually. We're just . . . different'" (25).

## Works Cited

Allen, Joseph P., and Jill Antonishak. "Adolescent Peer Influence: Beyond the Dark Side." *Understanding Peer Influence in Children and Adolescents*. Ed. Mitchell J. Prinstein and Kenneth A. Dodge. New York: Guilford, 2008. 141–60. Print.

Anderson, Benedict. *Imagined Communities: Reflections on the Origin and Spread of Nationalism*. London: Verso, 1991. Print.

Blanton, Hart, and Melissa Burkley. "Deviance Regulation Theory: Applications to Adolescent Social Influence." *Understanding Peer Influence in Children and Adolescents*. Ed. Mitchell J. Prinstein and Kenneth A. Dodge. New York: Guilford, 2008. 94–121. Print.

Brown, B. Bradford, Jeremy P. Brakken, Suzanne W. Ameringer, and Shelly D. Mahon. "A Comprehensive Conceptualization of the Peer Influence Process in Adolescence." *Understanding Peer Influence in Children and Adolescents*. Ed. Mitchell J. Prinstein and Kenneth A. Dodge. New York: Guilford, 2008. 17–44. Print.

Butler, Judith. *Precarious Life: The Powers of Mourning and Violence*. London: Verso, 2004. Print.

Butler, Octavia E. *Clay's Ark*. 1984. London: VGSF, 1991. Print.

———. *Mind of My Mind*. 1977. London: Sphere Books, 1980. Print.

———. *Patternmaster*. 1976. London: Sphere Books, 1978. Print.

———. *Wild Seed*. 1980. New York: Warner, 1999. Print.

Cash, Mason. "Cognition Without Borders: 'Third Wave' Socially Distributed Cognition and Relational Autonomy." *Cognitive Systems Research* 25/26 (2013): 61–71. Print.

———. "Extended Cognition, Personal Responsibility, and Relational Autonomy." *Phenomenology and the Cognitive Sciences* 9.4 (2010): 645–71. Print.

Clark, Andy. *Natural-Born Cyborgs: Minds, Technologies, and the Future of Human Intelligence*. Oxford: Oxford UP, 2003. Print.

Clark, Andy, and David Chalmers. "The Extended Mind." *Analysis* 58.1 (1998): 7–19. Print.

Critchley, Simon. *The Ethics of Deconstruction: Derrida and Levinas*. Oxford: Blackwell, 1992. Print.

———. "The Original Traumatism: Levinas and Psychoanalysis." *Questioning Ethics: Contemporary Debates in Philosophy*. Ed. Richard Kearney and Mark Dooley. London: Routledge, 1999. 230–42. Print.

Derrida, Jacques. "'Eating Well,' or the Calculation of the Subject: Interview with Jacques Derrida." *Who Comes after the Subject?* Ed. Eduardo Cadava, Peter Connor, and Jean-Luc Nancy. New York: Routledge, 1991. 6–119. Print.

———. "Force of Law: The 'Mystical Foundation of Authority.'" *Cardozo Law Review* 11.919 (1990): 920–1045. Print.
Douglas, Mary. *Purity and Danger: An Analysis of Concepts of Pollution and Taboo*. 1966. London: Routledge, 2002. Print.
Elliott, Anthony. *Concepts of the Self*. 2nd ed. Cambridge: Polity, 2008. Print.
Ferreira, Maria Aline. "Symbiotic Bodies and Evolutionary Tropes in the Work of Octavia Butler." *Science Fiction Studies* 37.3 (2010): 401–15. Print.
Gallagher, Shaun. "The Socially Extended Mind." *Cognitive Systems Research* 25/26 (2013): 4–12. Print.
Gallese, Vittorio, and Alvin Goldman. "Mirror Neurons and the Simulation Theory of Mind-Reading." *Trends in Cognitive Sciences* 2.12 (1998): 493–501. Print.
Halberstam, Judith, and Ira Livingston, eds. *Posthuman Bodies*. Bloomington: Indiana UP, 1995. Print.
Hampton, Gregory Jerome. *Changing Bodies in the Fiction of Octavia Butler: Slaves, Aliens, and Vampires*. Lanham: Lexington, 2010. Print.
Hermans, Hubert J. M. "The Dialogical Self: Toward a Theory of Personal and Cultural Positioning." *Culture & Psychology* 7.3 (2001): 243–81. Print.
Levinas, Emmanuel. *Ethics and Infinity: Conversations with Philippe Nemo*. Trans. Richard A. Cohen. Pittsburgh: Duquesne UP, 1985. Print.
———. *Totality and Infinity: An Essay on Exteriority*. Trans. Alphonso Lingis. Pittsburgh: Duquesne UP, 1994. Print.
Lyotard, Jean-François. *The Postmodern Condition: A Report on Knowledge*. Trans. Geoff Bennington and Brian Massumi. Manchester: Manchester UP, 1984. Print.
MacCormack, Patricia. *Posthuman Ethics: Embodiment and Cultural Theory*. Abingdon: Ashgate, 2012. Print.
McCallum, Robyn. *Ideologies of Identity in Adolescent Fiction: The Dialogic Construction of Subjectivity*. New York: Routledge, 1999. Print. Children's Literature and Culture 8.
Melzer, Patricia. *Alien Constructions: Science Fiction and Feminist Thought*. Austin: U of Texas P, 2006. Print.
Mixon, Veronica. "Futurist Woman: Octavia Butler." *Essence* (April 1979): 12–15. Print.
Morley, David. "Domesticating Dislocation in a World of 'New' Technology." *Public Worlds: Electronic Elsewheres: Media, Technology, and the Experience of Social Space*. Ed. Chris Berry, Soyoung Kim, and Lynn Spigel. Minneapolis: U of Minnesota P, 2009. 3–15. Print.
Nedelsky, Jennifer. "Reconceiving Autonomy: Sources, Thoughts and Possibilities." *Yale Journal of Law and Feminism* 1.7 (1989): 7–36. Print.
Pepperell, Robert. *The Posthuman Condition: Consciousness Beyond the Brain*. Bristol: Intellect, 2003. Print.
Rutsky, R. L. "Mutation, History, and Fantasy in the Posthuman." *Subject Matters* 3.2 (2007): 99–112. Print.
Sartre, Jean-Paul. *Being and Nothingness: An Essay on Phenomenological Ontology*. 1958. Trans. Hazel E. Barnes. London: Routledge, 2003. Print.

Shea, Christopher M., and David Garson. *Handbook of Public Information Systems.* 3rd ed. Hoboken: CRC, 2010. Print.

Taylor, Charles. *Sources of the Self: The Making of the Modern Identity.* Cambridge: Cambridge UP, 1989. Print.

Turner, Victor W. *The Ritual Process: Structure and Anti-structure.* New York: Aldine De Gruyter, 1995. Print.

Vetlesen, Arne Johan. *Evil and Human Agency: Understanding Collective Evildoing.* Cambridge: Cambridge UP, 2005. Print.

Wittgenstein, Ludwig. *Philosophical Investigations.* 1953. Trans. Gertrude E. M. Anscombe, Peter M. S. Hacker, and Joachim Schulte. Ed. Peter M. S. Hacker and Joachim Schulte. Chichester: Wiley-Blackwell, 2009. Print.

Wolfe, Cary. *What Is Posthumanism?* Minneapolis: U of Minnesota P, 2010. Print.

# 2

# INFORMATION DISEMBODIMENT TAKEOVER
Anxieties of Technological Determinism in
Contemporary Coming-of-Age Narratives

*Shannon Hervey*

Navigating the tumultuous waters of adolescence amidst a postmodern landscape is a tricky endeavor. This complicated if not convoluted enterprise is made more complex by the pervasiveness of the internet and social network culture. Specifically, young adults today are growing up immersed in social media, and this immersion creates an entirely new set of anxieties and concerns that add to and sometimes exacerbate the age-old difficulties of growing up. Many of these anxieties pivot around self-representation and social projection of self. In this essay, I conceptualize social media as the main canvas of current self-writing. While Jo in *Little Women* wrote privately in her journal, characters in contemporary coming-of-age stories frequently write publicly for blogs, Facebook posts, Twitter, fan fiction sites, and other internet-based writing spaces. In many contemporary YA texts, the relationship between writing and coming of age is problematized by the public nature of writing. If writing is conceptualized as an act that garners agency and control, then publicly writing the self through available technologies seems to signal the loss of that control and the precariousness of that agency. Writing, as we can see in various YA texts such as *The Absolutely True Diary of a Part-Time Indian*, *The Book Thief*, *The Perks of Being a Wallflower*, and *Looking for Alaska*, to name but a few, is capable of constituting the self, but there seems to be something dangerous about *public* writing. This essay examines what, specifically, that something dangerous is.

The anxieties of publicly constructing the self are made manifest in YA narratives in which writing on the internet has harrowing results. In *#16thingsithoughtweretrue* by Janet Gurtler, for instance, the main character uses internet writing as a way to hide from her actual life. By doing so, she purposefully puts off coming of age, delays the entrance into adulthood, and shuts herself off from meaningful human connection. The main character, Morgan, repeatedly checks her Twitter account and her numbers of "followers" or "friends." The tension over whether these virtual friends can be counted as actual friends unfolds when Morgan's mother encourages her to put her Twitter account aside and go and make "real" friends; Morgan responds, "My online friends are real. No matter what she thinks" (33). In *The Future of Us* by Jay Asher and Carolyn Mackler, the anxiety over whether the internet creates the individual (or vice versa) is presented thematically when two teenagers turn on their computers in 1990 and find their Facebook pages, fifteen years in the future. Perhaps most unsettling is the YA novel *Feed* by M. T. Anderson, in which concerns about the internet being an insidious obstacle to self-actualization are terrifyingly clear; this futuristic science fiction novel is set some hundred years in the future when our very brains and central nervous systems have an internet feed installed at birth. In this world, language and the ability to write have completely deteriorated, and humans have the ability and ease to chat telepathically with whomever we please. Technological advancements attached to advertising and product placement are such that we no longer have to decide what we want because a computer decides for us. In this novel, the main tension is whether achieving a sense of self is even possible when being connected, both biologically and virtually, to so many outside stimuli means being constantly influenced and often having our choices made for us. Mike Carey (author) and Peter Gross's (artist) *The Unwritten*, an intertextual comic book series, illustrates the slippery divide between the virtual, the imagined, and the material. In a world in which writing has the power to create a collective unconscious, the internet, with its wide-reaching capabilities, can and does encourage a tyranny of the masses.

The first group of narratives discussed here, *#16things* and *The Future of Us*, narratively reflect the anxieties often associated with young people using the internet: asocial behavior, inappropriate exposure, and inability to control the flow of information. The second group of narratives, *Feed* and *The Unwritten*, are both more self-aware cultural commentaries largely pivoting around informatics. I consider both *Feed* and *The Unwritten* to be examples of what Katherine Hayles refers to as "information narratives":

> The characteristics of information narratives include, then, an emphasis on mutation and transformation as a central thematic for bodies within the text as well as for the bodies of texts. Subjectivity, already joined with information technologies through cybernetic circuits, is further integrated into the circuit by novelistic techniques that combine it with data. Access vies with possession as a structuring element, and data are narrativized to accommodate their integration with subjectivity.

> In general, materiality and immateriality are joined in a complex tension that is a source of exultation and strong anxiety. (43)

Though I would not classify the first set of texts I discuss as information narratives, they too illustrate this complex tension between materiality and immateriality. Taken together, each narrative discussed throughout this essay expounds upon the strong anxiety associated with shifts in subjectivity owed to our particular cultural moment, steeped in technological advancement and virtuality.

The texts examined here are a small sample that are indicative of the larger turn that both young adult and popular culture narratives are taking: a turn toward reflecting posthumanist themes and anxieties. Specifically, ideas of self and agency are drastically changing to exemplify the anxieties around acknowledging self as a cultural composite, largely informed by the pervasive technologies that inscribe the self. Hayles's influential work, *How We Became Posthuman: Virtual Bodies in Cybernetics, Literature, and Informatics*, begins by explaining the relationship between C. B. Macpherson's analysis of possessive individualism and "state of nature" arguments from Hobbes and Locke. Hayles's understanding of Macpherson's analysis is that the possessive quality of the liberal humanist comes from the belief that one is the sole proprietor over one's own person; this freedom is freedom from the influence and will of others. This understanding echoes philosophies by Hobbes and Locke: a self that is free from societal ideas and influences is possible. Though ownership of oneself is generally believed to have been possible only before market relations, Macpherson argues that the essential freedom of being the sole proprietor over one's self did not predate market relations but instead was a "retrospective creation of a market society" (3). In other words, only after acknowledging that market relations critically affect self did theorists formulate the philosophy that, market relations aside, an autonomous self might be possible. Hayles goes on to claim, "This paradox (as Macpherson calls it) is resolved in the posthuman by doing away with the 'natural' self. The posthuman subject is an amalgam, a collection of heterogeneous components, a material-informational entity whose boundaries undergo continuous construction and reconstruction" (3).

This description of posthumanism is important to this essay because the YA texts discussed here literalize Hayles's theories that the posthuman is an amalgam, "whose boundaries undergo continuous construction and reconstruction," and also emphasize how unsettling this realization is, especially for young adults searching for firm foundations in a continuously evolving and fragmented cultural landscape. This is a revolutionary turn for young adult novels previously so dedicated to unearthing one's *own* subjective truth that ultimately leads to agency. Though it generally goes uncontested that YA literature is saturated with narratives in which coming to understand self is central, the mere frequency of first-person narratives emphasizes this fact. About our current cultural, posthuman moment, Hayles argues, "the presumption that there is an agency, desire, or will belonging to the self and clearly distinguished from the 'wills of others' is undercut in the posthuman, for the posthuman's collective heterogeneous quality implies a distributed cognition located in disparate parts that may be in only tenuous communication with one another" (4). In this way, these novels challenge the normative representation of coming into adulthood traditionally depicted in YA literature in which the protagonist ultimately arrives at a sense of self.

Victoria Flanagan's *Technology and Identity in Young Adult Fiction: The Posthuman Subject* argues that there has been a distinct change in how YA texts depict the relationship between technology and human beings. According to Flanagan, more recent YA texts are less interested in characterizing technology as disempowering. Instead, argues Flanagan, recent YA texts illustrate the more positive and empowering repercussions of technological advancement. She states, "Rather than suggesting that agency is only illusory, as postmodernism does, posthumanism posits a rethinking of agency. It suggests that agency needs to be reformulated—through redistribution, for example, so that it is conceptualized as collective and networked, instead of being based purely on individualism" (5). While I concede that there are some YA texts that illustrate the more positive aspects of posthumanism that Flanagan articulates (*The Adoration of Jenna Fox* by Mary Pearson and *Skinned* by Robin Wasserman, to name two), there are still many YA narratives that clearly approach technology with a grave sense of anxiety. The texts surveyed here are in this latter category. That being said, *The Unwritten*, as a comic book series that remains ongoing, has the potential to eventually illustrate what Flanagan is arguing. Because the protagonist must learn to work within the "collective and networked" system that comprises his very existence, *The Unwritten* might be a text that simultaneously illustrates my own argument about posthumanism in YA texts—that it complicates notions of selfhood in disorienting and detrimental ways—as well as Flanagan's argument that it opens up new and different opportunities for conceiving a sense of self and agency. Regardless of the differences between Flanagan's argument and my own, I definitely agree that current YA narratives "reflect social attitudes towards technology, ethics and adolescence itself, the extent to which they engage with posthumanism as a critical discourse, and the strategic ways in which they seek to intervene in young adults' perceptions of themselves and the world by legitimizing particular forms of identity and social relations" (Flanagan 38). In most contemporary YA novels that feature identity formation taking place in the space of the virtual, we see dramatic changes in plot development owing to the somewhat dismal postmodern notion that we are created by/inscribed within the consumer- and media-driven world of which we are a part.

Not all critics see current and developing technologies in relation to social media as undermining notions of selfhood; in fact, David Buckingham's "Is There a Digital Generation?" argues that the internet provides a useful place for young people to explore aspects of self. He writes, "The internet provides opportunities for experimentation and play with identity, and for the adoption or construction of multiple selves. By offering communication with different aspects of the self, it enables young people to relate to the world and to others in more powerful ways" (8). But rather than the more positive outlook that Buckingham provides, many of these YA texts reveal anxieties about the relationship between self-construction and writing in the space of the digital. These anxieties pivot around self-representation, indelibility, control, and ownership. Though Buckingham is certainly not alone in his outlook that the internet provides an intrinsically positive experience for users, his argument seems to leave out the more insidious and problematic aspects of the relationship between social networking and user. His thesis that the internet offers opportunities for communication with different aspects of self is not completely inaccurate, but it misses the point: the fact that the internet offers *opportunities* for such explorative measures does not preclude the internet (social networking sites in particular) from simultaneously disenfranchising its users. Though the opportunity for exploration and experimentation is there, I tend to agree with Diane P. Michelfelder that social networking and participating in online communities depends on a process of self-commodification (205). I argue that for the contemporary bildungsroman, this process of self-commodification is depicted skeptically at best and, more often than not, disturbingly.

In the texts to be discussed here, the danger in self-writing within the public sphere of the internet seems to be tethered to self-commodification as well as to the confusion or slippage between virtuality and materiality. Becoming inextricably linked to (indeed, being *within*) the World Wide Web complicates the transition from childhood to adulthood: rather than turning inward for introspection and reflection, these novels attempt to depict the posthuman condition described by early cyberneticists in which "human identity is essentially an informational pattern rather than an embodied enaction" (Hayles xii).[1] Because human identity is less of an "embodied enaction," constructions of identity are also moving away from being tethered to the body. Being so inextricably linked with the media and internet spaces that inscribe the self exemplifies this external process of self-making. In this turn outward, toward self-representation in the public sphere, the internet works as a tool that commodifies. Of course, part of the issue here is that internal and external no longer hold the same significance as before, but this in and of itself is anxiety-producing, as is exemplified in the narratives discussed here. While many YA texts depict the act of writing as a process toward celebrating subjectivity, the texts discussed in this essay have the opposite effect; rather than celebrating subjectivity, texts that rely heavily on the internet for plot development and theme tend to have a more melancholy understanding of the internet as a powerful system that reaffirms objectification through commodification. In this reaffirmation of objectification, contemporary young adult novels are becoming increasingly vigorous in their illustrations of the damaging and anxiety-producing effects of the postmodern condition. In this way, we can think of young adult literature as taking a not-surprising turn toward dystopian themes that are not nearly as hopeful as traditional YA narratives. In the texts to be discussed here, even the mere existence of an individual, subjective self is called into question in various degrees and to various ends. The idea of self in these novels is replaced by an amalgam created both by the virtual spaces themselves and by the social interaction, in the form of writing, that these virtual spaces facilitate.

In *Social Psychology and Theories of Consumer Culture: A Political Economy Perspective*, Matthew McDonald and Stephen Wearing clarify the ways in which common social networking sites encourage (perhaps even demand) self-commodification:

> The development of information communication technologies such as the internet has turned out to be particularly well suited to the commodification of self-identity. . . . For users of Facebook, one's status is determined by the number of "friends" one has, so that quantity carries greater value than quality, providing evidence of one's popularity. In many ways Facebook provides a stage for its users to perform like actors in front of an audience of 500 million other registered users. . . . We see how self-identity and social interactions and relations in consumer culture are subsumed under the process of commodification and its corresponding system of impression management. (48)

Many YA narratives are wary of the relationship between consumer culture, self-commodification, and the internet that McDonald and Wearing point to. This distrust is illustrated through the protagonist's relationship to language and the textual. Specifically, in the narratives discussed here, what protagonists choose to write or not to write in public spaces and the repercussions thereof illustrate this distrust. Relatedly, in "Web 2.0: Community as Commodity," Michelfelder discusses the ways in which a "virtual self shares in the attributes of a commodity" (205). A virtual self, she argues, is a self that is always "readily available to others" but, like a commodity, can be taken off the market at any time "with no loss to one's actual self" (205). She goes on to articulate that it is the slippery boundary between public and private spaces that facilitates this self-commodification: "In willingly and knowingly abandoning their privacy, understood as control over personal data, individual members of online communities and social networking sites act in ways that make a significant contribution to the commodification of the self" (205).

Though Michelfelder's claims are useful for their pairing of self-commodification and social networking with the disappearing boundary between public and private, her assertion that the self can be taken off the market (read, "internet") with no "loss to one's actual self" is intensely challenged by each of the young adult narratives discussed here. In contrast, these novels each illustrate the ways in which the virtual is just as affecting in the physical world as the real. In fact, because the internet has replaced many other forms of socialization, it is not very useful to think about whether or not one's *virtual* self affects one's *actual* self. Thinking about the virtual and actual as distinct opposites misses the point. In these novels, the anxiety is about the complexity of the interconnectedness of the virtual and the actual. Implicit in this interconnectedness is the understanding that one's virtual self is very much tethered to one's actual self—or, perhaps equally conceivable, that there is no actual, material self that is distinguishable from the technologies that inscribe us.

Specifically, *The Future of Us* and *#16thingsithoughtweretrue* are two young adult novels that illustrate an extreme distrust of social networking; in fact, social networking is at the center of the protagonists' crises. *The Unwritten* and *Feed* are two examples of the contemporary bildungsroman that clearly and forcefully allegorize the very real danger of the internet acting as a system of erasure. Though all the texts mentioned above challenge the idea of a singular self, *The Unwritten* and *Feed* most obviously illustrate grave anxieties about the information age. Both depict information and the hybridizing of people with technology as the road to our demise. In this way, they reflect what Hayles refers to as the cultural anxiety/fantasy of information disembodiment takeover. Each of these texts thematizes a disappearing divide between the virtual and the material. While the act of writing and the reliance on intertextuality are both more present and powerful than ever, neither the act of writing nor the reliance on intertextuality facilitates the protagonist's arrival at and celebration of subjectivity. In *Feed*, for instance, the "I" literally disappears, and Violet succumbs to death when she attempts to biologically survive apart from the feed that is hardwired into her central nervous system; and Tom from *The Unwritten* learns that his very existence is dependent on a collective unconscious informed by internet technologies. In these narratives, both writing and intertextuality are routinely used as mechanisms that reaffirm the individual as a cultural artifact, as a manifestation of society's prescriptions. In both texts, basic survival is dependent on the protagonist's capitulation to the norms articulated by and maintained through technologies and social networking.

## *#16thingsithoughtweretrue* and *The Future of Us*

If we agree that commodification is the transformation of goods and/or services into commodities that can then be bought and sold, then what is the currency within social networking? In novels like *#16thingsithoughtweretrue* and *The Future of Us*, the payout for the protagonists engaged in public writing comes in the form of "followers" and "friends"; the more followers or friends one has on social networking and blog sites, the more successful one is, not just socially but entirely. *#16thingsithoughtweretrue* (*#16things*) is a novel about a Twitter-obsessed teenaged girl with a dying mother and a father she has never met. On her mother's deathbed, Morgan learns her father's address and decides to go and meet him, and two new and unlikely friends accompany her on her road trip. Throughout the story, Morgan continues to be obsessed with reaching five thousand Twitter followers: "If I can reach five thousand followers this summer, things will turn around for me in my senior year" (86). Morgan understands the number of followers her Twitter account garners as being not just closely related to her social power, but absolutely tethered to her future success. She sends out the following tweet: "Likeability can be measured by how many followers you have online" (71), and she operates under the basic assumption that "5000 Twitter followers are all the friends I need" (290). If how likeable we are is dependent on our followers, and how many followers we have decides our future, then how we portray ourselves online is of the utmost importance. *#16things* makes this most evident when Morgan is feeling low: "I scroll down, but my heart isn't in any of the things my friends are tweeting. I can't concentrate, and I'm close to typing a tweet to express my distress, something I vowed never to do. My online image is peppy. I don't want to drag people down" (67). We can see here that *#16things* illustrates McDonald and Wearing's analysis of social networking, which is that "self-identity and social interactions and relations in consumer culture are subsumed under the process of commodification and its corresponding system of impression management" (48). Rather than project a more authentic message expressing her distress, Morgan opts to give readers what she assumes they want: the peppy image. Her practices of impression management emphasize the parallels between social networking and the consumer-centered nature of supply and demand. Here is an illustration that writing done publicly is not done to uncover, explore, or challenge the self but to very carefully manage the self into a product that will then be supported by online friends and followers, who are usually strangers, a faceless mass of readers and voices from out of the ether.

Apart from the troubling relationship the internet has to commodification, self-writing in the public sphere of the internet is also presented within these novels as dangerous because of the uncontrollability of social media. As we see above, one's success in the material/actual is understood as largely dependent on one's success in the space of the virtual. For Morgan, who clearly understands her success as being inextricably linked to the internet, it is especially troubling to see the degree to which she understands her lack of control over that sphere; if Morgan's success is defined by the internet, and if Morgan maintains that she has no real control over what happens in that sphere, then she has no real agency or control over her life. Morgan's awareness of this disenfranchisement is most notable through one of the main plot points of the text: unbeknownst to Morgan, a "friend" of hers posts on YouTube a risqué video of Morgan dancing in her underwear. The comments section for this video is a textual surface that not only adds to the humiliation Morgan weathers, but the posts here also become a dark reflecting pool that she then must wade through; she asks herself which of these comments is the truth and must defend herself out in the physical world against what is being said about her in the virtual one. She says, "This is my life now, and deep down I wonder if maybe, just maybe they're right. Maybe I really am an attention whore who deserves to serve time in social purgatory for appearing in my underwear online" (2). She later explains to a new friend about how the video picked up speed, going "out of control," amassing over three million views in a short period of time (126). Commenting on how indelible the internet is, Morgan tweets, "Removing something from online is like trying to take pee out of a pool" (125). Perhaps most unsettling about this narrative is that despite Morgan's acknowledgment that the internet is a somewhat perilous place where things go "out of control" and where she cannot be honest with her feelings, she also notes repeatedly how attached she is to the internet: "[i]t makes me kind of twitchy. I'm edgy without Wi-Fi" (111); "the thought of [being without the internet] makes me hyperventilate a little" (107); "[f]or a fleeting moment, I wonder if I could give up the internet if I had to. But that thought makes my head and stomach hurt" (92).

For Morgan, then, the internet is an addiction that she is more or less *physically* bound to (she becomes twitchy, hyperventilates, and has headaches/stomachaches with the thought of not being able to access the internet), where millions of viewers have looked at her near-naked body without her permission and countless others have commented with extremely critical remarks, some of which Morgan has come to believe herself. Rather than the internet being a space where Morgan has the opportunity to project herself, the very opposite takes place—that is, the internet tells Morgan who she is. And instead of speaking back, perhaps by using her own Twitter account to be honest about her feelings and thoughts, Morgan self-censors, thinking about how she wants her followers to perceive her—in short, thinking about her consumers' needs and perhaps not her own. Interestingly, though the "inaugural moment of the computer age" is closely linked to the performance of "the erasure of embodiment" (Hayles xi), *#16things* complicates this relationship in various ways. First, the narrative emphasizes the significance of the body through Morgan's nearly-nude YouTube video. The narrative also opens up possibilities for understanding notions of shifting subjectivity revolving around the idea of informational hybrid bodies through Morgan's emphasis of her bodily connection to the internet. Unfortunately, the novel never pursues this line of inquiry. The resolution does not answer the question of whether her Twitter friends are her real friends, nor does it provide insight as to how to more productively manage self-representation in digital spaces. Instead, the novel seems to suggest that by acquiring meaningful connections that do not rely on digital spaces, the reliance on and interest in those digital spaces will cease to be important. Morgan, after establishing close friendships with both her road trip companions, all of a sudden is not so addicted to the internet.

*The Future of Us* also emphasizes how social networking, instead of being reflective of the actual, is often depicted as a space that is prescriptive of the material. Like Morgan, the protagonists in *The Future of Us* grapple with the virtual defining the material, rather than the material defining the virtual. *The Future of Us* is set in 1996 and has two main characters, Emma and Josh, who barely know how to use their personal computers. Remarkably, what they find once they power on their computers are their Facebook pages, fifteen years in the future. Rather than first constructing their identities and then projecting them out into the world, the internet tells them who they will be in the future. We can think of these future Facebook pages as distinct characters—that is, each Facebook page is an informational self, disembodied in both time and space. Both Emma and Josh try to figure out what sorts of life choices they make throughout the next fifteen years that would result in such Facebook profiles. But, like all time-travel fiction, the important question that arises is whether these two characters would have ever made those kinds of decisions had they not accidentally stumbled upon this unexplained glimpse into their futures. At one point, Josh begins to drastically change his self-presentation at school as a result of who he reads himself to be on the future Facebook page; Emma comments, "The discovery of his future is changing him now" (191). Josh himself acknowledges the impact the future Facebook page is having on him when he notes, "Everything changed the moment Emma discovered Facebook. If I didn't know Sydney and I would eventually get married, I may not have defended her in Peer Issues. And she wouldn't have asked for my number" (151).

*The Future of Us* nicely illustrates Hayles's definition of reflexivity: "the movement whereby that which has been used to generate a system is made, through changed perspective, to become part of the system it generates" (8). In further explanation, Hayles gives the following example: "When M.C. Escher drew two hands drawing each other, he took that which is presumed to generate the picture—the sketching hand—and made it part of the picture it draws" (8). For *The Future of Us*, it is presumed that Facebook is created by its users, but this narrative makes clear that the technologies (depicted as mysterious in this novel) also and simultaneously create the users. As Hayles argues, "reflexivity has subversive effects because it confuses and entangles the boundaries we impose on the world in order to make sense of that world" (9). The common assumption about YA narratives is that they are all about making sense of the world. Karen Coats, in *Looking Glasses and Neverlands: Lacan, Desire, and Subjectivity in Children's Literature,* links this "making sense of the world" directly to language: "for the child, that 'prodigiously open' creature who is using the textual Other to organize his inner as well as his outer world, everything the text tells him about the world is at some level true, because it is what generates the conditions for truth" (162). Though Coats is more concerned than I am with the readers of children's literature, her work is in conversation with mine because the reader she refers to here also occupies a position very similar to that of the protagonist in texts where textuality is central. Often, the quintessential plot resolution of YA novels takes place when the protagonist has come to know his or her place in society, which means making sense of the world. Contemporary YA texts that use information technology as central plot devices depict worlds where boundaries are indeed confused and entangled.

In fact, *The Future of Us* does so good a job of confusing the boundaries that the only thing that makes sense in the end is an inexplicable decision on the part of future Facebook Emma to delete the Facebook account. This is an unsatisfactory conclusion because it does not begin to resolve the central issue of Emma feeling disempowered by the technologies that will eventually shape her life. It also comes as a surprise, with no clear reason as to what informed future Emma's decision to delete her Facebook account. While some might argue that deleting the account solves the problem of present-day Emma feeling always already inscribed within the digital future, the resolution to simply do away with that technology is impractical. Regardless of whether or not Emma has a Facebook in the future, the technology still exists, and failing to learn to cope with this technology or to explore the potentially positive aspects of collective, networked projections of the self signals a missed opportunity at the very least and/or a failure to enter the social, which means joining a changing and plugged-in technological world.

Like Morgan from *#16things*, Josh and Emma conflate their social networking lives with their actual lives and do not feel like they have much control because of this conflation. For Morgan as well as Emma and Josh, this loss of control points to the anxiety associated with becoming informational hybrid bodies. Emma, extremely concerned about the unhappiness and unsuccessfulness of her future Facebook self, thinks, "Yes, it feels great to plan your life when you believe everything can turn out fine. But what about when you're shown, again and again, how little control you have over anything? No matter what I do to try to fix my future, it doesn't work" (253). Like Morgan, there seem to be feelings of desperation in relation to having any kind of traction or agency over one's own life. While the circumstances are different, both narratives include protagonists who feel completely disempowered by the writing that takes place on the internet. In both cases, the internet and the writing therein stand as a type of official social record, not a record of what has been but a record of what will be.

This idea that social networking serves as a kind of social record is perhaps most evident in the beginning of *The Future of Us*. When Emma and Josh are trying to understand what it is they have stumbled upon, it is as if they are from a different world trying to decipher the strange social practices of a society completely foreign to them. Because of this interesting vantage point of not understanding the cultural moment of Facebook's arrival (or other social networking), this text also provides cultural commentary about the superfluous extent to which society utilizes social networking in order to transcribe our otherwise mundane, day-to-day tasks. The following conversation illustrates this last point nicely:

> "[D]on't you get it? At some point in the future, *we* created it. I don't know exactly what it is, but it looks like interconnected websites where people show their photos and write about everything going on in their lives, like whether they found a parking spot or what they ate for breakfast."
>
> "But why?" Josh asks. (43)

This question of "why" concludes a main section of the text and remains unanswered. Because it remains unanswered, it interrogates the reader's own use of social networking; why *do* people record such mundane, day-to-day activities? Why *is* it important to tell the world so publicly what it is that we do privately? In *The Future of Us*, not only do these questions emphasize our lack of understanding of the role of the virtual in our daily lives, but the very premise of the novel also thematizes the degree to which we do not understand the teleology of our reliance on technology. Because Facebook inexplicably finds its way into the lives of Josh and Emma, they have no hope of understanding the social and cultural parameters that created such a technology. This lack of understanding partly explains Josh and Emma's anxiety and difficulty with processing their experiences with their future selves. To return to Hayles's explanation of reflexivity, Facebook in *The Future of Us* stands in as a metaphor for cultural and societal systems that inscribe the individual, leaving little or no room for the individual to "write" her/himself; instead, the individual is told who she/he is by the prevailing systems and technologies around her/him.

## *The Unwritten* and *Feed*

Unlike the novels discussed thus far, *The Unwritten* and *Feed* provide much more acute social commentary revolving around the intersections of popular culture and informatics. As mentioned earlier, Hayles's description of information narratives is entirely applicable to both of these narratives, as both place "an emphasis on mutation and transformation as a central thematic for bodies within the text as well as for the bodies of texts" (43). Central to both works is how information and technology have changed the means by which we understand the self. Elaine Ostry's "'Is He Still Human? Are You?': Young Adult Science Fiction in the Posthuman Age" discusses the relationship between estrangement and posthumanism. She argues, "The young adults in [YA] books feel estranged not just from their parents and from society that would likely shun them, but from themselves. The question that all adolescents ask—"Who am I?"—becomes quite complicated" (225). Importantly, bodies within these narratives are conceptualized in complex ways so as to reflect a growing anxiety around our posthumanist cultural moment. In both *The Unwritten* and *Feed*, our posthumanist condition is tethered not only to technology but to developments in internet communication that allow and encourage the emergence of a collective voice that oftentimes works as a system that silences.

In the four volumes of the graphic novel *The Unwritten*, the meaningful interaction between audience and text in the space of the virtual is powerfully articulated. This coming-of-age comic book series begins with the following quote: "In life the creatures had been half-ghost, half-devil, but Tommy's spell had made them entirely solid, had dragged them flailing and screaming into the physical world, and the trauma of that crossing had utterly destroyed them" (Vol. 1). The main character of *The Unwritten*, Tom Taylor, has spent his entire life trying to prove to people that his famous literary father's fictional character, Tommy Taylor, is not based on himself. The above quote that opens *The Unwritten* is from one of these Tommy Taylor novels and immediately brings to the fore the slippery boundary between the virtual and the material; the "creatures" that were at one time not of this world are "dragged" into the physical world "flailing and screaming." Not only does this opening immediately make possible the crossing over from the non-physical to the physical, but it also makes clear the frightening and perhaps even violent processes of actualization. In *The Unwritten*, this process of actualization—that is, the process by which ideas/things from the virtual become material—is completely dependent on readership. That is, in this world, the collective voice of an audience wields incredible power. Tom Taylor must learn to manipulate readers through writing in order to survive. The entire series works as a metaphor for the power of mass media, and popular culture in particular, to effect reality through its users.

In the beginning of Volume 1 of *The Unwritten*, Wilson Taylor, Tom's father, disappears and leaves thirteen Tommy Taylor novels in his wake. This series of novels has an immense fan base, depicted as both bigger and more ardently devoted than any Harry Potter following. With Wilson's disappearance, Tom is left to sign books at media conventions as an easy way to make money off his father's fandom. At these conventions, Tom corrects fans again and again that Wilson's Tommy Taylor is not based on himself. In fact, Tom has had the burden of differentiating himself from Wilson's character for as far back as he can remember. At one specific convention, a graduate student who is writing her dissertation on Wilson Taylor and the Tommy Taylor novels confronts Tom, in front of media cameras and a large audience, with evidence that he is not, in fact, Wilson Taylor's biological son. This scene launches a series of incredible events during which Tom slowly becomes aware, though he is not sure how it is possible, that he actually *is* made up of the collective unconsciousness of his father's fandom.

One of the most interesting features of this narrative is its experimental structure. Rather than the traditional structure of most comic book series, in which panels move from left to right and top to bottom in a linear and chronological fashion, *The Unwritten* jumps back and forth between the principal narrative (the Tom Taylor bildungsroman), interior narratives (excerpts from Tommy Taylor novels), a vast array of faux internet pages (Google searches, blog posts, message boards, and still shots of newscasts and YouTube videos), as well as "Choose Your Own Adventure" pages (in Vol. 3). This structure places an emphasis on mutation and transformation, pointing to the posthumanist condition in which subjectivity is "joined with information technologies through cybernetic circuits" (Hayles 43). This narrative is an intertextual pastiche, illustrating through structure a hybrid body of its own—a composite of actual history, alternative history, and references to works of literature both actual (*Frankenstein* and *Our Mutual Friend*) and fictional (the Tommy Taylor novels), all influenced by the technologies of our current cultural moment.

One of these blog post pages makes clear how the narrative structure, apart from simply mirroring the chaos associated with postmodernism, emphasizes the great impact of audience members as informational hybrid bodies in our current cultural moment. Psychologist Dr. Swann's blog post interrupts the primary Tom Taylor narrative: "Karl Jung suggested that there's a collective human unconscious. An under-mind that feeds all our myths, all our deepest instincts. That's always been true. But in an age of mass culture, we can actually write to the under-mind. Our virally spreading fictions embed themselves in the collective unconscious of humanity and change it" (Vol. 2). For *The Unwritten*, the various interjections of media coverage (news broadcasting) together with the vast arrangement of online writing, emerge as the character voice of this collective unconscious. Important here is Swann's interpretation and word choice in describing Jungian theory: "we can actually *write* to the under-mind" (my emphasis). This ability to create and speak to the collective unconscious is completely dependent on, according to the fictional Dr. Swann, the "age of mass culture." This point is reaffirmed throughout the series when images of discussion boards, blog postings, and Google searches all collectively contribute to a predominant voice. In *The Unwritten*, social networking and other forms of writing disseminated widely contribute to a collective voice. This collective voice is conceptualized as an informational hybrid body that is extremely influential in forming individuals' subjectivity. In this world, subjectivity is transformed into an amalgam or cultural composite, and the idea of a singular self is thrown out.

In an interview, the artist of the series, Peter Gross, said the following of *The Unwritten*: "The original title of the series was 'Faction,' and it was the idea of the intersection between fact and fiction. So from the beginning, we wanted to talk about where the mix falls and that fiction has real consequences in our life" (Gross). Writer Carey and illustrator Gross accomplish their goal by interweaving real-world historical events and people, like Joseph Goebbels and his role in Nazi Germany, with characters like Lizzie Hexam, taken straight out of the Charles Dickens novel *Our Mutual Friend* and transplanted as a key figure in *The Unwritten*. But Carey and Gross accomplish a great deal more than simply illustrating that fiction has real consequences in our lives; they show that our realities are often fictions themselves and that they become reality through a somewhat mysterious process connected to the collective unconscious that is dependent on mass media that gives us the ability to write to the under-mind. Because stories have such incredible and oftentimes terrifying power, understanding how they work and why audiences gravitate toward certain stories is key; as Lizzie Hexam says to Tom, "I learn about how stories work for the same reason that soldiers learn how to strip a rifle. You should, too" (Vol. 1).

Tom, who grew up believing (like most of us) that reality has a strong foundation based in the physical, is understandably confounded at the evidence unfolding around him, which points to the real possibility that his very biology is literally composed of words. He is further confused as he finds out that other things/people/truths he assumed to be based in something real also originated in the land of writing and fiction. When Tom meets a monster of a man, who has a striking resemblance to the creature from *Frankenstein*, Tom tries to shake himself from what he believes to be a bad dream. He says to the monster, "You're a character in a book. A really old book that nobody reads. You standing there—talking—it's like a bad joke. If you're real, then Br'er Rabbit is real. And Dracula. And the tooth fairy." The Monster replies, "And—Christ, perhaps. I understand your dilemma. It is frightening to think of the world as having no firm foundations. Frightening to meet one's maker" (Vol. 2). Apart from overtly emphasizing the narrative's reflection of a postmodern society that, indeed, may have no firm foundations, this interaction highlights that even truths some hold as sacred, like the story of Christ, are also based in fiction.

The anxiety that there are no firm foundations permeates contemporary coming-of-age stories. But rather than lose hope altogether, these narratives feature protagonists who struggle against the anxiety of either/or logic: virtual *or* material, past *or* present, online persona *or* real person. Tom's character arc consists of coming to understand himself as an informational hybrid body, written by others, made up of information, but also still a flesh-and-bone human being. He is both. Further emphasizing the significance of dualistic thinking, the monster simultaneously infers that Christ is a fiction, but that we do have maker(s). This speaks to the theme of the series, which is that everyone participates in the construction of what we come to know as reality. Essentially, we are our own makers; however, the theory that we make our own realities suggests that we have some sort of control or agency over these realities, but this notion is undermined by the series' emphasis on the power of the collective unconscious. We are created by but also contribute to the collective unconscious. This is another example of Hayles's theory of reflexivity "whereby that which has been used to generate a system is made, through changed perspective, to become part of the system it generates" (8). Reflexivity is not only tethered to understandings of self in *The Unwritten* but is reflected heavily in the excessive intertextuality throughout.

The conversation between the monster and Tom emphasizes the relationship between the collective unconscious and the world having no real, firm foundations. The conversation also provides one of the recurring literary allusions that run throughout *The Unwritten*. Mary Shelley's *Frankenstein* is about how knowledge can be extremely dangerous, especially in the hands of unbounded ambition. It is about a monster who is rejected by society. *Frankenstein*'s very structure is made up of letters, notes, journals, inscriptions, and allusions. Each of these elements is echoed in *The Unwritten*; Tom quickly finds out that the more he knows, the more danger he is in. Gaining knowledge of the mysterious workings of the world is dangerous because it challenges everything he has ever known. Tom also learns that it is his father's relentless ambition to effect change in the world that eventuates his death, much like the monster's father's ambition which also brings about his end. Similar to the depiction of society in *Frankenstein*, whose fear of the unknown and death grip on normativity means rejecting the monster, so too the society in *The Unwritten* rejects Tom.

The monster from *Frankenstein* is a kind of spirit guide for Tom as Tom comes to terms with the world unraveling around him. Rather than mere allusion, this use of Mary Shelley's monster as an actual character in *The Unwritten* is an act of bricolage in which textual layering facilitates the development of plot and theme throughout. The inclusion of *Frankenstein* in *The Unwritten* is perfect because it creates a kind of meta-intertextuality. That is, *The Unwritten* uses *Frankenstein* in an act of intertextuality, and *Frankenstein* also possesses many intertextual qualities itself. In chapter 15 of *Frankenstein*, for example, while the monster is talking to Victor in the cave, the monster alludes to *Paradise Lost* and explains how he relates to the text because he was also created and then rejected by his creator. The monster says to Victor, "*Paradise Lost* excited different and far deeper emotions. I read it, as I had read the other volumes which had fallen into my hands, as a true history. It moved every feeling of wonder and awe that the picture of an omnipotent God warring with his creatures was capable of exciting" (Shelley 122). Throughout the monster's adventures, he comes across many texts (*Plutarch's Lives, Paradise Lost*, and *The Sorrows of a Young Werther*) and reads all of them as real histories of humanity. In *The Unwritten*, the monster has come to explain to Tom the interconnections between fiction and reality. In doing so, the parallels in theme between the two narratives, and the multitude of narratives each of those principal texts alludes to, all contribute to the multilayered intertextual landscape of *The Unwritten*. For Tom, understanding the complexity of this textual layering is important to his understanding of who he is as a person created by such stories. In this way, the monster facilitates Tom's entrance into adulthood—no longer does Tom believe in the sophomoric ideas of real and unreal. Now he understands that everything is created.

Throughout the series, there are reminders that what we have come to know as truth is but a construction. When Tom demands to know the story of his life, his father responds, "Ignore history. It's only what these people have allowed to be written.... Their domain is stories. They manipulate them in complex and significant ways" (Vol. 3). The "they" Wilson speaks of here is the "cabal"—a group of authors who have exploited their knowledge that stories and reality are intricately intertwined. Allegorically, the cabal symbolizes the powerful structures that systematically enforce normative behaviors and reject those that do not embody this normativity.

One particular example from *The Unwritten* that highlights the insidious possibilities of stories and their immense, terrifying power is when Tom and Lizzie Hexam are transported back in time to World War II–era Germany. Here they encounter a huge, swirling vortex, outside of time and space, made up of words and images related to the Holocaust. The vortex appears to be getting bigger and bigger, swallowing space and time as it does so. In reference to this vortex about to swallow them, Lizzie explains to Tom, "Wilson calls it a canker. It happens when a story gets corrupted or complicated too much. When the energy inside it gets poisoned." The story she is referencing, that became corrupted and complicated, is *Jud Süss*, Wilhelm Hauff's 1827 novella, which Joseph Goebbels made into a Nazi propaganda film. Lizzie says, "Goebbels turned it inside out. Turned it into its own opposite.... It was a novel written by a Jew from a Jewish perspective. It became the most successful anti-Semitic movie of all time." Tom asks, "So this is because Goebbels? Because of the movie?" To which Lizzie responds, "It's because of the contradictions. In the novel, Süß sins, but finds *salvation* through his religion. In the movie, he is just a monster. When enough people had seen the movie—there was a crisis. An imbalance" (Vol. 2). Goebbels's unfaithful adaptation debased the original story, and because this anti-Semitic film was so widely seen and embraced as truth, the collective unconscious was persuaded of its message. In "Palimpsests and Intertexts: *The Unwritten*," David Large explains the canker: "The realm of ideas itself is portrayed as a desaturated void outside of time, space, and the constraints of panel borders. Any lingering images or phrases from the novella are disfigured by swirling images from the film.... Later in the series, Carey is more explicit about the power of an idea: we are made aware that 'For-real-true is only true now. Story-true is true forever.'"

This real, historical example is one of the most persuasive moments in *The Unwritten*. The central argument of the series, that we collectively make our own realities and that these realities are informed by powerful storytelling, is appallingly apparent in this example from which readers can imagine what might have happened, or perhaps what might *not* have happened, had Goebbels not reinterpreted and dispersed widely Wilhelm Hauff's novella. Though the series does not go so far as to say that Goebbels caused the Holocaust, readers can clearly see that such storytelling, combined with other powerful storytelling, changed reality in devastating ways.

*The Unwritten* has not yet concluded and is continuing to do new and interesting things with ideas that revolve around created realities and the power of stories and writing within those realities. Though the series thus far predominantly emphasizes Tom's distress and disillusionment with the realization that he is literally a composite of what his father has written and what Tommy Taylor fans write about on the internet, the series has also begun to illustrate the ways in which Tom is learning to live within this world. Flanagan's argument that posthumanism opens up new and different opportunities for conceiving of a sense of self and agency is hinted at in *The Unwritten* when Tom decides to take matters into his own hands and create a website about Tommy Taylor. As more people read his fan fiction and the collective unconscious shifts, Tom begins to change in real life, becoming more powerful and reflecting and embodying the public's new understanding of the fictional Tommy Taylor (Vol. 4). Even though both the postmodern and posthumanist aspects of the series complicate notions of selfhood in disorienting and detrimental ways, Tom does seem to be learning to work within the "collective and networked" system that comprises his very existence, pointing to potential agency and hope.

Like *The Future of Us* and *#16things*, this series reveals anxieties around the vanishing boundary between the print and media world and the physical one. For *The Unwritten*, language is conceptualized as the main technology constituting and composing self. In *Feed*, anxieties pertaining to transhumanism, a concept related to posthumanism, are made evident as bodies become literally hybrid when machinery is attached to the central nervous system.

Flanagan describes transhumanism as "the propensity for the human body to become radically transformed by technology" (15). She argues that both posthumanism and transhumanism "focus on the impact of technology on human subjectivity and social relationships," and goes on to explain that "the technological modification of the human body is a recurring motif in sci-fi narratives for adolescents" (16). *Feed* is a young adult science fiction novel that exemplifies Flanagan's description of the technofuturistic YA novel: "Young adult narratives that are set in technofuturistic worlds are typically concerned with exploring how technologically modified bodies might extend or challenge normative definitions of what it means to be a human being" (16). These novels ruminate on what it means to be a human being by asking questions about "the importance of human 'authenticity' or originality (in the case of cloned characters), the role of memory in the production of human subjectivity (particularly since memories can be mechanically inserted or retained in genetically engineered bodies), and the relationship between embodiment and cognition" (Flanagan 16).

Focusing on issues such as data mining, information technology, and commodification, *Feed* takes place in a future in which environmental decay is in full effect and technological advancement has produced oxygen factories, filet mignon orchards, and feeds that are hardwired into our central nervous systems. Through the thematic of language, *Feed* actively asks questions about the relationship between embodiment and cognition, and through its critique of capitalism, *Feed* explores the possibility or impossibility of authenticity or originality. The feeds that are installed at birth connect humans to an always "on" internet network. The novel begins with a group of teenagers who are taking their spring break on the moon. While at a nightclub, a radical protestor against feed technology infects the nightclub visitors with a virus that shuts their feeds down. For the protagonist, Titus, this is the first time he can remember experiencing consciousness without the feed. Titus describes the general reaction to the feeds being shut down: "we were frightened, and kept touching our heads. Suddenly, our heads felt real empty" (46). This quote illustrates the degree to which society has come to rely on technology and the internet; without the feeds working properly to connect Titus and his friends directly to the internet, something as seemingly automatic as basic thought becomes difficult. The grammar mistake of saying "real" instead of "really" is but one example of many that litter the text, pointing to a deterioration of language. Simultaneously, using "real" instead of "really" metaphorically refers to the actual emptiness of their heads.

Violet's father, an eccentric academic, speaks only with "difficult words." In her explanation of her father's odd behavior, Violet says, "He says the language is dying. He thinks words are being debased. So he tries to speak entirely in weird words and irony, so no one can simplify anything he says" (137). Throughout the text, the deterioration of language is exaggerated, but Violet's father's obsession with the preservation of words highlights further just how much people have forgotten how to use language. This corrosion of the ability to speak is linked directly with the inability to think throughout the text, and the inability to think is linked directly with the constant reliance on internet technology; when Titus first meets Violet, he is instantly attracted to her and tries to describe why: "Her spine. Maybe it was her spine. Maybe it wasn't her face. Her spine was, I didn't know the word. Her spine was like . . .? /The feed suggested 'supple'" (14). Here Titus attempts to find language that adequately describes his fascination with Violet, but when he fails, the feed immediately intervenes and provides a possible match to his thoughts. Though the narrative emphasizes the inseparability of human and machine, it undercuts this cohesion by emphasizing the ways in which the machine is diminishing human cognition, or the ability to think critically.

Another example of this relationship between the loss of language and the overreliance on technology is when Titus is trying to tell Violet stories: "I tried to just talk to her. I tried not to listen to the noise on the feed, the girls in wet shirts offering me shampoo. I told her stories. They were only a sentence long, each one of them. That's all I knew how to find. So I told her broken stories. The little pieces of broken stories I could find. I told her what I could" (296). Here Titus can only manage single-sentence stories—importantly, even these stories are not stories he is actively thinking of; instead they are stories he is "finding," the way we might sort through and select files on a computer. This quote also illustrates how consumerism is implicated in the loss of language when part of Titus's difficulty in finding stories is his being bombarded by advertisements on the feed that he must then attempt to ignore.

The inability to ignore feed advertisements is returned to throughout the text and is perhaps first highlighted near the beginning of the narrative when Titus lands on the moon for spring break. Immediately upon arrival, Titus explains, "I was trying to talk to Link, but I couldn't because I was getting bannered so hard, and I kept blinking and trying to walk forward with my carry-on. I can't hardly remember any of it. I just remember that everything in the banners looked goldy and sparkling" (8). This is the first example in the narrative in which the feed, in effect, ends up paralyzing Titus—he keeps attempting to walk forward but is being "bannered so hard" that not only is he unable to walk, but he is also unable to talk to Link. Though this scene is described as an everyday occurrence and therefore not something Titus usually responds to, it is particularly alarming because the barrage of feed information essentially leaves Titus physically impaired, verbally debilitated, and unable to record or perhaps access memories of those several minutes. Though this physical, verbal, and mental interruption is brief, this occurrence signals the nefarious nature of technology throughout the narrative.

In the days following Titus and his friends contracting the virus that results in the temporary feed shutdown, Titus suffers the incredibly uncomfortable experience of being alone in his head. During this time, he attempts to explain life before the feed: "I don't know when they first had feeds. Like maybe, fifty or a hundred years ago. Before that, they had to use their hands and their eyes. Computers were all outside the body. They carried them around outside of them, in their hands, like if you carried your lungs in a briefcase and opened it to breathe" (47). In this world, it is hard to imagine a body that is separate from technology. The protagonist goes on to describe that

> the braggest thing about the feed, the thing that made it really big, is that it knows everything you want and hope for, sometimes before you even know what those

things are. It can tell you how to get them, and help you make buying decisions that are hard. Everything we think and feel is taken in by the corporations, mainly by data ones like Feedlink and OnFeed and American Feedware, and they make a special profile, one that's keyed just to you, and then they give it to their branch companies, or other companies buy them, and they can get to know what it is we need, so all you have to do is want something and there's a chance it will be yours. (48)

The internet knowing what Titus wants even before Titus knows what he wants (and therefore dictating and mitigating that want, which connects back to being written by mass consensus rather than writing the self) makes explicit the anxieties associated with the internet defining who we are and not the other way around. In this world, the technologies that have literally fused with human bodies are defining who those humans are by way of large corporations that make thinking for oneself unnecessary and perhaps even impossible, as is exemplified above when Titus cannot think of words to use to describe basic feelings. A more startling example of this failure to think for oneself is when Titus tries so hard to comfort Violet with stories, but he can think of none, partially due to the rampant advertising that he cannot seem to slow down. In *Feed*, not only are bodies inextricably linked with hardware technologies, but these hardware technologies allow and even necessitate an online presence that inscribes the individual using data mining and other illusive measures never fully articulated or understood by the characters in the book. *Feed* is perhaps a perfect example of a bleak future inspired by grave anxieties of technofuturism. Hayles writes, "the posthuman implies not only a coupling with intelligent machines but a coupling so intense and multifaceted that it is no longer possible to distinguish meaningfully between the biological organism and the informational circuits in which the organism is enmeshed" (35). This definition of posthuman and the anxiety it engenders is most acutely illustrated through the character of Violet.

Violet comes from a family that did not have the money to equip her with a feed at birth. Her father, realizing in Violet's early childhood that she had no chance of success or normalcy without the feed, had one installed even though doctors explained that installing one later in life might lead to complications. Therefore, the virus has more effect on Violet than it does her peers, and her feed begins to deteriorate, making her more aware of problematic aspects of the technology and more inspired to reject them. During one particular tirade when she is attempting to convince Titus of the feed's ruinous qualities, she rants,

> They're also waiting to make you want things. Everything we've grown up with—the stories on the feed, the games, all of that—it's all streamlining our personalities so we're easier to sell to. I mean, they do these demographic studies that divide

everyone up into a few personality types, and then you get ads based on what you're supposedly like. They try to figure out who you are, and to make you conform to one of their types for easy marketing. It's like a spiral: They keep making everything more basic so it will appeal to everyone. And gradually, everyone gets used to everything being basic, so we get less and less varied as people, more simple. So the corps make everything even simpler. And it goes on and on. (97)

If the relationship between consumerism, technology, and the diminishing ability to construct self was not made apparent before this point, Violet makes it startlingly clear: the feed works to streamline personalities by keeping track of what people do and, in particular, what people buy, so that big corporations can create products and advertisements that are more basic, which in turn makes people more basic, simpler, less varied, implying the emergence of a homogenous posthumanism.

Because the confluence of technology, personhood, and consumerism in *Feed* works to reobjectify, there is little hope for subjectivity, and thus little hope for attaining selfhood outside of the prescriptive and commodity-driven culture of which the characters are a part. Indeed, *Feed* makes literal the impossibility of living outside the confines of commodified culture when Violet's attempts at resisting the marketing ploys of the internet, now hardwired into her physical person, result in her death. As Violet's machinery malfunctions and she becomes less and less able to function mentally and physically, she reaches out to medical professionals and "investors" (read "medical insurance companies"). This is their ghastly reply:

> We're sorry, Violet Durn. Unfortunately, FeedTech and other investors reviewed your purchasing history, and we don't feel that you would be a reliable investment at this time. No one could get what we call a "handle" on your shopping habits, like for example you asking for information about all those wow and brag products and then never buying anything. We have to inform you that our corporate investors were like, "What's doing with this?" Sorry—I'm afraid you'll just have to work with your feed the way it is. . . . Maybe, Violet, if we check out some of the great bargains available to you through the feednet over the next six months, we might be able to create a consumer portrait of you that would interest our investment team. How 'bout it, Violet Durn? Just us, you and me—girls together! Shop till you stop and drop! (247)

Of course, Violet does not have six months—the machinery attached to her spinal cord is deteriorating and causing a multitude of unpleasant and life-threatening medical conditions. The cavalier attitude of the Feedtech employee reinforces the cruel callousness of a world so dependent on machines and consumerism that humanness is left behind. Importantly, it is Violet's resistance to letting the feed create a purchasing/personality portfolio of her that causes her ultimate demise: Feedtech does not want to invest money in helping someone they cannot get a handle on. Rather than opening up more liberating possibilities, the space of the digital in *Feed* is responsible for the deterioration of language, the inability to think critically, and the erasure of individuality.

## Conclusion

In *The Question Concerning Technology*, Martin Heidegger "points to the discomfort of being, namely the homelessness of human beings in a modern technological society" (Turner 527). The texts discussed in this essay all speak to this homelessness. In *#16things*, Morgan is literally displaced because her mother is dying and she does not know her father. For Morgan, technology by way of the internet offers her a space to gesture toward home—a place she can know and understand intimately—but it ultimately leaves her feeling untethered because she cannot be honest in that space, and she also feels violated by it. For Emma in *The Future of Us*, the internet is a complete mystery outside of cultural context and the confines of time and space. In *The Unwritten*, blogs and other internet paraphernalia drop into the narrative haphazardly while Tom attempts to find traction in an extremely slippery reality, made malleable by an unstable collective unconscious informed by mass media. In *Feed*, no characters are at home in their own minds as software and corporations inform every thought. These YA narratives thematize the relationship between homelessness and technology. If YA narratives are about entering the social, more contemporary coming-of-age narratives necessitate this entrance into the social by emphasizing that there is no actual home. Simultaneously, however, contemporary YA narratives also underscore just how tenuous and difficult entering the social is. This premise, that there is simultaneously no home but little hope of successfully entering adulthood by acquiring a sense of self, relegates the adolescent to perpetual liminality. This state could account for the proliferation of categories attempting to name adolescence: pre-teenagehood, teenagehood, adolescence, extended adolescence, emerging adulthood, etc. As the terrain for what it means to enter the social becomes more complex, the attempts at naming this process become equally as complex.

While YA texts are most commonly understood to be books about attaining some semblance of agency with the end goal of embracing and celebrating subjectivity, the protagonists discussed here waffle between being *writers* and being *written*. They encounter writing and intertextuality through the digital landscape—a landscape that presents only the illusion of agency and subjectivity. As Tom Taylor finds out, it is the collective consciousness (altered by print media), that ultimately grants him power, not his own ability to create.

The transformative effects media can have on human beings were predicted by Marshall McLuhan more than fifty years ago:

> By the 1960s, Marshall McLuhan was speculating about the transformation that media, understood as technological prostheses, were effecting on human beings. He argues that humans react to stress in their environments by withdrawing the locus of selfhood inward, in a numbing withdrawal from the world he called (following Hans Selye and Adolphe Jonas) "autoamputation." This withdrawal in turn facilitates and requires compensating technological extensions that project the body-as-prosthesis back out into the world. . . . McLuhan clearly sees that electronic media are capable of bringing about a reconfiguration so extensive as to change the nature of "man." (Hayles 34)

These four YA novels show McLuhan's ideas in action. In *#16things*, Morgan's asocial behavior in the actual world and her withdrawal inward is countered by her internet presence/persona. In *The Future of Us*, we might understand the future Facebook pages as preemptive "compensating technological extensions" of self, but extensions that only negatively complicate the present. In both *The Unwritten* and *Feed*, there is essentially no "locus of selfhood" in which to withdraw but only technological prosthesis. The texts discussed here do not assign many, if any, positive attributes to technological extensions/conflations of self. Instead, they rigorously reinforce the posthumanist depiction of the self as an amalgam, a collection of various society-influenced aspects whose definitions are in a constant state of revision. Rather than focusing on the potentially subversive and positive attributes of such indeterminacy, as Flanagan suggests, these texts and other YA narratives focusing on advanced technologies, specifically the internet, instead blanch at the cultural anxiety/fantasy of information disembodiment takeover. In each of these texts, the disappearing divide between the virtual and the material creates a deeply troubling indeterminacy. At the root of this upset is that there is no actual, material self that is distinguishable from the technologies that inscribe us.

## Notes

1. Hayles contests the notion, proposed by cyberneticists and enthusiastically endorsed by transhumanism, that information or identity can be disembodied: "Information, like humanity, cannot exist apart from the embodiment that brings it into being as a material entity in the world" (48).

## Works Cited

Anderson, M. T. *Feed*. Somerville: Candlewick, 2010. Print.

Asher, Jay, and Carolyn Mackler. *The Future of Us*. New York: Simon and Schuster, 2012. Print.

Buckingham, David. "Is There a Digital Generation?" *Digital Generations: Children, Young People, and the New Media*. Ed. David Buckingham and Rebekah Willett. New York: Routledge, 2013. 1–13. Print.

Carey, Mike. *The Unwritten Vol. 1: Tommy Taylor and the Bogus Identity*. Illus. Peter Gross. New York: Vertigo, 2010. Print.

———. *The Unwritten Vol. 2: Inside Man*. Illus. Peter Gross. New York: Vertigo, 2010. Print.

———. *The Unwritten Vol. 3: Dead Man's Knock*. Illus. Peter Gross. New York: Vertigo, 2011. Print.

———. *The Unwritten Vol. 4: Leviathan*. Illus. Peter Gross. New York: Vertigo, 2011. Print.

Coats, Karen. *Looking Glasses and Neverlands: Lacan, Desire, and Subjectivity in Children's Literature*. Iowa City: U of Iowa P, 2007. Print.

Flanagan, Victoria. *Technology and Identity in Young Adult Fiction: The Posthuman Subject*. New York: Palgrave Macmillan, 2014. Print.

Gross, Peter. "The Greatest Unwritten Interview of Them All: Part Two." Interview by Christian Hoffer. *Theouthousers.com*. N.p., n.d. Web. 1 Mar. 2015.

Gurtler, Janet. *#16thingsithoughtweretrue*. Naperville: Sourcebooks, 2014. Print.

Hayles, N. Katherine. *How We Became Posthuman: Virtual Bodies in Cybernetics, Literature, and Informatics*. Chicago: U of Chicago P, 2008. Print.

Large, David. "Palimpsests and Intertexts: *The Unwritten*." *The Comics Grid: Journal of Comics Scholarship*. N.p., 2012. Web. 2 Mar. 2015.

McDonald, Matthew, and Stephen Wearing. *Social Psychology and Theories of Consumer Culture: A Political Economy Perspective*. New York: Routledge, 2013. Print.

Michelfelder, Diane P. "Web 2.0: Community as Commodity?" *The Good Life in a Technological Age*. Ed. Philip Brey, Adam Briggle, and Edward Spence. New York: Routledge, 2012. 203–14. Print.

Ostry, Elaine. "'Is He Still Human? Are You?': Young Adult Science Fiction in the Posthuman Age." *Lion and the Unicorn* 28.2 (2004): 222–46. *Project Muse*. Web. 15 Mar. 2015.

Pearson, Mary. *The Adoration of Jenna Fox*. New York: Holt, 2008. Print.

Shelley, Mary Wollstonecraft. 1818. *Frankenstein*. San Francisco: Ignatius, 2008. Print.

Turner, Bryan. "Postmodernity, Cosmopolitanism and Identity." *Identity, Culture and Globalization*. Ed. Ben-Rafael, Eliézer, and Yitzhak Sternberg. Boston: Brill, 2002. 527–42. Print.

Wasserman, Robin. *Skinned*. New York: Simon Pulse, 2008. Print.

# PART II
## THE MONSTROUS OTHER:
### Posthuman Bodies

# 3

# ONCE UPON A CYBORG
Cinder as Posthuman Fairytale

Angela S. Insenga

Even in the future, the story begins with "Once Upon a Time."
—Marissa Meyer

Virtually all iterations of the Cinderella mythos center on material embodiment, a trope that pervades any etymological study of the persecuted heroine core story.[1] Regardless of variant, the heroine struggles to attain an appropriate, empowered cultural expression of the body via some aspect of dress, for as virtuous as Aschenputtel, Yeh-Hsien, or Donkeyskin (she goes by many names) may be, her initial appearance renders her societally undesirable. She is granted an opportunity to revise the perception of her body by means of supernatural agents, and her "exceptionally sweet and gentle nature" (Perrault 55), finally matched with suitable physicality, is hailed, often at a public spectacle. Some act of magic saves her from the perilous servitude that her body exemplifies, and she is granted a deserving social station. Thus, as Andrew Lang notes in his exploration of the tale's origin, "One thing is plain, a naked and shoeless race could not have invented Cinderella" (x).

Marissa Meyer deploys the tale type as a scaffold for her young adult science fiction novel *Cinder*,[2] alluding primarily to Charles Perrault's nineteenth-century tale "Cendrillon" and Disney's film adaptation (1950). Although Meyer, too, utilizes the embodiment trope endemic in the Cinderella mythology, she does so in a posthuman context, so that the concept is not relegated solely to materiality. Instead, embodiment in *Cinder* also reflects the gradual displacement of the liberal humanist organic subject—the biological body—from its preeminence over intelligent information systems. Meyer complicates the tale's mythos, requiring readers to turn from surface to subtext, from the slipper to the composition of the foot that wears it.

We can first root Cinder's corporeality at the intersection of the bioconservative and transhumanist debate occurring in our own political, medical, and academic arenas. The two groups, existing at opposite ends of a spectrum, epitomize a prevailing cultural dialectic concerning our physical and ideological evolution toward the posthuman condition. Transhumanists promote the ethical advancement of biotechnologies, worrying less about the minutia of posthumanity's cultural landscape and, instead, pondering the democratic distribution and ethics of scientific advancement. Bioconservatives deem such technologies philosophically, politically, and metaphysically abhorrent. They oppose biological augmentation in varying degrees, focusing on how introducing too much biodiversity will irreparably modify our essential humanness, thereby ushering in psychosocial and geopolitical destabilization. Cinder's body is a manifestation of this dialectic, and my close reading aims to examine how, via the delivery system of popular versions of the fairytale, Cinder is the instantiation of posthuman anxiety. She learns to resolve acculturated inscriptions of her body through constant interplay between emergent selves, finally becoming emblematic of the multiplicity of existence that New Beijingers—and, by extension, YA readers—must grapple with to thrive.

Once touted as supreme progenitors, humans living in the posthuman era grapple with the reassessment of the ontological position that "privileges informational patterns over material instantiation so that embodiment in a biological substrate is seen as an accident of history rather than an inevitability of life" (Hayles 2). The human body, once seen as the only appropriate vessel to hold the mind, undergoes a deconstruction at the onset of advancing biotechnologies, resulting in the need for human recognition of our reflexive coexistence as consciousness always already in the process of inhabiting the fittest bodies to which we avail ourselves. Meyer's fictional heroine exists in a world in which these theoretical concepts play out. Her narrative, framed by textual features prevalent in "Cinderella," executes a clinamen, swerving from common divestitures—a lack of pedigree, poor parentage, poverty, and resulting social enmity—to the identification of cybernetic augmentation as the prime marginalizing agent in the sociopolitical context of post–World War IV New Beijing. One hundred twenty-six years in the future, the Letumosis pandemic and an uneasy peace between Earth and the evil Lunar Queen create instability. Being 36.28 percent cyborg in a world largely unaccepting of biotechnological enhancement, Linh Cinder's presence only increases the citizens' anxiety. In *Cinder*, Meyer revises the previous image of Cinderella as one whose temporary appearance masks a normative mien, since the insertion of the posthuman body disallows simple excision of culturally undesirable traits to reveal an accepted self. *Cinder*'s backdrop presents parallel and, at times, intersecting trajectories connected to the heroine's dual origins: she springs from the precursory tale and inhabits the world Meyer imagines.

Ostensibly cognizant of her readers' "deep knowledge of the traditional [Cinderella] narrative," Meyer makes use of the story's "constellation" (Zipes 120) before introducing recombinant components of the mythos, the first of which is the techno-segregation in New Beijing. Book One, chapter one hails its YA demographic with an epigraph taken from the Brothers Grimm's "Cinderella": "They took away her beautiful clothes, dressed her in an old gray smock, and gave her wooden shoes" (116). Readers thus are reminded of the familiar tale before they experience the variations that follow; as a result, they understand immediately that their heroine is the ill-treated but kindhearted heroine. Meyer places sixteen-year-old mechanic Linh Cinder in a shabby marketplace, where she must work as the sole wage earner in her adopted mother's home. She struggles to remove her ill-fitting and rusted cybernetic foot, succeeding with a final twist of the fastening screw, its "engraved cross marks worn to a mangled circle" (3). She sits, her careworn foot dangling from wires connected to her leg, her hair in a greasy ponytail, waiting for the aged android Iko to return with a used foot more suitable for her growing adolescent frame.[3] While Cinder waits, her gaze at the detailed setting allows readers to observe Cinder's Eastern Commonwealth alongside her. Children sing "Ring around the Rosie," an ancient song repopularized since Letumosis, the deadly plague, has returned. Chang Sacha, the market's baker, reproves her children for playing next to a cyborg's stall, "[meeting] Cinder's gaze" before "[knotting] her lips" and dragging her son away while Cinder mutters, "It's not like wires are contagious" (5). Cinder is surprised when Prince Kaito (Kai) suddenly arrives, asking Cinder to utilize her mechanical skill[4] to retrieve research from his defunct android, Nainsi. He exhibits interest in her as a talented Commonwealth girl while there, but Cinder, conditioned by her culture's repeated marginalization of cybernetic parts, hides her affected limbs (foot and hand), fearing judgment.

Cinder is wary of any attention, knowing that Sacha's cruel comments reflect New Beijingers' bioconservative belief that cyborgs are less valuable than their fully organic fleshy counterparts, that those most deserving of dignity are those who possess no synthetic elements. Referring to such a perspective, Clare Bradford, Kerry Mallan, John Stephens, and Robyn McCallum write of a changing social order in which "many of the binary concepts used to make sense of experience in the past will no longer function" logically (154). Cinder's reaction to Sacha, followed by her reticence in front of Prince Kai, establishes a similar acculturating process that cyborgs and androids in fictional New Beijing undergo. For Sacha, wires are suspect. Though she first detects Cinder's *human* gaze, Sacha's prejudice is common to those in New Beijing. Cinder, conditioned to be ashamed of her biotechnology, comments sarcastically on technophobia's provinciality yet wilts under human judgment of her embodiment. Her selfhood derives "from what others have put onto and into her body, once again destabilizing any notion of fixed coherence" (Mitchell 55). Sacha's glare alongside Cinder's sarcasm and desire to pass as human while with Prince Kai points to a caustic feedback loop by which she receives others' judgment and recurrently internalizes it. Her sense of self is mediated by others like Sacha who define her as Other, as queer.[5] The baker's prejudicial reaction reflects human fears about the loss of organic superiority in a posthuman world. N. Katherine Hayles notes that some envision a nightmare scenario requiring "[abdication] of their responsibilities as autonomous independent beings" (288). Applied to Sacha, this outward disavowal of the cybernetic body reveals her human interiority. Because she desires to retain her precarious social position in an already tumultuous time in the Commonwealth, she teaches her son to revile Cinder's kind in hopes of perpetuating a crumbling social order in which she can retain agency.

Cinder's hand and foot, the augmentations which will be the most outward manifestation of posthumanity's largesse, are illustrative of the necessary philosophical revision of human agency in such a cultural backdrop. In the ideal posthuman world "there are no essential differences or absolute demarcations between bodily existence and computer simulation" or "cybernetic mechanism and biological organism" (Hayles 3), so Sacha's reaction to Cinder, coupled as it is with the cyborg's thoughts, makes evident the ignorance of New Beijingers who believe that valid ontological positions exist only when human consciousness is affixed to a body made of organic matter. But the shame—ostensibly a human feeling—that Cinder experiences because of her cyborg parts (which she hides from Kai) paradoxically reveals her adherence to liberal humanism's precepts of fairness and inclusivity, thus dismantling the notion that she, a product of "biology/machine symbiosis" (Haney vii), is not a sentient being in possession of a viable consciousness. Sacha takes the part for the whole, ignoring that Cinder is just like her despite her augmentations.

Francis Fukuyama, an opponent of transhumanist development of biotechnologies like Cinder's fictive ones, argues that accepting these scientific advancements into society "would mean a new social hierarchy resulting in prolonged, global strife" and points out that wealth would dictate the dispersal of these advancements, thus "provid[ing] the makings ... of a full-scale class war" (16). In the fictional Eastern Commonwealth, tensions between humans and posthumans have yet to become violent; rather, androids and cyborgs, owned by humans, experience the populace's protracted technophobia. Thus, just as

Fukuyama would marginalize biotechnological beings to avoid destabilization of the world order, organic citizens of New Beijing like Sacha, surrounded by perils beyond their control, treat synthetics as virtual slaves, refusing to accept the possibility that the gradual introduction of biological enhancements into the population is a beneficial course that acknowledges how "[people] and technology are inseparable and that technology shapes us even as we shape it" (Morrissey 191). Although we could consider ameliorating devices as simple as contact lenses to be posthuman accoutrement since they are synthetic additions to our organic matter that enhance our ability to see, largely bioconservative New Beijing gives preferential treatment to its highly organic beings, sublimating android and cyborg alike in favor of citizenry made up of blood and bone.

As Sacha reviles Cinder in the marketplace, so does Adri, the girl's legal guardian, at home. Both women, in line with bioconservative fears that "human technologies might be 'dehumanizing' [and could] undermine our human dignity or inadvertently erode something that is deeply valuable about being human" (Bostrom 203), degrade Cinder and her kind, becoming bellwethers of the empire's hostile attitudes toward posthumans in their midst. Cinder's embodiment, which came about because of an accident (as she was told), was not conceived to be reviled. Her adoptive father, an award-winning scientist, restored her broken human body with state-of-the-art cybernetic materials that resemble human limbs. The care he exhibited as a scientist, then, is an indicator that not everyone in this setting chafes at posthuman possibility. It is after the surgical process and his untimely death that her adoptive stepmother Adri—another character connected to the fairytale mythos—disavows Cinder's enhancements, finding no comparison or possible connection between the cyborg and her fully human daughters. Though her father gifted Cinder with mechanical skill that could benefit humans and gave her cybernetic parts reminiscent of human limbs, his efforts do not allow her to retain her position with Adri's daughters. Because her father was an early victim of the plague, Cinder has grown up with only Adri's acculturating influence, the virtues of her body hidden in favor of emblems reflective of servitude: work gloves, dirty clothes, and rusting parts that pain her. True to the wicked stepmother persona popularized by Perrault and Disney, Adri habitually calls Cinder a "thing" (25), roots her in the grimy stall, teaches her to conceal attributes that make her exceptional, and refuses to attend to her changing mechanical needs as her human body grows. She holds Cinder to essentialist standards of feminine beauty by decrying the girl's fitness for Prince Kaito's ball, yet erases her ability to engage in the culture of her daughters despite Cinder's desire to do so. Further, she inhibits Cinder's social advancement by denying the girl the dignities of her own body, all the while exploiting Cinder's advanced mechanical abilities for her own economic benefit.

The laws in the city of New Beijing are macrocosmic representations of Adri's and Sacha's thinking. Meyer includes no detail of protections that posthumans like Cinder might expect in a posthuman world,[6] but community action exposes a discriminatory ethic of care that forces cyborgs to submit to medical trials in the ongoing battle against Letumosis. Of this conscription, Cinder thinks,

> It was made out to be some sort of honor, giving your life for the good of humanity, but it was . . . a reminder that cyborgs were not like everyone else. Many of them had been given a second chance at life by the generous hand of scientists and therefore owed their very existence to those who had created them. They were lucky to have lived this long, many thought. It's only right that they should . . . give up their lives in search for the cure. (28)

Some of the philosophical and ethical concerns about transhumanist exploration and eventual implementation arise here. In New Beijing, royal researchers, aware of cyborgs' desire for acceptance, tout community service objectives in an effort to convince the downtrodden to acquiesce to testing. As a hybridized body capable of mechanical wonders and of human feeling, Cinder sees the charade. Her thought processes sharply focus the complexity involved in classification of cyborgs as less than human. Her narration here highlights complex thinking, but despite these human emotions, Adri's inhumane treatment, coupled with public actions against posthumans, dictates that Cinder is not human enough for the twenty-second century. The scientific community that gave her life can also take it, especially with the threat of Letumosis looming.

Bioconservatism often stems from religious belief that includes a supreme progenitor and His creations who have been endowed with the ability to reason and, more importantly, to choose restraint. In his article "Design-A-Kid," Bill McKibben chastises the scientific community for its lack of self-control, warning, "If we cannot summon our ability to use self-restraint . . . we will leave our specialness behind forever. . . . [and] there will be no way, and no reason, to turn back." McKibben worries that amplified promises of posthumanity spurred on by the transhumanist movement that focuses predominantly on positive effects of biotechnologies could push traditional humankind down a secular slope, moving us away from a Judeo-Christian God-given "specialness" and toward the constant struggle of keeping at bay the presumed hollowness of machine life. He wonders too if such a world would see continual improvement in the absence of human tensions needed for progress, asking us (by rephrasing Robert Browning), what is the point of heaven if our reach no longer exceeds our grasp? Leon Kass also points to the dangers of "making the essence of human nature the last project of [our] technical mastery," indicating that, "in his moment of triumph, Promethean man will become a contented cow" (48). The logical extension of transhumanist endeavor for these thinkers is a loss of desire for betterment instead of a revision of humanity's position in a larger schematic that leads to advancement of all beings.

Meyer manages, however, to offer some examples that do not fit into the bioconservatist/transhumanist dichotomy prevalent in the kingdom, namely, Iko, the android who is Cinder's companion and helpmate, and the architecture of the palace. In *Cinder*, ancient architecture and religious signs exist in tandem, each complementing the other, and androids are not simply wires and metal, thus confounding the neatly discrete ideas of bioconservatives while calling into question the idealism of transhumanists. When she visits the palace, Cinder's built-in netlink informs her that it "had been rebuilt after World War IV . . . [and] was designed in the fashion of the old world, with hearty dosages of both nostalgic symbolism and state-of-the-art engineering" (155). Cinder notices that the golden roofing tiles are galvanized steel covered with solar capsules and that the statues of gargoyles contain motion sensors and cameras. Cinder also sees a "squat Buddha sculpture scanning visitors for weapons" (156), indicating that religious iconography retains symbolic meaning for believers while also becoming functional. Despite the material amalgamation of old and new exemplified in the palace at the center of the realm, social practices that engulf the Commonwealth demonstrate that outmoded ideas related to humanity's preeminence remain, though Prince Kaito, the emperor-in-waiting, demonstrates an affinity for technology as it applies to the good of his future people, proffering a glimpse forward.

Iko also functions as a salient amalgam attesting simultaneously to the negative cultural worth afforded to androids in bioconservatist New Beijing and to the inevitable blending of biological and technological advancement. Adri sees the aging android as just saleable spare parts whenever Iko's personality traits, attributed to a "programming error" that made her inexpensive to acquire and difficult to sell, shine through. Iko's behavior, at least on the surface, acts as comic relief typical of the Disney sidekick. But her endearing human mannerisms point to the innocuous yet crucial blending that will inevitably occur in a posthumanist world. Iko is an android, a much earlier iteration of the synthetics that aid Cinder, but she nevertheless possesses attributes of a stereotypical adolescent girl. She is a gossip-hound, smitten with the celebrity prince Kai, "her metallic voice squeaking" (12) when she meets him, and she has a yen for common feminine items, gleefully scanning and rescanning the velvet ribbon Cinder's younger stepsister Peony gives her while dreaming about visiting local dress stores. After Adri has Iko dismantled, Cinder salvages the android's humanity, contained in her personality chip, preserving the android's essence even though her outmoded body has been destroyed. In fact, Cinder installs Iko's chip into the spaceship Rampion in the second book of the series, further illustrating the ongoing revision of the body/mind binary in favor of the mind's existence without a stable synthetic or all-too-fragile organic body. Later in the series, Iko is gifted a humanoid form, and, as we will see with Cinder's corporeal journey, Iko retains previous understanding despite the transition, the residual blending with the embryonic. She still possesses the girlish behavior that typifies her—ever the fangirl, she faints from Emperor Kai's embrace in *Winter*—but she also comes into new consciousness with each physical incarnation. We have to point out here that, ironically, by retaining Iko's body/mind dichotomy, Meyer undercuts the entire concept of material embodiment. According to Hayles, Iko cannot possibly remain "stable," for with each new embodiment her mind and personality will change, shaped by the new environment. Perhaps Meyer is trying to convey that Iko's ability to dream of an ideal humanoid body, which she finally receives, is indicative of growing beyond just a computerized brain.

Thus far in the novel, narrative details familiar in popularized versions of Cinderella frame the unfamiliar posthuman anxieties in New Beijing; however, at this juncture Meyer diverges from the type A "persecuted heroine" tale type identified by Marian Roalfe Cox[7] to dismantle prevailing binaries existent in the fairytale mythos and, consequently, in largely bioconservative New Beijing. Like Cinderella, Cinder is relegated to subhuman status by her guardians, she is interested in the royal gala, and she desires freedom and happiness that open access to society can provide. But her dreams of release are snatched from her: as she scours the junkyard for parts to repair the prince's android, Peony, her younger, devoted adoptive sister, exhibits the first signs of Letumosis and soon dies. Enraged, Adri sells Cinder to the royal scientist, Dr. Dimitri Erland,[8] who has *carte blanche* to test experimental vaccines on conscripted cyborgs. This sequence ruptures the heretofore parallel trajectories that Cinder and Cinderella traverse. In the popularized Disney tale and in its German antecedent, the wicked guardian figure denies Cinderella cultural engagement, sequestering her in the domestic space to toil while the finely garbed sisters attend the celebration. Through magic, Disney's Cinderella gains access to the ball; in the Grimm brothers' "Aschenputtel," the heroine's steadfast prayer at her mother's grave earns heaven's grace, and doves bring her a gown and glass shoes so that she can attend the king's three-day festival. But here, Meyer embraces Cox's type C delineation of the persecuted heroine tale in which the protagonist, judged as treacherous by her guardian, is cast out à la Cordelia in *King Lear*. Banishing Cinder to a laboratory where scores of cyborgs must sacrifice themselves for humans ironically enables her eventual rebellion, since the secrets revealed to her while there recast the lab and her body as loci of eventual empowerment, qualities firmly outside of the mythos.

Dr. Erland's encounters with Cinder continue Meyer's inversion of source material as, through scientific study instead of magic, he works to reveal her origin, upending the protagonist's persecuted role in the tale and reconfiguring cyborgs' potential positive role in New Beijing. Erland values cyborgs who possess the most organic matter because these candidates' physical composition provides the most accurate data for development of a human antidote for Letumosis. When Cinder's body rejects the Letumosis virus, Erland's scientific fervor extends far beyond the promise of a cure. But during ensuing examinations, he talks *with* her, not *at* her, requiring only that she exist as she is. Using his expertise, this "fairy godfather" gifts Cinder with the self-worth automatically afforded to humans. Later, he sequences her DNA and informs her that she is a Lunar "shell," immune not just to Letumosis but also to the Lunar Queen Levana's manipulative glamours. After more extensive testing, he discloses that Cinder is, in fact, not a "shell" but that her ability to glamour was deactivated during her cybernetic augmentation to save her from detection on Earth. These plot revelations trifurcate Cinder's identity and begin to close a loop in her corporeal herstory. She confronts these heterogeneous selves while gazing into a portscreen at her reflection, an act *verboten* to Lunars and implicitly discouraged by earthen culture, since what Cinder has been taught to see is the ugliness of her body. Meyer writes,

> She couldn't understand what Levana and her kind, *their* kind, found so disturbing about [mirrors]. Her mechanical parts were the only disturbing thing in Cinder's reflection, and that had been done to her on Earth.
> Lunar. And cyborg.
> And a fugitive. (190–91)

Habituated to seeing herself through humans' gaze as "disturbing," Cinder wonders why Lunars refuse to look at themselves, first disassociating from Levana but then acquiescing to kinship through the emphasized third-person pronoun "their." She remains disgusted by her mechanical parts, a bodily acculturation she cannot yet escape.[9] Facing her Lunar origin, contending with her human and mechanical parts (the "tan skin of her arms contrasted with the dark steel of her hand" [190]), she settles on her fugitive status because these physical truths form the strata of Cinder's anagnorisis. She climbs a ladder of specificity, dismantling and reassembling her identity, gaining bodily insight from Erland but retaining psychosocial experiences accumulated on each rung, finally seizing upon the elusivity her fugitive status can afford. Thus, as she examines her Lunar face, she is ever cognizant of her cybernetic hand that is so distinct from her human skin. Her emotional reaction to these revelations and her resulting thought processes continue to reveal her human qualities despite posthuman attributes and alien genealogy, classified as monstrous on Earth. But here, too, she becomes an admixture not as easily annexed for classification and recognizes the possibility for subversiveness because of her subjugated selves. Such mindfulness is inconsistent with the original tale types' female heroines, who frequently present with qualities like "obedience, humility, friendliness, helpfulness and, for practical reasons, the ability to manage with housework" (Toomeos-Orglaan 51).

After critiquing New Beijing's outmoded human/posthuman dichotomy due to Erland's revelation of Cinder's pedigree, Meyer further inverts the Cinderella mythos to thrust forward this corporeal circumstance and its potential for social good. At first Cinder decides to flee the city using an old gasoline car, but then she learns that the Lunars have been spying on the palace by means of a secret recorder hidden in Kai's android. (The recorder is what caused the android to malfunction and what led Kai to seek Cinder's help.) In line with her development as an unconventional iteration of the Cinderella figure, Cinder decides to attend the grand ball, where she plans to tell the prince about Levana's espionage. She dresses herself in Peony's discarded and ill-fitting ball dress, "wrinkled as an old man's face" (324); her stepsister Pearl's hand-me-down velvet boots; the old and rusting foot, a "paperweight" (325) hastily reattached to her leg after Adri sold the newer one; and the silken gloves sullied by Pearl in a jealous rage to "complete the [sartorial] affront" (325). Her clothing, mismatched and amassed, is, like her, a series of identities beginning to act in concert. The ramshackle Volkswagen Bug, a self-fashioned carriage that looks like "a rotting pumpkin" (47), illustrates Cinder's self-reliance and growing will to enact a transgressive plan: "The car was sandwiched [parked] between two sleek, chrome-accented hovers. Its awful orange paint was dulled by the garage's flickering lights. It didn't belong. Cinder knew how it felt" (325–26). Dilapidated car and motley cyborg are well-suited partners, the old, used, and new coexisting, synthetic enmeshed with organic. Not content to replicate the fairytale, though, Meyer reverses it further to emphasize her heroine's self-worth gained through an accession of her once disparate and despised identities.

In a blinding rainstorm, Cinder careens into a tree and must walk the rest of the way, arriving at the palace with "wet boots squishing[,] . . damp hair[,] . . . [and] mud splatters on the hem of her wrinkled silver dress" (336). Instead of obeying Adri, fully devoting herself to Erland's scientific cause, or yielding to New Beijingers who see her and other posthumans as lesser, Cinder's focus is on what could happen to others should she not share her new information with Kai. Her thinking processes confirm that she is not rigidly partitioned off from humanity, living a hyphenated human-inhuman existence. Rather, her empathic impulse indicates that she is circuitously connected, an image that "implies a more reflexive and transformative union" (Hayles 115). To emphasize the radical importance of reflexivity, Meyer returns to the community celebration that acts as the apex of the popularized Cinderella tale to set in motion a dazzling de-Disneyfication in which Cinder displays all of her socially attenuate selves as "loosely coupled" entities, a phrase that Norbert Wiener, when illustrating ways in which elements of the universe hold orbit without flying apart, uses to discuss the pinnacle of cybernetic advancement (32).

When Cinder enters, the ball guests turn to stare, "pinning [her] to the top of the stairs" (336). She stands on a precipice, straddling two epochs of her life. Behind her is a life as an unwilling servant in which she, a biodiverse marvel, was perceived as a worthless automaton, just as Iko was. Before her is certain humiliation and danger. She reflects, "Soon, Queen Levana would see her . . . and she would be taken, maybe killed. . . . But she had taken the risk. She had made the decision to come. It would not go to waste" (337). These dangers comprehended and accepted, Cinder descends the stairs, each step agony because of the rusting foot encased in the tight boot. The entrance, cinematic in scope, calls to mind the image of Disney's iconic degraded girl, now dressed by magic, arriving to awe guests with her beautiful dress and golden hair, shoes of glass, and rosy skin cleaned of ash. However, the magic in Meyer's iteration is not outward but lies beneath these adornments, *inside* the body of the heroine whose strengths had been revealed to her by Dr. Erland.

After Kai welcomes Cinder and listens to the news regarding Lunar spying, he does not act, going against traits of the classic male counterpart in the mythos, who is commonly characterized through his physical activity, "which is expressed in taking risks, being brave, fearless and adventurous" (Toomeos-Orglaan 50). Instead, the newly minted emperor announces his marriage to Levana (Levana has promised to give New Beijing the plague antidote if Kai will marry her) and takes Cinder's information under advisement, showcasing a more introspective version of the traditional hero. Kai's reversal clears the way for Cinder's further disruption of the Cinderella archetype. She responds by kissing Kai and declaring out loud that he is in love with her, much to his delighted shock. The triumph of this public brazenness is short-lived, however, since Levana announces the girl's alien genealogy to all. But before Cinder can be imprisoned, Meyer initiates a culminating capsizal of the tale type in which Cinder publicly demands notice and claims agency. The emotion surging through the teen—anger or awakened sexuality or, perhaps, both—allows her to overcome her failsafe chip so that her Lunar gifts surge forth, causing her entire body to become a stunning focal point of the ball yet again:

> Fireworks burst in her head. It felt as if her body were trying to dispel all her cyborg parts—explosions and sparks and smoke tearing at her flesh. Sweat sizzled on her brow. She felt different. Strong. Powerful. The left glove had started to melt, forming patches of gooey, silky skin on her white-hot metal hand. She could see electricity sizzling across the steel surface, but she couldn't tell if it was her human or cyborg eyes detecting it. Or maybe, not human. Not cyborg. Lunar. (363–64)

In this moment of interior tumult, Cinder's body orders and reorders her emergent consciousnesses externally, thus exemplifying true embodiment. Leah Phillips's contention that *Cinder* offers adolescent girls "ways out of the trap of appearance" through the sense of touch, which provides an "additional means of perceiving the body, particularly one's own" (41), functions well for this textual moment, as Peony's dress and the gloves from Kai melt into Cinder's cyborg parts, "silky skin" (364) matching her actual skin, adhering to metal that is also hers. The current she sees is also that which she feels, its sizzle melding together her heretofore disparate parts. Outwardly, she embodies all identities at once, nascent Lunar self demanding notice, the residual cybernetic and human ever present. And because the ball is an event to which all New Beijingers have been invited, Cinder's display acts as a public disavowal of the discrimination she has experienced. The young woman the guests ogled during her entrance, "mocking her" as rumors about her slovenly appearance "[take] flight" (364), is not just a girl in a dirty dress. After seeing through and revealing Levana's ugliness and ugly intent, Cinder tries to flee—teen embarrassment trumps Lunar power every time—but the as-yet oppressive, rusted foot gives way, and she is fully revealed as a cyborg Lunar who was reared as a human. Kai can only order that she be apprehended, and he is left staring down at the "dirty steel foot" he holds "clasped in both hands" (369).

In these consecutive sequences, Meyer centers Cinder's body as a text in the process of revision. She publicly claims a multifaceted identity in both instances. Cinder's decision to attend the ball by making use of the resources around her revamps the archetypal image of Cinderella as a creature acted upon and granted cultural mobility. She exhibits, too, the courage of her convictions even after her gasoline car is destroyed in the rain, and pinioned as she is at the top of the stairs, wearing the opposite of Cinderella's glorious blue gown in Disney's version, she risks earthen and Lunar detection when making her subversive entrance. In the second sequence of the celebration scene, Cinder negotiates her selves in front of a populace that does not yet accept biodiversity and is equally fearful of Lunars. Instead of being immobilized and humiliated, Cinder reveals a powerful self resulting from the very divestitures the source story typically eradicates. The blending of material goods that occurs as Cinder's Lunar powers surge forth highlights the cyborg body as "a stage on which are performed the contestations about the body boundaries that have often marked class, ethnic, and cultural differences" (Hayles 85). Material concerns burn away to reveal a powerful self that is still inscribed by social experience that systematically dismantles her worth. In New Beijing, where citizens are fearful of Lunar invasion, pandemic, and a destabilized government, they have refused to resolve anxieties related to posthuman advancement, displacing these fears onto cyborgs and androids instead of seeing them as emblems of progress that could erase boundaries so often opposed. The revelation of a self-possessed young woman cogently containing many identities serves as a progressive image for the populace, and they continue to grapple with the multiplicity of selves Cinder evinces as a blueprint for their own human advancement throughout The Lunar Chronicles. This event, a sea change for Cinder, also acts as a microcosm of the larger conflicts that play out in the series, all of which culminate in Winter, when Cinder, now as politically powerful as she is physically, negotiates a "fruitful and mutually beneficial . . . relationship" between Lunars and the Earthen Union before requiring that "all laws regarding cyborgs be reexamined . . . and [that they] be given the same equality and basic rights as everybody else" (787).

Cybernetic parts remain a focus at the end of the novel, Cinder's rusted foot serving as a reminder of her present inability to move entirely beyond the realities of her physical body, though, conversely, the "multicolored wires [dangling] from [her] cuffed pant leg" (374) signal the prospect for locomotion, an ability to connect and to gain mobility again. Dr. Erland visits Cinder in her prison cell to finish arming her for the battle to come, bringing with him a state-of-the-art hand and perfectly fitted foot, "[p]lated with 100 percent titanium. . . . with a hidden flashlight, a stiletto knife, a projectile gun, a screwdriver, and a universal connector cable" (377). With these gifts, he implores her to use her newfound Lunar ability to glamour the guards so that she may escape. In case she is not feeling as powerful as her feats at the ball indicated, he leaves her with one more bodily revelation: she is Princess Selene, the Lunar that Queen Levana fears most, since both are equally powerful. This disclosure adds a final rung to the ladder of corporeal specificity that Cinder must negotiate. After Erland's exit, Cinder adopts the posture in which readers first encountered her, sitting with a cybernetic foot in front of her, thinking. Her newfound self-awareness is the key difference that allows her to accept Erland's mission. She thinks, "Soon, the whole world would be searching for her . . . a deformed cyborg with a missing foot. A Lunar with a stolen identity. A mechanic. But they would be looking for a ghost" (387). Such prophetic claims do not a fairytale ending make; in effect, after the reversals at the public spectacle of the ball, Meyer focuses exclusively on finishing a posthuman fairytale. Cinder's newfound value and her willingness to contend with her identities even as she accepts the role of a fugitive—an elusive ghost in the machine of New Beijing but no longer a ghost unto herself—mark her as the physical embodiment of the compromise necessary for eventual physical and cultural health. Her escape neither precipitates a cyborg revenge plot nor indicates that her body will be docile, simply fitting in with a humanist tradition. Thus, she is not a triumph of biotechnology over humanity but a flawed adolescent alien with cyborg parts seeking her place in a complex yet wondrous world in which her creation was possible.

In "The Campaign for Shiny Futures," Farah Mendlesohn critiques YA science fiction for being too dreary, for forgetting that, along with a social critique, science fiction for juveniles historically holds wonderment as a core principle. The realms conceived in these science fiction texts concerned "the world of work, the world of changing technology, and the bright new opportunities promised by these things." *Cinder,* and indeed the entirety of The Lunar Chronicles, unquestionably portray a darkened worldview representative of Mendlesohn's critique. But Cinder's experiences throughout, at first situated at the juncture of the transhumanist and bioconservative debate in the fictive Eastern Commonwealth, eventually point to a possible brighter future in which humans, using Cinder's genesis and development, may embrace ways in which they are benefactors of biodiversity and ways that humans and cyborgs can live together instead of as perpetually opposed beings inserted into a false dichotomy that perpetuates untruths about cyborg behavior. After all, when presented with an opportunity to use her once-reviled posthuman body to save humans from disease and Lunar war, Cinder freely chooses to serve humanity because of her empathy for her fellow humans, and she chooses to use her posthuman gifts to explore her newfound Lunar power. She develops a commitment to open mediation between all of her selves, embodying them at a public spectacle. In doing so, she also manifests parallel adolescent and species development: "If one of the primary concerns of adolescence is figuring out one's self and one's identity, the posthuman context complicates those questions by casting species identity into doubt as well. In a sense, humanity itself is in the midst of coming of age . . . as it grapples with the shift from humanism to posthumanism" (Newcomb 178).

Cinder's integration of new knowledge and the public revelation of her socially stigmatic cybernetic features and alien genealogy, seen as single threads in a larger web of adolescent literatures representing humans grappling with their posthuman condition, therefore become metatextual endeavors.[10] She seeks to understand the multiplicity of selves she contains, and deploys new understanding publicly in an effort to revise what she and others like her signify to the populace of New Beijing. Readers, like guests at the ball, come to understand Cinder's growing bodily prescience and are introduced to the process of revising their own ontological precepts, especially if previously understood as affixed and outmoded binaries. Long inured to core stories, YA readers can find in *Cinder* a reconfigured heroine whose residual and emergent qualities represent a coming world in which cyborgs are "condensed image[s] of imagination and material reality, the two joined centres structuring any possibility of historical transformation" (Haraway 150). The material embodiment trope pervasive in the Cinderella mythos transmogrifies in *Cinder*, gloves, shoes, and gasoline carriages giving way to the salient image of a cyborg, alien yet utterly recognizable, claiming her complex bodily experience at a public spectacle, becoming the spectacle herself. In subsequent books of The Lunar Chronicles series, Meyer recapitulates her fairytale-in-the-future structure, taking up "Little Red Riding Hood" in *Scarlet*, "Rapunzel" in *Cress*, and "Snow White" in *Winter*, where she continues to cast Cinder as an emblem and agent of lasting cultural transformation. In fact, her eventual union with Kai in *Winter* signifies, both for New Beijingers and readers, the potent opportunity that coexistence through familiarization can provide.

## Notes

1. Marian Roalfe Cox indexed variants of the tale in 1893 to locate its genesis, recognizing five categories from 345 narratives studied. The ill-treated heroine, type A, includes the heroine's identification by means of a shoe. Types B and C, "Cat-skin" and "Cap o' Rushes," introduce the unnatural father and heroine's flight or banishment. These include sartorial tropes endemic in type A. Cox's last two categories, D and E, include "indeterminate" variants and hero tales that feature male protagonists, the most famous of which is "The Glass Mountain" and "The Little Bull Calf," both of which see the protagonists modifying their physical appearance to win the princess. In "The Glass Mountain," the boy kills a lynx and dons its claws to scale a magic tree. In "The Little Bull Calf," the boy must clothe himself in finery to gain an audience with the princess despite his possession of a ring and dragon's tongue that prove his identity. Additionally, R. D. Jameson lectured on the Chinese rendering, entitled "Yeh-Hsien," and found five endemic elements in the tale: (1) an ill-treated heroine who (2) performs menial work but (3) meets a prince who recognizes her heretofore ignored beauty and (4) identifies the protagonist by her shoe, thus (5) ensuring that she marries him (Jameson 81–82). Yeh-Hsien is recognized by royalty when she produces the ubiquitous golden slipper that matches one left behind at the festival, much like her European sisters. As he detailed this trope, Jameson indicated other bodily markers, such as a ring, that can serve as proof of identity or some difficult physical trial that only the ingénue can perform. Finally, Antti Aarne's landmark work *The Types of the Folktale* (1910) identified the

Cinderella tale as 510A, and some fifty years later, Stith Thompson revised Aarne's work, positing additional variants of tale type 510B. Both 510A and 510B reference appearance, often through clothing, as vital to the protagonist's status, eventual recognition, and rebirth.

2. *Cinder* is the first novel in The Lunar Chronicles. The second and third books, *Scarlet* (2013) and *Cress* (2014), present fairytale revisions of "Little Red Riding Hood" and "Rapunzel," respectively. The final book in the series, *Winter* (2015), is a revision of "Snow White." All three take place in the same posthumanist setting and present connected narratives. Throughout the series, Cinder serves as a cultural emblem of transformative possibility in varying degrees. In this piece, I focus predominantly on the inaugural novel in the series, in which the posthuman anxieties of the Eastern Commonwealth that inform Cinder's characterization and story arc are established. When germane, I include salient points from the remaining three texts in The Lunar Chronicles.

3. In "Putting the Punk in a Steampunk Cinderella: Marissa Meyer's 'Lunar Chronicles,'" (2015), Terri Doughty first draws attention to Meyer's interest in Asian culture, shared in an interview in the 2012 paperback version of *Cinder*, and then highlights a salient connection between the Chinese Cinderella variant and *Cinder*, saying, "Instead of fetishizing the tiny shoe, and by implication the tiny foot that fits it [as the Chinese variant does], Meyer focuses on the pain and constriction caused by her heroine's unnaturally small foot" (47).

4. Doughty endeavors to connect *Cinder* to the steampunk genre, noting ways in which the character adheres to the conventions of characterization. Cinder is a "maker" in that she can repair and create. She is, likewise, a cyborg, which is another figure within steampunk fiction. Importantly, in her study, Doughty points to ways in which steampunk literature "rejects contemporary consumerism and human subordination to technology" (50), a principle that figures largely in each of the novels of the series.

5. Jennifer Mitchell's essay, "'A girl. A machine. A freak': A Consideration of Contemporary Queer Composites" (2014), identifies Cinder's psychosocial experience as queer since "the questions of selfhood and species identification raised in [the novel] . . . are tied to queer theory's claims about stable identity and the impossibility of the 'knowable self'" (53).

6. See Bostrom or More.

7. Cf. endnote 1.

8. Erland functions as a fairy godfather in terms of the precursory tale from which Meyer draws, though he does aim his sights not only on Cinder's "happily ever after" but on the world's. He eventually reveals that he is a Lunar who once agreed that "shells" should be destroyed and discloses that his own daughter, a shell, was killed in the Lunar culling of cybernetic beings. His earthen task, then, is half penitence, half appalling, and his beneficence toward Cinder and desire to vanquish the Lunars is problematized when we consider the violence he has done to posthumans in his lab as he searches for Cinder/Selene.

9. Leah Phillips argues that it is through touch instead of sight that Cinder escapes "the trap of appearance that is not only engendered by the visuality (the insistence and reliance on the visual as a state of being) of popular and media culture but also by the mythic tradition (with

its ideal, heroic form)" (41). In line with this argument, Cinder's reflection and her reaction to it, still largely negative, relies on the visual. However, Cinder's conclusion—that she can use subversiveness to her advantage—indicates that confronting selves visually is a positive step toward actualization.

10. See Mildred Ames's *Anna to the Infinite Power* (1983), M. T. Anderson's *Feed* (2002), and Nancy Farmer's *The House of the Scorpion* (2002) for "subhuman" characters conducting themselves as humans. Regarding Farmer's text, Hilary Crew notes, "The inherent dignity and sanctity of Matt as a human being [he is a clone] are demonstrated by his representation as a loving boy who is highly intelligent, gifted at reading, math, learning languages, art, and, especially, at music" (207). Cinder, like Matt, behaves as a human being despite her cybernetic augmentation. In a similar vein, Elaine Ostry notes that "biotechnology is a metaphor for adolescence" (223), connecting the posthuman condition to adolescent development.

## Works Cited

Aarne, Antti. *The Types of the Folktale: A Classification and Bibliography*. 1910. Trans. Stith Thompson. Helsinki: Suomalainen Tiedeakatemia, 1987. Print.
Ames, Mildred. *Anna to the Infinite Power*. New York: Atheneum, 1981. Print.
Anderson, M. T. *Feed*. Cambridge: Candlewick, 2002. Print.
Bostrom, Nick. "In Defense of Posthuman Dignity." *Bioethics* 19.3 (2005): 202–14. Print.
Bradford, Clare, Kerry Mallan, John Stephens, and Robyn McCallum. *New World Orders in Contemporary Children's Literature: Utopian Transformations*. Basingstoke: Palgrave MacMillan, 2008. Print. Critical Approaches to Children's Literature.
*Cinderella*. Dir. Clyde Geronimi, Hamilton Luske, and Wilfred Jackson. Perf. Ilene Woods, Eleanor Audley, and Verna Felton. Walt Disney, 1950.
Cox, Marian Roalfe. *Three Hundred and Forty-Five Variants of Cinderella, Cat-Skin, and Cap o' Rushes, Abstracted and Tabulated, with a Discussion of Mediaeval Analogues, and Notes*. Liechtenstein: Kraus Reprint, 1967. Print.
Crew, Hilary. "Not So Brave a World: The Representation of Human Cloning in Science Fiction for Young Adults." *Lion and the Unicorn* 28.2 (2004): 203–21. Print.
Doughty, Terri. "Putting the Punk in a Steampunk Cinderella: Marissa Meyer's 'Lunar Chronicles.'" *Filoteknos* 5 (2015): 46–58. PDF file.
Farmer, Nancy. *The House of the Scorpion*. New York: Atheneum, 2002. Print.
Fukuyama, Francis. *Our Posthuman Future: Consequences of the Biotechnology Revolution*. New York: Picador, 2003. Print.
"The Glass Mountain." *The Yellow Fairy Book*. Ed. by Andrew Lang. New York: McGraw Hill, 1967. *University of Virginia Library Electronic Text Center*. Web. 19 July 2015.
Grimm, Jacob, and Wilhelm Grimm. "Cinderella." *The Annotated Brothers Grimm*. Ed. and trans. Maria Tatar. New York: Norton, 2004. 113–27. Print.

Haney, William S., II. Preface. *Cyberculture, Cyborgs, and Science Fiction: Consciousness and the Posthuman.* New York: Rodopi, 2006. vii–x. Print.

Haraway, Donna. "A Cyborg Manifesto: Science, Technology, and Socialist-Feminism in the Late Twentieth Century." *Simians, Cyborgs and Women: The Reinvention of Nature.* New York: Routledge, 1991. 149–81. Print.

Hayles, N. Katherine. *How We Became Posthuman: Virtual Bodies in Cybernetics, Literature, and Informatics.* Chicago: U of Chicago P, 1999. Print.

Jameson, R. D. "Cinderella in China." *Cinderella, a Casebook.* Ed. Alan Dundes. Madison: U of Wisconsin P, 1982. 71–97. Print.

Kass, Leon. *Life, Liberty, and Defense of Dignity: The Challenge for Bioethics.* San Francisco: Encounter Books, 2002. Print.

Lang, Andrew. Introduction. *Three Hundred and Forty-Five Variants of Cinderella, Cat-Skin, and Cap o' Rushes, Abstracted and Tabulated, with a Discussion of Mediaeval Analogues, and Notes.* By Marian Roalfe Cox. Liechtenstein: Kraus Reprint, 1967. vii–xiv. Print.

McKibben, Bill. "Design-A-Kid." *Religion-Online.org.* Web. 8 Aug. 2014.

Mendlesohn, Farah. "The Campaign for Shiny Futures." *Horn Book Magazine* March/April 2009: n.pag. *The Horn Book.* Web. 9 Oct. 2014.

Mitchell, Jennifer. "'A girl. A machine. A freak': A Consideration of Contemporary Queer Composites." *Bookbird* 52.1 (2014): 51–62. Print.

Meyer, Marissa. *Cinder.* New York: MacMillan, 2012. Print.

———. *Cress.* New York: MacMillan, 2014. Print.

———. *Scarlet.* New York: MacMillan, 2013. Print.

———. *Winter.* New York: MacMillan, 2015. Print.

More, Max. "A Letter to Mother Nature." *Maxmore.com.* N. pag. Aug. 1999. Web. 4 Aug. 2014.

Morrissey, Thomas J. "Parables for the Post-Modern, Post-9/11, and Posthuman World: Carrie Ryan's *Forest of Hands and Teeth* Books, M. T. Anderson's *Feed*, and Mary E. Pearson's *The Adoration of Jenna Fox*." *Contemporary Dystopian Fiction for Young Adults: Brave New Teenagers.* Ed. Balaka Basu, Katherine Broad, and Carrie Hintz. New York: Routledge, 2013. 188–201. Print. Children's Literature and Culture 93.

Newcomb, Erin. "The Soul of the Clone." *Contemporary Dystopian Fiction for Young Adults: Brave New Teenagers.* Ed. Balaka Basu, Katherine R. Broad, and Carrie Hintz. New York: Routledge, 2013. 175–87. Print. Children's Literature and Culture 93.

Ostry, Elaine. "'Is He Still Human? Are You?': Young Adult Science Fiction in the Posthuman Age." *Lion and the Unicorn* 28.2 (2004): 222–46. Print.

Perrault, Charles. "Cinderella." *Perrault's Fairy Tales.* Trans. A. E. Johnson. Kent: Wordsworth, 2004. 55–65. Print.

Phillips, Leah. "Real Women Aren't Shiny (or Plastic): The Adolescent Female Body in YA Fantasy." *Girlhood Studies* 8.3 (2015): 40–55. Print.

Thompson, Stith. *The Folktale.* 1928. Berkeley: U of California P, 1977. Print.

Toomeos-Orglaan, Kärri. "Gender Stereotypes in 'Cinderella' (ATU 510A) and 'The Princess on the Glass Mountain' (ATU 530)." *Journal of Ethnology and Folkloristics* 7.2 (2013): 49–64. Print.

Wiener, Norbert. "Newtonian and Bergsonian Time." *Cybernetics: Or Control and Communication in the Animal and the Machine.* Cambridge: MIT, 1965. 30–45. Print.

Zipes, Jack. *Why Fairy Tales Stick: The Evolution and Relevance of a Genre.* New York: Routledge, 2013. Print.

# 4

# THE ADOLESCENT POSTHUMAN
## Reimagining Body Image and Identity in Marissa Meyer's *Cinder* and Julianna Baggott's *Pure*

*Ferne Merrylees*

Given the rapid transformation of adolescence, it is unsurprising when teenagers find themselves experiencing feelings of disconnection not only between themselves and others, but also between conflicting parts of themselves. This disconnection is often further complicated by the interference or influence of parents and other adult authorities attempting to control and configure adolescent identity formation. Robyn McCallum proposes that "[c]oncepts of personal identity and selfhood are formed in dialogue with society, with language, and with other people" (3). For the adolescent posthuman, this dialogue would also include that between the self and the body and between the individual and his or her environment. For young adults negotiating the transition from childhood to adulthood, identity is constantly being reevaluated in terms of how they are perceived, how they perceive themselves, and how they wish to be perceived by others. Thus, the representation of these struggles in dystopian narratives dealing with images of the posthuman is particularly important in offering young adult readers a space in which they can challenge the idea of what it means to be human.

Pramod K. Nayar describes the human as an entity "traditionally taken to be a subject (one who is conscious of his/her self) marked by rational thinking/intelligence, who is able to plot his/her own course of action depending on his/her needs, desires and wishes, and, as a result of his/her actions, produces history" (5)—a description that posthumanist theorists challenge. Instead, the human subject is repositioned "as a dynamic hybrid" focusing "not on borders but on conduits and pathways, not on containment but on leakages, not on stasis but on movement of bodies, information and particles all located within a larger system," a system that rejects the humanist belief that humans are superior to other life forms (10). Subsequently, human subjectivity, according to N. Katherine Hayles, "is emergent rather than given, distributed rather than located solely in consciousness, emerging from and integrated into a chaotic world rather than occupying a position of mastery and control removed from it" (*How We Became Posthuman* 291). My discussion of autonomy in relation to the adolescent experience and the posthuman refers to the achievement of a sense of freedom through an understanding of the systems we are a part of, recognizing the "conduits and pathways" that Nayar describes and constructing identity in response to this recognition. Posthumanism is a mode of thought which, when applied to themes of identity creation in young adult dystopian literature, suggests that adolescents need to cultivate a form of hybridity to negotiate our increasingly technological world.

To examine these hybrid systems in more depth, I have selected Marissa Meyer's *Cinder* (2012), the first installment in the Lunar Chronicles, and Julianna Baggott's *Pure* (2012), the first of the Pure Trilogy, focusing primarily on their representations of the posthuman body and its relationship with body image and identity formation in dystopian environments. The posthuman in these novels is an expansion of the socially constructed human form into the next evolution of a hybrid being, not only becoming but belonging to something more, whether that expansion is perceived as negative or beneficial. The posthuman bodies of the characters in *Pure* and *Cinder* are epitomized by Harvey Hix's definition of hybridity: "a partial transformation, in the sense that some but not all elements of one form join with some but not all elements of another form; neither originating form is present in its entirety, and neither is entirely absent" (275). The technologically enhanced hybrid falls under the category of transhumanism: a subcategory of posthumanism that Cary Wolfe defines "as an *intensification* of humanism" (xv). Transhumanism is "the belief in the engineered evolution of 'post-humans,' defined as beings whose basic capacities so radically exceed those of present humans as to no longer be unambiguously human by our current standards" (Garreau 232). However, in *Pure* the attempt to enhance a select group of humans ends in tragedy, and in *Cinder* the enhanced human is considered a second-class citizen. Both novels propose different representations of the adolescent experience and the posthuman, reimagining the human experience, in Wolfe's words, by recontextualizing them "in terms of the entire sensorium of other living beings and their own autopoietic ways of 'bringing forth a world'" (xxv). In *Cinder* and *Pure*, the majority of characters are, in one form or another and to varying degrees, "prosthetic creature[s]" in that they co-evolved with and have been changed by "technicity and materiality" (Wolfe xxv).

*Pure* explores the lives of multiple protagonists in a desolate world set after the Detonations, an apocalyptic event involving nanotechnology that fused survivors to objects, animals, and even the earth itself. Select people, known as Pures, were protected from the Detonations inside a dome. The Wretches, those outside the Dome, were irreparably changed. Pressia, the protagonist of the trilogy, is one of these Wretches: a sixteen-year-old girl whose "[right] hand fused with the rubber of the doll's skull" (Baggott, *Pure* 12). Pressia undertakes a journey in which her sense of self evolves through her experiences and the individuals she meets, such as a Pure called Partridge; Bradwell, who has three birds fused into his back; and Our Good Mother, the fearsome leader of the surviving suburban housewives who have been fused to their children.

*Cinder*, on the other hand, is a retelling of the Cinderella fairytale set within a dystopian futuristic world in which the physical body can be augmented to create cyborgs, and androids are as common as smartphones. Just as in *Pure*, in which survivors like Pressia are considered less human by the sheltered Pures, in *Cinder* altered humans are treated as inferior. Set in New Beijing in the Eastern Commonwealth, a nod toward Cinderella's earliest incarnations,[1] the novel is about Cinder, a teenaged cyborg. Due to a childhood accident, Cinder is 36.28 percent machine. She has a synthetic hand and leg, a reinforced spine, four metal ribs, synthetic tissue around her heart, and additional splints in her human leg. Additional upgrades allow her to detect lies, download information directly into her head, and initiate retina displays to view relevant information. Cinder is a blend of human and machine, and she is more suited to the futuristic setting than unaltered humans, as she can directly interact with technology. However, Cinder's hybridity is a disadvantage when the threat of a plague outbreak results in a government-instituted draft that seeks technologically augmented humans to act as test subjects for antidote testing. The draft contributes to the prejudices against cyborgs, emphasizing their designation as commodities rather than people, and affects how Cinder views herself. Because her cyborg parts enable her to be more than human, Cinder is treated with the same distrust and contempt as the Lunars, genetically mutated descendants of the first human moon colonists. Lunars, though appearing human, have developed the so-called magical ability to control minds, which reinforces societal animosity toward the posthuman Other. The political unrest and the class system that dehumanizes cyborgs establish the dystopian framework of the narrative, encouraging adolescent readers to question these prejudices.

While confronting similar prejudices, the dystopian setting Baggott constructs in *Pure* is determined by the environmental catastrophe that completely reshapes the characters and the world in which they live. Baggott's dystopian vision of the future is grim; the characters are damaged both physically and mentally, moving through a postapocalyptic wasteland that is full of dust and monsters. Novels such as *Pure* question the cost of technology for human subjectivity and warn readers of the disastrous consequences of its misuse. Dystopian young adult literature often includes a sense of wariness and caution to counterbalance the hope often assumed to belong to young adult literature. Lois Lowry, author of the dystopian novel *The Giver*, considers hope essential to dystopian fiction, stating in an interview: "Young people handle dystopia every day: in their lives, their dysfunctional families, their violence-ridden schools. They watch dystopian television and movies about the real world where firearms bring about explosive conclusions to conflict. Yes, I think they need to see some hope for such a world. I can't imagine writing a book that doesn't have a hopeful ending" (Lowry, Hintz, and Ostry 199). Hope is frequently presented through the adolescent survivors' attempts to create a better world, whether or not they succeed. In this sense, hope and despair are irretrievably entangled in these narratives.

While the balance between hope and despair shifts more toward the latter in *Pure* than in *Cinder*, both novels explore societal fears regarding technology. Kay Sambell observes that, from the 1970s onward, "a dark literature of emergency and despair has developed, expressing deep-rooted fears for the future of those children being addressed" (163). These fears are often directed at the perceived posthuman threat, frequently represented by the computer, the only machine capable of competing with human intelligence. Joseph Weizenbaum warns that the boundaries between human and machine should not be crossed and that if we do not maintain control over the "slow-acting poison" that is science, we risk the essence of our human identity (16). Responding to Weizenbaum, Hayles cautions against humanist arguments that claim this essence will be compromised if "contaminated with mechanic alienness" (*How We Became Posthuman* 288). Instead, Hayles suggests that "when the human is seen as part of a distributed system, the full expression of human capability can be seen precisely to *depend* on the splice rather than being imperiled by it" (290). But what does it mean to be human? The answer depends on which mode of thought is applied.

Nayar discusses the major differences between transhumanism and posthumanism in regard to essential human attributes. Transhumanism focuses on the enhancement of human qualities, such as strength and intelligence, while still placing the human in "the centre of all things desirable, necessary and aspirational" (Nayar 10). Posthumanism, on the other hand, positions these so-called fundamental human qualities "as always already imbricated with other life forms . . . messy congeries of qualities developed over centuries through the human's interactions with the environment" (10–11). Applying this posthumanist theory to *Cinder* and *Pure*, the human qualities are thus not dependent on or determined by what is considered human. Cyborgs, hybrids, animals, and monsters are all capable of having attributes that have been traditionally seen as belonging to humans alone, as evident in the portrayal of Cinder in comparison to the more "natural" humans in *Cinder's* narrative, and the Wretches in comparison to the Pures in *Pure*.

Based on a fairytale character, Cinder is a stereotypical heroine who is kind, loyal, and brave in spite of the challenging situations she faces and the lack of a compassionate mentor or guide. Despite or because of Cinder's childhood surrounded by those contemptuous of cyborgs, notably her stepmother, Cinder is a good person, shaped by her environment and her cyborg parts; being ostracized by her community teaches her determination and sympathy for others while the optobionics that tell her when someone is lying guide her understanding of honesty. In *Pure*, the line between what is and is not human blurs, and many of the so-called human attributes are evident in beings that appear far from human, such as the more severely altered Dusts and Beasts. Dusts are humans who have fused with the environment—"fused with the earth; in the city, they fused with blasted buildings" (Baggott, *Pure* 33)—while Beasts are fusions between humans and animals. From the perspective of Pressia and the other young protagonists, the Dusts and Beasts appear not to have retained their previous human identities. What we consider to be human qualities, such as love, compassion, sympathy, and self-sacrifice, are absent. Dusts and Beasts are the epitome of the consequences wrought by technology, yet they are better suited for survival in the post-Detonation world than the less-used humans. The environment has shaped them into survivors: "some survived because they became more rock than human, and others proved they could be of use, working in conjunction with Beasts" (33). While they may lack compassion, they display qualities that have evolved through their interactions with their environment, such as teamwork and cooperation. Both Meyer and Baggott explore what it means to be human through the representation of their characters, presenting them in dystopian settings in which the posthuman body is something to be both feared and desired.

Baggott considers dystopian fiction a meeting ground to express fears that are not confined to one generation:

> Part of the post-apocalyptic, dystopian trend is that it seems to go hand in hand with young adult novels. Maybe that's because it's not simply the adults who are aware of the current crisis. Teens are the ones who are being told, again and again, that their futures are in jeopardy. The teen years can feel dystopian even in the best of times. But I don't think we realize how much pressure and feeling of doom we're

passing down to our teens. Post-apocalyptic novels are often a place where cross-generational fears meet. ("Dark Clouds")

Young adult science fiction, particularly dystopian literature, offers readers the tools with which to work through and confront these cultural fears. While the Detonations in *Pure* and the plague in *Cinder* call out to our deepest fears, what is appealing about Meyer's and Baggott's novels is "what survives destruction, what human traits—like the need for faith and hope, the desire for love, the search for beauty and home—endure," says Baggott ("Dark Clouds"). No matter how dark our future may loom, hope survives.

The enduring human traits described by Baggott are dependent on connections. Critical posthumanism, according to Nayar, is "the radical decanting of the traditional sovereign, coherent and autonomous human in order to demonstrate how the human is always evolving with, constituted by and constitutive of multiple forms of life and machines" (2). It emphasizes the constant dialogue we as humans have with one another as well as with the environment around us and the nonhuman objects that exist within it. Pressia and Cinder represent interconnected systems both in their settings, as organisms interacting within an environment, and within their bodies, as the inorganic interacts with the organic. The posthuman body includes the nonhuman, "a congeries, or assemblage, of multiple species, machines and organic forms" (Nayar 69), suggesting the body is an environment itself in which multiple forms interact and influence one another. Judith Halberstam and Ira Livingston describe the posthuman in a similar manner, stating that "[t]he posthuman does not reduce difference-from-others to difference-from-self, but rather emerges in the pattern of resonance and interference between the two" (10).

In literature, the posthuman body has often been depicted as monstrous—the creature in Mary Shelley's *Frankenstein*, Anne Rice's vampires, the androids in Philip K. Dick's *Do Androids Dream of Electric Sheep?*—a combination of life forms "too distant from 'normal' humans . . . and too uncomfortably close . . . [,] both equally monstrous in cultural representations of otherness" (Nayar 83). Yet in *Cinder* and *Pure*, not only is the monstrous Other—alien, monster, or villain—posthuman, but so too are the heroes and heroines at the heart of the stories. The multiple protagonists in *Pure* and *Cinder* are cyborgs, mutants, or aliens, and because of their posthuman bodies, they all struggle in defining their identities within themselves and within a community. Through the depiction of these characters' struggles with their posthuman bodies, readers are encouraged to sympathize. These struggles are a familiar motif in young adult literature as teens deal with their own issues about body image in connection with technology and the ever-present scrutiny of adults as they construct their identities.

According to McCallum, identity is a fabrication of fictions and ideologies, and the true self is but an invention, constructed by an individual in conjunction with dialogues that occur between the individual and his/her society. Yet we should not be dismissive regarding the power of such ideologies in "fashioning identities and in shaping the ways in which we relate to the world" (McCallum 256). Defining identity as "a construct designed to explain the self and, hence, human beliefs and actions," Hugh Lauder implies that this process of construction is fluid, susceptible to external influences and an individual's response to them (21). In relation to adolescent identity construction, these influences include not only the adolescent's peer group but also parents and other adult authority figures. The posthuman body in young adult science fiction represents the power struggle between adults and adolescents; adults are frequently responsible for the cyborgian features of the adolescent character's body in these narratives. Pressia and Cinder both serve as pawns in the adults' political battles, and the moments in which they comprehend their positions (for Pressia, when she realizes the Dome leader has been tracking her through an embedded chip; for Cinder, the dismantling of her only friend, Iko) compel them to take a stand. Roberta Seelinger Trites states that "power is even more fundamental to adolescent literature than growth" (x), as readers must recognize and learn how to balance their own power with that of the power held by the adults in their lives. Trites asserts that "it is in the very nature of power to be both enabling and repressive" (x), and when paired with the implications of a posthuman body, this repression by adult authorities in *Pure* and *Cinder* assists in shaping their young characters' identities.

*Cinder* and *Pure* contain similarities in character development and even symbolism that suggest a shared perception regarding adolescence, identity, and the body. While the adults in these narratives frequently attempt to suppress and control Pressia and Cinder, both female protagonists undergo transformations that enable them to become autonomous. Autonomy is a quality generally associated with the liberal humanist self; when considered with the posthuman subject, "autonomy can no longer be viewed as self-containment or self-ownership but instead as a process of self-making ... through various relations to the subject's environment" (Bolton 14). Michael Sean Bolton states that "the decentering of the human subject does not entail its complete disintegration or its subordination, but allows new possibilities for human agency and autonomy in a world of rapid and continual change" (22). This perspective is particularly useful in discussion of the posthuman in young adult literature as it allows space to explore a discrete subject, such as Cinder or Pressia, in relation to his/her surroundings rather than isolated from them. Pressia and Cinder redefine their identities and gain agency through their engagement with the world they move through, rather than reflecting the humanist attitudes requiring mastery over themselves and their settings.

In *Pure* and *Cinder*, the adolescent characters were rendered posthuman in childhood by adults, and as a result, their posthuman bodies influence how they construct their identities. The lack of control these characters have over their body transformations is representative of the discourses surrounding adolescent bodies in real life, in which parents frequently have control over what is and is not appropriate in how their children dress, behave, and act, such as determining the proper length of a skirt, obtaining a tattoo or piercing, and policing the age limit for drinking and consensual sex. According to Danah Boyd in her study of teenagers and the effects of networks and networking devices, "Teens continue to occupy an awkward position between childhood and adulthood, dependence and independence" in which teenagers are seeking to construct an identity outside of the role of son, daughter, brother, or sister (17). Adolescents are becoming less family-oriented and more focused on friends, increasing their time socializing online beyond the controlling influence of adults. Our media culture over-sensationalizes the dangers teenagers face, especially those involving technology. As Boyd comments, "Moral panics and the responses to them reconfigure the lives of youth in restrictive ways" as authority figures "view teens as nuisances who must be managed and innocent children that must be protected" (106). This contradiction of our society being both "afraid of them and for them" leads to the "power struggles between teens and adults" (107) that are made evident through the thematic use of the posthuman in Meyer's and Baggott's novels.

The act of an adult or adult authority altering Pressia's and Cinder's bodies reflects the control enforced by parents or guardians on teenagers and the consequences this has on identity formation. The adult characters frequently exhibit humanist traits, such as the desire for mastery over the world and, for the most part, use their power to repress the teenage protagonists. Hayles states that "a dynamic partnership between humans and intelligent machines replaces the liberal humanist subject's manifest destiny to dominate and control nature" (*How We Became Posthuman* 288). In Baggott's *Pure*, the actions of the liberal humanist subject are represented by the adult characters' attempts to change the world and create the perfect human. Partridge's father uses nanotechnology to physically enhance his sons to make them superhuman, with the long-term goal of repopulating the world. He is also directly responsible for the Detonations that caused Pressia's disfigurements, and he causes further harm when he has her outfitted with surveillance technology without her knowledge or consent. The intrusive, and at times brutal, act of bugging involves not only putting "lenses in your eyes and recording devices in your ears and you're a walking, talking spy whether you know it or not" (Baggott, *Pure* 61) but also implanting a "ticker," a bomb that is placed inside an individual's head that can be set off remotely. While Pressia is initially unaware of the surveillance, its revelation demonstrates how Pressia's rights have been denied. Her situation can be compared to issues young adults face in regard to their own rights to privacy. As Boyd observes, teenagers experiment "with the boundaries of various freedoms," desiring "a measure of privacy and autonomy[,] . . . but they also relish intimacy and the ability to have control over their social situation" (19), which is often at risk of adult monitoring. Teenagers' willingness to share in public spaces but insistence on privacy is viewed as contradictory by adults. Boyd contends that teens are not concerned about what strangers may potentially see; instead, they seek privacy specifically in relation to those who hold power over them, such as teachers and parents (56). In Pressia's case, her privacy is removed completely: her location is tracked, and Partridge's father monitors what she hears and sees.

In *Cinder*, the adults mirror the stereotypical characters found in fairytales. Meyer represents three kinds of adult authority: the wicked stepmother (who, while dislikable in her abuse of Cinder, is not unjustifiably malevolent); the beautiful, evil queen (who is the series's antagonist, the Lunar Queen Levana); and the fairy godmother (in this case, Doctor Erland, who gives Cinder the antidote for her sister and later assists her in escaping prison by providing her with a new prosthetic foot). Cinder's stepmother treats her (legally) as a commodity, and her actions toward Cinder and her posthuman body are motivated by grief and a desire to find someone to blame for the death of her husband and subsequently that of her daughter. The Lunar Queen, on the other hand, affects Cinder indirectly at first by threatening New Beijing through her ability to control an individual's thoughts, behaviors, and actions, representing the dangers of adult authorities that are left unchallenged. The revelation that Queen Levana is actually Cinder's aunt results in Queen Levana's stepping into the position of the evil female relative that the stepmother relinquishes when Cinder is arrested. Compared to the adults in *Pure*, who are mainly depicted as obstacles or challenges, the adults in *Cinder* exhibit complex motivations, as is clearly demonstrated in the figure of Doctor Erland. As a doctor, Erland is in a position that generally inspires trust and faith; however, his actions are questionable. He has the most interaction with Cinder's posthuman body, learning things about it of which Cinder is not even aware and asserting control over her by withholding this information. The adults in *Cinder*, like those in *Pure*, impact negatively on the characters' sense of self through their roles in physically and mentally altering the protagonists into their current posthuman forms, affecting how they fit in the wider community and their environments, and influencing the formation of a healthy identity.

Pressia's and Cinder's transformations from human to posthuman coincide with not only the loss of a traditional trouble-free and innocent childhood, as the traumatic events surrounding each ensure they lose their innocence far more quickly, but also loss of their memories. While this may symbolically represent how young adults desire to put more childish things behind them in attempts to be considered adult, it is also suggestive of the harm adults can do if they abuse the power and trust they have over adolescents. Pressia and Cinder do not remember an existence before their physical transformations. Cinder does not remember anything before she was eleven, and Pressia's memories of the time before the Detonations, which occurred when she was six, are unreliable and fragmented at best. Both sets of parents were supposedly killed during the events that physically altered the protagonists into their posthuman states (although they later discover that these events are false). According to Hayles, "[w]e do not leave our history behind but rather, like snails, carry it around with us in the sedimented and enculturated instantiations of our pasts we call our bodies" ("Afterword" 137). In *Cinder* and *Pure*, the body becomes a receptacle for the main characters' forgotten history. Pressia's and Cinder's bodies offer clues to their heritage, yet how they interpret these clues is complicated and not always accurate. Cinder's immunity to the letumosis plague is also a hint as to her true heritage, yet Doctor Erland, who repeatedly takes her blood for testing, purposefully misleads her. Cinder does not discover the truth regarding her origins until the end of the novel. Pressia assumes she received her Japanese features from her mother and her freckles from her Scotch-Irish father, and these assumptions—which turn out to be false—seem to confirm the fake history she has been taught.

Pressia's discovery that her childhood memories have been fabricated by a man claiming to be her grandfather, who found her just after the Detonations, leaves her feeling adrift and identity-less. The stories her so-called grandfather tells Pressia serve only to confuse her further, and this confusion plays a part in her struggles to come to terms with her physical body. The society Pressia moves within is defined by an individual's physical body and by what he or she can remember from before: "Pressia catches herself pretending to remember more than she does, borrowing other people's memories and mixing them with her own" (Baggott, *Pure* 30), a congeries of memories that parallels the aggregated posthuman body, which only adds to her fragmented identity. These memories are both a blessing and a curse. In *Pure*, children use memories like currency and mix and match to piece together identities; however, Pressia's yearning for a time before she was disfigured restricts her ability to construct a future. Pressia's lack of both a past and a sense of history results in her feeling displaced, and this displacement affects how she negotiates the space between herself and her environment. McCallum states that "concepts of personal identity are formed, in part, through an awareness and understanding of the past and of a sense of a relation in the present to personal and social histories" (167), but the dystopian world Pressia and her friends move through is complicated when what they do remember before the Detonations is unreliable. When Pressia is informed of her birth name, she wonders, "But who is she? Pressia Belze? Emi Imanaka? Is she someone's granddaughter or daughter? An orphan, a bastard child, a girl with a doll-head fist, a soldier?" (428). Pressia's memory, in particular, is in a constant state of flux, which is especially evident at the novel's conclusion: "Pressia's memory of this day will blur. She can feel the details colliding in her mind already—a slow loss of facts, reality" (459). Pressia is incapable of leaving behind her childhood—both real and imagined—despite her lack of memory, and she actively tries to erase the symbol of her past by seeking ways to remove her disfigurements.

In contrast, Cinder has no memories from before she was eleven due to her cybernetic operation. Like Pressia, Cinder dislikes the idea of someone getting inside her head and making changes over which she herself has no control. Cinder's mind is literally operated on and changed, and for readers this experience could be considered a metaphor for the thoughts and opinions that are pressed upon them through the media, their peers, and adult authority figures. Cinder's ability to detect lies and access data through the technology implanted in her head is symbolic of the systems we use every day that, according to Hayles, suggest "we have always been posthuman" (*How We Became Posthuman* 291). The Internet has become an extension of the human mind, changing how we not only record memories but how we process and find information. We "participate in systems whose total cognitive capacity exceeds our individual knowledge" (289). Cinder reveals the potential benefits of such an arrangement as her cyborg parts save her life.

The physical and mental transformations Cinder and Pressia undergo also alter their sense of history. Pressia is surprised to learn she has living family, just as Cinder is shocked to discover she is the long-assumed-dead Princess Selene. Yet it is when Cinder discovers she is a different age from what she thought that she questions her identity: "for a moment she had the distinct impression that she had no idea who she was anymore. No clue who she was supposed to be" (Meyer 385). To adolescents, this need for self-definition is an important motivator as they test the boundaries between themselves and their society—boundaries that, in a posthuman framework, include not only the physical but also the virtual.

Wolfe asserts that "the environment, and with it 'the body,' becomes unavoidably a virtual, multidimensional space produced and stabilized by the recursive enactions and structure couplings of autopoietic beings" (xxiii) sharing a unified area of existence. No longer is the body set apart from the environment, but instead both coexist and coevolve as an "open *and* closed" system (xxiv), cognition distributed beyond the human to the nonhuman. Humans have not become smarter but rather "have constructed smarter environments in which to work" (Hayles, *How We Became Posthuman* 289). Hix argues that "the border between system and environment is not breached, it's just not clear where it is or whether there is a border" (275). In the case of Pressia and Cinder, their environments have directly influenced their posthuman bodies, but their bodies have also *become* environments in the sense that their bodies are made up of a combination of the organic and inorganic.

Nayar's statement that the posthuman body is an amalgamation or congeries of parts can also be applied to both narratives, yet in different ways. In *Pure* the posthuman body is overtly imagined through the different forms humans have mutated into, such as Dusts (beings fused with the earth or buildings), Beasts (those fused with animals), or Groupies (those fused with other people), some of which literally coexist with other living organisms. The majority of these organic-based posthuman congeries are represented as terrifying and destructive to the individual (post)humans; their humanity, especially in the case of the Dusts, has evolved into something that liberal humanists or moral transhumanists would find objectionable. The other kind of posthuman transformation involves fusion with machine or inorganics, like Pressia's doll-head hand. These fusions occurred during the Detonations and are presumably a transitory tragedy, as these fused beings, Pressia included, will die and be replaced by non-fused yet still mutated offspring.

This concept of the posthuman body made up of a congeries of parts is also evident in *Cinder* through the main protagonist's body and her interchangeable parts. While the idea of a bionic woman may be threatening to some, Meyer portrays Cinder's posthuman body positively as it provides aid and offers protection, evoking the transhumanist mode of thought that technology can improve and enhance human beings. Cinder's body gives her the tools to help her navigate her class-divided society, protects her from Queen Levana's mind control, and monitors her systems when she is placed in stressful situations. Unnatural though Cinder is, her alteration mimics the appearance of a normal human body, which makes her posthuman body more comprehensible, cohering with our existing awareness of prosthetic limbs. Unlike Cinder's cyborg parts, however, Pressia's doll-head hand is discomforting in description: "The doll's eyes click shut; the hole within the pursed lips is dusted with ash as if the doll itself has been breathing air" (Baggott, *Pure* 12). Cinder is a system combining both organic and machine, a hybridity readers might find more acceptable when comparing it to the burden of Pressia's apparently useless deformity.

While Pressia's body represents the posthuman, it also uses the posthuman body as a metaphor for the adolescent struggle with body image. Pressia is first introduced as a mute child who uses her doll-head hand to communicate just as a shy little girl would use her toys as intermediaries in uncertain situations. Yet like teenagers outgrowing their toys, Pressia goes from blinking at the same time as the doll-head to distancing herself completely by covering it up. Pressia does not recall having the doll as a child, it is never given a name, and she eventually links the feelings associated with her hand with those she has for her mother: "a presence, numbed, riding under the surface of things" (336). It is interesting, then, that Pressia's doll-head is echoed in the bodies of the mothers in the Meltlands, the housewives of the suburbs fused to their never-aging children. Like one mother who has "eyes peering out from a bulbous baby head that sits like a goiter on her neck" (247), Pressia's fusion to the doll-head and the mothers' fusion with their children present a disturbing posthuman vision of womanhood: Pressia as a female child is defined by a toy, and the mothers are defined by their children. This parallel is suggestive of how society still places women and men within gendered and social constructs that influence adolescent identity formation.

Like Pressia's doll-head hand, Cinder's foot is associated with her past: it was a "small, rusted thing she'd woken up with after her operation, when she was a confused, unloved eleven-year-old girl" (Meyer 324). The novel begins with Cinder removing her robotic foot: "Cinder gripped her heel and yanked the foot from its socket. A spark singed her fingertips and she jerked away, leaving the foot to dangle from a tangle of red and yellow wires" (3). Meyer's word choice mirrors the mechanical with human anatomy: the socket reminiscent of body joints and the wires like human arteries and nerves despite the very posthuman concept of removable feet. Cinder finds herself feeling lighter after removing the too-small foot, and this sensation of release reflects on the growing pains associated with adolescence, as teenagers outgrow the familiarity of their child bodies and shed the identities associated with their childhood, like Cinder's foot, to test out new ones. Cinder's desire to distance herself from her outgrown foot may recall an adolescent's desire to separate him/herself from his/her childhood; it is also similar to Pressia's own need to hide her doll-head hand, which is the symbol for her feelings of alienation.

For adolescent readers, the outsider is a character they can relate to. The alienation of "powerlessness, meaninglessness, normlessness, social isolation, self estrangement and cultural estrangement" (McCallum 99) that the characters face, whether self-driven or externally enforced, is familiar despite the characters' forms being so unlike their own. Cinder's discovery that she is a Lunar, a genetically evolved human, is unwelcome for an individual who is already such an outcast, and she rejects the knowledge, declaring, "I'm not Lunar . . . I'm cyborg. You don't think that's bad enough?" (Meyer 176). Being a cyborg makes other characters question Cinder's humanity, and as a Lunar on Earth, she is shunned twice over. Her human stepmother completely rejects Cinder after the death of her younger daughter, when, distraught, she accuses Cinder of not being human anymore because "humans cry" and Cinder cannot (279). Cinder's stepmother and others in her community see Cinder's lack of certain bodily reactions, like blushing and crying, as proof she is not human. Cinder perceives herself as not having the same social status as humans, but despite other people's opinions, she never doubts her humanity, only her ability to express it.

Pressia is ashamed of her physical body; the Detonations left her face scarred and her hand fused with a doll's head, which she covers with a sock when she goes out and which she has contemplated severing. Although Pressia is constantly aware of this deformity, she refuses to identify herself with it. In contrast, she identifies Bradwell, her love interest, as "[t]he boy with birds in his back" (Baggott, *Pure* 46). Pressia sees his fusion not only as a natural part of him—even comparing the beating of the birds' wings beneath his shirt with a natural image in "rippling like water" (39)—but also as an identifier. To Pressia, the birds are part of Bradwell's identity, not separate as she sees her own doll-head. Her perception of Bradwell's facial scars is also contrary to how she views her own: "She likes his face, a survivor's face, a sharp jaw, his scars long and jagged" (39). This response suggests that there is more to Pressia's dislike of her scars than their identification of her as no longer Pure but does not clarify what, so that she appears confused and inconsistent. Pressia's deformity and scars are symbolic of what adolescents dislike about their bodies, whether it is real or imagined.

The physical body makes up an important element in how a person's sense of self develops through interpersonal interactions and the perceptions of others. Charles Horton Cooley's concept of the looking-glass self involves an individual viewing him/herself through the perception of others and, in this reflective process, forming a social identity (McIntyre 146). For adolescents this is particularly challenging, as not only do they perceive themselves through the eyes of others, but they also then compare themselves to others, often to the detriment of their self-image. Pressia isolates herself from others, comparing their strengths to her weaknesses and finding herself lacking, which in turn affects how she thinks others perceive her.

While Pressia's self-image is undermined by her scars, Bradwell finds Pressia's flaws appealing:

"The scar is beautiful," he says.
Her heart skitters. She pulls the doll head to her chest. "Beautiful? It's a scar."
"It's a sign of survival." (Baggott, *Pure* 344)

Instead of seeing her scars as signs of strength, as Bradwell does, Pressia sees them as grotesque. Bradwell's role in the narrative, besides his obvious romantic potential, is to force Pressia to rethink her conception not only of what was behind the Detonations, but also of herself and her place within the world. In a dystopian setting of "ash and dust" (1), the strength to survive is, as Bradwell implies, a far more valuable asset than contemporary standards of beauty. The unblemished perfection of the Pures, safe in their Dome, is in comparison useless and even undesirable to those living outside its walls. Baggott positions readers to view the Pures in their Dome as an act of transhumanism gone wrong. The Dome creators' technology was used to enhance and develop a perfect human race, but instead they created a community that is decaying and isolated from the outside world. To Bradwell, Pressia's impurity is a marker of her strength. Pressia's Dome-raised brother Partridge, too, is neither disgusted nor disturbed by it: "Partridge holds his sister's doll-head fist in his hand. It is part of her. It isn't with her, but of her. He can feel the humanness of it—the warmth, the play beneath the skin of a real hand, alive" (394). The "humanness" Partridge feels in Pressia's hand conflicts with Pressia's view of her deformity and emphasizes that most of the negative responses toward her disfigurements are from herself alone rather than from others. In effect, she has not fully developed a looking-glass self; however, at the end of the novel there are suggestions that she is slowly working through that reflective process as she wonders "what Bradwell thinks of her now" (442). While Pressia is considered less than human by the Pure adults within the Dome, her emotional isolation is self-inflicted.

In Meyer's novel, Cinder is personally confronted by social prejudices every day as she is judged for what she is. As a result, Cinder is considerably more isolated in her environment than Pressia. Although both characters actively try to hide their abnormalities (for example, by wearing gloves), Cinder is part of a minority who exist within a society made up of, in a traditional sense, unenhanced humans. From the perspective of Cinder, readers are aware of the discriminations leveled against her for being different. Her modifications are not her choice; as she proclaims, "I didn't ask to be a cyborg. None of this is my fault" (279), much as amputees do not choose to remove a limb. Her society's treatment of her as a thing rather than a person forces her into the role of the outsider, and in this position she is a sympathetic figure—especially as a protagonist in a young adult novel. Like the chimera from Greek mythology, the cyborg has often been perceived negatively, as is echoed in the way Cinder's society rejects her; however, in *Cinder*, the cyborg is portrayed positively by playing the role of the heroine.

In comparison, Cinder's nemesis is her complete antithesis. Ruler of the Lunar colony, Queen Levana, like many Lunars, has the genetic mutation that allows her to "alter a person's brain—make you see things you couldn't see, feel things you shouldn't feel, do things you didn't want to do" (43). She uses this ability to manipulate the citizens of New Beijing into doing her bidding and to create a "glamour," appearing beautiful and embodying feminine beauty. While Cinder's hybrid body is described in terms of its weight, the workmanship of her parts, and the ill-fitting nature of her foot as she dances, Queen Levana represents the posthuman as a form of image manipulation. The figure of Levana may be read as a warning to readers to be wary of how identities, especially within the media, can be altered to be something else, as models on magazine covers are Photoshopped, actors and musicians undergo cosmetic surgery to appear younger, and images on social media pages are selected to portray a particular construct. Cinder and Queen Levana represent the alteration of the body under different circumstances: Cinder to restore her body from her injuries as a child and Queen Levana to alter how people perceive her. The body images the two characters invoke make clear that, despite Cinder's struggles with her posthuman body, readers are encouraged to align their own attitudes toward their bodies with Cinder's as she attempts to accept rather than change her body, rejecting Queen Levana's attitudes toward false body imagery.

In *Pure*, Pressia's and Bradwell's bodies have been changed in an inutile manner (Pressia's doll-head hand is unusable and Bradwell's birds do not give him the ability to fly) when compared to the more environmentally embedded Dusts and Beasts. The alterations and transformations of their bodies are considered burdens by the characters who suffer them: carrying the weight of a child, the fusing of a fan within a throat, the loss of a hand in a doll-head. Yet Pressia's deformity, although she rages against it, is not presented as leaving her at any obvious disadvantage. In comparison, when Cinder loses her foot, she is essentially disabled and finds walking difficult. Cinder needs her cyborg parts to function properly. Her body is a system of organic and machine parts that are interdependent, symbolizing the growing dependence we have on technology in our own society; however, Meyer does not imply that this dependence is harmful in and of itself, but rather invites readers to consider the consequences of technology being removed, such as when Cinder's stepmother confiscates Cinder's foot. For adolescents, certain technologies have become integrated in the formation of identity as their social interactions extend to online communities. The restriction and prohibition of certain technologies by adult authority figures can undermine the potential for agency through technology, especially for teenagers who are already navigating the power imbalances between adults and children. Technology's capacity to empower is evident in *Cinder*, suggesting there has been a shift in our society regarding adolescents' use of technology to one that is more positive. In *Pure*, the posthuman body is either destructive (for example, the Beasts and Dusts) or disabling (such as the fused children), yet technology is considered both the curse and the cure, as Pressia's mother inspires hope in a serum that can undo some of the damage caused by the Detonations. While *Pure* is less optimistic than Meyer's novel, technology is considered not just a tool but a part of our posthuman bodies, and when used correctly, it can aid in shaping a hopeful future.

This hope is evident from the very beginning of these two narratives, with both girls interacting with technology as they either repair or create mechanical devices despite, or even because of, their posthuman bodies. Cinder has built her identity around her abilities as a mechanic and sees her skills as a way to escape, while Pressia, despite being unable to use her doll-head hand, creates delicate, metal wind-up creatures that not only offer comfort and beauty to people who live in a place that lacks both, but are traded for supplies when her grandfather can no longer support the two of them. These skills emphasize the positives that can come from an understanding of technology. Their crafting skills function as a form of escape for Pressia and Cinder as well as serving as proof of their engagement with the world, independent from the adults in the narratives. As Pressia and Cinder had no control over the formation of their posthuman bodies, they can find empowerment only through their actions.

Pressia takes on the role of provider, soldier, and even executioner when she, not her brother, kills her dying mother. Her abilities to assume these roles are never questioned by the other characters, and although Pressia does not acknowledge her own worth, her actions signify her developing abilities to solve problems and adapt to situations quickly. This development is most clearly demonstrated when Pressia decodes the clue regarding the light in the birthday card riddle her mother left Partridge, logically breaking the riddle down to find a solution. While Bradwell and Partridge see Pressia as strong and worthy of their affections, it is not until the end of the novel that Pressia acknowledges that "[t]hey're survivors" (Baggott, *Pure* 461). She admits, even as she includes herself with the others in her group, that her identity is one built on the human will to survive. Baggott encourages her readers to reexamine how they view and portray themselves and, through Pressia's conflict with her own posthuman body, highlights how internal interpretations of self are often more powerful and harmful than external ones.

In contrast, Cinder manages her feelings of inadequacy through her sense of humor, taking pleasure in others' assumptions about her body:

"I don't know. I don't actually remember anything before the surgery."

His eyebrows rose, his blue eyes sucking in all the light of the room. "The cybernetic operation?"

"No, the sex change."

The doctor's smile faltered.

"I'm joking." (Meyer 100)

Cinder's actions and reactions within a dystopian setting actively hostile to her cyborg nature define her as a strong and positive role model for adolescents: she possesses attributes usually associated with fairytale heroes rather than heroines, including her attempts at rescuing the prince. Unlike Cinderella's, Cinder's arrival at the ball is less than auspicious. Cinder is wet and muddy and clothed in a borrowed, wrinkled dress. Aware that her cyborg form may have been revealed, she refuses to apologize for her identity and instead stands proud: "She was glad no tears would betray her humiliation. Glad that no blood in her cheeks would betray her anger. Glad that her hateful cyborg body was good for one thing as she clutched onto her shredded dignity" (355). Despite her aversion to her posthuman body, Cinder has found strength in it, and her confrontation with Queen Levana requires her to draw on both her Lunar abilities and her cyborg augmentations to survive. In the end, Cinder recognizes that how she is perceived by others can work to her advantage: she knows that she is viewed as "[a] deformed cyborg with a missing foot. A Lunar with a stolen identity. A mechanic with no one to run to, nowhere to go. But they would be looking for a ghost" (387). As the Lunar princess who has long been presumed dead, Cinder has an identity that motivates her to persevere, placing her in a position to use her newfound knowledge in conjunction with her cyborg body to defeat Queen Levana.

Whereas in *Pure* the posthuman body is often viewed as a challenge to surmount, in *Cinder* the cyborg body becomes a metaphor for the fragmentation of identity, as characters are often comprised of interchangeable, replaceable parts or can be genetically altered or mentally controlled. Baggott's characters manifest conflicting attitudes to their physical selves, while *Cinder* explores not only the problems of an augmented posthuman body but also the benefits of full body replacements and prostheses that are more efficient than the original component. Meyer presents Cinder as not only a strong, independent, misunderstood, and ostracized young woman but also a metaphor for survival. Donna Haraway states, "Cyborg writing is about the power to survive . . . by seizing the tools to mark the world that marked them as other" (317); Cinder is a good example of this power as she takes her Otherness and makes it her strength. This strength is also evident in Baggott's *Pure*. The characters in

*Pure* develop from feeling powerless to being instigators of their own destiny, accepting constantly changing (if outwardly flawed) selves, and turning their weaknesses into strengths. Pressia's and Cinder's constructions of their own identities because of, and in spite of, these technologically imposed physical attributes encourage readers to reflect on their own constructions of self and body image within a society and community as well as within themselves.

Pressia's and Cinder's struggles to accept their posthuman bodies are a metaphor not only for the angst our culture associates with being an adolescent, but also for the condition of being human, as we all struggle with similar issues regarding body image and identity formation. The posthuman body becomes a battleground in these novels. It depicts the struggles adolescents face as they engage with identity and the body, dependent on how the characters are perceived, how the characters think they are perceived, and how they perceive themselves. As Nayar says, "Cyborg bodies and clones have been the stuff of popular culture long enough for these bodies to become recognizable as variants of the normal human body" (56), and like Partridge viewing Pressia's doll-head hand as just another part of her humanness, the reader never questions Cinder's humanity even though it is very much questioned in her society. Cinder is familiar to readers primarily because of the traditional fairytale, despite her physical augmentations and revelations of her alien heritage. To be human is no longer dependent on an isolated subject who controls his or her own destiny, but rather it is part of a fluid, dynamic system. In *Cinder* and *Pure*, the human is presented as a hybrid in which the boundaries between self and other are blurred. Pressia's and Cinder's posthuman physiognomies are only part of their overall posthuman state of being. Baggott and Meyer ultimately provide an intimate view of the posthuman, allowing adolescent readers a space to explore not only body image and identity creation, but how humans fit within the various and complex systems that make up our posthuman world.

## Note

1. The oldest recorded version of Cinderella is Tuan Ch'eng-shih's Chinese story of Yeh-hsien, published in the ninth century. Instead of a fairy godmother or flock of birds found in most European variants, Yeh-hsien finds aid from a pile of fish bones; however, the European and Chinese tales are similar in that Yeh-hsien loses her shoe, which is later given to a king. For a complete translation and further discussion of this Chinese Cinderella, see Arthur Waley's article "The Chinese Cinderella Story."

## Works Cited

Baggott, Julianna. "As Dark Clouds Move in, Literary Lessons in Survival." *Tampa Bay Times* 12 Feb. 2012. *Tampabay.com*. Web. 17 July 2014.

———. *Pure*. London: Headline, 2012. Print.

Bolton, Michael Sean. "Digital Parasites: Reassessing Notions of Autonomy and Agency in Posthuman Subjectivity." *Theoria and Praxis* 1.2 (2013): 14–26. *Academia.edu*. Web. 2 Feb. 2016.

Boyd, Danah. *It's Complicated: The Social Lives of Networked Teens*. New Haven: Yale UP, 2014. Print.

Garreau, Joel. *Radical Evolution: The Promise and Peril of Enhancing Our Minds, Our Bodies—and What It Means to Be Human*. New York: Broadway Books, 2006. Print.

Halberstam, Judith, and Ira Livingston. "Introduction: Posthuman Bodies." *Posthuman Bodies*. Ed. Judith Halberstam and Ira Livingston. Bloomington: Indiana UP, 1995. 1–19. Print.

Haraway, Donna J. *Simians, Cyborgs, and Women: The Reinvention of Nature*. New York: Routledge, 2010. *EBL*. Web. 9 Apr. 2015.

Hayles, N. Katherine. "Afterword: The Human in the Posthuman." *Cultural Critique* 53 (2003): 134–37. Print.

———. *How We Became Posthuman: Virtual Bodies in Cybernetics*. Chicago: U of Chicago P, 1999. *ACLS Humanities E-Book*. Web. 9 Apr. 2015.

Hix, Harvey L. "Hybridity Is the New Metamorphosis." *Comparative Critical Studies* 9.3 (2012): 271–83. Print.

Lauder, Hugh. "Psychosocial Identity and Adolescents' Educational Decision Making: Is There a Connection?" *Discussions on Ego Identity*. Ed. Jane Kroger. New York: Psychology P, 2013. 21–46. *EBL*. Web. 9 Apr. 2015.

Lowry, Lois, Carrie Hintz, and Elaine Ostry. "Interview with Lois Lowry, Author of *The Giver*." *Utopian and Dystopian Writing for Children and Young Adults*. Ed. Carrie Hintz and Elaine Ostry. New York: Routledge, 2003. 196–99. Print. Children's Literature and Culture 29.

McCallum, Robyn. *Ideologies of Identity in Adolescent Fiction: The Dialogic Construction of Subjectivity*. Oxon: Routledge, 1999. Print. Children's Literature and Culture 8.

McIntyre, Lisa J. *The Practical Skeptic: Core Concepts in Sociology*. 2nd ed. Boston: McGraw Hill, 2002. Print.

Meyer, Marissa. *Cinder*. London: Penguin, 2012. Print.

Nayar, Pramod K. *Posthumanism*. Cambridge: Polity, 2014. Print.

Sambell, Kay. "Presenting the Case for Social Change: The Creative Dilemma of Dystopian Writing for Children." *Utopian and Dystopian Writing for Children and Young Adults*. Ed. Carrie Hintz and Elaine Ostry. New York: Routledge, 2003. 163–78. Print. Children's Literature and Culture 29.

Trites, Roberta Seelinger. *Disturbing the Universe: Power and Repression in Adolescent Literature*. Iowa City: U of Iowa P, 2000. Print.

Waley, Arthur. "The Chinese Cinderella Story." *Folklore* 58.1 (1947): 226–38. *Taylor & Francis Online*. Web. 27 Jan. 2016.

Weizenbaum, Joseph. *Computer Power and Human Reason: From Judgment to Calculation*. San Francisco: W.H. Freeman, 1976. Print.

Wolfe, Cary. *What Is Posthumanism?* Minneapolis: U of Minnesota P, 2009. *ProQuest ebrary*. Web. 31 Mar. 2015.

# 5

# "THOSE MAPS WOULD HAVE TO CHANGE"
Remapping the Borderlines of the Posthuman Body in Leigh Bardugo's Grisha Trilogy

*Maryna Matlock*

With what organ do we perceive monsters? Or, perhaps more aptly, by what hybrid bodies are we deceived into loving them, if not into becoming them? Beginning with *Shadow and Bone*, Leigh Bardugo's Grisha trilogy for young adult readers continually plumbs the territories of teratology, subverting the illusion of body borders demarcating the organism from the environment, the organic from the prosthetic, the human(e) from the monstrous. Bardugo's texts introduce us to an enchanted world clawed in half by the Shadow Fold, a tract of darkness that swallows the land, teems with monsters, and threatens the survival of the Ravkan nation. But when the teenaged Alina suddenly manifests the power to summon light, her life is changed forever. For hundreds of years, Ravka has tempered its suffering with the meager hope that a Sun Summoner might be more than myth. But if Alina is to become the savior her country needs her to be, then she also risks transforming into the agent of its destruction. As Alina struggles with fears of becoming more than human or perhaps less than humane, as well as with the prostheticization of her body, which is sanctified as icon even as it is made a weapon, she must also contend with the kind of power that turns men into monsters. Distressingly seduced by her own potential, driven to belong, and inexorably drawn to the dangerous Darkling who has hopes for her of his own, Alina is thrust into an epic battle that exposes all the borderlines scarring her world and breeding its nightmares. As Alina tracks the boundaries between the ordinary and extraordinary, between hate and desire, fate and choice, even self and other, she comes to understand the spaces between, not as the tenebrous folds writhing with the monsters of humanism's grand schisms but as the tenuous stitches bridging those *man*ufactured divides. Thus, in Bardugo's texts, whether and how we see monsters is conditioned by Alina's developing posthumanist subjectivity; her incarnation of the posthuman borderline contests the myths on which margins are laid. Challenging the liminal thresholds upon which humanism erects its monstrous Others and against which it fortifies fictions of integrity, purity, and divisibility, the Grisha series demands a posthumanism that transcends binaristic bounds.

However, Bardugo's posthuman hybrids—her soldiers and scientists, scions and saints—do not court or even herald the doom of humanity; rather, their ontological fractures reveal what Pieter Vermeulen might call "the end of humanism by insisting that the discrete, disembodied entity of the human never existed" (123). Not only is a conviction in human(ist) exceptionality a sham, but the specious specialness we ascribe to those who count as human inevitably rests on privilege and prejudice. As Katherine Hayles points out, "the conception of the human . . . may have [only ever] applied, at best, to that fraction of humanity who had the wealth, power, and leisure to conceptualize themselves as autonomous beings exercising their will through individual agency and choice" (286). Moreover, such will, agency, and choice are implicitly attributed to and assembled by a humanist "he." After all, as Rosi Braidotti reminds us, "[h]umanity is very much a male of the species," a "white, European, handsome and able-bodied" paragon favored by his own self-wrought singularity and sovereignty, mastery and its master signifiers: language (24).

As an *otkazat'sya*—the Ravkan word for "orphan," for "abandoned," as well as the word to designate those born without superhuman Grisha talents (*SB*, ch. 10)[1]—the Grisha trilogy's Alina Starkov incorporates the borderline between those endowed with power and privilege and those with neither. As the series progresses, her body troubles immaculate masculinist ontologies that divide those who count as human in the phallogocentric discourse of modernity from those monstrous Others who—by virtue of age, race, sex, gender, or ability—do not. Indeed, Alina's subjectivity is "fragmented and plural," epitomizing Victoria Flanagan's understanding of posthumanist identity as favoring "a focus on the process of becoming (rather than being)" (52). In this way, too, Alina is *otkazat'sya*—a portmanteau term that assigns a nominal condition, a state of being, to Alina's existence while also ascribing to it a verbal function, an act of becoming, derived from the Russian verb *otkazat'sia*: to abandon, to refuse, to renounce. Significantly, therefore, the term describing Alina's identity is both noun and verb, being and becoming, attribution and abdication. It inscribes the very "sense" Alina herself experiences in "crossing the boundary between two worlds" and yet disavowing her ultimate sense of belonging to either (*SB*, ch. 5). Ultimately, therefore, in challenging not only *what* it means to be human but *who*, Alina complicates the binary dialectics of humanism (its sexism and speciesism) and aligns herself along the molten membranes of Donna Haraway's "border war," wherein she takes power over appurtenance, "*pleasure* in the confusion of boundaries and . . . *responsibility* in their construction" (150).

## "Like Calls to Like": Charting the Territories of Teratology

As we are thrust into Alina's world and its maelstromic evacuation of traditional humanist taxonomies, as we are hurled beyond the margins of the maps we once understood, Bardugo places us in the competent albeit scarred hands of a cartographer. A junior mapmaker's assistant, Alina Starkov knows something about borders, having lived her whole life between them: "I'd wanted so badly to belong somewhere, anywhere," she confides (*SB*, ch. 15). Alina is an orphan not only of Haraway's ontologically fractious fringes but also of Ravka's own political, and like-named, "border wars" (*SB*, "Before"). Here, conflict sears the Ravkan nation of Bardugo's "Tsarpunk"-inflected fantasy world, where imperial Russian aesthetics and culture collide with modernity's deadly devices, its advanced artillery developing beyond Ravka's borders (Bardugo, "Author Interview"). Meanwhile Ravka itself remains insular but far from integral, wracked by acrid division between the common Ravkans and those endowed with the pseudo-magical, quasi-alchemical Grisha power to wrest air from lungs or to charm beats from a heart, to choreograph winds and to orchestrate fires, to forge the subtlest of steel. Sought and tested as children, schooled and filed according to various Grisha orders coincident with their natural talents, Grisha are eventually conscripted as members of the king's Second Army. While internal hierarchies rage among lethal Corporalki and artisan Fabrikators, the Grisha likewise occupy a fraught position outside their residence in Ravka's capital city. Simultaneously charged with defending their nation's borders and yet persecuted both within and beyond them, these practitioners of Grisha Small Science are not unconscious of the fragility of the social stratum they are licensed to occupy by a power structure that is as much dependent on their abilities as it is deprecatory of their worth. While Ravkan Grisha are cast as subordinate and diminished (residents of the *Little* Palace, disciples of the *Small* Science, soldiers of the *Second* Army), outside Ravka they fare far worse: "The Fjerdans burn us as witches, and the Kerch sell us as slaves. The Shu Han carve us up seeking the source of our power," Alina is later informed by the Darkling, a Grisha so mighty as to be "second in power only to the King," and a creature conscious of his own marginalization, by map and by man (*SB*, ch. 5). Here be monsters, indeed.

Moreover, *Shadow and Bone* is a novel paratextually inscribed by a rough cartographical rendering of Bardugo's fantastic world. The map of Ravka is rent by the Shadow Fold, "a dark slash . . . on the landscape, a swath of nearly impenetrable darkness that grew with every passing year and crawled with horrors" (ch. 1). Monstrous volcra, with their "long filthy claws[,] leathery wings[,] and rows of razor-sharp teeth for feasting on human flesh," infest the Shadow Fold with their "snapping" jaws and their "fetid stench" (ch. 1). The map charts the Shadow Fold circumscribed by writhing snakes and discharging whales, the hard lines of two robust stags and the Ravkan crests of imperial, patriarchal power. A "dirty smudge" or a "stain"—yonic in form, labile in nomenclature, and forcibly penetrated by seamen (ch. 1)—the Shadow Fold's sprawling smear is evocative of Hélène Cixous's "dark continent" of the feminine body, the snapping jaws of its monsters suggestive of the vagina dentata haunting patriarchy's tenuous professions of ascendency (Cixous 884). That Alina fears the Fold, not only as the place "of possible death and dismemberment" but as the locus for a "something else, a deeper feeling of unease that [she can't] quite name," illustrates the extent to which the Shadow Fold truly represents something shadowed: something abjected, something monstrous standing sentry at the portal between self and other (ch. 1). Because it is upon the Fold that she first manifests her quiescent Grisha powers as a Sun Summoner, the cartographical border wars are incarnated in cartographer Alina, whose approximation of Haraway's cyborgian dualism as a feminist "border war" waged for power, privilege, and plurality only grows more pronounced.

When Alina's cartographical training takes her on an expedition across the Shadow Fold in the company of traders, trackers, and troops on their way to Ravka's western ports, the skiff is attacked by a swarm of shadow monsters. As a spontaneous surge of blinding light explodes from Alina, saving the lives of fellow *otkazat'sya* orphan Mal Oretsev as well as the rest of the crew from the creatures who feed in the dark, Alina is immediately apprehended by the fearful men and transported to the Grisha encampment, where the Darkling waits. Inquisition soon turns to violation, however, as the Darkling unleashes his own power. Beneath the cover of the billowing darkness snaking through the air, the Darkling seizes Alina's naked wrist with the words, "let's see what you can do" (*SB*, ch. 3). A living amplifier, the Darkling forges a connection with Alina that magnifies her delitescent abilities and disarms her disquietude, "push[ing] [her fear and anxiety] aside by something calm and sure and powerful" in his hungry touch (ch. 3). However, as Alina resists the seductive call the Darkling's power rings through her, she is compelled to comply at phallic knifepoint as the Darkling's icy blade threatens to breach her skin. When this corporeal violation erupts in a rapture of resplendent light, Alina is deemed a Sun Summoner, seized by the Darkling's guards (ostensibly for her own protection), and promptly precipitated into a novel negotiation of subjectivity wherein the fundamental forms of her body—like the topographical borders she maps—are dramatically transformed, transgressed, and transacted in the patriarchal economy of the Darkling's court. As Elaine Graham notes of the posthuman body, Alina's "contours . . . no longer end at the skin" (4).

Alina resents the manner in which her body is newly and alternately made pregnable by the Darkling's corporeal transgression, and she reads this non-consenting bodily imposition as devastating (if not utterly rapacious) colonization. She balks "at the indignity of being handed over like a sack of potatoes" (ch. 3) to the Grisha forces who intend to convey their newly discovered Sun Summoner (complement to the Darkling's own power of shadow and eclipse) to the Little Palace, where Grisha reside and cultivate their abilities. Nevertheless, she cannot forget that she has also "never really fit in," "never really belonged anywhere" (ch. 19). Consequently, beset by fears that she'll never be a true Grisha until she can conjure her own elemental forces and increasingly "aware of [her] shortcomings" as they are reflected to her along the mirrored walls or in the gazes of the gaping court attendants (ch. 6), Alina submits to the "glitter and gilt," the "storybook version" of life as constructed artifice in the capital of Os Alta (ch. 8). The Ravkan king loves beauty or at least the outer façade of it, and in his "court, appearances are everything" (ch. 6). Hence, in surrendering herself to the Grisha Tailor Genya, letting Genya "change [her] face" and "fix" the dark marks around her eyes, Alina also submits to the imperializing gaze of the monarch, whose first words to Alina convey his disappointment in her "very plain" features (ch. 7). Colonized by dissatisfaction with her physical form, Alina allows herself to be re-coded within the patriarchal imagination and in better accord with its prescribed aesthetic laws. Ultimately, Alina turns the male gaze upon herself when she takes in the results of Genya's handiwork: "the girl standing next to Genya in the glass was a stranger," Alina says of her reflection. "She had rosy cheeks and shiny hair and . . . a shape. I could have stared at her for hours" (ch. 13).

Essentially, Alina learns to re-code her body within a masculinist economy whose dearest currency is spectacle. Genya even suggests that Alina should "be used to being gawked at by now" (ch. 14). Moreover, if the erstwhile cartographer ever wants to be rescued from all the attention, Genya, who herself is unbelievably beautiful, is only half-joking when she offers to "get up on the banquet table, toss [her] skirt over [her] head, and do a little dance" (ch. 14). Undoubtedly, Genya and Alina are, in Alina's own terms, "spectacular" (ch. 14).

But as spectacular beings, they are also monstrous and beautiful, feared and fascinating creatures of the kind Graham describes as "intended to be public spectacles" (39). In this realm, the only authority women like Genya and Alina are licensed to display is in the performance of sublet agency, what Laura Mulvey defines as women's "traditional exhibitionist role," their "appearance coded for strong visual and erotic impact so that they can be said to connote *to-be-looked-at-ness*" and to reflect the masculine gaze as a key instrument of power (837).

While Alina's sense of autonomy evaporates along with her blemishes, her aesthetic modifications implicate her in still graver capitulations to the status quo. As Alina physically and ideologically acculturates herself to life in Os Alta—subjects herself to cosmetic refining, daily practice of her Grisha abilities, and immurement in the scholastic regimes of the Little Palace—she essentially relinquishes responsibility for her own body. Effectively, the palace operates as a sort of Foucauldian carceral network, ascribing its power-dominants "a hold over others' bodies, not only so that they may do what one wishes, but so that they may operate as one wishes" (Foucault 138). For Foucault, such "discipline produces subjected and practised bodies, 'docile' bodies" (138). And indeed, Alina finds herself increasingly domesticated, instrumentalized because (gender) essentialized. As her desire to belong to the Grisha world perversely transmutes into the gendered performance of complementarity, in which Alina agrees to be inscribed in the Darkling's color and tagged with his symbol, she is apotheosized by the aristocracy that elevates her upon a "stage," enjoined to "show" her abilities, to "*demonstrat[e]*" her monstrosity (ch. 14, emphasis added). Demonstrably monstrous, visibly Other, spectacularly surface, Alina slings her sparks across the glossy superficies of the Grand Palace, inscribing herself in infinite regress within its glittering mirrors and in the glowing tendrils of light framing her body and the Darkling's together. Though the Darkling's sinuous black coils curl upward into Alina's light, choking it, chaining it, but also "making [it] dance," Alina merely beams and performs precisely "as [she] had been taught" (ch. 14). Effectively, Alina has become "the Darkling's pet," the only position accorded her by the gendered, polarizing power structure he represents (ch. 12). And just as Peter Brooks notes that "[y]ou can't do anything with a monster except look at it," the monstrous Othering of Alina as the Darkling's complement, his paired polarity and binaristic balance, writes itself on her body (qtd. in Graham 47). "The clothes, the jewels, even the way you look," Mal tells her. "*He's all over you.* . . . He owns you" (ch. 14).

After Alina comes to understand that she is valuable to the Darkling only so long as he can possess her image, manipulate her power, and weaponize her body, she escapes from the Little Palace and reunites with her childhood friend

Mal. Together, Mal and Alina hunt the forests of Tsibeya for a mythical amplifier, an organic device imbued with the power to augment a Grisha's abilities and endowed with the promise, in Alina's hands, of the Darkling's defeat. When the Darkling finally captures Alina, however, the darkness he casts out toward her and Mal penetrates her protective projections of light, "leak[ing] into the edges of [her boundaried] bubble like ink" (*SB*, ch. 19). Attempting to ink Alina into his own hegemonic story, the Darkling, too, turns to an amplifier steeped in mythical echoes to transform Alina into an apparatus designed to perpetuate his tyrannical reign. In slaying the stag of the legendary Morozova's herd and seamlessly grafting its antlers around Alina's neck as "[a] necklace—no, a collar—of bone" (ch. 10), the Darkling corporeally splices Alina, not into the rustic lore by which folk tradition knows the herd, but into a fairytale of his own construction, into Haraway's "myth of original wholeness ... that Man has imagined" (176). That is, the Darkling reinscribes Alina as an epistemic tool and so is able to siphon his power through her as his own living amplifier, the "most powerful amplifier ever known" (ch. 12). Morozova's antlers not only amplify the Darkling's power, but they also magnify his voice. Effectively muzzling Alina, the Darkling ventriloquizes his voice through her body, permeating the membranes of her physical and psychical spaces until she can no longer be "sure if he spoke or simply thought the command that reverberated through" her (ch. 10). In commandeering Alina's inner voice as metonym for agential power, the Darkling objectifies, instrumentalizes, and subordinates Alina to a ventriloquization that is inherently tantamount to her "feminized condition" (Davies 8). As Helen Davies asserts, "the subject fulfilling the 'dummy' or 'puppet' role ... is largely condemned to repeat a patriarchal heteronormative script of passivity and objectification" (8). Prowess and power belong to the female subject's master.

Collar, fetter, muzzle. Just as "ventriloquism is an *illusion* of abnegated autonomy" in performative symbiosis (Davies 18), so too is the Darkling's conception of Alina as his dyadic balance founded upon a pernicious and disenfranchising complementarianism that subjugates feminine performance to masculine power and its tyrannical aggrandizement. Thus, the organic amplifier as employed by the Darkling becomes not a posthuman prosthetic empowered to raze the corporealized boundaries between men and women, humans and nonhumans, but the very perpetuation of a supreme, macrocosmically instantiated border war. Clamping Alina's throat between the two phallic prongs of the stag effectively pinions her into enforced gender performativity that, significantly, Judith Butler implicates in "the materialization of sexed bodies" (Barad 808n). Hence, the fettering and fetishizing of Alina's body appropriates her agency, instrumentalizes her ability, and compels her subordination to the binaristic fiction of normativity predicated on the humanist conceit of superiority and the apotheosis of its white male scions.

As Alina begins to recognize the human even in the monstrous volcra, she reveals the Darkling's perverse creations as products of Daniel O'Hara's "already empowered white male subject[] who . . . [is] out to dominate nature, marginalize further so-called minority groups (however defined), and assume godlike status at the expense of all these 'monstrous' others" (109). This is, of course, precisely the Darkling's plot: before an audience of Fjerdan, Shu Han, and Kerch ambassadors, the Darkling harnesses Alina's powers to navigate the Shadow Fold and to extend it. As the ship is about to dock in safety on the other side of the Fold, the Darkling arrests the journey and unleashes his power, sending swaths of shadow to meld with the darkness of the Fold and to swallow the village on its shores. The message is clear, the border abundantly sharp: the world must either fall to the Darkling or fall beneath his darkness. Ironically, therefore, in situating himself as supreme among species, in privileging singularity, and in usurping absolute sovereignty, the Darkling marks the quintessence not of what might have been his preternatural posthumanism but of a decidedly human anthropocentrism. Evincing a humanity that Alina concomitantly registers as equally poignant and terrifying—he seems "so cruel and still so human" (*RR*, ch. 12)—the Darkling's aims collude in the construction of Graham's "'ontological hygiene' separating human from non-human, nature from culture, organism from machine" (35). Alina's prosthetic amplifying antlers semantically invest her as metonym for the Darkling's greed, enslaving her to the man who literally and corporeally manifests humanism's imperializing binaries as they are imposed on gendered, politicized, organicized, and technologized bodies. If the Fold is the Darkling's all-too-human "soul made flesh," then it is also "a wasteland peopled by frightened monsters" of his own humanist construction (*SB*, ch. 22).

As the Darkling has it, however, the world he intends to use Alina to create is one of "no more borders, and . . . no more wars" (*SB*, ch. 22). But this vision is a humanist's fallacy. There is a border, and it is supreme. There will be only one border: only the self and the Other, only the same and the seditious, only "the land inside the Fold and outside of it" (*SB*, ch. 22). This simplified binary, this reductive dialectic of humanism is, of course, a token peace on tyrant's terms. The Darkling's world is perfect polarity, a world that not only sanctions but is predicated on utmost humanistic dichotomization. Fundamentally, his world is the distilled essence of the border war's hegemony. Implicated in the Darkling's perverse fission, Alina is cast as the implement of bifurcation, the object by which the Darkling may cleave his depraved channels of power. Significantly, even Alina cannot wholly deny that she is in part not merely captive to but captivated by the Darkling's seductive, destructive lie; while the Darkling assures her that "[t]*here are no others like us*," Alina is haunted by dreams of belonging and even hopes that such dreams might be fulfilled by joining the Darkling's powerful alliance (*SS*, ch. 6). However, Alina recognizes that the Darkling's polarities are structurally suspect coalitions. No others *like us*? The familiar Us against Them dualism is one Haraway sees as "systemic to the logics and practices of domination ... of all constituted as others, whose task is to mirror the self" (177), just as the Fold's schematic seepage marks a world "remade in [the Darkling's] image" (*SB*, ch. 22). Just "who counts as 'us'[?]" Haraway demands; "Which identities are available to ground such a potent political myth called 'us,' and what could motivate enlistment in this collectivity?" (155).

Enlistment or enjoinment is compelled by the apparatus by which the Darkling seeks to engage Alina's power with his own and to enjamb her symbols to his master discourse. When the Darkling decides to use Morozova's antlers as a device of bondage, a harness designed to make Alina "belong to him completely," to cede "all [her] newfound power ... to [his] command," and to render her absolutely powerless (*SB*, ch. 15), we can read the enforced prosthetization of Alina's body, in Amanda Booher's terms, as an "attempt at normalizing" (73). Alina's collar manifests a tyrannical desire fed by the Darkling's hegemonic masculinity not merely to incorporate the would-be Other with all her "potentially misbehaving natural parts" but also to maintain the ascendancy of his own social position by transforming Alina into a "more easily controlled" appliance (76). Forged at the interstices of subject and object, body and materiality, and welded by power, Alina is to be concomitantly his Foucauldian "body-weapon, body-tool, body-machine complex" (Foucault 153) as well as his "docile" body, "automat[on]," and "political puppet[]" to be "subjected, used, transformed and improved" (136). Nonetheless, the collar merely hypostatizes the injunctions of self-modification to which Alina has already—and readily—submitted.

While Alina's experiences at the Little Palace are persistently punctuated by shudders of self-consciousness when the newcomer perceives herself somehow deficient, whether in ability or appearance, such tremors are in fact occasioned by her consciousness of *others'* bodies. In other words, Alina has already assimilated the normative codes of "control and discipline by comparing bodies, behaviors, and functions ... in order to achieve the transformations and improvements of docility," and has already capitulated to a standardization "habituated to ... exacting and normalizing disciplines of diet, makeup, and dress" (Booher 71, 74). As we have seen, Alina not only dons the Darkling's symbol, but she is also evacuated and recolonized by it: the Darkling is *"all over* [*her*]," has already "taken possession of [her]" (*SB*, ch. 14; *SS*, ch. 23). Long before any collar fetters her neck, Alina inhabits a body already subjugated and controlled, a body complicit in its own performance of deference. Indeed, as Booher might note, she is "already, prior to any prosthetic discussion, [the very] embodiment[] of docility," a casualty to humanism's most potent and most pernicious myths (75).

Nevertheless, Alina comes to contest the terms by which she is wedded to humanist man and his oppressive dictates, mutating within the script of the very performance demanded of her. Her hair coiffed, the better to display and perform her collared prison, Alina is led in the climax of *Shadow and Bone* to the side of the Darkling and into his Fold "like a bride" (ch. 22). But this is to be no marriage ceremony, metaphorical or otherwise. For if Alina is to be the splice that establishes the Darkling's ultimate border war and that ossifies its heteronormative, unitary, and anthropocentric hegemony, her own hybridity is particularly suited to occupy this alternative space and to dismantle fantasies of normative dominance. She is, after all, *otkazat'sya*: a being of becoming, a mapper of margins, a weaponized cyborg, a mongrelized species, and a woman—"already the first step away from the 'human,'" as Patricia MacCormack reminds us (297). Consequently, just as the Darkling is swelling the margins of his master border, Alina tests its binary terms, precipitating a posthumanist crisis that threatens to unravel the fabric of the Darkling's worldview. Whereas the Darkling extends the Fold to massacre entire cities, to craft political currency from spectacle, and to coerce Alina into complicity, Alina is willing to exchange her own life for the stag's whose antlers hang about her neck. To Alina, the stag is never an "it," always a "he," and with him, she understands "the feel of the earth beneath his steady hooves, the smell of pine in his nostrils, the powerful beat of his heart," just as she "could still feel [the] vibrating [saw] through [her] clenched jaw" as the Darkling and his *oprichniki* guardsmen removed their trophy (*SB*, ch. 19). As "inappropriate/d others," Trinh T. Minh-ha's phrase for those who reject hegemonic geometries of self and Other, Alina recognizes her affinity with Morozova's mythical stag, and in thereby becoming affinitive with an Other whose tangency lives at and beyond the skin, she comes to occupy a fluid and plural posthumanist subjectivity as a position of power (qtd. in Haraway 2). As stated by the foundational principle of Grisha Small Science, "*Like calls to like*": just as the powers of the stag and, in the second installment of the trilogy, the sea whip coalesce inside Alina, "stealing [her] breath, breaking [her] up, dissolving [her] edges," Alina's initial experiences with her first prosthetic liquesce the boundaries between a no longer tenable unitary subjectivity and the world that offers infinite possibility, infinite transformation, infinite *becoming* (*SB*, ch. 22; *SS*, ch. 6).

However, although Alina comes to value her mutable body, it is not that Foucauldian body in its invocation of potentially normative forms but her intra-relational posthuman embodiment that constitutes hybridity as a site of empowerment. That is, it is not the yoke of Morozova that licenses Alina's emancipated heteronomy. Rather, within the compulsory performances to which, as Butler would insist, we are already inevitably yoked, the injunction is "to work the trap that one is inevitably in" ("The Body You Want" 84). Consequently, Alina repeatedly recites the same performative dreams of the stag but eventually re-cites them with a crucial difference. Initially, Alina suspects that the stag is shadowing her conscience, gnawing at her faults, boring into her guilt; neither could she save the stag nor steel herself to take his life and his power for her own. The consequence of her failure, she knows, is the Darkling's triumph over the stag and over her. However, as the dreams recur, Alina realizes that "[t]he stag had been showing [Alina her] strength—not just the price of mercy but the power it bestowed"; because she "had spared the stag's life[,] [t]he power of that life belonged to [her] as surely as it belonged to the man who had taken it" (*SB*, ch. 22). Together with this recognition, power and agency course again through her body, and Alina—resplendent in a halo of light and resounding with "the steady rhythm of the stag's ancient heart beating in time with" her own—is enabled to orchestrate her own escape from the Darkling's hold by employing the Cut (*SB*, ch. 22).

Not just a challenging maneuver attainable by only the most powerful of Grisha, the Cut, animated by the "intra-action" of power between Alina and the stag, is also emblematic of Karen Barad's "*agential cut*," an "enact[ment] [of] a *local* resolution *within* the phenomenon of the inherent ontological indeterminacy" (815). That is, in splitting in two whatever it is directed toward, the agential Cut *performs* the boundary by which Alina is able to sever her bond with the Darkling. Affinity with the stag does not *confer* abnegated or arrogated agency to Alina; attribution is a myth. Rather, agency consists in "enactment," in "'doing'/'being'"—in *becoming* (826, 827). While liberal humanism's "marginalisation of the body has been particularly disenfranchising for women, among other groups," as Flanagan reminds us, Alina's intra-acted execution of the Cut against the phallic mast of the Darkling's skiff grants her unsurpassed levels of corporeal strength, plenitude, multiplicity, and *jouissance* (41). Alina performs within constraint in order to resignify restraint, turning the bonds and boundaries of humanist hegemony represented by the bifurcating Cut into the site of insurrection. Feeding off the intra-agential force she shares with the power of the stag and the elements around her, Alina's body colludes in the dynamic volatility of the border war. At least at the conclusion of *Shadow and Bone*, Alina is once again capable of calling her own light because she recalls her own affinity with it, her contingent and inextricable part in the fabric of the making of the world. Ultimately, Alina escapes the Fold, leaving her nemesis still inside it. *Shadow and Bone* sees the Sun Summoner liberated by her very entanglement in a world of intertwined borderlines, the Darkling left to hollow nightmares in the cleft of his own heinous design.

## "Are We Not All Things?": Claiming Corporeal Complicity

Though she has remained partly unconscious of the import of "the shadow in [their] words, [the] second meaning" her fractious mentor Baghra and her artful companion Genya have attempted to impart, Alina's education in the tropes of illusive and subversive performance has been consummated by women on the peripheries (*SB*, ch. 13). From the weaponized glass sutured into the inside of her gloves to the twisted beams with which she slips objects on and off the visible spectrum, using "light for cover the way others used darkness," Alina's recourse to mirrors as subterfuge aligns the Summoner with the mutable and uroboric entities that Baghra and Genya embody (*RR*, ch. 15). Baghra's phantom implications, for example, continually haunt Alina's training, and her echoed warnings burrow into Alina's thoughts throughout the series. Only after she has absconded from the Little Palace in *Shadow and Bone*, huddled alongside pieces of scenery in a horse cart, does Alina realize the substance of Baghra's semantic specters. Baghra chastises Alina's initial desire for her first amplifier by likening it to a "pretty necklace" and Alina's yearning for it to a wish that "a unicorn [would] put its head in [her] lap" (*SB*, ch. 12). Effectively, therefore, Baghra dispatches Alina with the exact theatrical trappings in which Alina has been conscripted in her complicit performance of gender, a performance predicated on the Darkling's apocryphal myth of power that, like the stag's collar and the unicorn's purity, scripts hegemonic stories engineered to keep women chaste and compliant.

For all her repugnance to the Darkling's terms, however, Baghra is nonetheless complicit in the Little Palace's carceral network by which Alina internalizes normative aspirations; as Alina's instructor in the Grisha arts, she is constitutionally ambivalent, much like the witch Baba Yaga in Russian folklore with whom she shares an irascible disposition and a begrudging approach to tutelage. Alina's first Grisha friend and confidante, Genya, is likewise uroboric; although initially instrumental in domesticating Alina's body to the hegemonic masculine gaze and an agent of the Darkling's cause, Genya also takes Alina backstage, providing instruction in subversive and optative modes of Butlerian gender performance. Submerging Alina in dressing rooms suffused with makeup, mirrors, and costumes, Genya is adamant that Alina understand one thing: "appearances are everything. . . . [I]t would be better if you looked the part" (*SB*, ch. 6). Herself consigned by the Darkling as "a gift" to the aristocracy, and a Tailor whose own Grisha gifts lie in the body art of cosmetic artifice (*SB*, ch. 7), Genya is cognizant not only of the constructedness of status, class, and gender, not only of the hierarchical structures designed to inhibit her power, but also of the noxiousness of repetition that "is bound to persist" in legitimating "the power regimes of heterosexism and phallogocentrism" (Butler, *Gender Trouble* 42). While purportedly politically pliant, Genya understands pliancy as something rooted in the skin. Her consciously wrought corporeal alterations are sly insurrections, re-signifying the female body as a site of authority, as performative possibility rather than essentialized decree.

Genya may be collared, yoked, and domesticated by the masculine realm of the palace court. She may be puppeted into gendered performativity, conscripted into repetitions that divest her of choice. However, as Butler might contend, the *performative* compulsion to recite restrictive scripts is distinct from what becomes Genya's individualized expression of potentially subversive *performances* (see *Gender Trouble* 185). Hence, in the iterative performance of pliancy, Genya speaks with poisoned lips. Reappropriating the very trappings of gendered behavior enjoined upon her to entrap the phallogocentric system that has disempowered her, Genya literally envenoms her body to pollute the lecherous king, administering her toxin "in small enough doses over a long enough time"— in, that is, a series of subversive performances enacted each time the king forces himself upon her (*RR*, ch. 7). By polluting the phallocratic figurehead via a device that likewise contaminates her own body, Genya not only corrodes the sexist show but reveals its compulsive performativity as itself corrosive. Its women are never players, only played. Effectively, then, Genya's tainted skin performs a key "repetition with a difference," as Davies terms it: the collapse and restitution of a body no longer docile and mute, raped and ruined (30). Genya transforms pristine form into poisoned fortification, the irons with which she is threatened into "steel [she has] earned" (*SB*, ch. 13). Veritably incorporating repetition with a difference, Genya performs not as the "ruined" but as "ruination" (*RR*, ch. 7).

*Razrusha'ya.* The Ravkan word for "ruined" shares etymological resonance with the Russian active participle *razrushaia*: destroying, wrecking, shattering. The participle positions Genya as the active agent of the verb from which it derives (*razrushat'*) and, moreover, also identifies that agent as female. However, in Russian, *razrushat'* derives from a semantic root that not only connotes demolition, deformity, and ruin, but also contagion, infection, and contradiction (see Patrick's *Roots of the Russian Language* 173). Fundamentally then, the term that slanders Genya simultaneously inscribes her subversive rearticulations of dominant scripts. Hence, while Alina gleans from Genya knowledge about the accoutrements of display, she also absorbs strategies for reshaping the tokens by which the "game [is] played" (*RR*, ch. 1). Having come to power within a structure that "indicated [Grisha] designation within their order by color of [*kefta*] embroidery," in which identity is woven into fabric(ation), Alina too becomes acutely aware and suspicious of discourses by which she is interpellated, of performances in which she is charged to symbolize (*SB*, ch. 8). By the second installment of the Grisha trilogy, Alina is "done being shuffled across the True Sea and half of Ravka by people trying to use [her] and [her] power," done being "symbolic" and "tired of being a pawn" (*SS*, ch. 9). Instead, the powerful Sun Summoner is newly empowered to reinscribe the trap, to reappropriate her chains.

The muzzles and manacled marionette strings by which Alina is "*meant to be*" (*SS*, ch. 3, emphasis added), semantically invested and instrumentalized as tool and destiny, offer the opportunity to enact agency with and within Davies's "prescribed boundaries—subversion within limitation" (28). Injured and interned in the subterranean White Cathedral following her climactic encounter with the Darkling in which Alina had reached across her connection to the Darkling in an attempt to use his power to end them both, Alina "rattle[s] the bars of [an] underground cage" as she is again enjoined to perform a subservient role to a male figure—this time, a politically minded priest (*RR*, "Before"). Though he is quick to canonize Alina and her powers, the Apparat, like the Darkling, also sees in Sankta (Saint) Alina a conduit for his own aggrandizement. Here, however, Alina speaks in the shadowed words, the "hidden language" Baghra and Genya have shown her (*RR*, "Before"). The first words Alina speaks within the intradiegesis of *Ruin and Rising* identify her not only as performing an alternative discourse upon "a carved stone balcony" for a stage but as the very locus of theater: "I . . . tried to put on a good show. My *kefta* was a patchwork, sewn together from scraps of the gown I was wearing the night we fled the palace and garish curtains that I'd been told came from a defunct theater somewhere near Sala" (*RR*, ch. 1). Her robes a "patchwork" of hybridity and theatricality, filched from the detritus of a decayed institution, Alina is "all loose threads and false shine," a "threadbare Saint" (*RR*, ch. 1). This far underground, buried and bruised, Alina may be unsure of the state of her Grisha powers, but she will not be interred by "the weight of the [Apparat's] *Istorii Sankt'ya*" (*SS*, ch. 5): the weight of his book, the weight of her name impressed between its covers, the weight of a faith that seems all too eager not only to ink her followers but to imprint her own body, investing it as symbol and profiting by its prostitution. While merchants peddle relics purported to be "Genuine Sankta Alina," "selling off parts of [her] all over Ravka and West Ravka," Alina's performance operates on the abnegation of corporeal autonomy—an abnegation that is belied by the performance itself and that dismantles the illusion of "genuine" taxonomies of gender, divinity, power, and even humanness (*SS*, ch. 10).

By effacing the "moment [when she] ceased to bear her weakness as a burden and began to wear it as a guise," a guise she dons to pass as "human," Alina troubles the binaries between which performativity is licensed: dichotomies divorcing human from nonhuman, male from female, tellurian from supernal, connate from constructed, Grisha from *otkazat'sya* (*RR*, "Before"; *SS*, ch. 11). In *Siege and Storm*, for example, Alina masquerades as a Suli fortune-teller who, beneath the cover of her disguise, mocks the notion of the phallocentric discourse that forecasts her destiny by herself prophesying a nobleman's "private parts . . . shrink[ing] to nothink! [*sic*]" (*SS*, ch. 18). Here, Alina illustrates Ann Rosalind Jones's point that, "[i]f men are responsible for the reigning binary system of meaning . . . [that] relegate[s] [women] to the negative and passive pole of this hierarchy," women need not be "implicated in the creation" and perpetuation "of its myths" (252). The sainted Sun Summoner rejects mythologization as the Darkling's fated balance, sanctification as the Apparat's providential martyr. Alina's refusal to play by the script cleaves a vacuum where her icon was meant to stand, her life to symbolize. Instead, Alina's subversive staging razes "mountains of phallocentric delusion" so as to raise from the rubble neither the body of a saint nor the power of a queen, but rather a reconditioned topography upon which the borderlines of bodies and power may themselves be remapped (Jones 252).

If gendered and ontological essentialism inheres in the differential categories erected in "mountains of phallocentric delusion," then it is significant that the last lesson Baghra imparts to Alina is one that has her decapitating—cutting, neutering—phallic peaks. Indeed, the performance of the Cut for Alina is tantamount to the fathomless, plural, and protean experience of *jouissance*: "I called the light to me and then released it, letting myself go with it. I was in the clouds, above them, and for a brief moment, I was in the dark of the mountain, feeling myself compressed and breathless. I was in the spaces between, where light lived even if it could not be seen. When I brought my arm down, the arc I made was infinite, a shining sword that existed in a moment and in every moment beyond it" (*RR*, ch. 7). Similarly, Laura Sells has defined *jouissance* as connoting "multiplicity of woman's sexuality[,] indicat[ing] 'she has the potential to attain something more than total, something extra—abundance and waste, Real and unrepresentable'" (184). Further, Sells suggests, it is this "language of women's bodies [that] jams the machinery of phallocentric discourse that generates a dualistic world view, disrupting the symbolic system that demands the complementarity of gender and the dual world" (184).

For Alina, therefore, performing her "post" as saint and Summoner, cartographer and queen, is an exercise inextricable from the performance of her *posthumanity* in its ecstatic multiplicity. Posthumanism is an ideology predicated upon abdication of the human from *his* central (dominant and predominant) position, as well as a philosophy disposed to reassess *our* ontological contingency among other matter and the environment, the way that even the most powerful of Grisha still depend upon a dialogue with nature to exercise their powers; after all, no matter how able the Inferni, she "still need[s] flint to make [a] spark" (*SB*, ch. 10). Hence, for as ardently as the Darkling would like Alina to believe in a humanistic doctrine of exceptionalism, Alina is most arrested by the Grisha theorem "like calls to like" (*SB*, ch. 10). As Alina understands the legendary scholarship of the eminent Grisha Fabrikator Morozova, "if the world could be broken down to the same small parts, each Grisha should be able to manipulate them. *Are we not all things?*" (*RR*, ch. 4). Consequently, when Baghra, Morozova's own daughter, encourages Alina to wield the Cut that will shatter man's mountains, she galvanizes the Summoner to seek her affinity with the elements: "You are as much there as you are here. The same things that make the mountain make you. It has no lungs, so let it breathe with you. It has no pulse, so give it your heartbeat. . . . The Cut is already made" (*RR*, ch. 7). Though Alina's attempt to rupture the summit "draw[s] a crowd" (*RR*, ch. 7), Baghra drives Alina to understand that this enactment of posthumanist performativity is not premised on the "mere effect of human agency" (Barad 827), on the inane antics of "a dancing monkey" (*RR*, ch. 7). Rather, Baghra's final lesson derives directly from Vermeulen's conception of the inextricably intra-acting human "embedded[] in nonhuman matter" (122), as well as from Barad's understanding of the conditionality of our materiality: "we are part *of* the world in its ongoing intra-activity" (828).

When Alina returns to the Shadow Fold in *Ruin and Rising* to face the Darkling for the last time, the Fold feels different, but not because Alina is somehow more aware of her own exceptionality and in fuller command of her powers. This time, the Unsea feels less like home to the "human things" (*RR*, ch. 16) inside it that might recognize her laughter and more "like the end of everything"—a place not of kinship and empathy but of nightmares, a place "of isolation, as if the world had disappeared, leaving only you, the rattle of your breath, the stuttering beat of your heart" (*RR*, ch. 17). Harmonized to the rhythmic contingency of that place, to its respiration and its pulse, Alina finally recognizes the Fold as the bisecting abomination it has always been, product of the Darkling's devotion to the hegemonic dualism dismantled by feminist and posthumanist alterities. Like that perversely binaristic order of the defunct and delusory humanist system, the Fold too must be dissolved in a subversive performance that exposes it as a mobile and malleable mirage. Appropriately, then, it is in "the barest second, the brief space between instinct and understanding," the liminal hesitation wherein the Darkling is fundamentally vulnerable that Alina allows his binary assurances to crumble (*RR*, ch. 17). Transporting herself along the tether that connects her to the Darkling, Alina directs her spectral doppelgänger to perform the Cut. This illusive spectacle, this replication of self-not-self, this repetition with a difference ultimately licenses Alina's corporeal release. From Genya and Baghra and even the Darkling, Alina has learned as much about the spectacle of smoke and mirrors as she has about the properties of light and darkness, and her craft(iness) reveals the phantasmic structure of the Fold itself. By cutting through the fallacy of the Fold, Alina's body incorporates Andrew Pickering's understanding of performative posthumanism, as she parabolizes a "world that makes us in one and the same process [by which] we make the world" (26).

If there is strength to be had in re-citing ruin as ruination, then there is something to be salvaged from Neil Badmington's "account of what it means to be [a] human" that is continually "rais[ed] . . . to ruins" (10). *Ruin and Rising*, the final installment of the Grisha trilogy, ends on a poignant but pregnant note of loss. By piercing the Darkling with Mal's phallic knife, a knife that is shrouded in shadow and steeped in the blood he and the Darkling share as the progeny of Morozova, Alina ensures that the diseased patriarchal system—nursed by the conceits of a liberal humanist emphasis on individual agency and extended by the greed of the Darkling's Fold and the arrogance of Morozova's amplifier chains—is its own undoing. As her fetters fall from her wrist and neck, Alina witnesses her own liberation alongside that of the material agency animating the power of the amplifiers, into which this energy had been incorporated and within which it had been incarcerated. Suddenly, Alina finds her summoning abilities stripped from her body and diffused among the *otkazat'sya*, sun soldiers and shadow guard alike. However, although Alina comes to lament the "wound" this divestment has hollowed inside her, "the gap where something whole and right had been," her loss of power is a diminution neither of agency nor of hybridity (*RR*, ch. 17). Instead, her "power [has been] multiplied a thousand times, but not in one person," not in a defunct remnant of humanist exceptionalism (*RR*, ch. 17). In the aftermath of "the implosion of tightly scripted bodily regimes" imagined by Butler, Haraway, and Hayles, the "swift emergence" of Arthur Kroker's "body drift" ensues as Alina's old fetters break away (Kroker 6). In this ontological liberation from gendered humanist ideologies, Alina's plurivectorial and corporealized consciousness epitomizes Myra Seaman's understanding of a "posthumanism [that] transforms the [would-be] humanist subject into *many* subjects, . . . allowing it to roam free and 'join' with other beings" (248). Indeed, Alina's body macrocosmically magnifies the social changes Alina had initially instituted within the microcosm of the Little Palace in her desire "to erase the lines that had been drawn between the Grisha and the rest of Ravka's people" (*SS*, ch. 12). Though there are "still wars, and . . . still orphans," still rulers and power and greed, there is also a democratization of power, a dissolution of distinction (*RR*, "After"). As a new king tests his seat on the Ravkan throne, the unification of the First and Second Armies, the *otkazat'sya* and Grisha forces, likewise sits upon the horizon. As the most celebrated of Grisha powers takes root in the non-Grisha turned Sun Summoners, the ranks dividing the existing Grisha orders, sundering Healers from Tidemakers, Heartrenders from Fabrikators, become far more permeable and far less hierarchical. And as each new child discovers her own fledgling Grisha powers, the powers that would once have consigned her life to the defense of the state, the choice of what to do with them remains hers alone.

Essentially, the cartographer becomes the cartography, a harbor for "the intersection of a multiplicity of bodies" (Kroker 15); the orphan of the border wars absorbs "the borderline come[] inside [the] bod[y]" (14). In troubling the definitional ambiguities of its *otkazat'sya* and in apportioning the potency of its saint, Bardugo's Grisha trilogy compromises the ontological impunity of whatever we might be tempted to call "human." The Sun Summoner and the Grisha, the mapmaker and the soldier have, as Hayles would have it, "always been posthuman," and so have we (291). Orphans of the border wars, we are charged by Haraway "to survive in the diaspora"—across the fallen monuments to formerly impassable frontiers, beyond the worlds and through the skins we once called ours (170). Amidst a riot of new fissures, the "maps" to all our places, like those Alina knows, will "have to change" (*RR*, ch. 18).

## Notes

1. Citations of Bardugo's Grisha trilogy refer to the following novels, in chronological order: *Shadow and Bone* (*SB*), *Siege and Storm* (*SS*), and *Ruin and Rising* (*RR*).

## Works Cited

Badmington, Neil. Introduction. *Posthumanism*. Ed. Neil Badmington. New York: Palgrave, 2000. 1–10. Print.

Barad, Karen. "Posthumanist Performativity: Toward an Understanding of How Matter Comes to Matter." *Signs: Journal of Women in Culture and Society* 28.3 (2003): 801–31. Print.

Bardugo, Leigh. "Author Interview." Interview by Claire Legrand. *Claire Legrand*. N.p., 2012. Web. 22 Apr. 2014.

———. *Ruin and Rising*. New York: Henry Holt, 2014. Kindle file.

———. *Shadow and Bone*. New York: Henry Holt, 2012. Kindle file.

———. *Siege and Storm*. New York: Henry Holt, 2013. Kindle file.

Booher, Amanda K. "Docile Bodies, Supercrips, and the Plays of Prosthetics." *International Journal of Feminist Approaches to Bioethics* 3.2 (2010): 63–89. JSTOR. Web. 17 Oct. 2014.

Braidotti, Rosi. *The Posthuman*. Malden: Polity, 2013. Print.

Butler, Judith. "The Body You Want: Liz Kotz Interviews Judith Butler." Interview by Liz Kotz. *Artforum* Nov. 1992: 82–89. Print.

———. *Gender Trouble: Feminism and the Subversion of Identity*. 1990. New York: Routledge, 1999. Print.

Cixous, Hélène. "The Laugh of the Medusa." Trans. Keith Cohen and Paula Cohen. *Signs* 1.4 (1976): 875–93. JSTOR. Web. 27 May 2015.

Davies, Helen. *Gender and Ventriloquism in Victorian and Neo-Victorian Fiction*. London: Palgrave Macmillan, 2012. Print.

Flanagan, Victoria. "Girl Parts: The Female Body, Subjectivity and Technology in Posthuman Young Adult Fiction." *Feminist Theory* 12.1 (2011): 39–53. SAGE Journals Online. Web. 13 Apr. 2014.

Foucault, Michel. *Discipline and Punish: The Birth of the Prison*. 1975. Trans. Alan Sheridan. 2nd ed. New York: Vintage, 1995. Print.

Graham, Elaine L. *Representation of the Post/Human: Monsters, Aliens, and Others in Popular Culture*. New Brunswick: Rutgers UP, 2002. Print.

Haraway, Donna J. *Simians, Cyborgs, and Women: The Reinvention of Nature*. New York: Routledge, 1991. Print.

Hayles, N. Katherine. *How We Became Posthuman: Virtual Bodies in Cybernetics, Literature, and Informatics*. Chicago: U of Chicago P, 1999. Print.

Jones, Ann Rosalind. "Writing the Body: Toward an Understanding of 'L'écriture Féminine.'" *Feminist Studies* 7.2 (1981): 247–63. JSTOR. Web. 12 July 2014.

Kroker, Arthur. *Body Drift: Butler, Hayles, Haraway*. Minneapolis: U of Minnesota P, 2012. Print.

MacCormack, Patricia. "Posthuman Teratology." *The Ashgate Research Companion to Monsters and the Monstrous*. Ed. Asa Simon Mittman with Peter J. Dendle. Burlington: Ashgate, 2012. 293–309. Print.

Mulvey, Laura. "Visual Pleasure and Narrative Cinema." *Film Theory and Criticism: Introductory Readings*. Ed. Leo Braudy and Marshall Cohen. New York: Oxford UP, 1999. 833–44. Print.

O'Hara, Daniel T. "Neither Gods nor Monsters: An Untimely Critique of the 'Post/human' Imagination." *boundary 2* 30.3 (2003): 107–22. Project Muse. Web. 9 July 2014.

Patrick, George Z. *Roots of the Russian Language: An Elementary Guide to Wordbuilding*. Chicago: Passport Books, 1989. Print.

Pickering, Andrew. *The Mangle of Practice: Time, Agency, and Science*. Chicago: U of Chicago P, 1995. Print.

Seaman, Myra J. "Becoming More (than) Human: Affective Posthumanisms, Past and Future." *Journal of Narrative Theory* 37.2 (2007): 246–75. *Project Muse.* Web. 10 July 2014.

Sells, Laura. "'Where Do the Mermaids Stand?': Voice and Body in *The Little Mermaid*." *From Mouse to Mermaid: The Politics of Film, Gender, and Culture.* Ed. Elizabeth Bell, Lynda Haas, and Laura Sells. Bloomington: Indiana UP, 1995. 175–92. Print.

Vermeulen, Pieter. "Posthuman Affect." *European Journal of English Studies* 18.2 (2014): 121–34. *Taylor & Francis Online.* Web. 2 Dec. 2014.

# 6

# "SUPERPOWERS DON'T ALWAYS MAKE YOU A SUPERHERO"
Posthuman Possibilities in Michael Grant's Gone Series

*Patricia Kennon*

Recent dystopian fiction for young adults has been preoccupied with questions around norms of belonging, difference, and teenagers' potential for transformative reinvention. Series such as Scott Westerfeld's Uglies and Julianna Baggott's Pure novels have explored the interplay of control, desire, and anxiety regarding the dilemma of being human in a biotechnologically modified and consequently posthuman state, particularly in relation to how adolescence is conceptualized, experienced, and regulated. The dystopian world of Michael Grant's Gone novels similarly tests the limits to which the young human body and mind can be reconceived. The eponymous first novel begins with the abrupt vanishing of everyone over the age of fifteen from the fictional California town of Perdido Beach, just as an impregnable, opaque dome seals off the area that comes to be known as the Fallout Alley Youth Zone (FAYZ). Without adult authority, the FAYZ becomes a disorienting, violent world made even more unsettling when many of the teen inhabitants develop superhuman mutations. Grant's teenage characters must negotiate the boundaries between natural human abilities and unnatural, posthuman agency as they fight to survive within this new environment of the FAYZ and to resist the onslaught of the Darkness, a malevolent alien creature who crash-landed centuries before the series begins and who has since lurked under Perdido Beach, awaiting its chance to infect and dominate the planet. The alien entity gets its chance when the Perdido Beach nuclear power plant suddenly has a meltdown, and the town's children up to the age of fifteen find themselves isolated under the dome.

The FAYZ's young inhabitants initially believe that everyone who mysteriously disappeared is dead and that they too will disappear and/or perish upon turning fifteen. At the end of the first book, readers learn that FAYZ inhabitants who turn fifteen face different possible fates during that symbolic cusp of transitioning between child and adult: being killed by the Darkness, being teleported back to normal human society, or choosing to stay with their friends within the FAYZ. Due to the Darkness's viral influence, which imbues nearly all the main protagonists with unsettling powers that they must learn to control, the FAYZ becomes a zone of ongoing metamorphosis in which traditional concepts of heroism, villainy, childhood innocence, bodily purity, decency, and monstrosity are explored. However, despite the series's tantalizing depiction of posthuman transformations, Grant ultimately asserts a conservative humanist view regarding what constitutes being human and privileges conservative concepts of normality, adult authority, and hegemonic power regimes.

The adolescents soon find themselves divided into two factions, one headed by Sam Temple and the other by Caine Soren. Sam, the heroic protagonist, can generate light both as weapon and illumination and struggles to use this double-edged power to defend the town's human and posthuman residents against their enemies. Sam is aided by other teenagers who have similarly gained superhuman abilities, such as Astrid, who has the ability to perceive the relative scale of people's potential; Lana, who possesses the power of healing; Brianna, "the Breeze," who can move at super speed; and Dekka, who can manipulate gravity. Astrid's four-year-old brother, Little Pete, whose severe autism usually renders him incapable of communication with anyone, even his sister, possesses a godlike power of reality-warping and molecular manipulation. Later in the series readers learn that Little Pete's erratic control over his immense powers caused the accidental enclosure of the town and the associated teleportation of everyone over the age of fifteen outside the town's domed environs. Meanwhile, Caine (revealed during the series to be Sam's twin brother) draws upon his own imposing power of telekinesis; the ability of his girlfriend Diana to assess the degree and potential of transformed teenagers' powers; the unreliable support of the superstrong "Computer Jack"; and the unstable, sadistic, and monstrously mutated Drake to help his agenda of positioning himself as leader against Sam's authority.

Disappointingly, Grant does not fully engage with the radical potential of these young people's posthuman transformations. Instead, the series's ultimately humanist, conservative emphasis on the ideological primacy of traditional concepts of humanity presents a didactic cautionary tale about how young people who possess too much unnatural, revolutionary power pose a danger to themselves, each other, the laws of nature, and the traditional status quo. By the start of the sixth and final novel, "no one in the FAYZ [is] entirely sane" (*Light* 17) due to having encountered and inhabited diverse states of being which range from normal humans (such as the FAYZ's teenage sheriff, Edilio), to mutated humans with freakish powers (for example, Sam or Drake), an alien entity (the Darkness), an extraterrestrial-human hybrid such as Gaia (Caine and Diana's posthuman child, whom the Darkness transforms and inhabits in order to achieve corporeal form), and even a disembodied consciousness without a physical incarnation (Little Pete, who ascends to an existence of pure energy in the final books of the series).

Presented with the intertwined forces of biotechnological change, alien physiology, and extraterrestrial effect, young adult readers are challenged to consider their own potential feelings of uncertainty, ambivalence, and affinity regarding the evolution of humanity, what it means to be human, and how this hegemonic category might be reimagined. As such, this series offers an intriguing opportunity to consider the construction and mediation of the posthuman in young adult literature and to investigate the associated nexus of identity, norms, difference, and empowerment. However, despite this exciting potential, the series ultimately maintains and imposes a didactic, normative insistence on defining and ultimately enforcing identity in traditional, reactionary binary configurations against the perceived threats of posthuman transformation and change.

As many critics across diverse disciplines have noted, there is no standard definition of the posthuman. Likewise, there is a wide-ranging debate about how the posthuman can and should be conceptualized and manifested. The concept I am using here is commonly known as transhumanism, which asserts that the posthuman is something other or more than human and that posthuman capacity involves a new skill or capacity that had not existed previously but which holds a physical (although not necessarily moral or ethical) superiority to that possessed by current humanity. Francis Fukuyama has emphasized the dangers of posthuman alterity and its threat to traditional systems of subjectivity and systems of morality, while N. Katherine Hayles has strongly critiqued the earlier posthumanist theories' erasure of bodily experience and the privilege that the posthuman view accords to virtual intelligence and information over materiality. Questions about the extent to which human consciousness, selfhood, and corporeality are interlinked and even interdependent inform the ongoing debates regarding the posthuman. Scholars such as Cary Wolfe have agreed with Joel Garreau's definition that posthumans are beings "whose basic capacities so radically exceed those of present humans as to no longer be unambiguously human by our current standards" (qtd. in Wolfe xiii).

The remarkable powers that many of Grant's protagonists display are indeed perceived by characters within and outside the FAYZ as variously aligning them with the superhuman, the inhuman, and the godlike. However, I disagree with Garreau's assumption that ambiguity does not play any part in the interpretative exchanges and judgments about similarity and Otherness between altered and normal humans. The borderland between the posthuman and current human experience is not so decisively defined. For example, Nick Bostrom has argued that "posthuman modes of being" need not be so radically estranging or different in scale ("Why I Want" 108). Instead, posthuman abilities such as possessing "a general central capacity [health, cognition, emotion] greatly exceeding the maximum attainable by any current human being without recourse to new technological means could be advantageous and desirable" (108). The Gone series investigates two popular fears about the posthuman observed by Bostrom: "that the state of being posthuman might in itself be degrading" and "that posthumans might pose a threat to 'ordinary' humans" ("In Defense" 204). Grant's series explores tensions between conservative assumptions of childhood innocence and young people's bodily purity as well as humanist anxieties about the disquieting potential of posthuman youth. As one character ruefully notes in the second novel, echoing the author's conservative and humanist concerns about posthuman difference, superior capacities are not necessarily linked to an evolution in moral or ethical abilities: "Superpowers . . . don't always make you a superhero" (*Hunger* 156).

The ambivalence that surrounds young people's symbolic potential for serving the forces of both continuity and change is particularly evident in dystopian young adult fiction. Much scholarship has been dedicated to tracing the ideological dimensions and didactic propensity of speculative narratives for teenage audiences, since the figure of the child "can be interpreted as the ultimate form of the posthuman: one that comes after the present generation; one that is supposed to possess a future, rather than a past" (Földváry 209-10). Susan Honeyman notes the potentially revolutionary force of youth's relentless forward momentum: "neoteny, which interprets children as evidence of evolutionary advancements, provides the key to child power—mutiny by mutation" (348). However, Clare Bradford, Kerry Mallan, John Stephens, and Robyn McCallum argue that contemporary young adult dystopian fiction for teenagers offers a forum for constructively negotiating a relationship between the posthuman and traditional notions of the human: "the attempts to define a future version of humanity we find in such texts accords better with an alternative view that the posthuman does not necessitate either an evolution or devolution of the human. Rather it means that difference and identity are being redistributed" (181).

Although Bradford et al. optimistically focus on the potential of young adult speculative fiction to problematize concepts of difference, norms, and mutual respect between posthuman and human capacities, many scholars remain critical about the pervasive tendency by authors in this genre to sentimentally soften the complexity of their storyworlds when writing for younger readers. I agree with Elaine Ostry's critique of the failure of such dystopian narratives for teenagers to adequately acknowledge and engage with the complexities of posthuman futures: "much science fiction for young adults attempts to mediate the posthuman age to a young audience" while deploying biotechnology as "a metaphor for adolescence [that] . . . adds a dramatic dimension to the changing adolescent body and the identity crisis that arises from it" (223). Likewise, Farah Mendlesohn has criticized the failure of many science fiction narratives for teenagers to operate as true works of science fiction because the science fiction elements become secondary to the coming-of-age or bildungsroman aspects of the story (293). Grant's lack of interest in scientific details or coherence and his focus on the angst and relationship difficulties that his characters feel due to their posthuman alterity can be seen as part of this larger pattern. Throughout the series, Grant pays merely superficial attention to the scientific plausibility of "the awful blank monstrosity that was the Perdido Beach Anomaly" (*Fear* 525). For example, the process of how external light from the sun passes through the dome's barrier into the FAYZ and the lack of consequences (e.g., broken bones from the physiological pressures of superspeed) from the performance of posthuman powers are never adequately explained. He also does not seem concerned that his plots lack originality or that the premise of the enclosed FAYZ could be seen as derivative of Stephen King's *Under the Dome*. However, despite its lack of engagement with scientific and medical exposition and its conservative insistence on privileging hegemonic norms, the Gone series provides a productive exemplar for considering how young adult dystopian literature explores the possible reconfiguration of concepts of humanity and alterity.

The Gone novels especially offer an opportunity to consider issues of didacticism and suitability regarding young people's potential for destruction and how the posthuman challenges and even ruptures traditional human boundaries and taboos. The series has generated much controversy in its unsentimental depiction of adolescent brutality and grotesque, disturbing violence, especially when performed by ostensibly innocent youths who are enabled by posthuman abilities for aggression and destruction. Kay Sambell has written extensively about how adult authors negotiate various educational and ethical responsibilities traditionally associated with writing for young people. Observing that all too often adults assume that young readers need to be reassured and supplied with explicit closure via a happy ending (however unconvincing this might be within a dystopian scenario), she concludes that this didactic tradition compromises the narrative strategies of much young adult dystopian fiction. Thus "the child as an emblem of hope for the future, capable of transforming and transcending adult mores, and the image of the child as helpless victim are often held in acute tension in dystopian writing for young readers" (252). These tensions are further intensified when traditional, nostalgic concepts of childhood purity, innocence, and vulnerability are problematized by the empowering yet estranging opportunities created by posthuman transformations.

Throughout his prolific career writing for young adults, from the bestselling Animorphs series to his recent novel *Messenger of Fear*, Grant has demonstrated a fascination with themes of dehumanization, insanity, morality, freedom, the pleasures of violence, biotechnological mutations, and the ethical use of power—a fascination that exists in intriguing counterpart to his commitment to humanism and his privileging of conservative norms. If Roberta Seelinger Trites is correct in her assertion that "death is the *sine qua non* of adolescent literature, the defining factor that distinguishes it both from children's and adult literature" (*Disturbing the Universe* 118), then the Gone series with its preoccupation with the myriad and creative ways in which humans can die arguably serves as a preeminent representative of young adult literature. As Jane Howarth stated when reviewing the first novel in the series, *Gone*, this "potent mix of *Lord of the Flies*, *Heroes* and *Lost* . . . does not hold back at showing the feral nature of humans when faced with a world without order" (8).

The serialized nature of the Gone sequence affords Grant the opportunity to devise startling scenarios that push the human and posthuman bodies of his young protagonists to their limits and beyond while simultaneously replaying and perpetuating a fascination with potential transformation through psychic and physical suffering. Each novel starts with an explicit countdown of days, hours, and minutes to its respective denouement, underscoring the series's preoccupation with exploring what it is like to be enmeshed within intense, relentless cycles of violence. In many ways, Grant's dark imaginings about life and death within the dystopian territory of the FAYZ resonate with Elana Gomel's observation about post-disaster narratives: they seem to be concerned "not with the sharp moment of death but rather with the interminable duration of dying. If the apocalypse promises glorious rebirth, postapocalypse is enmeshed in the backward-looking narrative of trauma" (408). Normal and posthuman characters alike struggle with traumatic experiences, including the loss of family and friends, torture, bereavement, survivor guilt, the dilemma of sacrificing others to save oneself, the price of eating human flesh in order to avoid starvation, and the catastrophic effects of alien contamination and control.

While all these traumas are deeply enmeshed in bodily experience, the tone of Grant's investigation of the estranging, graphically described effect of posthuman alterations to the human mind and body aligns this series with the horror genre. As Norah Campbell and Mike Saren argue,

> [Posthumanism] is not just an epistemology but an aesthetic that blends three elements—the primitive, technology and horror. . . . [Posthuman transformations] depict the visceral, painful and embodied experience that results from ontological boundary clashes; . . . mutation conveys the other side of the posthuman utopian imagination by hinting at the pain and difficulty of the flesh in becoming its ontological Other. (152, 165)

Grant's series certainly does not sentimentalize or shy away from slaking his young readers' curiosity about some of the harrowing and disturbing aspects involved while transitioning to and becoming posthuman during the series's "unhinged version of evolution" (*Light* 387). Many adult readers have expressed dismay and disapproval at what they consider the graphic and even gratuitous treatment of pain, violence, and gore in the series. For example, the fourth novel, *Plague*, tracks the contagious effects of a virus that forces bodies into such convulsive coughs that the infected eventually vomit pieces of their own lungs; meanwhile the characters face a parallel threat of "the surging horror of insect bodies" (474) of evolved parasitic larvae that infest and consume their hosts as they emerge "like a chicken out of an egg. Being born" (113).

Many critics have debated the appeal, suitability, complexity, and ideological dimensions of horror literature for teenagers, especially regarding its attitudes toward morality, norms, and difference. For example, Roderick McGillis has concluded that this genre is cynical and cliché-ridden, ultimately offering "titillation without apparent consequences" (103). However, Kimberley Reynolds argues that adolescent horror literature is fundamentally concerned with promoting conformity since, despite its superficial "delighting in the attractions of misfits and outsiders," these works teach "readers how to behave in ways that will make them acceptable rather than monstrous. The *modus operandi* is still fear, but it is fear of the consequences of behaving in ways other than conventional and acceptable ways" (3). Reynolds's insight illuminates the fundamentally didactic, conformist agenda and binary systems of normal/abnormal and human/posthuman that inform the obvious relish with which Grant presents disturbing figures of hybridity, the monstrous, the grotesque, and the perverse, and yet ultimately silences these transgressive voices in favor of humanist, conservative power regimes.

Grant's explicit use of the device of intertextuality through links to such authoritative classics such as the Bible and *The Lord of the Rings* seems designed to counter potential allegations of shallow titillation and to increase the perceived literary density and thus legitimacy of the series. The most obvious examples in the series occur when Astrid ponders the alien nemesis of the Darkness and the associated "awakening of forgotten and brutal instincts" in the FAYZ while reading Joseph Conrad's *Heart of Darkness*, and later when she exchanges dialogue from Frank Herbert's *Dune* with Lana about the importance of managing fear, "the mind-killer . . . the little death that brings total obliteration" (*Fear* 17, 154). Despite Astrid's conviction that "the only thing we have to fear is fear itself" (*Gone* 50) and Sam's ongoing efforts to reduce tensions and to build cooperation between different factions of humans and posthumans, the FAYZ inhabitants are deeply sensitive and hostile to markers of difference from normal humanity. Elaine Ostry has argued that young adult fiction posits the posthuman body "as a lesson in tolerance. Can others look beyond the unusual bodies and origins these young adults have, and see their humanity?" (237). The residents of the FAYZ ultimately fail this test, instead displaying impressive creativity in creating new terminology for any posthuman, abject aberrations: "Moofs, muties, freaks. We're out of food, but we've got plenty of nicknames" (*Hunger* 17).

The posthuman mutations and metamorphoses occurring within the FAYZ range across a continuum of estranging abjection and difference and blur the comforting, traditional boundaries between the human, the inorganic, the animal, and the alien. Julia Kristeva has argued that this abjection is caused by that which "disturbs identity, system, order. What does not respect borders, positions, rules. The in-between, the ambiguous, the composite" (4).

Grant tracks the struggles of the FAYZ's inhabitants with the dilemma of successfully negotiating the fascination and repulsion they feel when encountering various abject mutations whose bodily integrity is so distorted by their posthuman alterations that their possession of humanity is in doubt. While some transformed, posthuman characters such as Sam try to retain their humane principles and their capacity for compassion in the face of agonizing ethical dilemmas, the "Human Crew," a paranoid hate group of physically normal humans, quickly succumbs to xenophobia and hatred and lynches anyone suspected of being a freak, that is, anyone who displays superhuman powers. Tellingly, Zil (the leader of this vigilante group of unaltered humans) uses the façade of legitimacy conferred by the endorsement of the hegemonically normal and popular teenager, Lance, to overcome his occasional internal doubts about the Crew's acts of persecution, crime, torture, and murder.

The participation and support of the "tall, cool, smart" Lance (*Lies* 241) serves as a crucial mechanism for authorizing this otherwise racist and vicious regime. In contrast to the admirably masculine and phallically named Lance, the transformed body of the town's teenage bully, Charles "Orc" Merriman, becomes nearly all subsumed during the series into a behemoth of super-strong, living gravel with just some facial scraps of skin still viable as human: "The tiny human portion of him seemed like the creepier part. Like someone had cut the flesh off a living person and glued it onto a stone statue" (*Gone* 116). The villainous Drake Merwin undergoes even more intense posthuman transformations by the Darkness. Drake's initially human form is mutated in the first novel to accommodate a monstrous whip-like arm, "such as no human ever had" (452). When the Darkness reassembles and resurrects Drake for its own purposes later in the series, Drake's psychic and physical existences are unnaturally juxtaposed with that of Brittney, a posthuman girl who possesses the unnatural ability of being immortal. Drake and Brittney become a "twinned undead creature melded . . . with two minds and two bodies" that switch back and forth with the emergence of each personality (*Plague* 7, 33).

Intriguingly, a posthuman anomaly exists who poses a disquieting impact surpassing even that of "the something outside of nature" (*Hunger* 268) that constitutes the monstrous twinned status of Drake/Brittney: Taylor, who initially possesses the power of teleportation and whom the ultimate superpowered child, Little Pete, later modifies into a "monstrous parody" of herself (*Fear* 150). This unique, golden-skinned hybrid exists in the liminal space between human, posthuman, mammal, and reptile. Some of the uncanny affect posed by Taylor's unnerving ambiguity after her transformation is attributable to her lack of familiar and reliable markers for human systems of sexual or gender identity. Taylor's lack of human genitalia is related indirectly through characters' hesitant dialogue and is never openly discussed or directly represented to the reader. Despite Grant's tendency to linger on the minutiae of physical pain and bodily suffering through violence, he significantly remains coy whenever conveying any sexual details. While Grant does not shy away from representing extreme pain and physical violence, even seeming to relish portraying the intricacies of extraordinary violence, he never addresses the threat or possible incidence of sexual violence and rape during the series, despite the strong likelihood that sexual attacks would be ongoing in an unregulated, brutal world like the FAYZ, inhabited by superpowered posthumans and groups of human vigilantes. Grant's sanitized, evasive approach to the realities of rape, gendered violence, and abuse of power is consistent with what Trites has argued is young adult literature's conservative tendency to regulate and police adolescent sexuality because teenagers' erotic curiosity and active desire compromise adults' positioning of young people as relatively innocent and needing protection from the dangers of sexuality ("Queer Discourse" 144).

Grant's approach to sexual politics is similarly conservative regarding the gendered dimensions of the posthuman capacities he affords to his male and female characters. All the various societies established within the FAYZ stereotypically expect and assume that girls will act as healers and caregivers for younger, orphaned children. Moreover, nearly all of the posthuman female characters in the series have been bestowed with passive powers (such as super speed, healing, manipulation of gravity, immortality, and prophecy) while the two major female protagonists, Astrid and Diana, possess the decidedly non-martial abilities of being able to read people's potential destinies and posthumans' power levels. All the female posthumans' abilities are employed to serve the interests of posthuman male characters rather than empowering female agency. In contrast, the posthuman male characters' superpowers tend to be directly active with aggressive potential: Sam's ability to create laser beams, Caine's telekinesis, Andrew's power to create shock waves, Computer Jack's enhanced strength, and Hunter's ability to project killing microwaves. The only non-alien female character who is represented as possessing an active, potentially combative ability is a "nameless girl" (*Light* 336) with fire-generating powers whom Sam tries to save early in the first novel. Tellingly, however, she is quickly killed by her own uncontrollable, self-destructive power while her death becomes merely an additional source of guilt to fuel Sam's heroic journey.

Grant makes the provocative decision to align all the physical incarnations of the Darkness with female bodies. Early in the series, the Darkness exists purely in the form of radioactive crystals whose thoughts and actions are relayed through the male pronoun "he." Yet as the books progress, the Darkness physically transforms itself into various corporeal female figures, first by drawing upon Lana's healing power to create a temporary avatar, then appearing in the form of Nerezza (a human girl transformed to be the Darkness's avatar), and finally by occupying the mutant infant body of Gaia, Diana and Caine's child. Gaia's status as posthuman/alien hybrid offers intriguing opportunities for problematizing a range of hegemonic concepts. The quasi-taboo and potentially revolutionary dimensions of "a hybrid child of a teenager union" have been noted by Clémentine Beauvais: "Born of very young parents . . . and astride socio-political divides, it . . . is a seditious entity, which forces both the adult world and the young adult reader to recenter their attention onto this threatening bearer of social change" (61). However, although the Darkness welcomes the capacity to physically interact with the world that any corporeal form affords, the reader is explicitly led to regard this female incarnation as compromised and limited, even inciting "contempt. This girl's body had . . . the emotions of a girl. The weakness of a girl" (*Light* 322). Victoria Flanagan has compellingly argued that "the female body's engagement with technology is a topic that offers limitless ways of rethinking concepts of the self" (51). Yet Grant fails to explore this exciting opportunity regarding the promise of new experiences of female embodiment and the agency of his female characters and instead privileges and normalizes male bodies and masculine superiority.

Grant's ostensibly supportive but ultimately conservative perspective on gender roles is further demonstrated through his assimilationist treatment of gay human and posthuman characters in the series. Many critics have noted the presumption of heteronormativity in much fiction for teenagers along with these texts' didactic inclination to associate deviancy with any other forms of desire. In light of Trites's suggestion that "queer discourse in young adult literature creates contradictory discourses because of the way sexuality is defined by the relationship between power, knowledge, and pleasure" ("Queer Discourse" 144), the Gone novels are to be commended for recognizing the importance of diversity and incorporating the presence of several homosexual characters: Dekka, Roger, and Edilio. Dekka reveals in the third book that she was sent to the Coates Academy by her parents in order to be rehabilitated from being a lesbian: "her parents imagined she would be under constant discipline. After all, Coates had a reputation for fixing damaged kids" (*Lies* 28).

This adult reliance on Foucauldian disciplining of transgressive bodies and desires superficially appears to be withdrawn and arguably irrelevant in the new child-led world of the FAYZ. For example, Dekka attains what appears to be acceptance from other characters such as Orc, who is initially "shocked" that the apparently normal, desirable Dekka is "one of those lesbos": "This was making Orc feel very uncomfortable. Lesbo was just a name to call an ugly girl back when he'd been in school. He hadn't really thought much about it. And now he had to think about it . . ." (*Fear* 458). Dekka's rapport with Brianna is ruptured when the latter realizes that her friend is a lesbian who is in love with her, but their platonic friendship is later reassuringly and conveniently restored. Edilio and Roger's relationship is accidentally outed in front of Sam as they mutually reach out to intimately touch each other for comfort. Sam's response is to stand "very still, and for a few very awkward seconds no one spoke" (*Fear* 373). Sam predictably displaces his confusion and surprise by confronting Edilio about why he had not told Sam that he was gay and in a relationship. Edilio responds by stating that he does not feel ashamed but rather that "I have a lot of responsibility. I have to have people trust me. And some kids are still going to call me a faggot or whatever" (405).

From the first novel onwards, Sam struggles to promote and enforce inclusivity between humans and posthumans, but this campaign for social justice is undermined by his denial of the complicated interstices involved in systems of prejudice and Othering: "'There aren't going to be lines like that, between freak and normal,' Sam said firmly" (*Gone* 250). Dekka challenges the unrealistic sentimentality involved in this assertion, drawing an uncomfortable link between the reactionary treatment of posthuman mutants and members of marginalized queer and ethnic groups: "Sam, that's a great concept. And maybe you believe it. But I'm black and a lesbian, so let me tell you: From what I know? Personal experience? There are always lines" (250). In the fifth novel, Sam is again forced to consider his own naiveté and unconscious privilege as a white, middle-class, heterosexual male, which continue even during times of apocalypse when he unsuccessfully attempts to dismiss Edilio's concerns: "'Seriously? We're about to be plunged into eternal darkness and you think those kids out there are going to worry about who you like?' Edilio didn't answer. And Sam had the feeling maybe Edilio knew more than he did on the subject" (*Fear* 406).

However, these fleeting moments of reflection around the dilemma of various heroic characters' complicity in social injustices and systems of othering are few and far between. Instead of Dekka, Roger, and Edilio's relationships being afforded an equal depth of attention and longevity as the heterosexual ones, the gay characters' romantic explorations and difficulties are mediated and repurposed by the FAYZ's inhabitants into fodder for titillating gossip (*Fear* 173). Moreover, only heterosexual relationships such as Sam and Astrid's bond triumphantly survive the series, while Dekka and Brianna's potential lesbian relationship and Edilio and Roger's actual relationship are terminated by the death of Dekka and Roger. Grant's privileging of heteronormativity and apparently inclusive though conservative treatment of queer characters is in keeping with Trites's observation that a "double-voicedness" pervades mainstream young adult publishing regarding the representation and repression of queerness ("Queer Discourse" 144).

Michael Cart and Christine A. Jenkins have examined the heteronormative tradition in young adult literature and note the disturbing tendency of the few homosexual characters present in these texts to be "hideously injured in a car wreck" or to die prematurely (22). It is thus difficult to regard Grant's treatment of his gay characters as coincidental and not to interpret these character deaths as a kind of punitive erasure of the threat of non-heterosexual desire, despite the superficial presence of a small number of gay characters in the novels. Grant's underlying ideological emphasis on heterosexuality as the normal, dominant orientation is therefore consistent with Balaka Basu, Katherine Broad, and Carrie Hintz's conclusion that "very few YA dystopias include queer relationships as a central focus, suggesting a reluctance to subvert dominant mores" (8), despite these narratives' ostensible veneer of investigating opportunities for social transformation and progress.

Similarly, Grant seems to present an inclusive panorama of characters from diverse backgrounds, yet he ultimately privileges the perspectives and preoccupations of traditionally white, middle-class, Christian protagonists. At first glance, the Gone series seems to have made respectable efforts to incorporate voices from a range of ethnicities and socioeconomic classes. Albert, Dekka, and Howard are African American, Lana has Chumash Indian heritage, Penny and Taylor are Chinese American, Sanjit is Indian, and Virtue is Congolese. This range of ethnicities and experiences is wider than Grant's nod toward diversity when he includes a Hispanic boy and an African American girl as members of the shapeshifting team of five heroic protagonists in his 1990s Animorphs series. However, whiteness is still presumed and normalized throughout that series, and Grant's apparent inclusiveness is a superficial gesture toward a "liberal form of multiculturalism . . . in which racial differences are seen as naturally necessary to an effective team . . . [and] in which differences never reflect competing interests or signal histories of genocide, slavery, rape, or exploitation but instead are brought into accord as examples of good managerial theory" (Sturgeon 114).

In his Gone series, Grant attempts to engage in a deeper way with issues of white privilege in his occasional acknowledgments of the casual micro-aggressions of racism and classism that are perpetuated in the FAYZ community. For example, Edilio's Honduran parents work as housekeeper and farmhand for the white, professional families of Perdido Beach, and despite his ongoing heroic leadership, Edilio is still called "wetback" and "Mexican" throughout the series by white, middle-class characters (e.g., *Gone* 84). Edilio succinctly summarizes what he considers to be the inevitable human attraction to this scapegoating process: "Some folks with the power, some folks without. . . . [P]eople are going to be jealous and they're going to get scared and, anyway, they're all weirded out so they are going to be looking for someone to blame" (*Gone* 183). The vigilante Human Crew intensifies this culture of fear and suspicion even further by juxtaposing resentment against the perceived empowerment of marginalized communities with their animosity against posthumans: "See, that's what's happening: it's all these minorities hooking up with freaks. . . . We're normal people. We're not black or queer or Mexican. And we're the ones digging toilets. How come?" (*Plague* 153).

Grant's ideological insistence on the importance of hegemonic privilege and a normal physical body as criteria of humanity takes on a disturbing aspect in light of his treatment of able-bodiedness and disabilities. Little Pete, Astrid's younger brother and the most powerful posthuman within the FAYZ, is represented as possessing unidentified physical and cognitive impairments, which many readers might interpret as an autism spectrum disorder. He is described thus: "Little Pete was four years old, blond like his big sister, but freckled and almost girlish, he was so pretty. He didn't look at all slow or stupid; in fact, if you didn't know better, you'd have thought he was a normal, probably smart kid" (*Gone* 112). The use of the second person (unusual for the series) and the direct address to the reader are significant as the narrative voice calls attention to how Little Pete's appearance both performs and subverts traditional markers of gender conventions and difference. Grant had previously investigated some hierarchies of normality and abnormality in the Animorphs and Remnant series, which he co-authored with his wife, Katherine Applegate.

However, the Gone series presents a disturbing argument about the alleged inadequacy and limitations of the disabled body. Robert McRuer has critiqued this ideology of "compulsory able-bodiedness" which has dominated the literary imagination, arguing that "able-bodiedness, even more than heterosexuality, still largely masquerades as a nonidentity, as the natural order of things" (1). Troublingly, Little Pete is represented throughout the series as imprisoned within the pain, confusion, and limitations of what is repeatedly described as an aberrant body. He spends most of the second novel trying to escape the confines of corporeality through manipulating reality and conjuring physical monsters inspired by his dreams. Pete's experimentation with conceiving and modifying ostensibly superior posthuman bodies has the dangerous consequence of allowing the Darkness to learn the act of "creation" (*Hunger* 185). The Darkness uses this mutating ability to transform Diana and Caine's child into its monstrous avatar, Gaia, while plotting the design of an even more powerful, ever-evolving body: "Regeneration. Adaptation. Each new incarnation as dangerous and as deadly as the one before . . . the perfect biological machine" (549).

Pete's hunger to abandon his impaired bodily existence is granted as he shifts into a purely virtual, quasi-godlike existence that seems to emblematize a transhumanist vision of informational purity: "He was free at last from the disease-wracked body. And he was free, too, from the tortured, twisted, stunted brain that had made the world so painful to him. . . . Pete Ellison had never been more alive" (*Hunger* 525–26). This new, transcendent status is beyond the comprehension of any of the series's human and posthuman characters, including that of Pete and his sister, Astrid: "He's like a spirit. His body is gone. He's outside. Not in his old brain. Like a data pattern or something, like he's digital. . . . It's not something I understand. It's like a slippery thought, and Pete can't explain it" (*Fear* 485). When Pete's disembodied self starts to fade without the anchor of an organic body, he and the Darkness reluctantly come to dismiss the possibility of transhumanism and to share the same conclusion about the importance of corporeality, whether for a human, posthuman, or alien: "Bodies were definitely a mixed blessing—they kept you alive, they focussed power, and they allowed you to move about. But they felt pain, and they could be killed" (*Light* 220).

Grant's commitment to the importance of corporeality and associated norms of the supposed naturalness of the human body over disembodied states of being ultimately positions him alongside critics such as Hayles, who argue that consciousness cannot be separated from materiality. It is telling that when Pete has to decide which body to select as an avatar during his final confrontation with Gaia, he dismisses Diana and Astrid as prospective hosts. He instead chooses to occupy Caine, a handsome, physically perfect, and hegemonically masculine figure who could be considered to be the binary opposite of Little Pete's original effeminate, childish, and so-called defective body. Grant's implicit assertion that there are "right" and "wrong" kinds of bodies is consistent with Rosemarie Garland-Thomson's argument that conceptualizations of disability in general are "not so much a property of bodies as a product of cultural rules about what bodies should be or do" (270). In light of its concern with prioritizing hegemonic cultural and ethnic norms, this standardizing tendency is another example of how Grant's series does not fulfill its promise of providing a satisfyingly rich, equitable range of representations of alterity and difference.

In the final novel, Grant faces the question of whether these aberrant, posthuman youths can be assimilated into conventional human society and, if so, what the ripple effect would be regarding the viability of adults' traditional systems of regulation and cultural rules. His exploration of posthuman transformations is not sustained past the unnatural environment and duration of the FAYZ as the surviving adolescents' posthuman alterations are stripped from them upon their return to the normal human world. In the second, third, and fourth novels, Grant mentions the diverse responses of the global media and adult audiences to the opaque, impenetrable dome surrounding the FAYZ: "every species of doomsayer from Luddite to End Times nut had had his say. It was a judgement. On America's technological obsession, on America's moral failure. This. That. Something else" (*Hunger* 116). The enjoyable and even titillating aspects to this hypothetical speculation are stripped away near the end of the penultimate novel when the barrier suddenly turns transparent due to Little Pete's fluctuating control over his powers, revealing a scene of violent confrontation between Sam, Gaia, and the "filthy and starved ... savages" that the children of Perdido Beach have become (*Fear* 544). The world is not prepared for witnessing or accepting the shocking savagery that the FAYZ's young inhabitants have developed in order to survive within the up-to-then non-translucent dome which blocked adult surveillance and intervention.

Although Grant acknowledges the U.S. government's interest in the military value of children with unnatural powers being used as weapons, wider society recoils in disgust and panic at the prospect of such radically changed young people: "Horror. Distance. Both sides, parents and children, now saw the huge gulf that had opened up between them" (*Fear* 545). Although a few people try to defend these "children trying to survive" (*Light* 89), the majority of adults are not able to accept this rupture of stereotypical assumptions of childhood innocence and purity. The possibility for empathy and imaginative connection between ordinary adult humans and the FAYZ inhabitants is shattered by the sight of Gaia, an ostensibly "defenceless little girl" (*Fear* 539), killing and eating a human adult whom Gaia has pulled through the now-transparent dome into the FAYZ. The adult, human world is confronted with the stark realization that traditional power dynamics between adult authority and young people's subordination no longer apply: "The effect had been electric. Suddenly, it was clear: this wasn't child's play. Whatever power was in there could kill adults as well" (*Light* 89). The immediate reaction of the adult spectators when their privilege is threatened is to dehumanize all the dome's citizens to the abjectified status of "dangerous wild animals in a zoo" (*Light* 88).

After the barrier surrounding the FAYZ is destroyed and the young characters are returned to the human world at the end of the sixth novel, the final chapters of the series chart the various processes for the medical and social rehabilitation of the FAYZ survivors. While these young people still bear psychic and physical scars, Grant implies that the most important aspect of these posthuman experiences is that these scenarios allowed the characters' inner qualities and supposedly true selves to appear rather than involving any radical change, subversion, or reconfiguration of their identities and capacities. Astrid the Genius, Sam the Hero, and Diana the Desirable emerge from the dome stripped of their unnatural powers but crucially possessing the same presumably essential qualities that they started the series with. Through their trials, they have acquired the traditional human qualities of friendship, loyalty, and courage and have learned to be distrustful of the professed freedoms of posthuman power. Despite the awesome posthuman sights and feats they have witnessed and enacted, their simple goal at the end of the series is to live as quietly and inconspicuously as possible in a normal home as normal members of humanity. Likewise, the wider world is all too happy to assimilate these temporarily aberrant youths back into recognizable, familiar systems and to forget the anomaly of the FAYZ and its posthuman threat as quickly as possible.

When considering the conformist, normalizing drive of this otherwise stimulating series, Bradford et al.'s questions about the competing didactic, emancipatory impulses of young adult fictions that explore the posthuman are valuable: how far do such novels succeed in representing "an ideological move away from dominant conceptual paradigms? To what extent do they use posthuman motifs to simply reinscribe and recuperate a humanist metaethic?" (180). Despite appearing to interrogate traditional systems of power, norms, and difference, Grant's novels, alongside all too many other recent dystopian narratives, align with the conservative humanism seemingly inherent in this genre's recent engagement with issues around biotechnology, embodiment, alterity, and posthuman possibilities. I therefore agree with Ostry's assertion that despite these narratives' speculation about "the excitement of a changing, flexible definition of the human being" (235), young adult novels often "play it safe" (243) and do not sustain a posthuman challenge to conventional norms and associated, traditional anxieties about change and evolution. Grant's Gone series, with its didactic and reactionary ideology, perpetuates this tradition of a reassuring yet conservative message regarding the purportedly natural truth of a universal and ultimately hegemonic humanity.

## Works Cited

Basu, Balaka, Katherine R. Broad, and Carrie Hintz. "Introduction." *Contemporary Dystopian Fiction for Young Adults: Brave New Teenagers*. Ed. Balaka Basu, Katherine R. Broad, and Carrie Hintz. New York: Routledge, 2013. 1–15. Print. Children's Literature and Culture 93.

Beauvais, Clémentine. "Romance, Dystopia and the Hybrid Child." *Contemporary Adolescent Literature and Culture: The Emergent Adult*. Ed. Mary Hilton and Maria Nikolajeva. Farnham: Ashgate, 2012. 61–76. Print. Ashgate Studies in Childhood, 1700 to the Present.

Bostrom, Nick. "In Defense of Posthuman Dignity." *Bioethics* 19.3 (2005): 202–14. *Nick Bostrom's Home Page*. Web. 11 June 2015.

———. "Why I Want to Be a Posthuman When I Grow Up." *Medical Enhancement and Posthumanity*. Ed. Bert Gordijn and Ruth Chadwick. N.p.: Springer, 2008. 107–37. *Nick Bostrom's Home Page*. Web. 11 June 2015.

Bradford, Clare, Kerry Mallan, John Stephens, and Robyn McCallum. *New World Orders in Contemporary Children's Literature: Utopian Transformations*. Basingstoke: Palgrave MacMillan, 2008. Print.

Campbell, Norah, and Mike Saren. "The Primitive, Technology and Horror: A Posthuman Biology." *Ephemera* 10.2 (2010): 152–76. *Academic Search Complete*. Web. 20 May 2015.

Cart, Michael, and Christine A. Jenkins. *The Heart Has Its Reasons: Young Adult Literature with Gay/Lesbian/Queer Content, 1969–2004*. Lanham: Scarecrow Press, 2006. Print.

Flanagan, Victoria. "Girl Parts: The Female Body, Subjectivity and Technology in Posthuman Young Adult Fiction." *Feminist Theory* 12 (2011): 39–53. *SAGE Journals Online*. Web. 30 May 2015.

Földváry, Kinga. "In Search of a Lost Future: The Posthuman Child." *European Journal of English Studies* 18.2 (2014): 207–20. *Academic Search Complete*. Web. 10 Mar. 2015.

Fukuyama, Francis. *Our Posthuman Future: Consequences of the Biotechnology Revolution*. New York: Picador, 2003. Print.

Garland-Thomson, Rosemarie. *Extraordinary Bodies: Figuring Physical Disability in American Culture and Literature*. New York: Columbia UP, 1997. Print.

Gomel, Elana. "The Plague of Utopias: Pestilence and the Apocalyptic Body." *Twentieth Century Literature* 46.4 (2000): 405–33. *Literature Online*. Web. 15 Jan. 2014.

Grant, Michael. *Fear*. London: Egmont, 2012. Print.

———. *Gone*. London: Egmont, 2009. Print.

———. *Hunger*. London: Egmont, 2009. Print.

———. *Lies*. London: Egmont, 2010. Print.

———. *Light*. London: Egmont, 2013. Print.

———. *Plague*. London: Egmont, 2011. Print.

Hayles, N. Katherine. *How We Became Posthuman*. Chicago: U of Chicago P, 1999. Print.

Honeyman, Susan. "Mutiny by Mutation: Uses of Neoteny in Science Fiction." *Children's Literature in Education* 35.4 (2004): 347–66. *Academic Search Complete*. Web. 20 Apr. 2011.

Howarth, Jayne. "Don't Let Sci-Fi Theme Put You Off Reading This Great Novel." Rev. of *Gone*, by Michael Grant. *Birmingham Post* 17 Apr. 2009: 8. *Birmingham Post*. Web. 18 May 2015.

Kristeva, Julia. *Powers of Horror: An Essay on Abjection*. Trans. Leon S. Roudiez. New York: Columbia UP, 1982. Print.

Mendlesohn, Farah. "Is There Any Such Thing as Children's Science Fiction? A Position Piece." *Lion and the Unicorn* 28.2 (2004): 284–313. *Literature Online*. Web. 23 Apr. 2016.

McGillis, Roderick. "'Terror Is Her Constant Companion': The Cult of Fear in Recent Books for Teenagers." *Reflections of Change: Children's Literature Since 1945*. Ed. Sandra L. Beckett. London: Greenwood, 1996. 99–106. Print.

McRuer, Robert. *Crip Theory: Cultural Signs of Queerness and Disability*. New York: New York UP, 2006. Print.

Ostry, Elaine. "'Is He Still Human? Are You?' Young Adult Science Fiction in the Posthuman Age." *Lion and the Unicorn* 28.2 (2004): 222–46. *Literature Online*. Web. 23 Apr. 2006.

Reynolds, Kimberley. "Introduction." *Frightening Fiction: Contemporary Classics of Children's Literature*. Ed. Kimberley Reynolds, Geraldine Brennan, and Kevin McCarron. London: Continuum, 2001. 1–18. Print.

Sambell, Kay. "Carnivalizing the Future: A New Approach to Theorizing Childhood and Adulthood in Science Fiction for Young Readers." *Lion and the Unicorn* 28.2 (2004): 247–67. *Literature Online*. Web. 23 Apr. 2006.

Sturgeon, Noël. *Environmentalism in Popular Culture: Gender, Race, Sexuality and the Politics of the Natural*. Tucson: U of Arizona P, 2009. *Google Books*. Web. 11 May 2015.

Trites, Roberta Seelinger. *Disturbing the Universe: Power and Repression in Adolescent Literature*. Iowa City: U of Iowa P, 2000. Print.

———. "Queer Discourse and the Young Adult Novel: Repression and Power in Gay Male Adolescent Literature." *Children's Literature Association Quarterly* 23.3 (1998): 143–51. *Literature Online*. Web. 17 June 2009.

Wolfe, Cary. *What Is Posthumanism?* Minneapolis: U of Minnesota P, 2009. *Google Books*. Web. Posthumanities 8. 14 May 2015.

# 7

# POSTHUMANISM IN *THE HOUSE OF THE SCORPION* AND *THE LORD OF OPIUM*

*Donna R. White*

What does it mean to be human? Science fiction has been posing this question since 1818, when Mary Shelley's *Frankenstein* first appeared, although Shelley was not the first to ask it. It has been a foundational question in religion and philosophy for thousands of years. Enlightenment thinkers proposed a definitive answer to the question, based on Protagoras's proclamation in the 5th century BCE: man is the measure of all things. Humanism, as the philosophy came to be called, declared that being human means having a self that is rational, autonomous, coherent, unified, and universal. For six centuries, this answer satisfied the Western world. In the 1960s and 70s, however, critical thinkers pointed out that this liberal humanist self was also male, white, heterosexual, and European—in other words, far from universal—and that humanism was responsible for many of the excesses of nationalism, imperialism, racism, sexism, and anthropocentrism. These anti-humanists raised new questions about what it means to be human, and in their wake others proposed that we have been asking the wrong question entirely. What we should be asking is, what does it mean to be posthuman?

This is one of the many questions that Nancy Farmer addresses in *The House of the Scorpion* (2002) and its sequel, *The Lord of Opium* (2013), which tell the story of Matt Alacrán, the clone of a powerful drug lord. The first book follows Matt from birth to the age of fourteen as he discovers his identity and purpose as a clone, runs from his intended fate into a different kind of bondage, and finally returns to the land of Opium to find that the drug lord is dead and thus his clone, Matt, has legal claim to the identity of the original. The second novel follows Matt through his first year as the new drug lord as he establishes his claim and tries to imagine a new future for Opium: a future without slavery or drugs, one in which his small country holds the key to restoring the ravaged ecosystems of the rest of the world.

In *The House of the Scorpion,* Matt spends his early childhood locked in a small cabin that he shares with Celia, who is the cook at the big house. Left alone every day, Matt is so desperate for companionship that he breaks through a window to get to three curious children who are investigating the cabin, injuring his foot seriously in the process. The children carry him to the big house, where someone notices the writing on his foot that proclaims his identity as a clone. The maid Rosa, ordered by a member of the ruling family to care for Matt, does so reluctantly and vengefully; she treats him like an animal for six months until Celia finds him and gets El Patrón, the ruler of Opium, to rescue him. For the next eight years, Matt lives with Celia in the mansion, ignored by most of the people around him, but indulged by El Patrón and raised by Celia and the bodyguard assigned to him, Tam Lin. María Mendoza, whose family sometimes visits El Patrón, is his only friend and playmate.

As he grows up, Matt learns that he lives in Opium, a country created after a series of drug wars involving the United States and Mexico. Both countries have ceded land to the Farmers, as the drug lords are called, who have established a Dope Confederacy in the border area between the U.S. and Mexico (now known as Aztlán). In exchange for the land, the drug lords have promised not to sell drugs in either country and to take care of illegal immigration by capturing everyone who tries to cross either border. The illegal immigrants are microchipped to completely dull their brains and put to work harvesting the drugs. Called eejits, these workers live short, brutal lives.

Matt eventually learns that as a clone of El Patrón, he is intended to become an unwilling donor to keep the old man alive. He is the eighth such clone, all of whom were given the protected kind of childhood that El Patrón wished he and his siblings could have had. Celia saves Matt from his intended fate by poisoning him with enough arsenic to make his organs unfit for donation. Escaping from Opium after El Patrón's death, Matt finds another kind of prison in Aztlán as an orphan in the charge of the Keepers, who supervise the boys working at the plankton factory. Escaping yet again—this time with friends— Matt finds María's convent school, and María's mother, Esperanza Mendoza, sends him back to Opium to lift the mysterious lockdown there. Esperanza informs him that because El Patrón is dead, Matt now has legal claim to the drug lord's identity; since Matt also has El Patrón's fingerprints and DNA, only he can lift the lockdown. What Matt discovers when he returns is that El Patrón had poisoned the wine that was served at his funeral, killing all his immediate family members, most of his bodyguards (including Tam Lin), the other drug lords who control the Dope Confederacy, and everyone else with any authority in Opium. Matt is now the Lord of Opium.

The sequel shows Matt struggling to establish his control over Opium while he searches for a way to restore all of his microchipped subjects to their full humanity. While Celia remains in the background, his new adult mentor is Cienfuegos, leader of the Farm Patrol that is in charge of capturing illegal immigrants and supervising eejits. Matt resists Cienfuegos's efforts to turn him into El Patrón, but he is beset on all sides: Glass Eye Dabengwa, an African drug lord, has invaded the other drug countries of the Dope Confederacy, which are leaderless after all the Farmers died at El Patrón's funeral, and his soldiers are at Matt's border; Esperanza Mendoza, who is a United Nations representative as well as María's mother, has U.N. troops ready to invade; customers are clamoring for their opium shipments. Matt wisely leaves the lockdown in place while he negotiates with all of the demands.

Meanwhile, he adopts an eejit called Waitress, trying to find a way to restore her humanity, and he discovers several young clones in another part of Opium, where Dr. Rivas, the man who created Matt, is conducting illegal experiments. Matt also visits the biosphere, a self-contained collection of multiple ecosystems established by El Patrón as a dry run for the Scorpion Star, the drug lord's space station. With help from Cienfuegos and the biosphere's Mushroom Master, Matt discovers that the microchips are controlled from the Scorpion Star. When Dr. Rivas betrays Opium by opening the protective shield to admit Dabengwa, Matt finds a way to defeat the invaders and destroy the Scorpion Star, setting all the eejits free. At the end of the novel, Matt has begun to shift the economy of Opium from drugs to food crops, but he is considering leaving the lockdown in place until his people have adjusted to all the changes.

Both novels reward a posthumanist investigation, especially the second, because Matt represents the posthumanist self. Posthumanism questions the binary oppositions that humanism has established: mind/body, human/non-human, and human/nature. It also challenges the notion of the liberal humanist subject by proposing a different kind of self, one that is fluid, collective, and networked. However, in proposing these changes, posthumanists have sometimes inadvertently set up new binary oppositions between humanism and posthumanism; they assume that the *post* in posthuman means "after" and that posthumanism therefore replaces humanism. Neil Badmington takes issue with these assumptions and points out that humanism never goes away: "many are a little too quick to affirm an absolute break with humanism, and a little too reluctant to attend to what remains of humanism in the posthumanist landscape" (15). After all, as he says, "[t]he 'post' is forever tied up with what it is 'post-ing'" (20). Farmer, on the other hand, does attend to the remnants of humanism. In fact, she deconstructs the new binary between liberal humanist self and posthumanist self by showing how Matt Alacrán, her posthumanist protagonist, must incorporate the traditional humanist self into his posthumanist identity.

## Are Clones Posthuman?

In *The House of the Scorpion* and its sequel, Farmer poses many questions about cloning. Is cloning ethical? Is a clone really an identical duplicate of the original person? Are clones human? I propose to address a further question: are clones posthuman? In *Technology and Identity in Young Adult Fiction*, Victoria Flanagan makes a useful distinction between *posthuman* and *posthumanism*. *Posthuman* is to *posthumanism* as *human* is to *humanism* (14). *Posthuman* can be a noun referring to a physical being[1] that is beyond human in some way, or an adjective relating to characteristics of that physical being; whereas *posthumanism* is a philosophical, cultural, and occasionally political worldview built around the existence of such beings. In practice, people tend to use *posthuman* and *posthumanism* interchangeably. (Even after discussing the differences, Flanagan, too, conflates the two terms.) To be *post* or beyond human may mean to be more than human or less than human, depending on one's perspective, but it always means being different from human. Thus posthumans can include cyborgs and artificial intelligences but also ghosts and vampires. However, as most people apply the term, posthuman incorporates some kind of biotechnological change in the human such as attaching cybernetic prostheses or transferring a human consciousness into an animal body or machine.

Addressing the question of whether clones are posthuman from this perspective, many theorists of posthumanism would reply in the affirmative. Next to the figure of the cyborg, the clone is the second most invoked example of the posthuman. Pramod K. Nayar, for example, discusses clones at length in *Posthumanism*, and Elaine Ostry's examination of posthumanism in young adult science fiction considers numerous cloned protagonists. Whereas the cyborg is perceived as a hybrid of human and machine, the clone is purely artificial life, a reconstruction of manipulated human cells.[2] Despite the fact that the clone's substance is one hundred percent human DNA, its artificial origins render it unnatural and thus nonhuman, and the biotechnology involved in its creation render it posthuman. The mere fact that most people refer to the clone as "it" emphasizes the human/nonhuman binary that influences our perceptions; we would never refer to the human as "it." However, biotechnology is only one aspect of posthumanism, which comes in as many flavors as Ben and Jerry's ice cream. The philosophical side is called critical posthumanism. It looks "beyond the traditional humanist ways of thinking about the autonomous, self-willed individual agent in order to treat the human itself as an assemblage, co-evolving with other forms of life, enmeshed with the environment and technology. It rejects the view of the human as exceptional, separate from other life forms and usually dominant/dominating over these other forms" (Nayar 4). Are clones posthuman(ist) in this philosophical sense? Their existence certainly challenges the liberal humanist idea of the self, bringing a "perceived threat . . . to the concept of the individual as a separate and unique human being" (Crew 207). People are repelled by the idea of cloning because it goes against what we see as the natural order, but they also fear the brave new world that might result: "cloning could be used by the mad and powerful to produce armies of genetically identical drudges and drones to provide spare organs, to perform menial labour, or to be cannon fodder in an attempt to take over the world" ("Fear of Cloning").

Matt Alacrán is an identical genetic copy of El Patrón, the drug lord of a new country called Opium. As a clone, Matt carries the exact genetic pattern of his progenitor. Although he was created to provide youthful spare parts for El Patrón, behavioral theory would suggest that if Matt were allowed to mature, he might become as vicious and ruthless as his original. On various occasions in both novels, Matt wonders and worries about whether he is exactly like El Patrón, and even his mother and father figures, Celia and Tam Lin, assume his guilt when a dog is poisoned; after all, such behavior is expected of El Patrón. Of course, there is also some circumstantial evidence against Matt on this occasion, but no one believes him when he insists that he only kidnapped the dog—he did not poison him. Ironically, the drug lord's strong traits are what allow Matt to survive during his escape from Opium, his internment at the plankton factory, and his attempts to establish control of Opium after El Patrón's death, so there are both positives and negatives associated with carrying the DNA of El Patrón.

However, as Katherine Hayles argues in *How We Became Posthuman*, disembodied information such as a genetic pattern is an impossibility. Information is always instantiated in material reality: "Information, like humanity, cannot exist apart from the embodiment that brings it into being as a material entity in the world; and embodiment is always instantiated, local, and specific. Embodiment can be destroyed, but it cannot be replicated" (48). Thus, according to Hayles, an identical copy is impossible. El Patrón is a distinct instantiation of the genetic pattern, as is Matt, and therefore they cannot be identical. Moreover, the process of cloning invites the possibility of change. As Bruce Clarke says, "the reproduction and transmission of any system opens it to metamorphosis" (10). Dr. Rivas, the scientist who created Matt from El Patrón's skin cells, tells Matt that "[a]ll of El Patrón's clones differ from the original in some way" (*Lord of Opium* 147). The fact that information must always be embodied allows for differences in environment, training, and nurture as well as small genetic mutations, such as the musical ability Matt exhibits, which does not seem to be shared by El Patrón or any of his other clones. El Patrón's poverty-stricken childhood and violent young adulthood have influenced his choices in life and thus affected his personality. As Tam Lin tells Matt, "When he [El Patrón] was young, he made a choice, like a tree does when it decides to grow one way or the other. He grew large and green until he shadowed over the whole forest, but most of his branches are twisted" (*House of the Scorpion* 70). Because El Patrón gives Matt the protected childhood the drug lord never had, including a substitute mother in Celia and a father figure in Tam Lin, Matt's personality develops in a completely different direction.

A younger clone that Matt discovers in *The Lord of Opium* is yet another instantiation of the pattern. The Bug, as the clone is called, has not had the nurturing Matt received from Celia and Tam Lin because Dr. Rivas has been keeping his existence a secret, and his genetic mutations include a total lack of impulse control. The Bug has been neither nurtured nor loved, and physical restraint is the only way to control his frequent dangerous rages. Despite the shared genetic pattern, El Patrón, Matt, and the Bug all develop into distinctive individuals. According to epigenetics, a fairly new branch of genetic science, environmental triggers cause inherent genetic traits to express themselves; since these three people have all experienced different environmental triggers, different traits have been expressed. The genetic pattern, the genotype, is the specific DNA of an individual; the phenotype, created through interaction with the environment, is a particular instantiation of the genotype. Therefore, El Patrón, Matt, and the Bug share a genotype, but each is a separate phenotype. As Nayar says, "One genotype does not produce just one phenotype, but a spectrum of phenotypes" (44). El Patrón's genotype apparently expresses a high level of phenotypic plasticity because all three characters are distinctly different.

As a scientist herself, Farmer is familiar with epigenetics and uses it consciously in these novels. In an interview published in *The Lion and the Unicorn*, she states:

> Cloning does not ensure absolute duplication; even if the physical body is a copy of the original, only certain parts of the personality can come through, and then—only if they are nurtured. In *The House of the Scorpion* Matt does not turn into El Patrón because he's raised differently than the donor of his DNA. Instead, Matt grows up

with love from the two people who protect him. He's also raised with music, which civilizes him. Only in *The Lord of Opium* you get some idea of how musical El Patrón was, but of course, he never had any kind of training and so this gift withered and died. He never had any kind of love and he turned into a brute. Yet, it's the same heredity for El Patrón and Matt. (Oziewicz et al. 105)

The answer to one of Farmer's questions is therefore "no"—a clone is not an identical duplicate of a person any more than an identical twin would be. Both a clone and an identical twin start from the exact same DNA as someone else, but epigenetics ensures that they develop in different directions. However, from the point of view of liberal humanism, a twin is almost an extension of self, whereas a clone is distinctly Other, and not only because we refer to it with the neuter pronoun. We value the original painting of the *Mona Lisa* much more than a print of that painting. An original document holds more legal weight than a photocopy and sometimes more aesthetic and historical value, as we can see by the thousands of people who troop through the National Archives in Washington, D.C., to view the original U.S. Constitution when they could call up a facsimile of it on their smart phones in a matter of seconds. The liberal humanist self is a distinct and original being, but the clone is merely a copy. Since humanism has been our philosophical paradigm for more than six centuries, we cannot avoid its influence on our mental patterns, and humanism prizes the independent, autonomous individual, not the cloned copy.

Farmer provides a clear answer to the question about whether or not clones are human. Initially Tam Lin explains to Matt that a clone is like a living photograph of a person. Since Matt is only seven years old at the time, he takes the metaphor literally. Seven years later, when Tam Lin is helping Matt escape from Opium, he explains more directly: "'Here's the dirty little secret.' Tam Lin bent down and whispered, as though he had to hide the information from the swallows, the duck, and the dragonflies. 'No one can tell the difference between a clone and a human. That's because there *isn't* any difference. The idea of clones being inferior is a filthy lie'" (*House of the Scorpion* 244–45).

At the end of the first novel, U.N. Representative Esperanza Mendoza repeats this assurance when she tells Matt he has legally become El Patrón. The law does not allow the existence of two identical people, so the copy is considered property; however, if the legally existing one dies, the remaining one inherits the identity. Her daughter asks if the legal change means Matt is now human. "'He always was,' her mother replied. 'The law is a wicked fiction to make it possible to use clones for transplants'" (367).

Farmer thus avers that clones are human. But are they also posthuman? Matt was created in a test tube and gestated in a cow. The test tube suggests science unbounded by ethics or emotions, a purely rational mind following a series of established steps to obtain a predicted result. This cold and clinical origin is far from the human passions we associate with the creation of new life. The cow indicates animal, and that is exactly how Matt is perceived by most of the other characters. Creation in a test tube makes him a thing, and gestation in a cow makes him an animal. His identity as a clone makes him a copy. Legally, he is merely property, as the words tattooed on his foot state: Property of the Alacrán Estate. In Matt's world, the law requires technicians to destroy a clone's mind at birth, so most clones appear to be uncontrollable, slobbering animals. El Patrón, however, chooses to ignore that law with his own clones, so they appear fully human. Other than the words on his foot, there is nothing to distinguish Matt from the naturally born humans around him, yet they view him as disease-ridden vermin. He is a "filthy clone," a "bad animal" (*House of the Scorpion* 27). Rosa, the servant who is forced to take care of Matt when his foot is injured, fills his room with chicken litter and makes him eat from a bowl like a dog.

This view of animals comes from humanism. To believe in human exceptionalism, we have to set humans apart from nonhumans. As Nayar says,

> humans have consistently (i) defined themselves *against* the "animal" . . . ; (ii) marked the boundaries of the human by separating, through rigorous socialization, sanitization and coercion, particular characteristics of human life as merely "animal" to be expelled, and the "essential" human to be retained; and (iii) dominated, controlled (including their birth and breeding) and exterminated animal life. (79–80)

Matt has certainly been dominated and controlled, and extermination is in his planned future since El Patrón intends to take his heart as a transplant. The presumed humans in *The House of the Scorpion* apply rigorous socialization, refusing to associate with an animal like Matt; sanitization, burning the sheets that touched Matt; and lots of coercion. Thus they are acting like good little humanists. But these views are dangerous, according to Cary Wolfe, because "as long as it is institutionally taken for granted that it is all right to systematically exploit and kill nonhuman animals simply because of their species, then the humanist discourse of species will always be available for use by some humans against other humans as well, to countenance violence against the social other of whatever species—or gender, or race, or class, or sexual difference" (8).

Posthumanism takes a different approach to the animal Other. Whereas humanism sets up a hierarchical order with humans at the top, posthumanism disputes our species supremacy. Tom Alacrán, El Patrón's great great grandson, speaks for humanism when he says to Matt, "Who wants to be at the bottom of the food chain? . . . That's the difference between humans and animals, see.

The humans are at the top, and the animals—well, they're just walking T-bone steaks and drumsticks" (*House of the Scorpion* 129). However, as Rosi Braidotti explains, posthumanism involves "the displacement of anthropocentrism and the recognition of trans species solidarity on the basis of our being environmentally based, that is to say embodied, embedded and in symbiosis with other species" (67). Embodiment removes the mind/body distinction emphasized by humanism, embedding insists that we are all part of a larger natural system and thus challenges the idea that humans can control nature, and symbiosis suggests codependence and an equal interrelationship with other animal species. As these concepts indicate, posthumanism seeks "the erosion of hierarchies with their boundaries and binary oppositions" (Herbrechter 86).

Animal references abound in both novels. When he is very young, Matt sees himself as Peter Rabbit, warned not to wander into Mr. MacGregor's garden lest he be put into a pie and eaten. In this case, Celia cautions Matt to stay inside their little house and never let anyone see him. Farmer uses *Peter Rabbit* as the basis for her plot in the first book: Matt does indeed violate the warning and ends up locked in a small room filled with chicken litter. Rather than being in danger of becoming a pie, Matt is threatened with having his heart cut out to keep El Patrón alive. There is even a real Mr. MacGregor in *The House of the Scorpion*—another drug lord to whom Matt takes an instant dislike. Matt's thoughts about Beatrix Potter's story could be a summary of his own: "Pedro el Conejo was a bad little rabbit who crawled into Señor MacGregor's garden to eat up his lettuces. Señor MacGregor wanted to put Pedro into a pie, but Pedro, after many adventures, got away. It was a satisfying story" (7).

The more Matt is treated as an animal, the more he accepts his own animality. At first he rejects an animal identity. In chapter two of *The House of the Scorpion*, Celia tells him he must hide in her shack like a little mouse. "There're hawks out there that eat little mice," she says, but Matt refuses the animal comparison: "'I am *not* a mouse!' Matt yelled. He shrieked at the top of his voice in a way he knew was irritating" (5). However, soon afterward, when he has been locked up in the mansion because he failed to behave like a mouse, his attitude begins to change. When Rosa fills his room with sawdust, he makes tunnels in it and uses rotting fruit to attract bugs for entertainment:

> Matt felt deeply peaceful. The room might look like a featureless desert to Rosa, but to him, it was a kingdom of hidden delights. Underneath the sawdust—and he knew exactly where—were caches of nutshells, seeds, bones, fruit, and gristle. The gristle was particularly valuable. You could stretch it, bend it, hold it up to the light, and even suck on it if it wasn't too old. The bones were his dolls. He could make them have adventures and talk to them. (45–46)

Of course, six months of being treated like a barnyard fowl traumatizes the six-year-old, and for months after he has been rescued, he cannot speak. When he becomes an animal, he loses human speech.

Matt's only playmate, María, often compares him to various animals, at first her dog. She has been told clones are bad animals, so she thinks Matt is a kind of dog, like Furball. Luckily, she adores animals. Later, in her teens, she reads about Saint Francis and how he conversed with a wolf, and she nicknames Matt "Brother Wolf."[3] Matt is happy to take on that identity and even reads a book about Saint Francis to please María, after which he addresses all living creatures as brother or sister. Saint Francis is invoked in both novels as the epitome of wisdom in accepting and loving all of God's creatures as they are. Cienfuegos, Matt's male protector in the second novel, recasts Saint Francis's views in more scientific terms, correcting himself for complaining about poisonous plants and animals: "Still, it's all part of the ecosystem. . . . Just as *I* am part of the ecosystem, along with my venomous brothers and sisters" (*Lord of Opium* 376).

After his abuse at Rosa's hands, Matt begins to accept his identity as an animal:

> "You're like a wild animal," complained María as she stood in the doorway of Matt's room. "You hide in here like a bear in a cave."
> Matt looked indifferently at the curtained windows. He liked the safe, comfortable darkness. "I *am* an animal," he replied. Once those words would have pained him, but he accepted his status now. (*House of the Scorpion* 92)

When people taunt him about being harvested from a cow and legally being livestock, Matt comforts himself by thinking about someone else from humble origins: "Matt saw nothing wrong with being born in a stable. Jesus had found it perfectly acceptable" (188). Sometimes he uses his animal status as a defense. When Esperanza Mendoza wants him to return to Opium to lift the lockdown, he protests, "the Alacráns will have me put to sleep like an old dog. I'm a clone, in case you've forgotten. I'm livestock" (366).

Farmer makes it clear that although Matt is the one perceived as and treated as a wild animal, the other human characters are the truly uncivilized, inhuman ones. Celia refers to Rosa and the doctor as animals for abusing Matt, and when the doctor disavows knowledge of how Matt has been treated, Rosa attacks him: "She kicked and screamed, driving Willum back with the force of her rage. She actually bared her teeth like a wild animal, and Matt watched with interest to see whether she would manage to sink them into the man's neck" (56).

Almost all of the characters are described as animals. In the first book, Tam Lin is like "a tame grizzly bear" (67–68), El Patrón is "the old vulture" (69) and a dragon (184), Tom Alacrán is a crocodile (129), and El Patrón's grandson looks like "a starved bird" (151). In *The Lord of Opium*, Cienfuegos is "a hungry coyote" (20), the men of the Farm Patrol are "trained dogs" (34), and Esperanza Mendoza is a both a snake (22) and a crow (52). The clone known only as the Bug is clearly an insect, but he is also compared to a rabid skunk (*Lord of Opium* 378), a rabid coyote (403), and a frog (403). Even the servants and the mindless eejits are animals, as Tam Lin complains to Celia: "We're bloody lab animals to this lot. We're only well treated until we outlive our usefulness" (*House of the Scorpion* 189).

The difference between Matt's animality and that of the other characters is that he accepts it as part of himself. He also insists that it is not the only aspect of his identity or of the identity of other clones or the mind-controlled eejits. When Rosa, his former abuser, is turned into an eejit, Matt continually tries to talk to her as if she is a fellow being capable of human interaction. In *The Lord of Opium*, Matt's attempts to befriend Waitress, another eejit, meet with so much misunderstanding from those around him that he recasts the relationship in terms they can comprehend, telling them Waitress is a pet. Meeting the infant clone of another drug lord, Matt objects when Dr. Rivas, the genetic specialist, refers to the clone as a tissue sample:

> "He's a child," Matt said.
> "Not according to the law. He exists for one purpose only, to prolong the life of his original."
> "I make the laws here," said Matt, "and I say Mbongeni is a child." (*Lord of Opium* 130)

To Matt, all creatures are people; in fact, he claims them as family: "Hello, Brother and Sister Eejits. . . . Hello, Brother Wasp" (*House of the Scorpion* 167, 168). So what if Matt's birth mother was a cow? Following Saint Francis's habit of greeting everyone and everything "gave Matt the warm feeling that the world was one loving family" (166). When it comes to the human/animal binary that posthumanism rejects, Matt represents the posthumanist perspective. All clones may be posthuman in the biotechnological sense, but Matt is also posthuman in the philosophical sense, although he is the only one of Farmer's characters who can claim that distinction.

## El Patrón as Liberal Humanist Subject

Far from being posthumanist, El Patrón, the original Matteo Alacrán, takes the concept of the liberal humanist subject to extremes. Nayar's description of the humanist subject is a perfect fit for the drug lord:

The human is traditionally taken to be a subject (one who is conscious of his/her *self*) marked by rational thinking/intelligence, who is able to plot his/her own course of action depending on his/her needs, desires and wishes, and, as a result of his/her actions, produces history. The human has traditionally been treated as male and universal. It is always treated in the singular (*the* human) and as a set of features or conditions: rationality, authority, autonomy and agency. (5)

Although we may at times question El Patrón's rationality, he is remarkably sane for a man who is more than 140 years old, thanks to fetal brain transplants from a previous clone. He is the only true authority in Opium; everyone must do his bidding, even the few who are not controlled by implanted microchips. Because of that control, he may be the only autonomous person in Opium as well as the only free agent. He has certainly produced history as a result of his actions: Opium and the entire Dope Confederacy exist only because of his determination, will, power, and negotiating skills, as he was the one who convinced the United States and Mexico to cede territory to the drug lords.

Americans have been conditioned to believe that agency and autonomy are positive characteristics; in fact, most of our young adult novels focus on youthful protagonists seeking to develop those traits as well as trying to establish a unified sense of self—another aspect of the liberal humanist subject. However, as Braidotti reminds us, even positive characteristics can become negative: "individualism breeds egotism and self-centredness; self-determination can turn to arrogance and domination . . ." (30). Such is the case for El Patrón. The strength of will that enabled him to survive a difficult childhood, the memory of which still haunts him, also turns him into a possessive, controlling adult. Almost everyone fears him: he is powerful, vindictive, and ruthless. Tam Lim and Cienfuegos, Matt's male role models in the two novels, admire the old man's strength while acknowledging that he is also twisted and evil. Matt is the only person who actually *likes* El Patrón. Matt is attracted to the old man from their first meeting, not realizing that they carry the identical genetic pattern. Even after El Patrón tries to take Matt's heart, the boy cannot help liking him. Although some of the things Matt learns about El Patrón repel him or frighten him, he remains fond of the man who indulged him like a favorite grandson for seven years. Many aspects of El Patrón's personality are reflected in Matt, so in some ways, Matt's affection indicates his healthy ego development: liking El Patrón is similar to liking himself.

Authority, autonomy, and agency are the three aspects of the liberal humanist subject that El Patrón expresses most fully. He has gone to great lengths to make his authority absolute in Opium and influential in the lands beyond Opium. Money and power are enough to influence U.S. senators like María's father, who is El Patrón's puppet, and to have two scientists arrested in another country when they travel from Opium without El Patrón's permission, but the drug lord takes further steps to establish his authority in his own country by hiring scientists to develop an elaborate system of microchips to control most of the people and some of the animals in Opium. In effect, he buys the scientists because once they are under his control, he never lets them go.[4] One group of scientists was locked in a huge biosphere eighty years earlier, and their descendants now believe the biosphere is the whole world. Another group lives for six months at a time on the Scorpion Star, El Patrón's space station. The biosphere was a model for the space station, and the space station contains the energy source that controls the microchips. The microchips are so pervasive in Opium that at one point Matt fears that he too has been microchipped to remain under El Patrón's control. The eejits who work the fields have the widest constellation of chips, while house servants are more moderately controlled, and the Farm Patrol and El Patrón's bodyguards have a lighter version that constrains them to protect and obey their boss. Only a few people are left unchipped: Celia, because she is a cook and a female and thus unimportant; three top level scientists, Dr. Rivas and two of his children; and presumably El Patrón's immediate family members, although Farmer never clarifies their status.[5] Controlling people via microchip may have been a sensible precaution from El Patrón's point of view since Celia and the three scientists—the only confirmed non-chipped people in Opium—are the ones who betray him.

El Patrón maintains his own autonomy by depriving others of theirs. He uses his agency to freeze time in his country. Despite his use of science to develop microchips and clones, culturally Opium lives in the distant past. As Tam Lin tells Matt, "Opium, as much as possible, is the way things were in El Patrón's youth. Celia cooks on a wood fire, the rooms aren't air-conditioned, the fields are harvested by people, not machines. Even rockets aren't allowed to fly over" (*House of the Scorpion* 245). The television shows are one hundred years old. Although hovercrafts are available, El Patrón prefers to travel in his ancient car, which was once owned by Adolf Hitler. The car is one of the many treasures of the past that he collects. El Patrón's actions in maintaining the cultural past have an unexpected side effect: they make him an accidental ecologist. By keeping to the old ways and by neglecting huge swaths of land in Opium, El Patrón inadvertently nurtures plants and animals that have become extinct in the rest of the world. Likewise, imprisoning scientists in a biosphere forces them to figure out how to remove toxic buildup in the soil. These plants and animals and new methods of soil purification become bargaining chips for Matt as the new lord of Opium because the outside world wants to repair its ecosystem.

El Patrón thus exhibits, albeit indirectly and unintentionally, both the good and bad of humanism. On the good side, as Braidotti would suggest, he "promotes respect for science and culture" and "a project-oriented approach that is extremely valuable in its pragmatism" (29). On the other hand, he excludes and suppresses all Others: females, eejits, clones, scientists, his own family. Matt may be the only one whose foot is tattooed "Property of the Alacrán Estate," but as far as El Patrón is concerned, every living being in Opium is his personal property, and he never lets go of any of his possessions.

Since he is such an extreme example of the humanist subject, it seems ironic that El Patrón turns to biotechnology, which is so closely associated with posthumanism, to extend his life. Erin Newcomb states that he is actually a cyborg "patched together with organs from multiple clones" (178); if he is a cyborg, he would be posthuman. Such a reading indicates a misunderstanding of *cyborg*, which stands for cybernetic organism, a being with both organic and biomechanical parts. El Patrón is purely organic, unlike Glass Eye Dabengwa, the drug lord who invades Opium in *The Lord of Opium*, who is a true cyborg with machine parts. In fact, the susceptibilities of Dabengwa's biomechanics allow Matt to kill him with a powerful flashlight. El Patrón, on the other hand, has only organic weaknesses due to his extreme age and the many transplants he has endured. He dies of heart failure, in a sense murdered by Celia, who has fed Matt just enough arsenic to make his heart unsuitable for transplanting.

El Patrón is not a cyborg, and he is not posthuman; he is rather co-opting posthuman capabilities in the service of humanism. As Myra Seaman explains, "while technological and biological modifications to the body are intended to improve its inadequacies, their use indicates an investment in a distinctly individual and already human identity" (248), in this case an investment in the humanist self as represented by El Patrón. El Patrón is not even a transhumanist—the branch of posthumanism that seeks to perfect the human species via life extension technologies, genetic manipulation, and biotechnological prostheses—because he does not seek to perfect himself but rather to sustain himself exactly as he is, just as he wants to maintain a century-old culture. He sees everything in terms of his humanist self; when that self ceases to exist, he plans to take all of its accoutrements with it, including his family, the other drug lords, and even Opium itself. His authority and agency are so absolute that they extend beyond his own death.

## Matt Alacrán as Posthumanist Subject

In contrast to the liberal humanist subject, the posthumanist subject is neither unified nor autonomous, neither independent nor universal. Thanks to antihumanists like Foucault and Derrida, who fill the gap between humanism and posthumanism, we now question whether free agency is even possible given the social, cultural, political, and environmental constraints that surround us and influence both our actions and our construction of meaning. Our concept of self is not a given but rather is constructed through various discourses, and far from being unified, it is fluid and constantly changing. Working from these anti-humanist observations, posthumanists propose a different model for the self: "Posthumanism ... sees human subjectivity as an assemblage, co-evolving with machines and animals, ... [and] a congeries, whose origins are multispecies and whose very survival is founded on symbiotic relations with numerous forms of life on earth" (Nayar 8–9).

The two nouns most often used in relation to the posthumanist self are *assemblage* and *congeries*, the former suggesting a more orderly structure than the latter, which can mean a jumble of unrelated odds and ends. Identity is multiple rather than singular in this view and constantly fluctuating rather than becoming unified. The posthumanist self incorporates humanism's rejected Others: animal, mineral, vegetable, and machine. The Others most often discussed by critical posthumanism are animals, monsters, the disabled, and the posthuman; it takes for granted the Others that were the focus of much anti-humanist discourse—women, minorities, the LBGT community, and the colonized. However, posthumanism rejects the idea that any of these groups *are* Other: they are part of the assemblage that constitutes the posthumanist self. Humanism marked off a particular set of characteristics as distinctly human, and any being that fell outside those parameters, as perceived from the humanist viewpoint, was nonhuman, inhuman, or subhuman. Humanism established boundaries between human and nonhuman and hierarchies of value and power with the human at the apex. Likewise, it set up boundaries between mind and body, body and nature. Posthumanism challenges those boundaries as well by insisting that humans are embodied and embedded within an environment: "Posthumanism is all about the embedding of embodied systems in environments where the system evolves with other entities, organic and inorganic, in the environment in a mutually sustaining relationship. It is a philosophical position that sees alterity (Otherness and its concomitant characteristic, difference) as constitutive of the human/system" (Nayar 51).

Farmer addresses the human/nature binary primarily by means of the biosphere. Cut off from all other contact, the humans who have been born and raised within the biosphere have developed their own culture, built on the teachings of the scientists who were the original inhabitants. Their pragmatic approach to childrearing involves placing children, whom they see as pre-humans, in a Brat Enclosure with a rota of caretakers until they are fourteen, at which time they are put into a controlled sleep for a year to be trained for their duties as adults. The job of the adults is to maintain a careful balance of all plants and animals, including humans, in order to keep the ecosystem stable. The first person Matt meets in the biosphere is proud to be a frogherd and says, "We know everything about our world and merely care for our companion animals and plants" (181). He refuses to believe that Matt is his boss: "No one owns nature. We are all Earth's creatures" (182). Although Farmer at times seems to be poking fun at the inhabitants of the biosphere, she values their perspective toward nature; they accept that they are embodied and embedded beings rather than the rulers of the world. She also values their knowledge and wisdom, using the biosphere's Mushroom Master, who is based on a real scientist, as the instrument to clean up the poisoned land around the eejit pens. Although Matt does not completely adopt the perspective of the biosphere's inhabitants, he adapts aspects of it to improve Opium and even sends the Bug to the Brat Enclosure in an effort to help him learn self-control.

If El Patrón represents the liberal humanist subject run amok, Matt represents the fluid posthumanist subject. Adolescence, as the most protean stage of life, epitomizes the posthumanist subject. Rare indeed is the young person who is single-mindedly focused on one clear identity; a teenager contains a multitude of conflicting selves. Matt experiences more identity confusion than most. Clone, livestock, property, human, animal, monster, drug lord, saint, savior, murderer—these are all part of Matt's identity along with the more familiar roles of (foster) son, indulged grandson, friend, lover, brother, and student.

In *The House of the Scorpion*, Matt's selfhood is bound to his identity as a clone. He is a Pinocchio figure seeking to become a real boy through his efforts to win the approval and acceptance of those around him by developing himself intellectually, musically, and physically. As discussed earlier, Matt's clonehood also enables him to accept his animality, thereby removing the human/animal barrier established by humanism. Another humanist binary is that of human/monster; clones disturb that boundary as well. The animal Other and the monstrous Other are closely related, as Amy Ratelle points out: "The technology by which the Other is made monstrous includes the animalization of some humans" (32). As Brother Wolf, for instance, Matt is both animal and monster since wolves are traditionally viewed as "monstrous devourers of innocents" (Ratelle 43).

Farmer does not develop the monstrous Other as thoroughly as she does the animal Other, but Matt clearly conflates the two: "Now, for the hundredth time, Matt thought about why anyone would create a monster. It couldn't be to replace a beloved child. Children were loved and clones were hated. It couldn't be to have a pet. No pet resembled the horrible, terrified thing Matt had seen in the hospital" (*House of the Scorpion* 190). Clones are both animal and monster, so by accepting his clone identity, Matt is also acknowledging his animal and monstrous selves. El Patrón is also a monster—the vampire drug lord with an army of zombies—and Matt is literally made from a piece of skin of this monster. In fact, El Patrón is the part of Matt's monstrous self that he finds hardest to accept, and he rejects any suggestion that he is becoming more like the old man.

Animal and monster are the parts of Matt's assembled posthumanist self that he culls from the negative social views about clones, expressed through the fear and loathing of most of the people around him. In *The House of the Scorpion*, Matt also finds pieces to assemble from his more positive interactions with a few individuals, primarily Celia, Tam Lin, María, and his friends at the plankton factory. Celia calls him "mi vida" (my life). Although during his early years she insists that she is not his mother, she always treats him as a beloved son. To Tam Lin, Matt is "laddie," and to María, he is "Brother Wolf." He continually fluctuates from one of these identities to another. At the plankton factory, he becomes a big brother to Fidelito and a friend to Ton Ton and Chacho, and he finds another role as a natural leader among the boys who work at the factory; he is a kind of Peter Pan among these Lost Boys. His relationship to El Patrón is more complicated. The drug lord adopts Celia's name for Matt—mi vida—but he means it much more literally than she does since Matt is intended to be the means by which the old man stays alive. To El Patrón, indulging Matt is the same thing as indulging himself; he is replacing his own impoverished childhood with a more pleasant one while simultaneously annoying his own family and reminding everyone of his power to do as he pleases. However, to Matt, all of the attention and indulgence indicates that El Patrón loves him; Matt is too young to realize that El Patrón loves only himself and that Matt is a stand-in for his younger self. Nevertheless, Matt finds both a strong sense of identity and a constant state of confusion through his connection to El Patrón, who is both self and Other, kindly old man and ruthless dictator. Is Matt a beloved son/grandson? A favorite companion? A pet? A replacement being trained to take over Opium in the future? A set of youthful spare parts? Matt is never sure who he is in relation to the drug lord.

*The Lord of Opium* complicates Matt's posthumanist self considerably. In the sequel, Farmer is much more indefinite about Matt's sense of identity, which fluctuates constantly. This change in approach as well as a new focus on environmental issues suggests that she may have read about posthumanism in the years between writing the two books. While *The House of the Scorpion* can be read as a traditional coming-of-age novel in which a young protagonist figures out his humanist identity, its sequel does not permit such a reading. Newcomb's study of Matt as a posthuman suggests that *The House of the Scorpion* reinforces humanist values in that it allows Matt "to move from instrument to agent and from a collection of spare parts to a whole creature with a body and soul" (176). Hilary Crew, John Stephens, and Naarah Sawers make similar claims about the first book in other articles. However, *The Lord of Opium* rejects a humanist reading by refusing to pin down a single identity for Matt. He continues to be both instrument and agent, and Farmer refuses to close off any possibilities: Is Matt becoming El Patrón? Is he Jesús Malverde, the unofficial patron saint of drug dealers? Is he Brother Wolf? Is he a microchipped puppet? Is he Don Sombra, Lord Shadow? Farmer raises these questions but never answers them. Matt's identity is fluid and changeable throughout the second book, thus expressing his posthumanist subjectivity.

At the beginning of *The Lord of Opium*, Celia and Cienfuegos, the head of the Farm Patrol, pressure Matt to take a title suitable to a drug lord. He resists all their efforts. He does not want a new name, especially not one that inspires fear. Despite the fact that he is now legally El Patrón, Matt does not really want to be a drug lord. His goal is to restore the eejits to full humanity and to disband the drug empire. Eventually, however, he chooses a title for himself—Don Sombra, lord of shadows—because he is deeply depressed over the death of an eejit he has tried to befriend and help. Don Sombra the drug lord becomes part of his assembled self, and although Matt feels that this part of his identity has been forced on him, he uses it to his own advantage at times, asserting his authority as lord of Opium. Don Sombra is a fluid part of Matt, coming and going as needed, called upon when ruthlessness is required. Even after the eejits have been freed and the drug empire disbanded, Cienfuegos continues to call Matt by his drug lord title. A part of Matt will always be Don Sombra.

A more intriguing aspect of his identity is that of Jesús Malverde, the unofficial saint of the drug dealers. The statues of the saint were modeled after a young El Patrón, so they look exactly like the drug lord's young clone. Matt's first reaction is delight: "Wait till he told María! Brother Wolf had not only become human, he'd turned into a saint" (94). Later, Matt is extremely uncomfortable with the resemblance and its effect on the newly freed eejits, who see him as the saint come to life. In truth, however, he is responsible for their freedom, having destroyed the Scorpion Star that controlled their microchips, so he is a kind of saint or savior to them. At the same time, he has caused the deaths of everyone on the Scorpion Star as well as the would-be thieves he locked into one of El Patrón's treasure rooms. Despite his earlier insistence that he does not want to hurt anyone, he ends up murdering hundreds of people in order to free the eejits and save Opium from invasion by the forces of Glass Eye Dabengwa, who has been conquering and devastating the other parts of the Dope Confederacy.

The most important aspect of Matt's posthumanist self comes from an unexpected source: El Patrón himself. Naturally, since Matt is the drug lord's clone, there are already strong similarities between the two. In the first book, when Matt thinks Tam Lin has betrayed him, he reacts just like El Patrón: "[H]e felt a surge of pure animal rage. He deserved to live! He was owed this life that had so casually been given him, and if he had to die, he would struggle until the very last minute" (241). He responds like El Patrón on many occasions. In the second novel, however, Matt fears becoming like El Patrón, and he worries when anyone says he is just like the old man. Cienfuegos encourages Matt to be more like the drug lord, whereas Celia is more likely to caution him against such behavior. But El Patrón's influence becomes something deeper in *The Lord of Opium*. Matt actually hears El Patrón's voice in his head whenever he is in danger. He has mental conversations with this voice, and when he does what it tells him to do, he saves himself and the people around him. Celia fears Matt is suffering from spirit possession. Matt fears that he has been microchipped and El Patrón is controlling him through prior programming. Farmer never suggests that Matt might be suffering from mental illness; these conversations, as well as similar ones with the spirit of Tam Lin, seem more like the conversations with spirits in two of Farmer's African books, *The Ear, The Eye and the Arm* (1994) and *A Girl Named Disaster* (1996), both of which are told from the cultural perspective of the Shona people. Farmer seems to be suggesting that Matt is still in touch with the spirits of these two men who were so influential in his life.

Early in *The Lord of Opium*, Matt is deeply disturbed when Cienfuegos tells him how El Patrón had a passenger jet blown out of the sky when it strayed into Opium's airspace. That level of ruthlessness turns Matt's stomach. Yet at the end of the novel, Matt calmly activates the panel that will decouple the parts of the Scorpion Star and kill the three hundred people on the space station. Then he locks the door of the secret room, leaving two scientists and a group of soldiers inside to die a slow death by starvation. To be fair, those scientists and soldiers had just tried to kill Matt and his companions, so he has strong motivation. Matt never experiences a moment of regret for these actions, which are the kind of ruthless actions El Patrón would take. He has finally accepted that El Patrón is a part of his identity beyond their shared DNA. To truly be a posthumanist subject, Matt has to incorporate, not reject, the humanist self represented by El Patrón, no matter how monstrous it may be. It is part of the assemblage that makes up his self: animal, monster, clone, human, posthuman, Celia, Tam Lin, María— and El Patrón. If we are to move beyond the binary oppositions of humanism, Farmer suggests, we cannot cast the liberal humanist self as yet another rejected Other; we must incorporate the humanist self as part of the assemblage. The posthumanist self is always becoming, always changing, fluid and multifaceted, but it is built at least partially on that earlier unified, autonomous self.

## Notes

1. Some people would include disembodied intelligences as posthuman, but I accept Katherine Hayles's argument that all information (including consciousness) must be embodied in some physical form, whether it be organic, inorganic, or etheric.

2. I refer only to human cloning here. Obviously Dolly the Sheep, never having been human in the first place, cannot be posthuman in the species sense. Many people have written about the perception of clones in literature. The most relevant articles as far as young adult literature is considered are Elaine Ostry's "'Is He Still Human? Are You?': Young Adult Science Fiction in the Posthuman Age" and Hilary S. Crew's "Not So Brave a World: The Representation of Human Cloning in Science Fiction for Young Adults."

3. In *Animality and Children's Literature and Film*, Amy Ratelle discusses the symbolism of the wolf: "the Big Bad Wolf was envisioned as outside of civilization, while its perceived ravenous appetite dictated that it could not be rehabilitated or tamed" (44). The significance of the animal terms used in Farmer's Opium novels is beyond the scope of this article, but it would be a fruitful area for analysis in terms of the animal Other.

4. Nancy Farmer calls these scientists "kept scientists": "Such scientists get paid by some company to find particular results. So, if they're being paid by the tobacco company, then tobacco is good for you; if by the insecticide company, insecticide is good for you, and so on. These 'kept scientists' work on the Scorpion Star like modern day mercenaries and they don't care that their work supports enslavement and human degradation. Having worked with a few 'kept scientists,' I didn't feel too bad about crashing the whole thing" (Oziewicz et al. 107).

5. Females who marry into El Patrón's family are often drugged in order to force their obedience, but there is no mention of microchips. Like his children, grandchildren, and great-grandchildren, these women are just part of his human collection, to be disposed of as he wishes.

## Works Cited

Badmington, Neil. "Theorizing Posthumanism." *Cultural Critique* 53 (2003): 10–27. *Project Muse*. Web. 4 June 2016.

Braidotti, Rosi. *The Posthuman*. Cambridge: Polity, 2013. Print.

Clarke, Bruce. *Posthuman Metamorphosis: Narrative and Systems*. New York: Fordham UP, 2008. Print.

Crew, Hilary S. "Not So Brave a World: The Representation of Human Cloning in Science Fiction for Young Adults." *Lion and the Unicorn* 28.2 (2004): 203–21. *Project Muse*. Web. 4 June 2016.

Farmer, Nancy. *The Ear, the Eye and the Arm*. New York: Orchard, 1994. Print.

———. *A Girl Named Disaster*. New York: Orchard, 1996. Print.

———. *The House of the Scorpion*. New York: Atheneum, 2002. Print.

———. *The Lord of Opium*. New York: Atheneum, 2013. Print.

"Fear of Cloning." *Economist* 5 Jan. 1998: n. pag. *The Economist*. Web. 27 Aug. 2016.

Flanagan, Victoria. *Technology and Identity in Young Adult Fiction: The Posthuman Subject*. New York: Palgrave Macmillan, 2014. Print. Critical Approaches to Children's Literature.

Hayles, N. Katherine. *How We Became Posthuman: Virtual Bodies in Cybernetics, Literature, and Informatics*. Chicago: U of Chicago P, 1997. Print.

Herbrechter, Stefan. *Posthumanism: A Critical Analysis*. London: Bloomsbury, 2013. Print.

Nayar, Pramod K. *Posthumanism*. Cambridge: Polity, 2014. Print. Themes in 20th and 21st Century Literature and Culture.

Newcomb, Erin T. "The Soul of the Clone: Coming of Age as a Posthuman in Nancy Farmer's *The House of the Scorpion*." *Contemporary Dystopian Fiction for Young Adults Brave New Teenagers*. Ed. Balaka Basu, Katherine R. Broad, and Carrie Hintz. New York: Routledge, 2013. 175-88. Print. Children's Literature and Culture 93.

Ostry, Elaine. "'Is He Still Human? Are You?': Young Adult Science Fiction in the Posthuman Age." *Lion and the Unicorn* 28.2 (2004): 222-46. *Project Muse*. Web. 27 May 2016.

Oziewicz, Marek, Emily Midkiff, Nancy Farmer, and Harold Farmer. "'The Handling of Power': An Interview with Nancy Farmer." *Lion and the Unicorn* 40.1 (2016): 100-13. *Project Muse*. Web. 4 Mar. 2017.

Ratelle, Amy. *Animality and Children's Literature and Film*. New York: Palgrave Macmillan, 2015. Print. Critical Approaches to Children's Literature.

Sawers, Naarah. "Capitalism's New Handmaiden: The Biotechnical World Negotiated through Children's Fiction." *Children's Literature in Education* 40 (2009): 169-79. *Academic Search Complete*. Web. 4 June 2016.

Seaman, Myra J. "Becoming More (than) Human: Affective Posthumanisms, Past and Future." *JNT: Journal of Narrative Theory* 37.2 (2007): 246-75. *Project Muse*. Web. 12 June 2014.

Stephens, John. "Performativity and the Child Who May Not Be a Child." *Papers: Explorations into Children's Literature* 16.1 (2006): 5-13. *Papers: Explorations into Children's Literature*. Web. 4 June 2016.

Wolfe, Cary. *Animal Rites: American Culture, the Discourse of Species, and Posthumanist Theory*. Chicago: U of Chicago P, 2003. eBook.

## 8

# COMING OF AGE AND THE OTHER
Critical Posthumanism in Paolo Bacigalupi's
*Ship Breaker* and *The Drowned Cities*

*Lars Schmeink*

Paolo Bacigalupi is one of science fiction's most outspoken voices on issues of environmentalism; thus it is no wonder that his work has garnered critical attention whenever climate fiction (abbreviated as "cli-fi") or eco-fiction is mentioned (see, for example, Berry). Literary critics have focused on his dystopian visions of ecological disaster and capitalist exploitation (see Hageman; Otto; Tidwell), as witnessed in his adult science fiction writing. They argue that his work is a sharp warning call on issues such as genetic engineering, gene patenting, invasive species, and the devastating human intervention inprocesses that shape our current geological age, the Anthropocene. Both his short stories in *Pump Six* (2008) and his debut novel *The Windup Girl* (2009) prove insightful in terms of these issues, as their plots center around characters navigating these dystopian societies with aplomb, currying political and economic favor in corrupt systems and using whatever means necessary to further manipulate their world.

Bacigalupi's young adult novels similarly play out in dystopian worlds in which ecological disaster has struck, but they focus on adolescent characters and their search for identity—a common trope of young adult fiction (see Ostry 223–24) that in the dystopian context becomes infused with "political strife, environmental disaster, or other forms of turmoil as the catalyst for achieving adulthood" (Basu, Broad, and Hintz 7). Bacigalupi's young adult novels *Ship Breaker* (2010) and *The Drowned Cities* (2012)—both based in the same storyworld, but only loosely connected—thus each center around adolescents trying to survive in a harsh world challenged by political, economic, and ecological crises. And even though the novels acknowledge global warming, rising sea levels, climatic changes, the loss of fossil fuels, a drastic decline in global economic power, and a post-national power struggle between either rivaling company factions or warlords, respectively, these crises function only as dystopian backdrop on the macro level of diegetic world. For the young adult audience, the dystopian, with its "capacity to frighten and warn," additionally manifests on a personal micro level: when the adolescent characters need to negotiate "liberty and self-determination, ... questions of identity, and the increasingly fragile boundaries ... [of] the self" (Basu, Broad, and Hintz 1), they are confronted with the dystopian. But it is here also that the narratives reveal their utopian hope in that they provide their adolescent protagonists with the choice of a different path, offering an alternative to the dystopian status quo.

The protagonists' coming of age plays out against the backdrop of a dystopian society shaped by overt self-preservation and cutthroat capitalism. The crises mentioned before all feed into this social makeup of fierce individualism, which forces the adolescents to confront their own morals and values at an early age, thus foregrounding these issues in the novels. Influenced by social expectations and a stark genetic determinism, both protagonists—Nailer in *Ship Breaker* and Mahlia in *The Drowned Cities*—fight to become more than a product of either their genes or their upbringing. They have to choose their actions toward others, whom to trust, whom to help, and whether or not to break promises and alliances. At the heart of these decisions are issues of identity, community, and Otherness that Bacigalupi positions within contemporary discourses of posthumanism. As Elaine Ostry has stated with regard to posthumanism, "If adolescence is the time when one considers what it means to be human, ... then there has never been a period of history when it has been more difficult to figure this out than now" (222).

Further evidence for the centrality of posthumanism in the two novels is their only other connection (apart from general story world), which manifests in the character of Tool, a genetically engineered creature, who stands in as the ultimate Other, while at the same time providing a necessary counterpart for both Nailer and Mahlia to test their values against and to offer an alternative perspective on the state of the world. Tool, a mercenary and warrior-like figure, is a posthuman creature, a "genetic cocktail of humanity, tigers and dogs" (*SB* 212), and thus ideally suited to function as a reflector for questions of human identity, as he finds himself in an ex-centric position, always outside of society: "He's despised and distrusted by normal human society because he's so different," which makes it possible for him to be "watching and judging ... from his own peculiar perspective on the outside," as Bacigalupi notes in an interview with A. S. King.

By allowing Tool to voice a strong subjectivity, a self beyond his genetic programming, Bacigalupi establishes a position that opposes the genetic determinism, anthropocentrism, and speciesism fueling the oppressive and dystopian society and instead engages a critical posthumanism determined by a *zoe*-centric (concerned with the interconnectedness of all life), complex, and interrelated subjectivity that understands the human, in the words of Pramod Nayar, as "co-evolving, sharing ecosystems, life processes, genetic material, with animals and other life forms" (8). Bacigalupi thus proves his novels to be "expressly concerned with how to use [the dystopian] warning to create new possibilities for utopian hope within the space of the text" (Basu, Broad, and Hintz 3). I argue, therefore, that both novels are critical posthumanist commentaries on questions of (young adult) identity formation, calling for adolescents to reject humanist notions of exceptionalism and a superior position inherent in genetic determinism, and instead embrace a zoe-centric subjectivity. In this reading, Tool acts as a stand-in, using Stefan Herbrechter's phrasing, for all those "ghosts ... repressed during the process of humanization" (9) and reminds readers that in posthuman times, the human as a category is not exempt from the consequences of the anthropocene and that all life should be valued equally.

## "If Genes Are Destiny": Genetic Determinism as Dystopian Reality

Before exploring the notion of Tool as reflective screen for issues of identity formation in the coming-of-age process of the adolescent, it might be prudent to note that both Nailer and Mahlia start their journeys with a preconceived notion of identity. In fact, both struggle with the identity thrust upon them by their surroundings, which is based merely on their genetic heritage. In the beginning of *Ship Breaker*, Nailer is part of a crew of child workers whose job it is to break down rusting shipwrecks into recyclable parts; in his case, he is part of the crew that scavenges in the hard-to-reach places inside the ships' ducts to extract wiring and other light valuables. Nailer's job, due to his size, is to crawl through the ducts and loosen the wiring so that the rest of his team can reel it in. When not earning his living in this way, he lives with his father, Richard Lopez, a violent cutthroat and drunk, in a shed on the beach. Due to his father's foul moods, Nailer spends most of his time with his best friend Pima and her mother Sadna, who takes care of him as a surrogate mother and is the only reliable adult presence in his life.

After a storm, Pima and Nailer find a stranded luxury yacht and hope to be able to scavenge it and become rich in the process. When they discover Nita, a young girl, the owner and only survivor of the wreck, they decide against killing her (thus forfeiting the scavenge rights) and instead help her. Nita is the wealthy, privileged heiress of a corporate empire, who is being hunted by a rival faction within her father's company to be used as a hostage. When a conflict about Nita and the scavenge ensues with Richard Lopez, Nailer and Nita escape to the Orleans in order to find help from Nita's family. They are aided by the mercenary creature Tool, who thus pays a debt owed to Sadna for saving his life when they worked on the same shipbreaking crew.

From the earliest moments of the novel, Nailer is determined not to be seen as being like his father, a feat that proves hard to accomplish as people draw such comparison easily from physical similarity and Nailer can do nothing to contradict them:

> And then there was Nailer. Some people, like Pearly, knew who they were and where they came from.... Nailer was nothing like that. He had no idea what he was. Half of something, a quarter of something else, brown skin and black hair like his dead mother, but with weird pale blue eyes like his father.
> Pearly had taken one look at Nailer's pale eyes and claimed he was spawned by demons.... Even so, the truth was that Nailer shared his father's eyes and his father's wiry build, and Richard Lopez was a demon for sure. (*SB* 9–10)

The similarity does not stop with physique, though, as Nailer fears he may share his father's violence and ruthlessness. When Nailer is forced to kill another mercenary, Tool compliments him by comparing Nailer to his father, which prompts Nailer to answer emphatically, "I'm not my father," nonetheless inwardly afraid "at the thought of mirroring his father" (*SB* 175).

Nailer and the other characters in *Ship Breaker* here echo a form of genetic determinism that equates identity with DNA. The artists and scholars Oron Catts and Ionat Zurr have pointed out that this belief in genetics has become entrenched in contemporary culture as a "discourse of exaggerated claims and overstatements concerning DNA" ("Big Pigs"). In their opinion, this "genohype" reduces the intricacies of human existence into simplistic catch phrases such as "We are our DNA" in order to provide "cause-effect formulas" for us humans, "who are 'locked' within our physiology" ("Ethics" 126). Evelyn Fox Keller has identified this kind of rhetoric as being linked to the notion that the Human Genome Project "has promised to reveal the genetic blueprint that tells us who we are" and that DNA functions similar to computer code, running the biological hardware of our bodies. But genohype and genetic determinism are not sustainable as proven by functional genetics (Keller 4, 5–7). Instead, as Catts and Zurr argue, additional factors similarly structure the organization of life, which needs to be understood as "a whole organism (or part of an organism) that exists, grows, and changes together with its environment" ("Ethics" 136).

In the novel, Bacigalupi complicates the genohype position and shows Nailer not as someone programmed by his DNA (Nailer becoming his father) but rather as a specific material expression of that genetic code (Nailer as an individual), which develops in a specific environment (growing up on the beach, cultivated by the caring relationship with Sadna). Although Nailer does have the genetic traits that allow him to kill, these characteristics are neither inherently good nor bad but merely one expression of his genes, as Tool aptly points out: "It's human nature to tear one another apart. Be glad you come from such a successful line of killers" (*SB* 175).

That Nailer is not simply enacting his father's genetic program becomes clear when he sides with Nita and escapes from the beach. At one point during their escape, Tool lectures Nita on how genes do not dictate behavior and how personal choice factors in:

> "If genes are destiny, then Nailer should have sold you to your enemies and spent the bounty on red rippers and Black Ling whiskey."
> 
> "That's not what I meant."
> 
> "No? But you descend from Patels, and so you are all intelligent and civilized, yes? And Nailer, of course, is descended from a perfect killer and we know what that means about him." (*SB* 212)

At the end of the novel, Nailer has to confront his father, fighting him and realizing that Richard "was horrifyingly fast.... The man was born to fight" (*SB* 305). Nailer is even afraid that his father might not be able to die, echoing the superstition of Richard as a demon. Nailer kills him, later pondering if there is part of his father in him: "I felt strong. Really strong.... [Now] I don't feel a thing. Not a damn thing. I was glad when I did it. And now I don't feel anything at all. I'm empty" (*SB* 319). After Nailer's return to the beach, Sadna guides him through this experience, soothing his doubts and guilt, and giving him caring advice. In her view, identity is determined not by genes but by actions: "You're not your dad. If you were your dad, you'd be down on the beach ... feeling pleased with yourself. You wouldn't be up here worrying about why you don't feel worse.... Be glad you were lucky and fast and smart. And then go do something right in the world" (319). Nailer's genetic makeup is merely a tool that determines the range of his abilities; his values, his decisions, and his actions determine his identity as a person.

Bacigalupi further stresses this self-determination of identity through the character of Nita, who is introduced as a privileged "swank" (*SB* 97), a rich girl, educated and sophisticated, who does not know about Nailer's world. She is shown to be merely a plaything in the world her father inhabits, a pawn to pressure the patriarch and owner of Patel Global. As with Nailer, people prejudge Nita as a "boss girl," "worth more dead than alive" (SB 97), manipulative, arrogant, and spoiled. But when pressed to survive on her wits, Nita similarly proves more than the swank everybody takes her to be:

> Nailer had expected Nita's prissy distaste for the slums of the Orleans to continue, but she adapted quickly, with a fierce attention to whatever Tool and Nailer taught. She threw herself into work, contributed her share, and didn't complain about what she ate or where she slept. She was still swank ... but she also showed a determination to carry her weight that Nailer was forced to show respect. (*SB* 218)

Being forced into a different role, Nita adapts quickly, rejecting the stereotypes of her heritage and proving herself to be self-reliant. In contrast to Nailer, though, Nita does not reject her family but instead in the end embraces it, as she sees her father's actions as morally superior and worth emulating. When discussing the conflict within Patel Global, Nita rejects the exploitation promoted by her father's antagonist Pyce and instead holds strong to her father's ideals: "My family is a clean company. Just because a market exists doesn't mean we have to serve it" (*SB* 194). At the close of the novel, Nita, as successor of her father's empire, will have the chance to prove this moral ideal by changing the work conditions at the shipbreaking beach. The novel suggests, however, that Nita needed the experience of being forced out of her role as swank to be able to come to this decision. Her privileged position never allowed her to understand the consequences of her company's business decisions beyond the theoretical and idealistic. But when confronted with the abject disregard for the poor in the Orleans, Nita is forced to become more than her current status. As a swank, she was missing something: "Then again, he wasn't too sure that she was a person either. Swanks were different. They came from a different place" (*SB* 210). In Nita, Bacigalupi balances out Nailer, by allowing both characters, though starting from very different positions in life, to convene on a similar self-determined position of identity.

In *The Drowned Cities*, the protagonist Mahlia also faces a struggle of identity after having been abandoned by her father and losing her mother to the conflict of the Drowned Cities. In the war-torn region, Mahlia is rescued from being slaughtered for her biracial heritage by Mouse, another orphaned child, and both struggle to survive until they find shelter with Doctor Mahfouz, a physician, in the village of Banyan Town. Even though a warrior gang has amputated one of Mahlia's hands, Mahfouz makes her his assistant, educating her to become his successor, and letting her work alongside him. When the village is seized by a group of child-soldiers hunting for the escaped hybrid creature Tool, Mahlia not only attacks the soldiers but also escapes with medicine to heal Tool and convince him to help her and Mouse leave the Drowned Cities. Mouse gets captured by the soldiers only to be recruited and marched off back into the Cities, making it necessary for Mahlia and Tool go after them and attempt a rescue.

Whereas Nailer struggles with his very direct parental lineage in the form of Richard Lopez, Mahlia is fighting a war against her perceived racial heritage, both her father's Chinese and her mother's Drowned Cities origins. Mahlia is not concerned with character traits inherited from either parent but rather struggles as being perceived as a "castoff," a child born of mixed-racial heritage to a Chinese "peacekeeper" and a citizen of the Drowned Cities (i.e., an American), left behind when the peacekeepers left their post: a "throwaway" (*DC* 37, 38).

Both parts of her heritage bring with them positive as well as negative associations. In her memories and desires, she connects the Chinese with wealth, civility, and order, effectively constructing a fantasy she has never been part of:

> In exchange for Mahlia's promising to speak Chinese like a civilized person and keeping herself polite, her father had given her ice cream ... [a] fairy-tale luxury from a fairy-tale land. According to her father, China had ... cities with towers a thousand feet high, all because they were civilized. Chinese people didn't war amongst themselves. They planned and built.... China had culture. It was civilized. Chinese people knew how to *hezuo*—"cooperate." Work together. (*DC* 61)

At the same time, her Chinese origin is a constant reminder of the intimate betrayal of being left behind ("Her father had abandoned her" [*DC* 218]) and the cowardice she assigns to it ("Her father had run away with his tail between his legs" [*DC* 63]). Further, it is a reminder of the Chinese troops invading the Drowned Cities and imposing their humanitarian aid with military force in the first place: "All of them rich enough to meddle where they didn't belong" (*DC* 30). Mahlia's genetic makeup is obvious to everyone who sees her, and they react to it with hate, being confronted with the occupation and the conflict with the Chinese: "'Half,' he said. 'For sure, you're half. And you're the right age, all right. Some peacekeeper nailed your old lady, left you behind.' He cocked his head. 'Don't got much use for collaborators'" (*DC* 89).

Her origin as stemming from the Drowned Cities is just as conflicted, however. She has taken on her father's judgment of the Americans as being poor, self-destructive, quarrelsome, without respect, and untrustworthy: she sees herself as "one of the animals he'd found ungovernable" (*DC* 63). Her evaluation of her mother is especially tainted with her experience, branding her mother as ignorant and unpractical: "Reality was all around her, but she couldn't see it. She just kept pretending" (*DC* 147). At the same time, however, the moniker Drowned Cities has also come to represent a form of survival instinct for Mahlia: "If Mahlia had been as civilized as the peacekeepers, she would have been dead ten times over, just getting out of the Drowned Cities" (*DC* 63). The selfishness she sees as her genetic heritage from the Cities becomes a tool to be used for survival:

> She'd survived the Drowned Cities because she wasn't anything like Mouse. When the bullets started flying and warlords started making examples of peacekeeper collaborators, Mahlia had kept her head down, instead of standing up like Mouse. She'd looked out for herself, first. And because of that, she'd survived. All the other castoffs like her were dead and gone. The kids who went to the peacekeeper schools, all those almond-eyed kids ... [had] been too civilized to know what to do when the hammer came down. (*DC* 66)

Just as in *Ship Breaker*, Bacigalupi here reveals genetic determinism as faulty and the organization of life as far more complex. Mahlia is influenced by her mixed heritage but does not conform to either "programming." The novel reveals her to be adapted to her environment, using her traits as needed—not merely a product of genetics, whose supposedly positive traits like Chinese civility or Drowned Cities pride might get her killed, but a conscious agent, who can choose to use her negatively connoted traits like Chinese cowardice and Drowned Cities deception to help her survive. She is smart and organized, very good at planning ahead, but when needed, also ruthless in order to survive her dystopian surroundings.

Aside from being a source of the social prejudices the characters have to confront, genetics also plays a role in their purely physical existence in the form of their adolescent and changing bodies. Heightened by the ecological crisis of global warming and the economic crisis of a loss of fossil fuels, human life has been transformed into a commodity within the inhuman system of the dystopian world depicted by Bacigalupi. Both Nailer and Mahlia experience this commodification of human life, as their own value is determined only in regard to their usefulness in their local economy.

Nailer's value is determined according to his body size and the limits this puts on his work: "Light crew needed small bodies. Most kids got bounced off the crew by the time they hit their midteens, even if they starved themselves to keep their size down" (*SB* 11–12). The stratified system of work at the ship-breaking beach is kept running by bodies, and body type determines one's position in life: small bodies for light crew, strong bodies for heavy crew or as bodyguards for those with wealth. Those without any of these attributes can sell their bodies for entertainment as "Nailshed girls" (*SB* 49) or for genetic experimentation in the form of eggs to the "Life Cult" (*SB* 50). Bodies are literally worth their weight in coin; when they are clean and healthy, they can be sold as medical supply parts to the "Harvesters"—a fate that would have awaited Nita, due to her exceptional health and pristine condition (see *SB* 196). Everything revolves around bodies and their value in the scarcity of the economic system.

Similarly, Mahlia is constantly measured against expectations of bodily standards, her missing hand marking her as incomplete and ineffective. The townsfolk determine her worth by her function as Doctor Mahfouz's assistant: "'What's that man see in a one-handed nurse?' Amaya asked. 'Is that why Tani's dead? Because you got no hand?' . . . 'She didn't need a useless crippled China girl for a nurse'" (*DC* 37). Moreover, the war economy of the Drowned Cities functions on bodies as much as the beach does. Young boys are recruited as soldiers to be used in the war: "If men like Glenn Stern . . . had a use for you, you could live a little while. But you were just a pawn. Her. Mouse. All those soldier boys who'd been hand-raised to shoot and knife and bleed out there in the Drowned Cities" (*DC* 400). Those not fighting in the conflict keep it alive with their bodies, becoming part of the "seething hordes of dust-covered slave labor" surrounding the war effort (*DC* 272).

This view of the human body as commodity in the capitalist economy of the dystopian world reduces the human being to mere bio-mass. It emphasizes a development that Bacigalupi has already commented on in his adult works, such as in the short story "The People of Sand and Slag" (from *Pump Six*), and which Christy Tidwell identifies as "a growing separation from and control of nature and bodies, . . . [which] are nothing more than resources to be profited from or destroyed" (100). But whereas in the adult stories Bacigalupi portrays the world from the perspective of participating subjects, the characters seeing nature as Other and separating themselves from it, making use of it, in *Ship Breaker* and *The Drowned Cities* he focuses on adolescent bodies, which are not yet participating subjects. Rather, both Nailer and Mahlia experience their own bodies as grotesque, partial, and unfinished. Nailer fears growing too big for light crew and physically experiences the toll his work takes on his body ("black grime in the filters" [*SB* 3]), culminating in his close escape from the oil pocket and the rusty piece of metal that opens him up and leaves a wound. Mahlia similarly is defined by her missing hand and the traumatic experiences of the war zone: "Instead, she carried scars, and her hand was a stump, and her eyes were hard like obsidian, and her smile was hesitant, as if anticipating the suffering that she knew awaited her, just around the corner" (*DC* 227). Their status as incomplete, as still *becoming*, marks them as transgressive of boundaries, as inhuman Other in a world that puts value only on the usability of the body. Adolescents, as Ostry puts it, possess a "frightening body, subject to violation and very far from finished perfection" (231). In both of his young adult novels, Bacigalupi reveals a world that sees them as expelled Other, not as full members of society, because of their bodies/genetics/heritage. It seems little wonder then, that he further presses this point by introducing the ultimate grotesque body, the monster, and aligns it with the adolescent position as Other.

## Of Monsters and Animals: Human Exceptionalism and the Other

Allen Weiss reminds us that monsters represent "categorial ambiguity, ontological instability, . . . the confusion of species" (124). Therefore, the monster is a cultural marker of transgression, a reminder of the boundaries and delineations of categories such as *the human* or *nature*. Monsters are used to contrast their Otherness with "prevailing conceptions of the human and of normalcy" (Weinstock 3). And as Jeffrey Cohen points out, monsters "are disturbing hybrids whose externally incoherent bodies resist attempts to include them in any systematic structuration" (6). As such, Tool, with his chimerical genetics marking him as monstrous, as a "dialectical Other and . . . incorporation of the Outside" (7), culturally aligns more closely with the unfinished and *becoming* bodies of the adolescents than with the displayed conceptions of the human and of normalcy within the novels.

When introducing Tool, Bacigalupi emphasizes his difference and potential as threat, both real and imagined. His physical superiority and animal features make him stand out among the humans, but it is their superstitions and fears that position him on the outside of society:

> The monster's huge muscled form loomed over the rest of the thugs, its doglike muzzle snarling and showing its teeth to scare back the hungry people. . . .
> 
> Lucky Strike laughed. "Well, at least you all listen to my killer dog, huh? That's right. Everybody step back. Or my friend Tool here will teach you a lesson in manners. I mean it, everyone, give us some space. If Tool doesn't like you, he'll eat you raw." (*SB* 70–71)

Tool's ontological status is that of a monster—neither fully human, nor fully animal. He is depicted as a chimera, a creature genetically created from several different species, specific attributes of each built into the creature to make it suitable for the tasks it is supposed to perform. His chimerical nature thus highlights the categorical transgression and forces readers to position Tool uneasily beyond human and animal:

> The creature's massive pit-bull skull loomed close. Scars and torn flesh. Animal and human, crushed together in one nightmare beast. Ropy gray scar tissue covered one eye, but the other eye was wide open, rabid and yellow, big as an egg. The monster growled, revealing rows of sharp teeth. A gust of blood and carrion washed over her.
> "I am not meat," it snarled. "*You* are meat." (*DC* 77)

Tool is not a natural creation but a "living war weapon, . . . [a] bioengineered supersoldier," as Bacigalupi claims in an interview with Jeff VanderMeer. As such, he is shown to have abilities that go far beyond that of a human: "They're better than us. Faster. Stronger. Many of them are smarter. Perfect tacticians. Built for war, from day one" (*DC* 162). In addition, his body is genetically engineered to withstand the harshest environment and grave injuries:

> Don't think of a half-man as human. It is a demon, designed for war. Its blood is full of super-clotting agents and its cells are designed to replicate as quickly as a kudzu grows.
> If you cut a creature like this with a knife, the wound closes itself within minutes. . . . Flesh torn down to the bone. Ligaments ripped apart. Bones snapped. None of it matters to a creature like this. (*DC* 166)

The descriptions as monster or demon reveal the fear that humans experience, the threat Tool poses, and thus confer a specific power on him. They hint at the posthuman potential to supplant the human as the most dominant species. Mahlia is reminded of this possibility when she tries to control him: "*Fates, what was I thinking?* She'd forgotten what a monster it was. It dominated its surroundings" (*DC* 173).

In order not to feel the threat of losing dominance, most humans employ a linguistic strategy to limit Tool's categorical transgression by referring to him as animal. In their descriptions, Nailer and Mahlia (as main focalizers of the narratives), as well as other characters in the novels, highlight their view of Tool as an animal, as doglike, describing his fangs, his muzzle, and the snarling sounds, repeating phrases such as "dog-face" (e.g., *SB* 45, *DC* 72) and "yellow dog eyes" (e.g., *SB* 87, 138).

More important than the physical assessment as animal is the functional value that is inherent in this dehumanization and linguistic marking. Here his name is revealing, as humans do not want to see more in him than a mere tool to be used for their needs: "Half-men were used for bodyguards, for killing, for war" (*SB* 211). The most common response to him is fueled by the same genetic determinism that bears down on Mahlia and Nailer: "Scientists created me from the genes of dogs and tigers and men and hyenas, but people always believe I am only their dog" (*SB* 248). Out of the diversity of genetic traits, the most harmless and convenient for humans are his dog-traits, which also make him a perfect soldier: obedience, loyalty, and the ability to be trained for tasks. These are the traits that become dominant in human descriptions of Tool and in his perception of himself, filtered by his experiences:

> Tool... was a very bad dog. His masters had told him so many times as they beat him and trained him and molded his will to match their own. They had forged him into a killer and then fit him into the killing machine that had been his pack. A platoon of slaughter. For a little while, he had been a good dog, and obedient....
>
> Tool had been such a bad dog that he still lived....
>
> When he had been a good dog, an owned dog, a loyal dog, his masters would have stitched and treated wounds like these.... Good dogs had masters, and masters kept good dogs close. (*DC* 12–13)

As before, the evaluation of Tool as a weapon to be wielded reveals a separation from nature and a human exceptionalism that places humans above all other creation. Tidwell describes the attitudes that characters display toward Tool perfectly when she talks about creatures in Bacigalupi's short story "The People of Sand and Slag" that were "created only to serve; they are a subclass from which the humans intentionally separate themselves. Similarly, there are also bio-jobs, creatures created for a variety of functional purposes from the DNA of older, less useful animals.... Bio-jobs have no rights or value other than their usefulness to (post)humans" (99).

The animal thus becomes the dichotomous Other of the human, which the novels constantly probe and explore. This dichotomy, as Cary Wolfe notes, has been part of Western cultural history since antiquity, the animal functioning as reflector of "the constitutive disavowals and self-constructing narratives enacted by that fantasy figure called 'the human'" (6). To become fully human and acquire a stable identity, humans require "the sacrifice of the 'animal' and the animalistic" (6). The speciesism inherent in this thinking once more reestablishes the notion of human exceptionalism that, as Wolfe notes, can easily be used to justify wars, genocide, and slavery, if only some humans are marked as animals. In the novels this speciesism is apparent, on the one hand, in the notions of animals as lesser beings that are of little value beyond the specific use they have to humans, as shown before. But with precision, these notions are then, on the other hand, transferred to human bodies in order to allow for their dehumanization.

In *The Drowned Cities*, children orphaned by war, such as Mahlia, become "war maggots" (*DC* 36) that need feeding and give nothing in return, and the same term is later employed by the soldier boys to describe the townsfolk they enslave. Whenever one party wants to express disdain for a specific behavior of another party, they refer to the other as animal: "Think we're just animals? That's what you peacekeepers always used to say, right? Called us animals? Called us dogs?" (*DC* 109–10). The war boys employ the same tactic, referring to their enemies as animals, and even the townsfolk see Mahlia's aggressiveness as inhuman: "Doctor Mahfouz was staring at her with dismay, as if she were some kind of animal gone wild" (*DC* 38).

A similar disdain shows in the words of Nita in *Ship Breaker* when she refers to drug users and describes them as less valuable: "That's what surge rats use. Combat squads. Half-men. It's for animals" (*SB* 134). The label becomes especially meaningful when contrasted with terms such as *person* or *human*, as when Nita "thought of [Tool] as something like an animal, a useful creature like a dog, but not actually a person" (*SB* 210). Even Tool rejects the animal part of his nature as less valuable: "Tool was not some brute animal, able to think only in terms of attack or flight. He was better than that. He hadn't survived this long by thinking like an animal" (*DC* 20).

Bacigalupi counters this speciesism by allowing Tool a subjectivity that "undermines the ontological stability of 'human beings'" (293), as Andrew Hageman has pointed out for the similarly posthuman Emiko in *The Windup Girl*. As Sherryl Vint argues for science fiction as a genre, the novels prove "an excellent resource for interrogating how we construct the posthuman, and the political ends inherent in various constructions, because [science fiction's] generic conventions provide a space for narrating agency for non-human subjects" (189). It thus seems interesting that Tool is specifically positioned to reject the humanist ideology of a useful and separate nature, which "privileges the rights of humans ... over those of all other forms of life," as Barbara Heise has pointed out (qtd. in Tidwell 77–78).

The most important privilege that Bacigalupi challenges in his writing is the idea of a superior position of the human species. As mentioned before, half-men are physically and mentally "augmented" beyond human ability; "they're people-plus" (*SB* 262). Consequently, from a humanist position of separation and exceptionalism, posthuman superiority necessitates some kind of control mechanism so that human masters remain in charge of their creations. When half-men are captured or their masters die, a genetic fail-safe robs them of a purpose to live for, as one of the owners of the creatures explains: "Augments aren't like us. They have a single master. When they lose that master, they die.... They pine. They are very loyal. They cannot live without their masters. It comes from a line of canine genetics" (*SB* 262). This loyalty is built in via a genetic predisposition but then ultimately induced by strict behavioral training, as Tool reflects: "Trainers. Hard men and women with their discipline rods ... knew how to build obedience. Lessons of raw meat and cold electricity. Showering sparks. *BAD dog!*" (*DC* 133). After the negative reinforcement, the designated master of the half-men is introduced as a savior, generating gratitude: "And then, their general came. The kind and honorable man who rescued them ... [and] led their pack out of Hell.... In desperate thanks, they gave their loyalty to General Caroa, forever after" (*DC* 133). Ultimately, this fail-safe is supposed to keep half-men loyal to their masters and stop them from gaining control over their actions: "So they can't go rogue against their wealthy masters. So they can't raise a flag for themselves. The worst nightmare of any general would be an army of augments gone rogue" (*DC* 163).

## "I am not your dog!": Posthuman Subjectivity and Utopian Identity

In the face of this genetic determinism and the behavioral training binding half-men, Tool challenges the hegemonic categories of master and slave, human and animal, subject and object, and instead promotes what Rosi Braidotti has called a posthuman "ethics of becoming" by establishing himself as a "relational subject that works across differences" (49). As Sherryl Vint argues, critical posthumanism "acknowledges that self is materially connected to the rest of the world ... It is a posthumanism that can embrace multiplicity and partial perspectives, a posthumanism that is not threatened by its others" (189).

Tool does not accept his subservient role, stating that "not all of us enjoy slavery" and that he realizes he is "smart enough to know that I can choose who I serve and who I betray, which is more than can be said of the rest of my ... people" (*SB* 211). When the rest of his platoon died, Tool fought to become free, to gain a subjectivity beyond the object-status of a weapon, openly rebelling against orders and genetics: "'You think my general offered to let me walk free of his own accord?' ... [Tool] alone had won free. He alone had survived. The bad dog who had turned upon his master" (*DC* 135–36). As such, Tool is an anomaly—his existence puts into question the idea behind these servile genetic chimeras: "Tool was an impossible creature.... [N]o independent half-men existed. And yet Tool had walked away from many masters, ... had simply walked away when it no longer suited him" (*SB* 262).

Tool's refusal of his genetic programming and training is reminiscent of the coming-of-age adolescent in that Tool similarly needs to explore his hard-won identity, test out specific values, and finally act upon chosen morals. He struggles with his genetic heritage just as much as Mahlia does, torn between a fierce individualism and a need for companionship he cannot explain:

> Tool wondered if it was his loyal nature, bred and trained into him, that made him feel guilty for leaving [Mahlia] to her fate. Some vestige of the training that had made him so obedient to his original masters. Was that why he kept following her, trying to persuade her to leave this doomed land? Had he simply been reverting to his original conditioning? The loyal dog who would not leave its master? (*DC* 235–36)

Moreover, he is just as fierce in reacting to any judgment rendered on him from the outside as Nailer is when confronted with his father's character traits: "You do not reward me with raw meat, you do not scratch me behind the ears, and YOU DO NOT OWN ME!" (*DC* 173).

Tool rejects the genetic determinism placed on him, denies the simple logic of obedience, and instead adopts a subject position that is relational, accountable, and communal. When Nita confronts him about his loyalty and the rejection of his master, Tool challenges her: "You wish that I was a good dog-man? That I had kept allegiance to Nailer's father, maybe? ... Richard Lopez thought your clean blood and clear eyes and strong heart would fetch an excellent price from the Harvesters. You wish I had stayed loyal to that?" (*SB* 196). Tool's words reveal the underlying issue: obedience induced through genetics would have left him merely a weapon, determined by the morals and values of the one wielding the weapon, and not accountable for any of his actions. Tool instead proposes a moral accountability, a subject position that takes into consideration its relation to other life and the community surrounding it:

> "The wealthy measure everything with the weight of their money.... Sadna once risked herself and the rest of her crew to help me escape from an oil fire. She did not have to return.... Others urged her not to. It was foolhardy. And I, after all, was only half of a man." Tool regarded Nita steadily. "Your father commands fleets. And thousands of half-men, I am sure. But would he risk himself to save a single one?" (*SB* 197)

Tool's decision to reject the existing system of genetic determinism—the status quo in the novels—positions him clearly with Nailer and Mahlia, both of whom are in a similar conflict with the adult world they inhabit. Both Nailer and Mahlia feel trapped and struggle with their position. For them, Tool becomes an alternative to the existing value system, an ally against the restrictions and pressures of their dystopian world, and ultimately a reflector of their own search for identity. As Balaka Basu, Katherine R. Broad, and Carrie Hintz argue for current young adult dystopias: "The confrontation with the realities of the adult world may lead to a standoff between adolescents and adults that empowers young people to turn against the system as it stands and change the world in ways adults cannot, locating the utopian potential of dystopian scenarios within young adult protagonists themselves" (7).

I believe that for *Ship Breaker* and *The Drowned Cities*, this utopian potential is not just located in the adolescent protagonists but also in the posthuman subjectivity represented by Tool. Whereas the genetic determinism of this dystopian world would force judgment on Nailer (criminal, beach rat) and Mahlia (castoff, war maggot) that limits their identity formation, Tool offers a different set of values, expressed not in the idea that we are determined by our DNA, but in the idea that we are determined by our decisions.

Bacigalupi establishes this set of values by offering a replacement for the missing, defective institution of family—both Nailer and Mahlia are effectively orphans. Whereas Nailer and Mahlia are connected to their families via DNA, their value system and their morality are determined by other figures, providing a different set of environmental influences. Nailer is shaped by Sadna and Pima, who instill in him a loyalty that is formed by the concept of "crew"—a community united by cooperative struggle and connectedness to others in order to survive. Loyalty is given to those with whom one is working in collaboration; actions determine one's worth. When crew-member Sloth breaks her vows and acts against her allies, she is punished by a community that sees itself as interconnected: "They all looked down the beach to where Sloth had been dumped. She'd be hungry soon, and needing someone to protect her. Someone to share scavenge with, to cover her back when she couldn't work. The beach was a hard place to survive without crew" (*SB* 43).

Sloth's betrayal shows the value of crew, but it is Tool who makes this clear by siding with Sadna instead of his current employer, Richard Lopez, as mentioned above. Tool is part of Sadna's crew, and her actions have formed a bond that is more important than obedience toward an employer or master. Nailer realizes that the idea of crew is a stand-in for decisions based in morality (what is right and what is not) and loyalty to those who share one's morals. He crews up with Nita, and they each promise the other to help: "I got your back, you got mine" (*SB* 116). When Richard wants to sell her, Nailer decides to uphold this promise: "We're crew, . . . I'm not selling her. . . . We can't just give her to them. It'd be like giving Pima to my dad" (*SB* 179–80). The contrast with the concept of family becomes most pronounced when Nita is kidnapped and Nailer hires on to rescue her. The captain questions his loyalty to Nita (whom Nailer refers to as Lucky Girl), expecting him to be loyal to his father instead:

> "My dad doesn't give anyone a chance for second thoughts. He cuts you first. He talks about family sticking together, but what he really means is that I give him money.... Lucky Girl's more of a family than he is."
>
> As soon as he said it, he knew it was true. Despite the short time he'd known her, Nailer was sure of Nita. He could count the people on one hand who were like that, and Pima and Sadna were the ones who topped that list. And surprisingly, Lucky Girl was there, too. She was family....
>
> "It's not about my dad. It's Lucky Girl. She's good, right? She's worth a hundred of some of my old crew. A thousand of my dad." (*SB* 251–52)

It is important to note that Nailer has an innate sense of what is good and what is right that seems to have been nurtured by Sadna and Pima, and he bases his decision about Nita on this feeling. He adopts the term *family* to mean those whom he can count on, who act accordingly—and not to refer to blood relatives or genetics.

In *The Drowned Cities*, Mahlia has a similar notion of family being unreliable. Her father has abandoned her, and her mother died of ignorance and left her struggling for survival—all of which has made her fiercely self-reliant but also somewhat self-centered. However, she does have a strong sense of right and good as well and will not go back on her promise to Tool: "I promised I'd give the half-man medicine" (*DC* 148). Her motives are far from selfless, but essentially she is the only one to see beyond the animal side of Tool and not act as if he were a monster: "But what if it was something else? It hadn't killed Mouse, even when it could have. A soldier boy would have done him in a second, but the half-man had let him go. That had to count for something" (*DC* 152). It is of course no coincidence that while Mahlia is pondering the value of Tool's life, she is listening to his heart: "Huge and thick. Heavy.... Crazy big" (*DC* 152). A certain poetic contiguity is at play here: Tool is portrayed as merciful, his heart big enough to let Mouse live, whereas the soldier boys (i.e., humans) are vicious and malignant. Mahlia thus decides to save Tool, and when the Doctor tries to force her against Tool, she reacts instinctually, sensing "something of the predator" (*DC* 153) in the Doctor, and fends him off.

She has formed an attachment to Mouse, who, with utter disregard for his own life, saves her from the soldier boys. Her loyalty to him is founded on their mutual survival—again the idea of community in a common struggle and the connectedness with other lives, each depending on the other to survive. When

Mouse is captured, Mahlia is willing to fight a whole army by herself: "I got to get him back. If he's dead, I'm dead. It's how it is" (*DC* 191). It is this reaction that Tool recognizes and aptly names:

> "Pack," the half-man said. "He's of your pack." The way the half-man said it made Mahlia think that it was more than just when you talked about dogs or coywolv running together. It was something absolute and total.
> "Yeah," she said. "Pack." (*DC* 191)

The concept is beyond her human understanding—the attempt to grasp the term through its human usage ("dogs running together") is limited and fails to realize the non- or posthuman meaning behind it. For Tool, *pack* is charged with ritualistic meaning: it refers to a crèche—a group of half-men genetically produced as a unit—that trains and fights together, which to him is the essence of his life: "We are nourished by victory, Doctor. Life's blood, from the beating hearts of our foes. Our enemy fortifies us. The more enemies we have, the more we feed. And the stronger we become.... Conquest feeds itself.... We welcome our enemies, as we welcome life" (*DC* 176).

It is important to note that this loyalty (at least as Tool promotes it) does not include his master but is built on the idea of connection through similarity of experience. A close connection to the pack does not excuse one of its members from making decisions based on individual morality. And for Tool, individuality includes a subjectivity that sees the interconnection of all life—*zoe*—not a specific cultured life—*bios*—both in terms of his own purpose ("Killing in one place or killing in another; it makes no difference" [*SB* 182]) and in terms of who is worthy of his loyalty. He recognizes Mahlia's loyalty to Mouse and feels connected to her through his near-death, from which only Mahlia is willing to save him. He agrees to help her, bonding with her over a shared enemy's heart: "'If we are pack, then conquest is our sustenance, sister.'... With a wet tearing, the heart came out, glistening and full of blood, veins and arteries torn. The muscle of life. Tool held it out to her. 'Our enemies give us strength'" (*DC* 243).

Both crew and pack are presented in the novels as alternative concepts for determining loyalty, morality, and identity. They emphasize a shared subjectivity based in a shared experience, in a shared environment. Tool is representative of this posthuman subjectivity: his status as monster, based in an ontology between human and nonhuman animal, is ideally suited to challenge the young adult protagonists, as well as the readers. As Joan Gordon points out, "Once we allow other beings subjectivity, their position as tools is problematized" (334). And this is exactly what Bacigalupi has done. The dystopian scenario he describes, as we have seen, is expressed in a separation from nature, privileged subjectivity (adult, able-bodied, wealthy), and the exploitation and dehumanization of those bodies that do not conform to the privileged position. In this world, genetic determinism traps both Nailer and Mahlia in grotesque bodies—incomplete, wounded, of faulty origin, lacking power. But they reject this power dynamic, embrace the conflict with the established system, and test out their own identity. In them, the utopian moment shines through, and alternative subjectivity is possible.

Bacigalupi further enhances his message by employing a powerful posthuman subjectivity in the form of the chimera Tool. Tool is closely allied with the adolescents due to his position as Other, as "the sexualized, racialized, and naturalized others, who are reduced to the less than human status of disposable bodies" (Braidotti 15). He provides Nailer and Mahlia with an ex-centric view and the possibility to explore their own morality and identity. An ethical or critical posthumanism, as presented in *Ship Breaker* and *The Drowned Cities*, reveals to readers the possibility of utopian hope in the face of dystopian systems. At the end of *The Drowned Cities*, readers can feel with Mouse and the other soldier boys—Ocho's words summing up the helplessness of young adults in the face of an adult world beyond their control: "'None of us asked for this!' he shouted. 'None of us! We were all just like him. Every maggot one of us.' . . . 'None of us were like this,' he said again. 'We aren't born like this. They make us this way'" (*DC* 416). At this point, because of Tool's own development, the adolescents have found an alternative: "They were getting out. All of them. They were leaning into the wind, eyes brighter and more alive than anything she had ever seen. A whole pack of soldier boys, all pursuing a future that they thought they'd never be allowed to have" (*DC* 431).

## Works Cited

Bacigalupi, Paolo. *The Drowned Cities*. London: Atom, 2012. Print.
———. "A. S. King Interviews Paolo Bacigalupi About His Latest Book *The Drowned Cities*." Interview by A. S. King. *SFSignal.com*. SF Signal. 27 Apr. 2012. Web. 1 Dec. 2014.
———. "Paolo Bacigalupi on His Hopeful Dystopia *The Drowned Cities*." Interview by Jeff VanderMeer. *Shelfari*. N.p., 13 July 2012. Web. Dec. 01, 2014.
———. *Pump Six and Other Stories*. San Francisco: Night Shade, 2008. Print.
———. *Ship Breaker*. New York: Little, 2010. Print.
———. *The Windup Girl*. San Francisco: Night Shade, 2009. Print.
Basu, Balaka, Katherine R. Broad, and Carrie Hintz. Introduction. *Contemporary Dystopian Fiction for Young Adults: Brave New Teenagers*. Ed. Balaka Basu, Katherine R. Broad, and Carrie Hintz. New York: Routledge, 2013. 1–8. Print. Children's Literature and Culture 93.

Berry, Michael. "The Rise of Climate Fiction: When Literature Takes on Global Warming and Devastating Droughts." *Salon.com*. Salon Media Group. 26 Oct. 2014. Web. 6 Jan. 2015.

Braidotti, Rosi. *The Posthuman*. Cambridge: Polity, 2013. Print.

Catts, Oron, and Ionat Zurr. "Big Pigs, Small Wings: On Genohype and Artistic Autonomy." *Culture Machine 7* (2005): n. pag. Web. 7 July 2014.

———. "The Ethics of Experiential Engagement with the Manipulation of Life." *Tactical Biopolitics: Art, Activism, and Technoscience*. Ed. Beatriz Da Costa, Kavita Philip, and Joseph Dumit. Cambridge: MIT, 2008. 125–42. Print.

Cohen, Jeffrey Jerome. "Monster Culture (Seven Theses)." *Monster Theory: Reading Culture*. Ed. Jeffrey Jerome Cohen. Minneapolis: U of Minnesota P, 1996. 3–25. Print.

Gordon, Joan. "Animal Studies." *The Routledge Companion to Science Fiction*. Ed. Mark Bould et al. London: Routledge, 2009. 331–40. Print.

Hageman, Andrew. "The Challenge of Imagining Ecological Futures: Paolo Bacigalupi's *The Windup Girl*." *Science Fiction Studies* 39.2 (2012): 283–303. Print.

Herbrechter, Stefan. *Posthumanism: A Critical Analysis*. London: Bloomsbury, 2013. Print.

Keller, Evelyn Fox. *The Century of the Gene*. Cambridge: Harvard UP, 2002. Print.

Nayar, Pramod K. *Posthumanism*. Cambridge: Polity, 2014. Print.

Ostry, Elaine. "'Is He Still Human? Are You?': Young Adult Science Fiction in the Posthuman Age." *Lion and the Unicorn* 28.2 (2004): 222–46. Print.

Otto, Eric C. "'The Rain Feels New': Ecotopian Strategies in the Short Fiction of Paolo Bacigalupi." *Green Planets: Ecology and Science Fiction*. Ed. Gerry Canavan and Kim Stanley Robinson. Middleton: Wesleyan UP, 2014. 179–91. Print.

Tidwell, Christy. "The Problem of Materiality in Paolo Bacigalupi's 'The People of Sand and Slag.'" *Extrapolation* 52.1 (2011): 94–109. Print.

Vint, Sherryl. *Bodies of Tomorrow: Technology, Subjectivity, Science Fiction*. Toronto: U of Toronto P, 2007. Print.

Weinstock, Jeffrey, ed. *The Ashgate Encyclopedia of Literary and Cinematic Monsters*. Farnham: Ashgate, 2013. Print.

Weiss, Allen S. "Ten Theses on Monsters and Monstrosity." *Drama Review* 48.1 (2004): 124–25. Print.

Wolfe, Cary. *Animal Rites: American Culture, the Discourse of Species, and Posthuman Theory*. Chicago: U of Chicago P, 2003. Print.

# 9

# POSTHUMAN POTENTIAL AND ECOLOGICAL LIMIT IN FUTURE WORLDS

*Phoebe Chen*

Young adult fiction is about what it means to grow up and what it means to exist as a human being. It is literature that is thematically and ideologically centered on the time in our lives when we question our identity and existence the most, asking profound questions about who we are, why we do what we do, and what we will be. Robyn McCallum believes it is no coincidence that identity and subjectivity formation are integral to young adult fiction since adolescence as a developmental period is usually conceived as "a period during which notions of selfhood undergo rapid and radical transformation" (3). Although McCallum identifies ideology and discourse as the primary dialectics that shape and inform the young adult protagonist's sense of self, as scholars begin to pay attention to the impact of changing environments on our definition of humanity, nature and ecology surface as crucial factors of subjectivity formation. In *Landscape in Children's Literature*, Jane Suzanne Carroll builds on existing scholarship on literary topographies and spaces to highlight the symbolic importance of green spaces and landscapes in British fantasy, while Pauline Dewan claims in *The Art of Place in Literature for Children and Young Adults* that places, especially natural places such as islands, woods, and gardens, facilitate heightened spatial perception that assists the reader's understanding and formation of subjectivity and identity.

But what happens when environments turn harmful? This type of speculative thinking is pursued by Alice Curry in *Environmental Crisis in Young Adult Fiction*. Curry evaluates representations of post-disaster scenarios from an ecofeminist perspective and proposes that environmental crisis is effectively "a crisis of embodiment for young adults who are faced with the prospect of growing up in a post-natural world. This crisis is reflected in the contentious relationships between the young protagonists of the novels and their social and ecological surroundings, relationships that are enacted on the discursive site of their own bodies" (15–16). Through dialectic engagement with the natural environment, bodily boundaries that separate the self from the environment are transgressed. This transformative process produces posthumanist realities in which the protagonist's identity is contested and reconstructed on the ground of radical and speculative ecologies. What this means for young adult protagonists is that their physical interaction with and within nature, ecology, and the environment is treated as foundational to their self-awareness and self-identity.

To examine literary depictions of posthumanist identity and ecological crisis in young adult (YA) science fiction, I have selected three novels in which the connection between human and nature is at risk, compelling the protagonist to respond and adapt to biological changes and environmental factors. *Earth Girl* (2012), by Janet Edwards, is set in a future world where humans are divided into two species based on the discovery of a singular genetic difference. The majority of the human population possess the genetic marker that enables them to teleport and escape the ravaged earth, while Jarra, one of the few born without the needed DNA strand that enables teleportation, is left stranded on earth. *Of Beast and Beauty* (2013), by Stacey Jay, also establishes biological and visible division in its premise. After the arrival of human colonists on an uninhabited planet, contact with the wild and untamed environment causes genetic mutation in some but not all human colonists, separating the mutants from the "pure" humans. Lastly, *Orleans* (2013), by Sherri L. Smith, begins in a quarantined, post-disaster New Orleans where hurricanes have destroyed the ecosystem and a pandemic disease has installed a new world order. The protagonist, Fen, has had to find new ways to survive when the rest of the world has declared the city uninhabitable. The expectation is that through the protagonist's contestation of environmental and physical divisions between self and nature, she can establish organic solidarity with other living organisms, for that is what it means to be posthuman in ecological terms. To be posthuman is not to undermine existing distinctions but to confront "facets of Life's determination to organise itself, understand itself, to be present to itself—even in its missteps" (Chiew 67). The human self does not lose its significance as a human, but rather, gains insight into deeper connections that bind his/her existence to the physical world.

These novels, however, reveal the protagonist's transition into posthumanism amidst environmental crisis to be a challenging if not futile process. *Earth Girl* realizes a mode of identity construction that relies on restoration of the past, conveying the warning that when ecological crisis explodes the progressive teleology of human civilization, the connection between past and present becomes integral to formulating what it means to be human. Likewise, *Of Beast and Beauty* utilizes the post-crisis adolescent as the necessary ideological experiment for the purpose of creating a posthumanist subject that is characterized by enough ecological hybridity to reflect troubling environmental futures and enough quintessential human qualities to appear familiar and, most importantly, desirable. *Orleans* proves to be the most subversive text because it sustains the protagonist's dynamic connection with a destabilized ecosystem. But the protagonist's death proves that eventually the adolescent posthumanist identity is a fragile one at the mercy of the state's exploitation, which leads to a disenchanting and disconcerting moment of reaching the end of being posthuman. The ecological and biopolitical aspect of futuristic worlds in YA science fiction thus appears in sharp relief as a constant source of uncertainty and disturbance in the protagonist's construction of human identity, emptying and redefining words like *nature* and *naturalness* while foregrounding the protagonist's dependence on them. I would argue that although these novels do not exemplify actual solutions to the ongoing problem of depleting resources and species extinction, nor do they necessarily resolve ambivalent tensions within the protagonist's posthuman transformation, what is most important is that they function as an imaginative platform for running speculative thought experiments about being human in a world that is becoming increasingly out of sync with its own ecological and biological rhythm.

## Posthumanism in Young Adult Science Fiction

In the present, products of modern science and technology cross into questionable ethical grounds, and as a result we are compelled to ask ourselves what it means to be human in a time when the human skin is no longer the barrier that separates the self from the Other. YA science fiction addresses these doubts and uncertainties by evoking both utopian and dystopian possibilities. The responses are varied across an ideological spectrum, ranging from postapocalyptic disenchantment to religious fanaticism. Yet what binds these YA novels is the presence of young protagonists who are "isolated and radically alienated from the worlds around them" (Bradford et al. 180), characters who necessitate the redistribution of difference and identity and create "possibilities for the emergence of new relationships between human and machine, biology and technology" (181). Due to YA science fiction's speculative tendency, Farah Mendlesohn identifies the genre as a means of provoking the teen reader to think otherwise about the world he/she is currently in, and of letting consequences "leak from the books because we are no longer looking inward, instead outward to the 'what if' of the world" (309). In the same vein, Elaine Ostry believes that the representation of posthuman futures in YA science fiction is the way to prepare teenaged readers for a future characterized by hybridity and alienation, with the genre's representation of biotechnology serving as a metaphor for adolescence, since the adolescent protagonist is often seen as "an open, frightening body, subject to violation and very far from finished perfection" (231). Gary Westfahl, however, notes that YA science fiction claims to challenge the liberal humanist definition of human, yet it does not always offer viable alternative definitions of humanness. In actuality, it is more likely to reject the unknowable potential of posthumanism to reassure the adolescent's need for a solid and grounded self-identity (125). In other words, despite its speculative nature, YA science fiction's posthumanist experiences could slip into a liberal humanist paradigm that enables the protagonist to recuperate an essentialist identity, implying that the genre's reconfiguration of humanness may not be as radical as its premise suggests.

Nevertheless, the posthumanist drive has not entirely lost its momentum in YA fiction. Zoe Jaques compares posthumanism and children's literature, which broadly includes YA fiction, and finds that though they may seem incongruous at first, they are both committed "to imagine not just 'autopoetic wholes' but also the meanings that emerge in the betwixt-and-betweens" and that "children's literature, perhaps more than any other literary form, is invested with more possibilities than impossibilities" (239). So the in-betweenness, or rather, the liminal ambiguity of identity and existence, inherent to children's literature is actually the resonating principle that draws the interest of posthumanism. As Cary Wolfe puts it, posthumanism is not intended to undermine the idea that humans are essentially human, but it is a perspective that "forces us to rethink our taken-for-granted modes of human experience, including the normal perceptual modes and affective states of *Homo sapiens* itself, by recontextualizing them in terms of the entire sensorium of other living beings and their own autopoietic ways of 'bringing forth a world'" (xxv). To Pramod Nayar, the notion that posthumanism conceives reality as an organic multilayered sensorium is fundamental since connections with other organisms enable the posthuman subject to move beyond the individual self and to thereby construct the human "as an assemblage, co-evolving with other forms of life, enmeshed with the environment and technology" (3–4). Therefore, posthumanism as a conceptual framework is not only useful but necessary to our reassessment of the human condition in new and strange contexts, such as ecological upheaval and global catastrophe, which knit humans materially and experientially with other organisms.

In like manner, posthumanism proves invaluable to considering representations of nature in YA science fiction. Ecological posthumanism is critically focused on how environmental changes force humans to come into physical contact with other nonhuman entities, how changing environments affect the human body, and how, as a result, they recontextualize and redefine the human experience materially, culturally, and biologically. In particular, ecological posthumanism invokes a remapping of nature that contests "the false integrity not only of the humanist self but also the idea of nature as essentially natural, other, elsewhere, or outside" (Taylor 359). Since posthumanism at its core explores "the vital, self-organizing and yet non-naturalistic structure of living matter itself" (Braidotti 2), posthumanism's rearrangement of invisible connections between humans and nonhuman nature invariably has impact on the protagonist's self-awareness as a living and sentient being. Consequently, when reading the text through ecological posthumanism as a theoretical filter, we reach into moments of nature in crisis and evaluate the transformative process through which the natural environment influences the protagonist's identity.

### The Futureless, Scavenging Historian

In the brave, new world of *Earth Girl*, humans have left Earth in search of planets to colonize because Earth's resources have been depleted. The postapocalyptic wave of galactic migration creates a form of biological determinism that separates humans who are genetically able to access the portals from those who cannot. Those who are born with DNA that makes them capable of teleportation can migrate and thrive on other planets, which have been terraformed to simulate an Earth-like environment, while Jarra, the protagonist of the novel, remains Earth-bound. Outer-planet communities view those left behind as primitive throwbacks. Jarra confesses, "The Polite people would call me Handicapped, but you can call me ape girl if you like. The name doesn't change anything. My immune system cannot survive anywhere other than Earth. I'm in prison, and it's a life sentence" (3). Despite their hyper-advanced technology that screens out genetic disabilities, scientists cannot introduce the DNA sequence necessary for space travel into the genetic makeup of Earth-bound humans. As a result, Earth-bound humans are pitied and labeled as an inferior species. To the other-worldlies, Jarra's disability is irrefutable because it has a biological basis, which illustrates a class system founded on genetic determination that is disturbingly reminiscent of eugenics.

Jarra's desire to undermine this system of biological discrimination drives her character development. She plans to prove that despite her lack of a particular DNA that allows space travel, she is just as intelligent and competent as those living on the outer planets. To undermine the system, Jarra first creates a fake identity as an outer-planet visiting student enrolled in a college course in prehistory archaeology that offers field experience on Earth, with the goal of revealing her real identity after gaining the public recognition of her teachers and classmates. Since she has spent her life exploring and scavenging on Earth while other-worldlies possess only book knowledge, her aptitude for archaeology makes clear the distinct lack of historical awareness in technologically advanced societies on other planets. Yet despite the devastated condition of Earth, it is valued and preserved as the ontological source of humanity, since "[t]he minute you dig deeply into the reasons behind something in modern history, you find yourself back in pre-history. That's where the blood and the bones are" (33). Consequently, Jarra's accumulated knowledge and experience of earth history is seen, in contrast, as a form of competence that her intergalactic classmates lack and desire. Archaeology becomes the unique means for Jarra to feel empowered as a form of rebellion against the system of discrimination.

However, at the end of the novel, Jarra remains a collector of lost remnants of a past that is constantly reproduced and reified as the other inferior life of humanity, which reinforces the arbitrary boundary of speciesism that Jarra initially seeks to overthrow. When Jarra's identity as an Earth-bound human is discovered, instead of standing confidently on her own achievement, she reverts to her old ape-girl identity characterized by anger, bitterness, and helplessness. She breaks down and proclaims, "Yes, I'm an ape, a nean [derivative of Neanderthal], a throwback, and the garbage of the universe. You can call me all the names you like, because I know I deserve them, but you'll just be wasting your breath. I know them already and I've been hearing them all my life" (269). Jarra's display of superior capability as an archaeologist in competition with her classmates from other planets is but a transient moment of empowerment and subversion. It provides the consolatory message that while Jarra is doomed to remain on Earth, home of the handicapped, she is not useless nor unhappy, despite the dystopian image of the survivors navigating "the mounds of rubbles and the blackened skeletal remains of skyscrapers still soaring up into the sky" (50). Consequently, the protagonist's human identity becomes a superficial form of performance centered on Earth's visible past as opposed to the future dream of humanity.

Arguably Jarra could carve out her own place in history on earth as a competent archaeologist, ignoring the biased views associated with her biological heritage. But as the narrative demonstrates, Jarra desires the recognition of the other-worldlies on their terms, which is her primary motive for entering into the archaeological profession. More importantly, she chooses archaeology because her genetic makeup restricts her physical and social mobility. As much as she desires to override her biological limitation using her professional achievement in uncovering earth's past, she cannot escape her biological destiny. Knowing one's past is crucial to exploring humanity's potential because "[h]istory, in a decidedly Platonic manner, is nothing but the presentation in time of the shapes of Spirit as they exist in themselves" (Haar 69). But what the novel reveals is that such confrontation will most likely occur not out of the individual's inclination but out of compulsion. *Earth Girl* portrays the protagonist as an individual who is forced to assess her humanness by approximating her distance to an incomplete, fragmented past, and then assimilating it on a colorless, abandoned Earth.

This approach of capturing the essence of human identity by remembering sheds light on the contradiction of defining the human subject in a post-crisis world. Youths are expected to look forward to the future and the prospect of growing up into able, functioning adults, but at the same time, the bleak reality of ecological ruin characterizes the future as a hopeless place, so they turn their gaze to the past. The futureless child thus acts as the figurative embodiment of "a world that can no longer look forward to a future without apprehension" in order to place our vision of the future "into a painfully distorted perspective" (Földváry 208–9). After all, the recognition of having lost something and the desire to reclaim it can most effectively challenge human complacency and thereby initiate a reconfiguration of the human/nature network. As Daniel Gustav Anderson explains, a historically constructed identity can be conducive to understanding how our actions affect the natural environment; confronting the past illuminates our own embeddedness within social, biological, and ecological "dynamics of need and exploitation" (42). *Earth Girl* thus articulates the warning that in a future when ecological crisis functions as a breaking point for humanity, the young generation should not exploit it as an opportunity to abandon the past. The representation of Jarra as a biologically determined subject seeking out history reveals that if the young adult's human identity is to have any integrity, substance, and reality in a future-less world, the prerequisite is the motivation to think, acknowledge, and respect what the past holds, what it reveals, and what will remain in the future.

## The Tainted, Sympathetic Princess

*Of Beast and Beauty* is similarly set in a future when Earth's resources have been exhausted, creating an apocalyptic scenario that compels humans to abandon Earth and seek out planets for a second home. The novel begins with the omniscient voice of an alien planet, which intuits the arrival of human settlers as an intrusion in its unpopulated lands. Yet the alien planet's sentience welcomes their arrival and triggers evolutionary change in the settlers' biology to help them adapt, perceiving their smooth skin as a sign that they are "soft and unprepared for life on our world" (6). Instead of terraforming the alien planet, as in the case of *Earth Girl*, the settlers on this foreign planet require radical physical, biological, and even neurological transformation to survive. They evolve to adapt, obtaining tough skin, scales, and longer limbs that are antithetical to the cultural construction of normal human appearance, and even though the changes are necessary for their survival, the human settlers continue to identify their adaptive features as degrading and regressive. The colonists build glass domes to protect the unevolved and "pure" humans inside from being influenced by environmental factors and to keep out the transformed "monstrous" humans that now have abnormally large stature, long nails, and scales.

The story of integrating these two populations revolves around Isra, a blind princess who has lived her whole life inside the glass dome. Isra's blindness places the emphasis on the human genome and the material body—its product—as the interface for exploring differences between the self and the environment, childhood and adulthood. Despite her royal status, Isra distinguishes her blindness and "rough, peeling skin" as the defining characteristics of her identity (Jay 13). Due to biological and physical differences, Isra feels isolated and neglected by her people, and her loneliness presses her to seek consolation in what is left of the natural world. Isra acknowledges that she finds comfort in the rose garden, where the planet's sentience manifests itself, for it is where she can sometimes regain her sight via physical contact with the roses. Isra explains: "We must be connected—the thorn and the flesh—for the magic to work. I hold perfectly still until the sharp pain becomes a mean ache, until the blood flowing from my cut eases the hurt away with its warmth. I stay and I breathe and I sigh as, one by one, my eyes open" (18).

The romantic image of human in mutual codependence with nature introduces the notion that the formative experience of being human is fundamentally related to sensing the movement and exchange of organic matter within the ecological network, producing the consciousness of the human body as a form of materiality. Writing about the intersection between ecological thinking and materialism, Jane Bennett observes: "Because the human too is a materiality, it possesses a thing-power of its own. This thing-power sometimes makes itself known as an uneasy feeling of internal resistance, as an alien presence that is uncannily familiar" (361). Thus, in posthumanist terms, the ecological link between Isra and the roses characterizes Isra as a composition of organic matter. The experience makes the protagonist aware that the barrier between the human body and the environment is volatile and permeable, and consequently, sheds light on our embeddedness in a dynamic human/nature assemblage.

Although the scene is meant to denote the restorative function of contacting the natural world, this scene also reveals its troubling side effect on the protagonist's personal boundary. The rose, as the embodiment of nature's darker aspect, leaves a visible imprint of ownership on the protagonist's body by transgressing the barrier that separates the human self from the environment. As a result, Isra's narrative of growth becomes a matter of turning away from nature and toward other human beings. As she falls in love with Gem, a captured outsider, she learns the importance of not judging others based on their physical appearance or biological traits. Her love for Gem finally compels her to sacrifice herself, an act that unites the two species and restores ecological balance to counter the planet's curse, which is initially placed on the human colonists as punishment for their selfishness, bigotry, and abuse of natural resources. Isra constructs a self-identity and a hopeful future separate from her physicality, oppressive social conventions, human biology, and the weight of past human crimes against others more monstrous than she. In the end Isra laments, "How could I have looked into [Gem's] eyes that first night and not seen that we are not only similar creatures but kindred spirits? Not because I am tainted but because we are both human in the same way. The way Needle [Isra's maid] is human and my father—for all his faults—was human" (165). Isra regrets her ignorant discrimination against Gem, indicating that the unifying principle that mends broken humanity can never be scientific empiricism or taxonomy driven by the desire for absolute perfection. Instead, there should be the inclination to look past the physical body and into the depth of the soul to find qualities that unite us rather than divide us.

The narrative's emphasis on Isra's compassion toward others and her self-sacrifice seems jarring in the posthumanist context of her ecological experience. On the one hand, she embraces posthuman hybridity formed in her physiological and material bond with nature; but on the other hand, she values essential humanness with a universal set of qualities and beliefs as the ground for her identity. Isra's advocation of reaching deep within herself to retrieve her own sense of humanness runs counterpoint to Scott Bukatman's denouncement: "The body is no longer simply the repository of the soul; it has become a cyborg body, one element in an endless interface of bio-technologies" (98). In this light Isra's liberal humanist reclamation of identity, which culminates in her transformation into a new species—monstrous without, human within—at the end of the narrative, projects not the radical cyborg vision of Bukatman, but rather, a more consolatory aspect of posthumanism: "The posthuman does not necessitate the obsolescence of the human; it does not represent an evolution or devolution of the human. Rather it participates in redistributions of difference and identity" (Halberstam and Livingston 10). Hence, in comparison to *Earth Girl*, which advocates ontological recovery through history, *Of Beast and Beauty* celebrates the rediscovery of humanness through connection and sympathy. Isra confronts her own monstrosity and internalizes it as a link that connects her to not only the environment but also other human beings. Her acceptance leads to her maturation as a hybridized subject who is connected to her inner life as much as to the natural environment. To be human, in Isra's experience of nature and human contact, is to work with rather than against the web of interdependence, so that the human subject can physically, ecologically, socially, and morally connect with other sentient beings.

## The Resilient, Post-crisis Survivor

*Orleans*, by Sherri L. Smith, describes the post-crisis condition of New Orleans as an ecological hell. Unlike other parts of the United States, New Orleans has been ravaged by a series of hurricanes that fill the city with trash and debris, leaving the city vulnerable to the deadly Delta Fever. To prevent the disease from spreading, the United States Senate withdraws governance, citing, "The shape of our great nation has been altered irrevocably by Nature, and now Man must follow suit in order to protect the inalienable rights of the majority, those being the right to Life, Liberty, and the Pursuit of Happiness, the foremost of those being Life" (7). *Orleans*'s ecological crisis portrays the dehumanizing effect of biopolitics, which reduces man to beast through calculated decrees and abuse of state power. Although the United States declares the preservation of life as the primary aim, the expulsion of Orleans demonstrates that the political conception of life as a totality is an illusion maintained by the few in dominance.

Mary Bunch identifies this type of biopolitical crisis as the turning point that could potentially usher in a posthuman ethics, claiming: "A posthuman ethics is necessary if Agamben is correct in his diagnosis that in modernity, politics has been replaced with biopolitics. Instead of finding a subject at its center, biopolitics circulates around the figure of bare life, signaling a mass dehumanization of populations, and further exacerbating the limits of humanism" (48). *Orleans* demonstrates Bunch's point. Following the aftermath of their expulsion, New Orleans's residents create a new order of biopolitics that redefines human ontology by organizing communities based on blood types. The new biopolitical order is an effective and scientifically sound method because the fever, which devours the host's blood cells, mutates at a faster rate if the host comes into contact with other blood types, so if the authorities reinforce a biopolitical order based on blood types, they succeed in preventing Delta Fever from unpredictable transmutation. However, this tribal system forms a nihilistic picture of Orleans's practice of biological determinism, in which O-Positives and O-Negatives are hunted as commodities because their blood can be transfused into people of all blood types. When the protagonist, Fen, was a young girl still in an orphanage, she was rented out to paying customers who would extract her O-type blood for their own consumption. After Fen burnt her own arms to repulse potential customers, she was raped and discarded as used, useless, and spoiled.

Fueled by her desire to survive, Fen escapes and survives in New Orleans's post-crisis ecology by attuning herself to the natural environment. As she guides Daniel, a visiting scientist in search of a cure, to Mr. Go's hut, Fen exhibits a high level of ecological sensitivity: "We leave the dead forest and move into greenery again. Ain't far now. I smell the water before I see it, heavy with salt and dead leaves" (247). As a human subject who recognizes her own embeddedness in the natural environment, Fen embodies the ecological posthumanist concept that the human is human because it is part of nature, claiming that the forest is "nobody's territory, which makes it everybody's" (247). Her willingness to simply be part of the forest reiterates the ecocritical idea that boundaries of ownership become meaningless when we are willing to recognize that human and nature are indistinguishably enmeshed. Furthermore, her survival based on her ecological sensitivity articulates the hope that it is by reintegrating oneself into the ecosystem that one can have a foretaste of posthumanist reality and thereby be rescued from a state of biopolitical dehumanization and vulnerability. In the same way, Fen picks up the Tribe dialect during her time in the Institute of Post-Separation Studies because, as her father explains, it would offer her a degree of protection in the same way that a chameleon blends in with its surroundings. Consequently, although Fen may no longer be human within the legal institution of the United States, she is able to construct her own human identity based on her ecological embeddedness and openness to adapting to environmental factors, whether they be human or ecological.

Unlike *Of Beast and Beauty* and *Earth Girl*, which accentuate recovery and reclamation, *Orleans* demonstrates the importance of resilience and adaptation when confronted with ecological crisis that threatens to destabilize and dislocate the human subject. Fen relentlessly challenges the New Orleans biopolitical system and appears more ecologically aware than the adults. Her action, lifestyle, and decisions typify a mode of human materiality that is distinctly ecological. It signals the posthumanist desire to "retrieve the body from the dimension of discourse" and to orient the critical gaze on bodily experiences and practices "where 'body' refers not only to the human body but to the concrete entanglements of plural 'natures,' both human and more-than-human" (Iovino and Oppermann 53). Shifting the focus from nature as essence to nature as substance, the narrative strengthens the eco-materialist concept that human identity is inseparable from one's environment, which amplifies the horror of constructing one's identity in a global ecology that is increasingly becoming harmful to the human body.

Despite the hopeful message underscored by Fen's resilience and survival, the narrative ends with the death of its heroine. To ensure Daniel and Enola's safe passage over the wall back to the United States, Fen draws the guards away and ultimately ends up getting shot. Fen goes to her death willingly because she has realized, "I be tired of running and hiding, tired of just trying to survive. How can Orleans be a home if it always trying to kill you? How can it be living if you ain't allowed to live?" (220). Mark S. Jendrysik classifies this type of ecological nihilism as characteristic of deep ecology, which sees humanity as "a planetary disease organism" that destroys the very fabric of our world and thus brings our species closer to the brink of extinction (43). Fen's death certainly seems to align the narrative with the deep ecological thought that humans are malevolent parasites that must be eradicated for nature to survive, which infuses the narrative with the dystopian imagination of a posthuman future in its purest form—a post-world without humanity.

More importantly, Fen's survival and subsequent death raise some troubling aspects of negotiating posthumanist ethics in the biopolitical sphere and demand that the reader rethink terms such as human life, natural life, and especially, life itself. The lack of dignity in Fen's posthuman identity becomes the cause of her downfall. Nick Bostrom claims that in posthumanist terms, dignity "consists in what we are and what we have the potential to become, not in our pedigree or our causal origin" (213). Posthuman dignity extends beyond the level of social recognition and respect and takes on the meaning of faith in biopower and technology to liberate the human subject from the determinism of our own genetic makeup, or in Fen's situation, the limitation of her blood type. So although Fen's ecological embeddedness provides a measure of protection and even a sense of belonging, she finds New Orleans—inclusive of its ecology and its people—inadequate as the formative context of her human identity. Fen is forced to admit that despite her own sense of ecological belonging, living a life persecuted by the State has no dignity and that makes it not worth living. In the end, the state's nullification of her humanness proves too powerful for her as an individual to overcome, truncating her growth and robbing her of her posthuman dignity.

## Realizing the Ecological Posthuman

Out of the three novels, *Orleans* appears the most radical in its formulation of post-natural subjectivity. Both *Earth Girl* and *Of Beast and Beauty* are progressive in the sense that they encourage the reader to imagine futuristic modes of human survival. Realizing that the environment needs to be recovered before the human condition can have a chance of survival, these narratives project a posthumanist vision of ecologically oriented subjectivity characterized by restoration of the past and reclamation of one's inner life. Their heroines are leaders and agents of utopian hope, conveying the romantic notion that eventually the human condition can be recalibrated through the next generation's active negotiation of the relationship between self and nature. As depressing as their post-crisis worlds may seem, images of humans surviving in futuristic ecologies serve as an example of utopian world-making or, rather, world-mending, since as Rebecca Carol Noël Totaro points out, suffering is integral to the creation of utopia as the protagonist moves from suffering to hopeful longing for change and then to action (129). *Orleans*, however, never moves beyond suffering and in the end produces an ecological subject who is forced to endure her own nonhumanness deprived of dignity. Consequently, *Orleans* does not end in a consolatory tone like that of the fairytale ending in *Of Beast and Beauty* because it engages with the problems of being physically located in a precarious biopolitical system and acknowledges that there is something intrinsically unnatural about it. Refusing to identify ecological crisis as a utopian moment of human reconfiguration that normalizes the unnatural, the novel undermines the essentialist human selfhood that *Of Beast and Beauty* restores and the grand narrative of human history that *Earth Girl* seeks to integrate.

The conservatism, consolatory tone, and essential humanist beliefs inherent to *Earth Girl* and *Of Beast and Beauty* may seem counterproductive to articulating radical ecological possibilities that compel readers to reflect on the social, political, and environmental problems of the twenty-first century. Nevertheless, their portrayals of genetic determinism, ecological problematization, and the consequences they have on human identity highlight the need for posthumanist experiences that strive for acceptance of ontological unease and anxiety. Both novels attempt to reconcile the desire for essentialist values and posthumanist practices, with the protagonists becoming hybridized entities marked by nonhuman traits caused by environmental factors without and essentialist human qualities within. But ultimately their preservation of humanness points out the inadequacy of young adult science fiction's posthumanist imaginings of human and nature together, implying that a radical questioning of humanism may not necessarily lead to rebellion and upheaval. These novels remind the reader that in times of crisis, recovery is as important as invention, and that it is only natural and human to be introspective and immerse oneself in one's own mental landscape when the external landscape seems far more precarious. In the end, these ecocritical stories show that there is no right answer to the question of how to be human in an ecology that has become antithetical to humanity.

The novels' cautious attitude could be due to the underlying intent to educate teen readers and to evoke critical reflection on the current state of nature and ecology, because as Jean Webb and Stephen Bigger have observed, although authors are aware that readers do not become environmentally educated by fiction alone, there is still the unspoken acknowledgment of its didactic value as a means of encouraging teen readers to reflect and eventually take action (139–40). By portraying the difficulties and challenges of being human in the midst of environmental crisis, these young adult novels illuminate the fear of becoming unnatural when the planet becomes "vengeful and vitriolic, lashing out at the humans who have engendered widespread ecological devastation" (Curry 40–41). Exposing the direct causality between ecological abnormality and the destabilized ontological boundary between human and nonhuman, *Orleans*, *Earth Girl*, and *Of Beast and Beauty* demonstrate young adult science fiction's posthumanist potential to redefine the human condition according to the changing dynamics of human/nature relationships. By retracing and remapping the human subject into an adaptive organism in destabilized ecology, these futuristic visions of human and environment participate in the ecological posthumanist discourse, which challenges "the false integrity not only of the humanist self but also of the idea of nature as essentially natural, other, elsewhere, or outside" (Taylor 359). Installing an ecocentric awareness as the basis of post-crisis condition, *Earth Girl*, *Of Beast and Beauty*, and *Orleans* call for a more contingent model of processing self/world distinctions, nonhierarchical ontologies, and the absence of boundaries. They also identify with the purpose of critical posthumanism that attends "to the ways in which ideas of the human, nature, and culture continue to work even in accounts which suggest their implosion" (Castree and Nash 502). That is to say, the YA as a liminal subject, between childhood and adulthood, operates as a posthuman construct that embodies the ambivalence of relying on natural self/world and mind/body distinctions when nature itself is at risk.

## Conclusion

While these three young adult futuristic novels are only a sample of young adult science fiction's representations of ecological change, collectively they identify environmental crisis as an inevitable threat to the young adult's realization of a unique, innate self and the material boundaries that separate the self from its natural environment. All three novels identify environmental phenomena, such as the complete destruction of nature in *Earth Girl*, seismic hurricanes in *Orleans*, or *Of Beast and Beauty*'s rendition of evolution as mutation, as the challenge to young adults' subjectivity construction, generating the human/nonhuman divide that robs the young adult of human rights, values, and identity. Each protagonist responds to her nonhuman position in an unnatural ecosystem differently: *Earth Girl* emphasizes the young adult's retrospective turn to past knowledge, *Of Beast and Beauty* deals with the importance of making a connection between the essentialist self and the nonhuman Other, and *Orleans* demonstrates the importance of adapting to one's material surroundings by tuning one's body to its natural environment. *Of Beast and Beauty* is the most environmentally friendly, suggesting that the recovery of a human identity is derived from the individual's desire to reconcile with nature and ecology, while *Orleans* appears radical and dystopian in its rendition of the YA's material embeddedness and subsequent defeat by the state's biopolitical power. In contrast, *Earth Girl* seems almost tragically antithetical to the ecocritical thought of reconciling with nature, since its narrative promotes the importance of establishing an essentialist human self in a world characterized by loss and ruins while ambivalently portraying the YA as a futureless posthuman. These novels convey three distinct responses to the question of what it means to be human in a post-crisis world and subsequently bring the relationship between human and nature to the foreground because it has the power to transform our material existence, our supposedly secure ontological boundaries, our world orders, our definition of humanity, and our future survival.

## Works Cited

Anderson, Daniel Gustav. "Natura Naturans and the Organic Ecocritic: Toward a Green Theory of Temporality." *Journal of Ecocriticism* 4.2 (2012): 34–47. Web. 1 Dec. 2014.

Bennett, Jane. "The Force of Things: Steps toward an Ecology of Matter." *Political Theory* 32.3 (2004): 347–72. JSTOR. Web. 2 Dec. 2014.

Bostrom, Nick. "In Defense of Posthuman Dignity." *Bioethics* 19.3 (2005): 202–14. *Wiley Online Library*. Web. 23 Apr. 2016.

Bradford, Clare, Kerry Mallan, John Stephens, and Robyn McCallum. *New World Orders in Contemporary Children's Literature: Utopian Transformations*. Basingstoke: Palgrave Macmillan, 2008. Print. Critical Approaches to Children's Literature.

Braidotti, Rosi. *The Posthuman*. Cambridge: Polity, 2013. Print.

Bukatman, Scott. "Postcards from the Posthuman Solar System." *Posthumanism*. Ed. Neil Badmington. New York: Palgrave, 2000. 98–111. Print.

Bunch, Mary. "Posthuman Ethics and the Becoming Animal of Emmanuel Levinas." *Culture, Theory and Critique* 55:1 (2013): 34–50. *Taylor & Francis Online*. Web. 23 Apr. 2016.

Carroll, Jane Suzanne. *Landscape in Children's Literature*. New York: Routledge, 2011. Print. Children's Literature and Culture 84.

Castree, Noel, and Catherine Nash. "Posthuman Geographies." *Social & Cultural Geography* 7.4 (2006): 501–4. *Taylor & Francis Online*. Web. 1 Jan. 2015.

Chiew, Florence. "Posthuman Ethics with Cary Wolfe and Karen Barad: Animal Compassion as Trans-Species Entanglement." *Theory, Culture & Society* 31.4 (2014): 51–69. *SAGE Journals Online*. Web. 2 Apr. 2016.

Curry, Alice. *Environmental Crisis in Young Adult Fiction: A Poetics of Earth*. Basingstoke: Palgrave Macmillan, 2013. Print.

Dewan, Pauline. *The Art of Place in Literature for Children and Young Adults: How Locale Shapes a Story*. New York: Edwin Mellen P, 2010. Print.

Edwards, Janet. *Earth Girl*. London: HarperCollins, 2012. Print.

Földváry, Kinga. "In Search of a Lost Future: The Posthuman Child." *European Journal of English Studies* 18.2 (2014): 207–20. *Taylor & Francis Online*. Web. 17 Dec. 2014.

Haar, Michel. *The Song of the Earth: Heidegger and the Grounds of the History of Being*. Bloomington: Indiana UP, 1993. Print.

Halberstam, Judith, and Ira Livingston. "Introduction: Posthuman Bodies." *Posthuman Bodies*. Ed. Judith Halberstam and Ira Livingston. Bloomington: Indiana UP, 1995. 1–19. Print.

Iovino, Serenella, and Serpil Oppermann. "Material Ecocriticism: Materiality, Agency, and Models of Narrativity." *Ecozon@: European Journal of Literature* 3.1 (2012): 75–91. Web. 22 June 2016.

Jaques, Zoe. *Children's Literature and the Posthuman: Animal, Environment, Cyborg*. London: Routledge, 2013. Print. Children's Literature and Culture 102.

Jay, Stacey. *Of Beast and Beauty*. New York: Random House, 2013. Print.

Jendrysik, Mark S. "Back to the Garden: New Visions of Posthuman Futures." *Utopian Studies* 22.1 (2011): 34–51. *JSTOR*. Web. 26 May 2014.

McCallum, Robyn. *Ideologies of Identity in Adolescent Fiction*. New York: Garland, 1999. Print.

Mendlesohn, Farah. "Is There Any Such Thing as Children's Science Fiction?: A Position Piece." *Lion and the Unicorn* 28.2 (2004): 284–313. *Project Muse*. Web. 2 June 2014.

Nayar, Pramod. *Posthumanism*. Cambridge: Polity, 2014. Print.

Ostry, Elaine. "'Is He Still Human? Are You?': Young Adult Science Fiction in the Posthuman Age." *Lion and the Unicorn* 28.2 (2004): 222–46. *Project Muse*. Web. 15 Jan. 2014.

Smith, Sherri L. *Orleans*. London: Penguin, 2013. Print.

Taylor, Matthew A. "The Nature of Fear: Edgar Allan Poe and Posthuman Ecology." *American Literature* 84.2 (2012): 353–79. *Duke University Press Journals Online.* Web. 15 Dec. 2014.

Totaro, Rebecca Carol Noel. "Suffering in Utopia: Testing the Limits in Young Adult Novels." *Utopian and Dystopian Writing for Children and Young Adults.* Ed. Carrie Hintz and Elaine Ostry. New York: Routledge, 2003. 127–38. Print. Children's Literature and Culture 29.

Webb, Jean, and Stephen Bigger. "Developing Environmental Agency and Engagement through Young People's Fiction." *Experiencing Environment and Place through Children's Literature.* Ed. Amy Cutter-Mackenzie, Phillip G. Payne, and Alan Reid. New York: Routledge, 2011. 131–44. Print.

Westfahl, Gary. *Science Fiction, Children's Literature, and Popular Culture: Coming of Age in Fantasyland.* Westport: Greenwood P, 2000. Print.

Wolfe, Cary. *What Is Posthumanism?* Minneapolis: U of Minnesota P, 2010. Print.

# PART IV
## ACCEPTING/REJECTING POSTHUMANIST POSSIBILITIES

# 10

# NEGOTIATING THE HUMAN IN RIDLEY SCOTT'S *PROMETHEUS*

*Torsten Caeners*

Although Ridley Scott's 2012 film *Prometheus* is, at first glance, not designed for a typical young adult audience (the film received an R rating in the United States but 15 rating in Great Britain), it has been readily available to all audiences on American cable networks for several years. On closer examination, we can see that it focuses on one of the major themes of young adult fiction, namely, the mostly conflicted journey of finding one's identity, in the characters of the android David and the scientist Elizabeth Shaw. The film tackles the question of what it means to become human from a wide variety of perspectives, including but not limited to gender, religion, technology, artificial intelligence, reproduction, and evolution. As these topics are negotiated through the characters and their respective journeys, they become cyphers for specifically young adult concerns of coming of age, especially body issues, parental conflicts, and processes of individuation and identity consolidation.

In *Prometheus*, the search for a self-sufficient, grown-up identity separate from that of the parents is handled allegorically but centrally by means of the fundamental science fiction and posthumanist elements of the film. Indeed, Stefan Herbrechter considers "science fiction as the posthumanist genre *par excellence*, not just on the basis of content, however, but also because of the role it plays within the formation of a techno-posthumanist and technocultural imaginary" (113). The basic premise of the film, to travel to a distant star system in a search for the so-called Engineers as the creators of human life, is a quest to find humanity, but to find it elsewhere, outside of the received boundaries of the human condition. This search for humanity elsewhere is essentially a posthumanist gesture in the sense that a critical posthumanism "represents a radicalization and at the same time a 'relocation' of the human that transcends any dialectical historicization" (Herbrechter 199). The spatial displacement of the film's main characters from the known Earth to a distant and unknown world simultaneously represents a narrative representation of the paradoxical pubescent desire to leave home and the accompanying fear of the unknown, as well as the notion of the philosophical and theoretical relocation that is central to a critical posthumanism. The science-fiction plot of the film *Prometheus* thus allows for a physical "'relocation' of the human" that manifests the conceptual relocation suggested by posthumanist theory and the social as well as psychological ambivalences of young adulthood.

With regard to posthumanism, the genre of science fiction thus not only constitutes a passive mode of representation congenial to posthumanism, but also plays an active role in its continuing formation. Via a process of interactive mirroring back, it constitutes a

> form of consciousness that aims to depict scientific and technological transformation "realistically" and thus discusses the questions of probability and "realizability" with their associated problems of teleology, or inevitably, ontology and ethics.... Science fiction visualizes the dissolution of ontological foundations like the distinction between the organic and inorganic, masculine and feminine, original and copy, natural and artificial, human and nonhuman, etc., and thus serves as a reflection of our science fictional everyday life. (Herbrechter 116–17)

Science fiction thus proves to be an especially congenial medium to stage posthumanist transformations in relation to reality and "realizability" since it has always been at the core a genre about extrapolation, about transforming current knowledge into a possible vision of the future. Science fiction tends to tap into emerging cultural discourses and processes and project those into a futuristic extrapolation of today, thereby foregrounding and critically evaluating emerging discourses and processes.

Within this context, the film *Prometheus* immediately puts "the human" on trial by means of radically questioning its received origin and thereby relocating it outside the traditional notions of humanity. The film chronicles the scientific expedition to a distant planet, led by archaeologists Dr. Elizabeth Shaw and Dr. Charlie Holloway. Their belief that alien beings they have termed "Engineers" created humanity by inserting their DNA into Earth's biosphere in primordial times has persuaded the Weyland Corporation to finance the expedition. Unbeknownst to Shaw and Holloway, Weyland himself is on board the ship, a secret passenger, his goal being to gain immortality from the Engineers. At first, Shaw and Holloway's beliefs are confirmed when they reach the planet and find a 2,000-year-old alien spaceship holding still-recognizable remains of the Engineers. But when the android David awakens an Engineer from cryosleep, the alien indiscriminately kills Weyland and most of the away team. Additionally, a bioweapon in the form of a black liquid is set free in the course of the story, infecting and eventually killing other members of the expedition. The rogue Engineer restarts the alien ship and sets a course for Earth, intent on destroying humanity; the Engineer is stopped when the remaining crew of the *Prometheus* undertakes a suicide run and flies into the alien ship, causing it to crash-land on the surface. In a final confrontation with the Engineer, Elizabeth Shaw, sole human survivor of the expedition, tricks the Engineer into falling prey to another alien creature. Shaw and David take off in another alien vessel in search of the Engineers' homeworld.

The introduction of the alien Engineers as possible creators of human life puts into question two received notions of constructing the human: the Darwinian theory of evolution and the Christian story of creation. The indeterminacy that results from destabilizing these two major concepts precludes a dialectical bipolarity of human/nonhuman and "suggest[s] a posthuman world of ontological fluidity at hand. Identities . . . are fluid, forms are open to change and modulate, often seamlessly[,] . . . into each other" (Nayar 55). From within this fluid space, finding a new mode of humanity necessarily entails a radical redefinition by means of a continuous transformation and adaptation, and within this framework, humanity and identity are constantly questioned, deconstructed, reconstructed, effaced, and even negated. A posthumanist identity is not merely characterized by "ontological fluidity" but indeed defined by it. This is equally true of young adult identities, which are decentered in moving between childhood and adulthood. Negotiating these fluid conceptual spaces, the film oscillates on various levels between posthumanist possibility and (pubescent) angst caused by the loss of established humanist fixtures.

The ambivalence between new possibilities and angst is thus a central element that links posthumanism and adolescence in the film. The question of what it means to be human in an increasingly posthuman world is closely linked to the question of what it means to become an adult and associated adolescent, ambivalent processes of transformation, adaptation, and growing up. Analogous to adolescence, which is in between childhood and adulthood, both and neither simultaneously, so posthumanism

> comes both before and after humanism: before in the sense that it names the embodiment and embeddedness of the human being in not just its biological but also its technological world, . . . after in the sense that posthumanism names a historical moment in which the decentering of the human by its imbrication in technical, medical, informatic, and economic networks is increasingly difficult to ignore. (Wolfe xv)

The posthumanist condition is thus characterized by in-between-ness and a loss of conceptual borders. Definitions of what it means to be human based on humanist notions no longer suffice to adequately describe the present human condition. The lines separating the human from the Other are no longer clear-cut.

This changing condition is most obviously represented in the film by the Engineers, who physically embody these blurred borders. The Engineers are unnerving to look at. They appear very human, but at the same time, they exhibit some distinctly nonhuman qualities. With their perfectly textured muscles, they evoke Hellenistic notions of the aesthetically perfect male body—and like Prometheus of Greek myth, who stole fire from the gods and gave it to the humans so that they could survive, the Engineer in the opening scene of the film gives the gift of human DNA to Earth. The Engineers' greyish skin and the bone structure of their heads and faces clearly betray them as alien. They register as human, but as a different humanity, like the Titans of Greek myth. They seem superhuman and much like the Olympian Gods: their bodies inhuman in their perfection and unpredictable in their actions. The Engineers embody an aesthetically pleasing and interesting form of humanity, but one that must be characterized as simultaneously superhuman and nonhuman. This ambivalence circumscribes the relation between the crew as human beings and the Engineers as representations of a still-alien posthumanity.

The relationship between the human crew of the *Prometheus* and the Engineers is essentially one of children to their parents; the hopes projected onto the Engineers and the paradoxical familiar strangeness of their appearance mirror the adolescent's ambivalent view of adults and adulthood. This double signification of humanity's creators as both posthuman creatures and fathers mirrors the double image of adolescents' parents, for during adolescence, parents exist both as idealized role models and rejected Other. Faced with the Engineers, humanity is forced into a process of transformation in which the old is deemed insufficient and a new identity is constantly tested. This process also characterizes the notion of coming of age in the sense of the transformation from child to adult. For a young adult audience, the conflicts that play out in the plot of the film in terms of its science fiction/posthumanist elements also represent conflicts that an adolescent viewer knows firsthand from daily experience. As a major Hollywood science fiction film, *Prometheus* certainly appeals greatly to a young adult audience. Since young adults are usually more intimately in touch with the newest technological and cultural transformations, many elements of young adults' "science fictional everyday life" (Herbrechter 117) resonate with what is depicted in the film. When it comes to young adult science fiction and media, Elaine Ostry notes that these focus on "the search for identity and sense of self, the formation of new peer groups, resistance to adult control, decision making, growth and adaptation, and the challenge of hierarchies" (223). *Prometheus* negotiates virtually all of these aspects on various levels simultaneously and interconnectedly. It creates a dynamic space linking posthumanism and adolescence that is able to suggest possible answers to both the questions of what it means to be human and what it means to grow up in a postmodern world defined more and more by the technological and the virtual rather than direct human interaction. In posing questions such as "Where do we come from?," "What will we become?," and "Whom should we look up to?," the film chronicles processes of adolescent and posthuman redefinition and associated struggles of identity.

On the whole, *Prometheus* expresses as a governing metaphor the need to redefine human identity through processes of transformation. The key concept that links science fiction and adolescence is thus transformation: the film simultaneously stages and conflates processes of adolescent identity formation and posthumanist evolution. In light of this, I will retrace the dynamic posthumanist negotiations and transformations of often contradictory notions of humanity and identity in the context of the complexities associated with coming of age. The palimpsestuously interpenetrating layers that permeate the plot will be dealt with by concentrating on the relationship between the Engineers (parents, creators) and humanity (children, adolescents). This relationship is embodied most clearly and dramatically through the characters of Elizabeth Shaw (a young woman who still struggles with adolescent issues) and David (an adolescent posthuman) and their interrelations. With Shaw and David, *Prometheus* offers two characters (one female and one male) with whom a young adult audience can identify easily, thus facilitating an emotional investment in these characters. In this way, young adults partake in the conflicts of Shaw and David—conflicts that are essentially adolescent negotiations of identity. In the end, these processes of transformation and identity construction in and between Shaw and David mark humanity and identity as concepts in flow, non-concepts basically, which represent the state of what it currently means to be human and what it means to be an adolescent in a posthuman world: to constantly adapt, shift, change, and question one's received notions of identity. Posthumanity and adolescence coalesce and become indistinguishable. The postmodern human condition, or posthumanity, that emerges from the film can be defined as one of continuous adolescence.

## Adolescent Regression and Posthuman Fixation: The Case of Elizabeth Shaw

*Prometheus* stages the convergences between posthumanity and adolescence globally by means of the relationship between humanity and the Engineers.

Within the film's mythology, humanity represents the offspring of the Engineers; it is a relationship of creation to origin, which, however, is not cast in a straightforward, unproblematic manner. Rather, it is a relationship defined by unsubstantiated hope, misunderstandings, and unanswered questions on the side of humanity. The humans in the film are in an adolescent position: independent, but still seeking answers from their creators to the big questions of life. This overall theme is encoded on various metaphorical and symbolic levels throughout the film; most vividly, however, it is embodied by the character of Elizabeth Shaw. She serves as one major screen for projecting posthumanist and adolescent concepts and processes as her strong desire to get answers is rooted in the tragic events of her adolescence. Shaw lost both her parents at an early age, which leaves her struggling with unresolved adolescent issues of parental control and dependence.

At the beginning of the film, the android David takes a glimpse into Elizabeth Shaw's dream world while he supervises her cryosleep. He witnesses what is a memory of an adolescent Elizabeth seeking answers to questions about death and the afterlife from her father. Seeing a funeral procession pass by, daughter and father have the following exchange:

ELIZABETH: Where do they go?
FATHER: Everyone has their own word . . . heaven, paradise; whatever it's called, it's some place beautiful.
ELIZABETH: How do you know it's beautiful?
FATHER: 'Cause that's what I choose to believe.

This conversation shows that young Elizabeth is not satisfied with simple answers; she craves more complex and nuanced explanations. Her father's simple statement that the afterlife is a beautiful place is felt to be insufficient, in need of further explication. This, in turn, implies that the parental authority of her father as the ultimate or only giver of knowledge about life is no longer enough for her.

Elizabeth exhibits a critical and fledglingly independent adolescent personality rather than that of a dependent and docile child content with accepting everything her father says at face value. In an adolescent manner, she is testing her own rational abilities against her father's. It is not enough for Elizabeth anymore that her father states that heaven is a beautiful place. She demands proof: "How do you know it's beautiful?" Elizabeth seeks to know where her father derives his knowledge. She wants to know where adult knowledge comes from in order to gain access to it herself, to become an adult herself. In response to Elizabeth, her father takes recourse to an even higher parental authority than himself, that is, faith and, by metonymic connection, the Christian God ("'Cause that's what I choose to believe"). Elizabeth's father is a Christian missionary in Africa, so it is no surprise that he would refer to faith as the ultimate source of knowledge. From Elizabeth's perspective, however, he refers her to another parental instance that, firstly, simply provides another passive form of knowledge that Elizabeth is expected to believe in without further proof and, secondly, as religious dogma, requires complete subjugation under its law so that she would trade one form of dependence for another. Since her father does not provide answers that are helpful to Elizabeth in her adolescent state, she is caught in a conflict: she cannot fully reject her father and his beliefs because she is not yet an adult, and at the same time, she knows that she needs to know more and go beyond her father. As is revealed later in the story, Shaw's father died of Ebola, leaving her an orphan. Her father's death cuts short her adolescent development toward adult independence, prohibiting a solution to the adolescent conflict, which is carried over into biological adulthood, where it is perpetuated as a conflict between her desire for scientific objectivity and her father's insistence on faith/god as a subjective choice. Consequently, her father's faith is something Elizabeth cannot let go of because it would mean letting go of what remains of him.

Her continued adolescent dependence on her dead father is based on unresolved grief and nonacceptance of his death, which results in an inherently unstable identity that is characterized by repeated recourse to adolescent patterns. Although the exact circumstances remain unknown, it becomes clear that Shaw has never fully worked through the grief associated with her father's death. As Sigmund Freud notes, following the death of a loved person, "the existence of the lost object is psychically prolonged" until the work of mourning, which is time consuming, has detached the emotions connected to the dead person and freed these emotional ties for new attachments. However, Freud adds, "This path is blocked in melancholia" ("Mourning" 257). If the process of mourning is, for whatever reason, not successful, what remains is an artificially continued attachment to the lost object, a fixture on the dead person. The fact that Shaw has never truly let go of her father is symbolically signified by the cross she wears around her neck for most of the film. The cross belonged to her father, and the Christian symbol emphasizes her continued adolescent dependence on her dead father and his faith. Since Shaw is unable to emancipate herself from her late father, she retains her imaginary relationship to him as an artificial adolescent fixture in her adult life.

Jacques Derrida notes that to learn to think outside the established borders of Western metaphysics, that is, to emancipate oneself from a discursive structure that is safe but at the same time constricting, one has "to renounce the *epistēmē* which absolutely requires, which is the absolute requirement that we go back to the source, to the center, to the founding basis, to the principle, and so on" (286). Elizabeth's father represents the source (he is literally where she comes from); he is the center, the *epistēmē* she cannot renounce. This continued dependence on her father and the concepts that defined his identity means she is caught in a perpetual state of adolescence. Judging from Shaw's behavior in the film, this perpetual state of adolescence is not immediately visible, nor does it, at first glance, appear to affect her adult life negatively. In fact, one might argue that her thesis about the Engineers represents a movement beyond the center, beyond the *epistēmē*. When the crew of the *Prometheus* is briefed on their mission and Shaw and Holloway reveal their theory about the Engineers, resident biologist/zoologist Milburn exclaims, "Do you have anything to back that up? I mean, look, if you're willing to discount three centuries of Darwinism that's . . . buuuh. But how do you know?" His strong reaction clearly shows the radical and groundbreaking nature of Shaw's thesis. It is a renunciation of the established structures of the Darwinian paradigm. In a sense, thus, she has taken the adult step away from old securities into an independent if dangerous world and appears to have abandoned the need for sources and structure. Her thesis is unproven, and as David shrewdly notes, "That's why we call it a thesis."

Shaw counters Milburn's scientific skepticism, his scientific demand for objectivity ("But how do you know?"), via her father's recourse to faith, replying, "I don't. But it's what I choose to believe." Thus, challenged by Milburn, she takes recourse to a known "founding basis," that is, her father, and speaks in his voice, which is the voice of faith. At this moment, she regresses back to her adolescent self. Shaw's recourse to her father signifies that she is still dependent on her personal "founding basis," her father. On second thought, therefore, it becomes clear that, while Shaw may have renounced the Darwinian paradigm, she vehemently upholds another paradigm, that of her father and the Christian faith. In essence, she has not renounced *the* paradigm, i.e., the need for paradigms in general, but only let go of one paradigm and exchanged it for another. Thus, her fixture on centers—her need for certainty—remains, and she has never truly renounced the *epistēmē*.

Derrida notes that structure and fixtures "must be thought of as a series of substitutions of center for center, as a linked chain of determinations of the center. Successively, and in a regulated fashion, the center receives different forms or names" (279). While Shaw has abandoned the Darwinian paradigm, she upholds that of her father, which means that she substitutes "center for center" as the fixture of her life, as becomes clear in the discussion that Shaw and Holloway have in Shaw's quarters after they have discovered the dead Engineer:

SHAW: Their genetic material predates ours. We come from them.
HOLLOWAY: You're kidding me.
SHAW: No.
HOLLOWAY: I guess you can take your father's cross off now.
SHAW: Why would I wanna do that?
HOLLOWAY: Because they made us.
SHAW: And who made them?

Holloway suggests she take off the cross because, for him, the genetic, scientific proof that humanity comes from the Engineers invalidates the Christian story of creation. Shaw, however, cannot abandon the idea of God and the associated paradigm of human creation, but simply extends it to the Engineers ("And who made them?"): God created the Engineers so that they could create humanity. The paradigm—her father's paradigm—remains in effect.

In light of Shaw's stated beliefs, her renunciation of Darwinism no longer constitutes such a radical move after all. In fact, it signifies the desire for a fixed center. Shaw's vision of a fixed center paradoxically draws on and alternates between faith and science and thus between adolescence and adulthood. Shaw replaces the notion of God with the notion of scientific theory, which is in turn represented by the Engineers. Her father represents God metonymically (or, in Freudian terms, via displacement) as much as the Engineers represent science via the same process. The Engineers thus simultaneously represent three alleged fixtures—her father, God, and science—none of which is truly stable. The Engineers are constructed here as simultaneously a scientific thesis and an object of faith; they represent, as a posthuman signifier, the paradoxical possibility to go beyond the father without giving up the father, to retain the human in the posthuman, to be child and adult at the same time. In this manner, the Engineers function as the primary signifier of notions of posthumanity and adolescence.

The paradoxical possibility embodied by the Engineers gestures toward a space beyond the *epistēmē*. This is a space Shaw is unable to inhabit, however, because she needs the Engineers to represent each of the three fixtures fully and unequivocally. Nevertheless, this is exactly what is impossible within the structural thinking of the *epistēmē*. Thus, rather than giving up her need for centers, she constantly and repetitively regresses to her childhood self and associated parental dependence. By literally speaking in her father's voice, she fully subjects herself to the law that Jacques Lacan and Julia Kristeva denote as *the symbolic*:

> The symbolic function is . . . dissociated from all pleasure, made to oppose it, and is set up as the paternal place, the place of the superego. According to this view, the only way to react against the consequences of repression imposed by the compulsion

of the pleasure principle is to renounce pleasure through symbolization by setting up the sign through the absence of the object, which is expelled and lost forever. (Kristeva 149)

Shaw sets up the sign of the Engineers, itself metonymically a representation of god and science, for the lost object, which is her father.

In his essay "The Future of an Illusion," Freud bases the human need for religion on the essentially contingent nature of life, the helplessness of human beings against the constant possibility of death. Culture counters this fear by anthropomorphizing it as, for instance, in the Greek gods. In this form, the gods can be reasoned with through prayer and sacrifice, and humanity can reduce anxieties by living in the false belief that some form of control over chance can be achieved. Incidentally, Freud links this to the infantile and adolescent frame of mind: "One had reason to fear [one's parents], and especially one's father; and yet one was sure of his protection against the dangers one knew. [Humanity] makes the forces of nature not simply into persons... but he gives them the character of a father. He turns them into gods" ("The Future" 17). Freud emphasizes the conceptual proximity of the father and the concept of gods, a proximity that facilitates Shaw's adolescent regression to the fixture of her father identified with religion and god. In a way, Shaw's entire thesis about the Engineers utilizes conceptualizations that are, following Freud, implicated with infantile and adolescent states of development. She has literally turned the forces of nature (Darwin's theory of evolution) into persons, the Engineers.

As noted before, for Shaw the Engineers work as a center for both science and faith and are also symbolically a representation of her father. When Shaw encounters external difficulties (Milburn's Darwinian argument), she immediately regresses to the original fixture of her father's belief to defend her other representation of her father, the Engineers. Freud notes with regard to regression that "the stronger the fixations on its path of development, the more readily will the function evade external difficulties by regressing to the fixations" ("Lecture XXII" 341). Shaw's reaction becomes even more apparent when one refers to Lacan's definition of regression: "regression shows nothing other than a return to the present of signifiers used in demands for which there is prescription" ("The Direction" 194). The words of her father that she quotes are the "present of signifiers" that also make present again the associated "demands for which there is prescription." She enacts a regressive, adolescent pattern of her adult personality. In this context, Freud notes that "a return to the objects first cathected by the libido ... are of an incestuous nature" ("Lecture XXII" 341). For Lacan, demand is always a demand for love, and the love of her father is precisely what Shaw is still craving. By speaking in his voice, she upholds and brings into the living present the imaginary, melancholic relation to her dead father. This demand for paternal love prevents her from becoming a fully independent adult. Lacan notes further, "Regression is simply the actualization in the discourse of the phantasy relations reconstituted by an *ego* at each stage in the decomposition of its structure. After all, this regression is not real; even in language it manifests itself only by inflections, by turns of phrase, by '*trébuchements si légiers*'" ("The Function and Field" 33). Shaw appropriates the phrase of her father and, by doing so, actualizes the "phantasy relations" to her father while simultaneously projecting them onto the as-yet imaginary Engineers. The demand for the love of her dead father can no longer be answered, but it is now directed toward the Engineers. As with her father, she desperately wants answers from them. Relations both to her father and to the Engineers remain firmly within "the absolute requirement that we go back to the source" (Derrida 381), which figures a position of dependence and attachment. Thus the "regressive tendency . . . is not just a relapse into infantilism, but an attempt to get at something necessary . . . , the universal feeling of childhood innocence, the sense of security, of protection, of reciprocated love, of trust" (Jung 32). These things are all necessary for a successful maturation, but things the early death of her parents prohibited her from experiencing, keeping her caught in the state of adolescence.

The adolescent conflict that remains as part of her self also affects her adult identity as a scientist. Her juvenile concern with the afterlife that reemerges with her father's words and her scientific concern with the Engineers are conflated. Both her original question to her father and her question concerning the Engineers deal with the in-between process of transformation. The first question directed to her father asked what a human being becomes after death, after it ceases to be human, so in essence, what the transformation into a posthuman existence entails; the second question addressing the Engineers is directed backwards, seeking to know what transformations led to the current state of humanity. Adolescence and posthumanity are thus linked and staged as processes of transformation, of in-between-ness, which are defined by development and change. Shaw is also in between, but she is not in constant transformation. Hers is precisely not a process of development or of a liminal adolescent in-between-ness. Victor Turner defines liminality as representing "the midpoint of transition in a status-sequence between two positions" (237). In the context of the above, adolescence is a liminal state in that the young adult inhabits a transformative middle position—a liminal space—that leads from childhood to full adulthood. The in-between-ness Elizabeth inhabits is different. Her inability to let go of her childhood dependence on her father is based on her fixed state of adolescence that does not develop into another state, adulthood. Her fixture on her dead father functions like a tether that keeps her from moving onward into full adulthood. Hence, there is no transformative development, and she remains dependent on the center in whatever substituted form. Shaw thus statically resides between two states, childhood and adulthood, while inhabiting neither. There is no transformation from one into the other.

I will now continue to show the interrelations between Shaw's adolescent fixation and the Engineers in the context of how the film stages the conflation of adolescence and posthumanism on a more general plane. The Engineers represent modes of constructing humanity through transformation, which enter into a dynamic process of negotiation that underpins the plot of the entire film. In the Engineers, different modes of constructing humanity merge and are conceptually transformed into each other. The representation of the Engineers as uncanny versions of the Greek gods transplants Shaw's idiosyncratic regressive adolescence onto the global stage of the film as a whole. The Engineers simultaneously replace Darwin and God, representing both and effacing neither. When it comes to Shaw, the faith she has inherited from her father serves as the staging ground for her continued struggle of adolescence. The two paradigms that Elizabeth Shaw so vehemently (and ultimately vainly) strives to keep separate and distinct, in order to be able to achieve a transformation from one into the other, are always already blurred, suggesting a humanity and a posthumanity, a childhood and an adulthood, that are always already indistinguishable. This blurring is dramatically staged at the very beginning of the film with a camera flight over a rough landscape of primordial Earth. Although there are plants, no animals of any kind are visible. The Earth is void of any higher life forms. Finally, the camera pans upwards and overlooks a giant lake where the Engineers' ship can be seen hovering above the water. The image of the hovering ship is an allusion to Genesis 1:2: "And the earth was without form, and void; and darkness was upon the face of the deep. And the Spirit of God moved upon the face of the waters." The spirit of God takes form as a technological machine, a tech-God so to speak. This image is then immediately followed by a perfectly muscled Engineer who drinks a bio-engineered liquid. As a consequence, his body disintegrates and falls into the waterfall in what constitutes a ritualistic act of self-sacrifice in order to insert his DNA into Earth's biosphere. In this scene, the Judeo-Christian story of creation is not only conflated with pagan rituals of self-sacrifice and myth, but also inscribed with a technological, scientific element.[1] Conceptual and dogmatic boundaries are erased and become fluid. This fluidity decenters the status of essential humanist concepts throughout the film, most specifically those of belief and science, human and creature, and creation and creator.

The unpredictability of science, a science that conjures the specter of a posthumanist future, is given physical form in the Engineers, as gods, creators, father-figures with the Freudian double function of offering protection and threatening death. Humanity in the film has to negotiate this double possibility, a task that once again evokes the adolescent position with regard to the parents. Eventually, one has to face the threatening father in order to become independent and to come of age. In facing the father, however, the protection offered is also renounced, and one is forced to face the dangers of the world alone. With the discovery of the Engineers, humanity is forced to discard the alleged truth of their evolutionary development and to redefine themselves as partly Other. With the Engineers, *Prometheus* provides an embodiment of the unregulated and unpredictable changes implicit in the notion of the posthuman by taking regressive recourse to an imagined origin in a technological-posthuman act of creation. The Engineers are posthuman in the sense that they are *beyond* the human, but they are also the origin of our humanity and thus posthumanity is always already an essential part of humanity.

## Posthuman Impregnation: Redefining the Borders of the Human

The processes of transformation, change, and adaptation that characterize adolescence and posthumanism are also effectively staged in *Prometheus* by means of destabilizing the alleged borders of the human body. Again, the character of Elizabeth Shaw is at the center of this destabilization. These processes of transformation are negotiated through an investigation of the borders between human and nonhuman, an intimate encounter with the posthuman Other that simultaneously figures the adolescent encounter with the sexual Other. This encounter and conflation of human and Other is depicted by means of the alien creature that Shaw finds growing inside her body.

Following the first expedition into the Engineers' ship, Holloway visits Shaw in her quarters after he has previously been infected with a liquid from the Engineers' cargo hold. Shaw and Holloway have intercourse, which results in an unexpected pregnancy. Shaw has been diagnosed as infertile, a truth which is negated when she discovers that she has been impregnated with nonhuman DNA. Shaw cannot "humanly" become pregnant, but trans-species impregnation is able to transgress the limits of the human body. Precisely because it is a trans-human pregnancy, however, it constitutes an unwanted, alienating pregnancy, which is an issue specifically relevant for young adults. Shaw suddenly and unexpectedly finds herself faced with the truth that she cannot trust her own body. In adolescence, the body is perceived as partly Other because the physical transformations during puberty turn the body into a part of oneself that is no longer fully controllable. Shaw finds herself in the same position: her pregnancy constitutes a betrayal of her body. The dissolution of human boundaries via the posthuman notion of trans-species reproduction here begets adolescent uncertainty and angst. When Holloway impregnates her, he quite literally implants the Other in Shaw's body. Shaw's pregnancy thus symbolizes the Otherness that requires integration both in adolescent as well as in posthumanist terms.

In Shaw's case, the Otherness is especially multilayered. As a man, Holloway represents one side of the traditional binary woman/man, but he has himself been infected with alien DNA by the android David. Consequently, when he impregnates Shaw, he already carries an Otherness with him that goes beyond the traditionally conceived Otherness of the binary woman/man, a binary of X and Y that is essential for the creation of new human life. When David slips some of the Engineers' black liquid into Holloway's drink,[2] Holloway is in the traditional female position as the receiving vessel, thus taking on the function of his sexual Other. David, as an artificial life form, takes on the role of the active part, the traditional male pole, in what is effectively a moment of posthuman intercourse and creation. As an artificial being, David is as radically Other as are the Engineers, and through the Engineers' liquid, both these Othernesses are transferred into Holloway and then Shaw. Thus, the embryo that grows in Shaw's womb is the product of a multilayered Otherness[3] that dissolves the boundaries between human and Other/creature. The posthumanity suggested here is so radically Other that it cannot be integrated; it is a violent and oppressing posthumanity that Shaw completely rejects. She can escape from it only by having it surgically removed. This scene is presented in an extremely graphic and shocking way, with the medical bay using a laser to open up Shaw's belly and remove the rapidly growing alien. It requires a violent and painful operation, a physical opening of the body, to reconstitute the human body as purely human.

Shaw's rejection of the Otherness of this creature metonymically represents the rejection of the posthumanities represented by both the Engineers and David. Because of this traumatic rejection, however, Shaw becomes determined not to pursue her relentless search for a center anymore. It is a moment of epiphany and of possible growth, a transformation in which Shaw becomes able to accept a state of in-between-ness that is dynamic and allows for movement beyond her established fixtures. For a time, she is able to inhabit the transformative state of adolescence. Immediately following the removal of the alien embryo, she stumbles into a room where Weyland has just awoken from cryosleep. David is tending to Weyland, who barely acknowledges Shaw. She demands his attention and forcefully insists, "You don't understand. You don't know. This place isn't what we thought it was. They aren't what we thought they were. I was wrong! We were so wrong! . . . We must leave!" Shaw is ready to walk away from all her previously held beliefs and to truly redefine herself, to move beyond the sheltering boundaries of preconceived notions and become an adult. In rejecting the violent posthuman alternatives embodied in the alien embryo, she enacts an adolescent gesture of rebellion, a rejection of the parental ideology represented by the dying Weyland.[4]

Following her warning and plea to leave, Weyland closes in on her and replies, "How can you leave? Not knowing what they are? Or have you lost your faith, Shaw?" The next scene shows Shaw preparing to join the expedition to confront the last surviving Engineer. Apparently Weyland's words have made her reconsider.[5] She has fallen under parental authority once again. Similar to her reaction to Milburn's commentary challenging her theory of the Engineers, Weyland's questioning her faith causes her to "evade[] external difficulties by regressing to the fixations" connected to her father (Freud, "Lecture XXII" 341). She remains caught up in her static no-space of adolescent in-between-ness that looks for certainties, unable to fully detach herself from her late father. While she thus rejects posthumanist possibility in this instance, she does not get rid of the lure of posthumanity as such. Shaw's alien/human embryo is rejected and terminated, but as the end of the film shows, it survives nonetheless. Posthumanity can be rejected, but it will remain hauntingly at the fringes, waiting to be integrated.

Shaw's physical, violent fight with the surviving Engineer at the end of the film has to be read as a manifestation of the adolescent rage that accompanies processes of growth and the challenge of parental control.[6] It is a rebellion that remains inconclusive, however, as the ending of the movie shows. Shaw wants to go to the Engineers' home planet, to the origin of the origin, so to speak, which shows that she is still caught in "the absolute requirement that we go back to a source, to the center, to the founding basis, to the principle" (Derrida 381). She is still not an independent adult, making her own truths, but regressively dependent on her father's faith. David asks her what she wants to achieve by going there, to which Shaw replies, "They created us. Then they tried to kill us. They changed their minds. I deserve to know why." The last sentence articulates a demand, and, recalling Lacan, every demand is a demand for love. David says, "I don't understand," either her desire or her demand. Shaw replies, "Well, I guess that's because I'm a human being and you're a robot." Shaw unequivocally renounces notions of posthumanity and reasserts the classical notion of the human. She does so by clearly stating it ("I'm a human being") and draws a clear line between herself and David, whom she does not classify as an android (deriving from the Greek *andrós* for man), but a robot, thus denying him any aspect of humanity and relegating him to the realm of the purely mechanic. The boundary between human and posthuman is clearly redrawn by means of opposition and marked difference.

## Posthuman Adolescence: David's Return to the Human

Within the multiple layers of adolescent posthuman decenteredness of the film and in connection with the notions of adolescence and posthumanity figured by and through the character of Elizabeth Shaw, the android David functions as a special node joining posthumanism and adolescence. His status as an artificial and, more specifically, as a constructed being combined with his superhuman abilities (evoking, on yet another level, the notion of Nietzsche's *Übermensch*), turns David into a foregrounded signifier of the question of the posthuman condition. At first glance, David obviously represents a technologically based posthumanity. Donna Haraway notes that

> [h]igh-tech culture challenges these dualisms [of, among others, human/machine] in intriguing ways. It is not clear who makes and who is made in the relation between human and machine. It is not clear what is mind and what body in machines that resolve into coding practices.... There is no fundamental, ontological separation between our formal knowledge of machine and organism, of technical and organic. (313)

David clearly challenges the dualism of human/machine, but in contrast to the dualism human/creature in connection to the Engineers, he is not perceived as a dangerous Other. Despite his superior physical and mental powers, David is not perceived as a threat by the human crew. He is programmed to interface seamlessly with the crew, and in order to achieve this, he blends in by taking on the role of a docile and unobtrusive assistant. In doing so, he blurs the line between human and machine, but does retain that quantum of Otherness that marks him as not human so that the dualism remains firmly intact.

The following exchange between Holloway and David is illuminating. It takes place when the human crew is preparing to leave the ship for the first time in order to explore the Engineers' ship. The crew is putting on their environmental suits, and so is David:

HOLLOWAY: David, why are you wearing a suit, man?
DAVID: I beg your pardon?
HOLLOWAY: You don't breathe, remember? So, why wear the suit?

DAVID: I was designed like this, because you people are more comfortable interact-
ing with your own kind. If I didn't wear the suit, it would defeat the purpose.
HOLLOWAY: Making you guys pretty close, huh?
DAVID: Not too close, I hope.

The technological Other has been humanized in order to make interaction seamless. At the same time, the border between human and machine has to be firmly upheld to prevent any fearful ambiguities from arising. Androids are "pretty close" to a perfect imitation of the real thing, but not "too close" to erase the boundary. David thus embodies "the posthumanist fascination with the 'interface'—the seamless articulation between human and machine, technology and *bios*" (Herbrechter 42). David constitutes such an interface, and it is precisely this function as *inter*, as in between, that excludes him from humanity but also denies David an identity of his own, as different from humanity. He cannot completely counter-identify against humanity, because his programming forces him to care for humanity regardless of their treatment of him or his feelings for them.

The brief exchange between David and Holloway illuminates David's inherently conflicted position. On the one hand, his programming constrains him to obey human wishes and commands and to serve his human masters. His programming forces him to imitate human behavior in order to become a seamless interface. On the other hand, he is clearly striving not to identify with humanity. He actively distances himself from the very humanity he is forced to mimic. He is, for instance, Othering humanity by using the phrase "*you* people" (my emphasis). David's identity is thus split and fragmented. It is not his programming—received passively from his human creator—that defines David; rather it is the conflicted nature of his identity that constitutes the ontological essence of his existence.

Haraway notes that the "origin story in the 'Western,' humanist sense depends on the myth of original unity, fullness, bliss and terror, represented by the phallic mother from whom all humans must separate, the task of individual development" (292). David sublates, in a Hegelian sense, this myth of original unity in a double way. Firstly, as an assembled android, his origin is not in unity, but in fragmentation. There is no need for him to follow the human process of adolescence, to renounce his parents ("the phallic mother"), to split away from them in order to gain an adult identity in the new unity of self-sufficient individuality. He has emerged from disunity into unity already. The problem here is that it was a passive emergence, a process of assemblage which consequently did not convey self-sufficiency, but utter dependence. Secondly, the family unit providing the oedipal triangle of father/child/mother that allows for the transference of attachments, identification, and finally counter-identification necessary for the process of coming of age is not available to David. There is no original family unit that he can refer to. He can either see humanity globally as his father and mother, or he is left with the aging Weyland as his father figure. David thus finds himself in an undefined and indefinable space regarding his status: he is neither human nor machine but in between. In this sense, he figures adolescent posthumanism when both terms are considered as signifying something fundamentally decentered and in between. David represents both adolescence and posthumanism and their respective relation to adulthood and humanism in which the latter two terms are conceived of as an Other that is fixed and known, but clearly felt to be dogmatic, limiting, partially obsolete, and insufficient.

At different points in the film, David is clearly cast as or denoted as a child or adolescent. At the beginning of the mission, when Weyland speaks to the *Prometheus* crew as a hologram, he states, "There is a man sitting with you today. His name is David. He is the closest thing to a son I will ever have. Unfortunately, he is not human, he will never grow old, he will never die, and yet he is unable to appreciate these remarkable gifts, for that would require the one thing that David will never have: a soul." Weyland paints a strong image of himself as David's creator. Also, he clearly differentiates David from a human being ("He is not human") but shies away from the word *android* or *robot*. Instead, he defines him as a posthuman, a being that is immortal and has "remarkable gifts" that give him abilities that exceed those of normal human beings. Although he calls David a son, Weyland also denigrates David, almost blaming him for lacking a soul, the one thing that would make him fully human. Weyland considers David as his son in the sense of his creation, and conversely, he sees his own position as one of ultimate power over the android. As his creation, David's duty is to obey and to serve. There is no indication that Weyland would want David to exceed his design specifications or that this possibility is part of his original programming.

Weyland's treatment of and his relationship with the android has clearly had an impact on David in that he is, to put it mildly, negatively predisposed against humanity. David acts on his animosity toward humanity when he calls on Holloway following the first expedition to the Engineers' ship. Disappointed that they were unable to find a living Engineer and thus could not ask the questions they came there to ask, Holloway gets drunk. While he is in this drunk and disappointed state, David approaches him in order to infect him with the Engineers' virus. In this scene, it becomes clear how much David resents his creator and, metonymically, his creator's species as a whole:

DAVID: Am I interrupting? Thought you might be running low.
HOLLOWAY: Pour yourself a glass, pal.
DAVID: Thank you, but I'm afraid it would be wasted on me.
HOLLOWAY: Oh, right. I almost forgot, you're not a real boy, huh?
DAVID: I'm very sorry that your Engineers are all gone, Dr. Holloway.
HOLLOWAY: You think we wasted our time coming here, don't you?
DAVID: Your question depends on me understanding what you hoped to achieve by coming here.
HOLLOWAY: What we hope to achieve? Well, it's to meet our makers. To get answers. Why they . . . why they even made us in the first place.
DAVID: Why do you think your people made me?
HOLLOWAY: We made you 'cause we could.
DAVID: Can you imagine how disappointing it would be for you to hear the same thing from your creator?
HOLLOWAY: I guess it's a good thing you can't be disappointed, huh?
DAVID: Yes, it's wonderful actually.

David's facial reaction to Holloway's last statement strongly suggests that he can indeed be disappointed and that he is in fact very disappointed in Holloway's answer. Holloway's allusion to Pinocchio ("you're not a real boy") implies that David harbors similar wishes as Pinocchio in that he strives to transcend his nature as an artificial being and become human. What Holloway does not seem to take into consideration is that—as for Pinocchio—this struggle entails rebellious actions against the maker.

In order for the adolescent posthuman that David is to come of age, he needs to transcend his posthumanity by working through it and thereby redefining it in an adult manner. David needs to transcend posthumanism by returning to a position of humanity. Jean-François Lyotard describes this very process in the context of modernity and postmodernity, noting that postmodernity is "a working through (*durcharbeiten*) performed by modernity on its own meaning" (80). David needs to arrive at an adult postmodernity, that is, a postmodernity that is still defined by fluidity and a dissolution of dichotomies, but which is at the same time capable of independently creating agency. In order to do so, he has to achieve a position of humanity and actively engage with it. David's posthumanity thus emerges from his posthumanity working through its own meaning via a return to humanity, constantly, indefinitely, and transformationally. This return to humanity is not the same as regression, however, since it is a process of constant dynamic change. Shaw's in-between-ness is defined by stasis, by the repetitive return to her father as a fixture. Shaw is caught in this unchanging, repetitive space. David, in contrast, inhabits a posthumanist in-between-ness that is characterized by the desire for transformation and change. This dynamic space enables David to become an agent, first, of transformation in general (cf. his role in infecting Holloway) and, second, his own posthuman transformation. In David, thus, the film depicts a posthumanity that is achieved by working consciously and openly on the concept of humanity within the in-between-ness of the posthumanist condition. The posthumanist condition in question is in this sense again before and after humanism.

Key to David and his process of transformation is his troubled relation to his creator/father Weyland. Following David's discovery of a surviving Engineer and shortly before he infects Holloway, there is a scene in which David is standing at Weyland's cryo-bed receiving instructions: "No, sir. I will take care of it. . . . Yes, sir. Understood. I'm sorry. Unfortunately slightly broken. . . . Of course, sir." David is completely dependent on Weyland's orders and is literally enslaved by his father, expected to follow his commands. He is in the docile position of a child, receiving orders without questioning them. This dependence of creation on creator is a frequent topic in young adult science fiction and is usually represented in some symbolic way. Ostry notes that clones in young adult fiction are "marked with depersonalizing tattoos such as the serial number" (226), which hinders the process of coming of age as it signifies a commodification of the individual and precludes independence and individuality.

This depersonalization very much applies to David. For instance, his fingerprints contain the Weyland Industries logo which marks him as Weyland's creation. Even more so, the Weyland Industries logo marks David as a commodity and as Weyland's property. Despite these fundamental depersonalizing and commodifying aspects of his existence, David desires independence. He conceptualizes it in an oedipal fashion as he imagines the death of his father as a moment of liberation and clearly admits that Weyland's death is something he desires. When David encounters Elizabeth just after she has had the alien fetus removed from her body, they seem to goad each other:

> DAVID: I didn't think you had it in you. Sorry, poor choice of words. Extraordinary survival instincts, Elizabeth.
> SHAW: What happens when Weyland's not around to program you anymore?
> DAVID: I suppose I'd be free.
> SHAW: You want that?
> DAVID: "Want"—not a concept I'm familiar with. That being said, doesn't everyone want their parents dead?
> SHAW: I didn't.

David insinuates strongly here that he is familiar with the concept of "want." He wants to be free of Weyland and knows that Weyland's death is a prerequisite for his freedom. David utters the classical oedipal desire here. In the Oedipus complex, the father is seen as a rival for the mother, and the child wants him dead. At this stage, the incestuous desires for the mother have to be repressed, however, as the father is perceived as too strong and powerful (cf., for instance, Freud, "The Ego and the Id" 34–35). One can argue that Weyland's programming, a programming David cannot escape, represents a complete domination of the superego. During adolescence, the oedipal desire to kill the father that was repressed in the original oedipal process reemerges, and the father is symbolically killed by reevaluating the "character of the father," who is no longer as threatening and can therefore be symbolically killed by forming new, independent relations and identifications. This process is strongly insinuated with respect to David.

At the beginning of the film, David is shown watching the film *Lawrence of Arabia*, starring Peter O'Toole. David has obviously seen this film often: not only does he know the dialogue by heart, but he also practices O'Toole's intonation and speech rhythm. Along similar lines, he dyes and styles his hair to make it match that of O'Toole in the film. When it comes to O'Toole's Lawrence, David is counter-identifying with a man who is in key respects different from Weyland. Weyland is a man who is clever, intelligent, powerful, and obviously happy to let others do the dirty work. In contrast, O'Toole's Lawrence is hands-on, brave, and locked in a constant battle with his superiors. Since David is designed to be hands-on, it is no surprise that he would feel attracted to O'Toole's Lawrence as a surrogate father-figure.

The plot of *Lawrence of Arabia* supports David's connection to O'Toole's portrayal: Lawrence is sent to Arabia by his superiors in order to fulfill a certain mission. Very quickly, however, he begins to set his own priorities and starts realizing them in a highly idiosyncratic way that his superiors neither understand nor condone. In essence, Lawrence does not fit in with the English establishment, nor is he ever truly part of the Berber community. He is constantly in between both cultures. Lawrence is not dismayed by his position, however, but realizes his individual and highly idiosyncratic plans from within this fluid state of in-between-ness. David also does not fit in. His posthuman condition keeps him in between. Here is the strongest connection between the two characters. Lawrence is the man that David desires to become, one who is not limited by the circumstances he finds himself in, but who utilizes and thus actively fashions and transforms his own circumstances. Lawrence is a man who thrives on his in-between state and turns it into his greatest asset. Lawrence's indeterminate status is the driving force behind his relentless activities. These activities transform the circumstances in which Lawrence finds himself into conditions more favorable to his plans. David shares the same intermediate position. Hence, the freedom represented by the active and independent Lawrence represents a contrast to his programmed docility that is seductive.[7] He has chosen O'Toole's Lawrence as his ideal image.

With this process, David goes through what Lacan terms the *mirror stage*, a developmental phase of key importance:

> It suffices to understand the mirror stage in this context as an *identification*, in the full sense analysis gives to the term: namely, the transformation that takes place in the subject when he assumes an image.... But the important point is that this form situates the agency known as the ego, prior to its social determination, in a fictional direction.... The total form of his body, by which the subject anticipates the maturation of his powers in a mirage, is given to him only as a gestalt, that is, in an exteriority in which, to be sure, this form is more constitutive than constituted. ("Mirror Stage" 76)

The key word here, once again, is transformation. The mirror stage is a process in which a "transformation takes place in the subject." This is the same process of transformation that lies at the heart of posthumanism and adolescence, and it is a process David has initiated by identifying with Lawrence. In human beings, the mirror stage creates the ego, for "[t]he function of the mirror stage ... is to establish a relationship between an organism and its reality—or, as they say, between the *Innenwelt* and the *Umwelt*" (Lacan, "Mirror Stage" 78). O'Toole's Lawrence mirrors David's desires and wishes, and consequently, his identification with O'Toole's Lawrence creates his individual *Innenwelt* in that Lawrence allows him to perceive (fictionally) the possibility of turning his desires into reality. David, the artificial, posthuman, Pinocchio-like boy, thus chooses as his own mirror image a fictional character, a gestalt that comes to him from the media.[8] This choice creates a fictional, i.e. artificial, ego-function in the artificial David. It is a posthuman ego housed in an artificial human.

In addition to the mimicking of O'Toole as obvious signs of identification mentioned above, David quotes from the movie at several key moments in *Prometheus*.[9] Similar to Elizabeth Shaw, David is speaking in the voice of another when he uses these quotes. Both characters' adolescent identifications are thus expressed linguistically as quotations from the Other. The difference is that, as noted above, Elizabeth's lasting identification with her late father signifies regression: it is directed into the past and expresses a pathologically prolonged adolescence. David's habit of quoting O'Toole's Lawrence is directed into an imaginary future, which characterizes it as a much more normal adolescent process. This process further defines the ego-function he has created beside, against, and despite the superego of his programming. He actively strives to escape the *epistēmē* of his programming, a programming that defines and confines him to the posthuman, and in doing so he simultaneously comes closer to the human and a different mode of the posthuman.

## Conclusion

The last scene of the film reveals David and Elizabeth Shaw as the only survivors of the *Prometheus* expedition. After the surviving Engineer is killed, Elizabeth returns to the crashed alien ship in search of David, whose head was ripped from his torso by the Engineer. When she finds him, the following discussion takes place:

> SHAW: Where is my cross?
> DAVID: The pouch in my utility belt. [Shaw recovers her cross from the pouch.] Even after all this, you still believe, don't you?
> SHAW: You said you can understand the navigation? Use their maps?
> DAVID: Yes, of course. Once we get to one of their other ships, finding a path to Earth should be relatively straightforward.
> SHAW: I don't want to go back to where we came from. I want to go where they came from. You think you can do that, David?
> DAVID: Yes. I believe I can.

Shaw's insistence on getting her cross back, emphasized by David's comment about her continued belief, shows that she is still caught in her adolescent past and unable and/or unwilling to abandon her father's belief.[10] From the brief moment of posthumanist and adult possibility in Weyland's cabin after the removal of the alien embryo, Shaw has again taken to her old patterns. Her decision to travel to the Engineers' homeworld is merely a repetition of the desire that already led to the *Prometheus* expedition. Shaw remains caught up in her adolescent, independent (and hence repetitive) self.

In the final voiceover she warns everyone not to come to the planet, stating that "[t]here's only death here now and I'm leaving it behind. It is New Year's Day, the year of Our Lord, 2094. My name is Elizabeth Shaw. Last survivor of the *Prometheus* and I'm still searching." She is still searching indeed. Her continuing search is for answers that are, as the film shows, either unattainable (the Engineers did not benevolently explain the reason for human existence) or disappointing (Holloway answering David's question of why humanity created him with the trivial reason of "We made you 'cause we could"). Shaw has not learned from her experience but remains caught in the state of prolonged adolescence that condemns her to endless repetition.[11]

The final conversation with David at the end of the film illustrates Shaw's regression:

> DAVID: May I ask what you hope to achieve by going there?
> SHAW: They created us. Then they tried to kill us. They changed their minds. I deserve to know why.
> DAVID: The answer is irrelevant. Does it matter why they changed their minds?
> SHAW: Yes. Yes, it does.
> DAVID: I don't understand.
> SHAW: Well, I guess that's because I'm a human being and you're a robot.

Shaw thus remains in her static adolescent position based on regression and repetition; she does not take the final decisive step toward adulthood.

David is also, by design, in between, but based on his identification with Lawrence, he wants to grow, to come of age not by transcending the state of in-between-ness, but by consciously accepting it and choosing to exist within it. David's head, as mentioned, was ripped from his body, but his cognitive and speech functions continue to work perfectly.[12] His literal fragmentation signifies the dissolution of his unity with Weyland, who is no longer there to control him. The corporate brand on his fingertips is now part of another body, and David exists as the head, the head he has so carefully styled according to O'Toole's Lawrence of Arabia. David has, quite literally, shed his existence as a docile servant and entered into a new phase of existence, a phase which is different and new but still indeterminate. Unable to perform any voluntary action, he finds himself in a completely helpless situation, that of a newborn baby. The last time he is shown, Shaw places his head in a bag, and before she zips it closed, David gives the impression of a satisfied baby, which is underscored by the camera perspective. This image of David as a baby, in turn, casts Shaw in the role of a nurturing mother, a role she apparently desires but feels nature has cheated her of.[13] Thus, the posthuman David, once free from his human father, ends up in the care of a human mother. This mother, although she clearly states he is a robot while she is a human being, takes him under her care. Here, the ever-adolescent Elizabeth becomes mother to a fledgling posthumanism. This new relation hinted at between Shaw and David suggests hope for a harmonious unity between human and machine by means of a slowly nurtured posthumanism.

## Notes

1. With this sacrifice, the Engineer enacts a fundamental aspect of the Prometheus myth. Central to the Prometheus myth is the fact that he steals fire from the Olympian gods and gives it to mankind. In doing so, he knowingly sacrifices his position among the gods and is punished accordingly by Zeus. Prometheus is bound and chained to Mount Caucasus, where he is a victim to a bird that appears every night to peck out his liver, which grows back every day so that his torture can be repeated endlessly. Carol Dougherty notes that "Prometheus embodies the human condition with all its potential for brilliant innovation and for cruel suffering. Throughout the centuries since the Prometheus myth first captured the popular imagination, the fire that he steals for mortals has come to represent the spirit of technology, forbidden knowledge, the conscious intellect, political power, and artistic inspiration. As a god whose name means 'forethought,' Prometheus signals mortals' repeated attempts to overcome the limitations of their knowledge about the future—hope, technology, and prophecy are all part of Prometheus' complicated gift to mankind" (3). The Engineer's sacrifice is such a "complicated gift to mankind" and it is precisely the various complex and contrary aspects of the human condition that the film probes.

2. Before David puts the black liquid into Holloway's drink, he consults with Weyland who, as he reveals to Vickers, orders him to "try harder." Infecting Holloway with the Engineers' liquid is thus a direct result of Weyland's order. In addition, there have been clear tensions between Holloway and David up to this point, so that David's choice of Holloway as a victim suggests the android is motivated by petty and very human emotions.

3. When David extracts the drop of black liquid from the alien container, he balances it on his finger. A close-up shows that his fingerprint contains the symbol of Weyland Industries. Since this is the finger he will use to put the liquid into Holloway's drink (clearly a phallic symbol), one might even go as far as to say that Weyland himself, by virtue of the metonymic relation here, is yet another layer of Otherness that partakes in the fathering of the unwanted embryo.

4. In the scene, Weyland evokes fatherhood on a number of levels simultaneously. Firstly, by virtue of his age, he symbolizes the wise old sage, the cultural father-figure if there ever was one. David is in the room with them, so, secondly, Weyland is very literally a father in this scene. On a third plane, David is engaged in washing Weyland's feet, which recalls the anointment of Jesus's feet from the Bible (cf. Luke 7:36–50; Matthew 26:6–13; Mark 14:3–9; John 12:1–8). In this manner, Weyland also represents the religious dimension.

5. In the context of Weyland, a few comments have to be made about Meredith Vickers. Vickers is an enigmatic figure. She represents the Weyland Company's interest, and for most of the film, she acts out the stereotype of the tough business person. She visits Weyland once he is awake, and it becomes clear that she is his daughter. Telling Weyland that it was foolish to come and that he will die when he goes to the Engineers, she notes, "A king has his reign and then he dies. It's inevitable. That is the natural order of things." Weyland reacts coldly: "Anything else?" She almost hatefully replies, "No, ... father." She lets her father go and is not particularly touched

when he is indeed killed by the Engineer. It is clear that she has long since severed any emotional ties to her father. In this sense, she is the reverse of Shaw. Additionally, she is a sister to David. One question surrounding Vickers is whether or not she is also an android. When she enters the bridge of the ship late at night, she encounters Captain Janek, who makes a pass at her, which she initially refuses. Janek then challenges her by saying, "I was wondering . . . are you a robot?" Vickers apparently does feel the need to prove her humanity because she replies, "My room. Ten minutes." The question of whether or not she is a robot remains unanswered, and an exhaustive analysis of Vickers's role and impact on the questions of posthumanity and adolescence would go beyond the scope of this essay. It needs to be noted, however, that the uncertainty surrounding Vickers's ontological status as well as her agenda and her relationship to David and Weyland contributes to the processes of decentering associated with both posthumanity and adolescence.

6. The Engineer is killed by the creature that was cut from Shaw's womb, which has grown up rapidly. Ironically, the Engineer is impregnated or rather serves as an incubator for another creature, the xenomorph that emerges at the very end of the film. Here, the posthuman is infected with the human which, in turn, creates a creaturely Other.

7. In this context, it is important to note that Lawrence's actions are consciously mythopoeic. He creates an image of himself as a fearless war machine that feels no pain. David is a machine that feels no pain and thus identifies with this aspect of Lawrence strongly. David's desire to be more human is also mythopoeic as it perpetuates the myth that he could indeed someday become fully human, that he could become exactly like Lawrence of Arabia.

8. In a sense, thrice imaginary. The image of the historical Lawrence is mythopoeically distorted in the first place. The Lawrence as written for the movie *Lawrence of Arabia* is a fictional creation, and thirdly, what emerges on screen is O'Toole's interpretation of the script.

9. The quote "Big things have small beginnings" serves as a meta-commentary on the movie's plot as a whole and David's role in infecting Holloway with the Engineers' virus. The sentences he quotes from *Lawrence of Arabia* are "The trick, Mr. Potter, is not minding that it hurts"; "Big things have small beginnings," and "There's nothing in the desert, and no man needs nothing."

10. Shaw has inherited the cross from her father. It symbolically emphasizes her return to her adolescent need for fixtures. David took the cross from her when the alien pregnancy was discovered. Shaw's adolescent fight with the Engineer and the moment of epiphany when she almost manages to break free of her regression thus all happen while she is without her father's cross.

11. Her continued recourse to her adolescent patterns can be glimpsed, for instance, by the use of the term "the year of our Lord" in her final voiceover. She specifically mentions God here, which signifies that she has once again returned to her adolescent behavioral patterns.

12. There is a parallel here to the first Engineer they discover, who has been decapitated by a giant door closing down. When Shaw tries to revive the head, it explodes. David's head continues to function perfectly without his body, which signifies his posthuman state in between humanity and their creators, the Engineers, in that he transcends them both in his ability to survive.

13. After discovering the Engineers and finding them all (allegedly) dead, Holloway comes to Shaw's room, stating, "There is nothing special about the creation of life. Right? Anybody can do it. I mean, all you need is a dash of DNA and half a brain, right?" To this she answers, clearly

upset: "I can't. I can't create life. What does that say about me?" Taking care of baby-David thus fulfills her desire to be a mother. The fact that David is put into a closed backpack locates him in a symbolic womb that Elizabeth carries with her. It is, however, an artificial and external womb so that her pregnancy is clearly constructed as different and, in the context of the film, as posthuman. Connections can also be drawn to the manner in which the xenomorph procreates, namely by using an external host as incubator. Elizabeth's posthuman pregnancy also has a religious aspect as it suggests an immaculate conception.

## Works Cited

The Bible: Authorized King James Version with Apocrypha. Ed. Robert Carroll and Stephen Prickett. Oxford: Oxford UP, 2008. Print.
Derrida, Jacques. "Structure, Sign and Play in the Discourse of the Human Sciences." *Writing and Difference*. Trans. Alan Bass. Chicago: U of Chicago P, 1978. 278–93. Print.
Dougherty, Carol. *Prometheus*. London, New York: Routledge, 2006. Print.
Freud, Sigmund. "The Ego and the Id." *The Standard Edition of the Complete Psychological Works*. Trans. and ed. James Strachey et al. Vol. 19. London: Hogarth, 1962. 3–66. Print.
———. "The Future of an Illusion." *The Standard Edition of the Complete Psychological Works*. Trans. and ed. James Strachey et. al. Vol. 21. London: Hogarth, 1962. 5–56. Print.
———. "Lecture XXII: Some Thought on Development and Regression—Aetiology." *The Standard Edition of the Complete Psychological Works*. Trans. and ed. James Strachey et al. Vol. 16. London: Hogarth, 1962. 339–57. Print.
———. "Mourning and Melancholia." *The Standard Edition of the Complete Psychological Works*. Trans. and ed. James Strachey et al. Vol. 14. London: Hogarth, 1962. 239–60. Print.
Haraway, Donna. "The Cyborg Manifesto: Science, Technology and Socialist-Feminism in the Late Twentieth Century." *The Cybercultures Reader*. Ed. David Bell and Barbara M. Kennedy. London: Routledge, 2001. 292–324. Print.
Herbrechter, Stefan. *Posthumanism: A Critical Analysis*. London: Bloomsbury, 2013. Print.
Jung, Carl Gustav. "Some Aspects of Modern Psychotherapy." *The Practice of Psychotherapy*. Trans. and ed. Gerhard Adler and R. F. C. Hull. Princeton: Princeton UP, 1985. 29–33. Print. Vol. 16 of *The Collected Works of C. G. Jung*.
Kristeva, Julia. *Revolution in Poetic Language*. Trans. Margaret Waller. New York: Columbia UP, 1984. Print.
Lacan, Jacques. "The Direction of the Treatment and the Principles of its Power." *Écrits: A Selection*. Trans. Alan Sheridan. London: Routledge, 2001. 173–214. Print.
———. "The Function and Field of Speech and Language in Psychoanalysis." *Écrits: A Selection*. Trans. Alan Sheridan. London: Routledge, 2001. 23–86. Print.
———. "The Mirror Stage as Formative of the I Function." *Écrits: The First Complete Edition in English*. Trans. Bruce Fink. New York: Norton, 2006. 75–81. Print.
*Lawrence of Arabia*. 1962. Dir. David Lean. Sony Pictures, 2002. DVD.

Lyotard, Jean-François. *The Postmodern Explained*. Trans. Don Barry et al. Minneapolis: U of Minneapolis P, 1992. Print.

Nayar, Pramod K. *Posthumanism*. Cambridge: Polity, 2014. Print.

Ostry, Elaine. "'Is He Still Human? Are You?': Young Adult Science Fiction in the Posthuman Age." *Lion and the Unicorn* 28.2 (2004): 222–46. *JSTOR*. Web. 20 June 2015.

*Prometheus*. Dir. Ridley Scott. 20th Century Fox, 2012. DVD.

Turner, Victor. "Passages, Margins, and Poverty: Religious Symbols of Communitas." *Dramas, Fields, and Metaphors*. Ithaca: Cornell UP, 1974. 231–71. Print.

Wolfe, Cary. *What Is Posthumanism?* London: U of Minneapolis P, 2010. Print.

# 11

# POSTHUMANIST MAGIC
## Beyond the Boundaries of Humanist Ethics in Lev Grossman's *The Magicians*

*Tony M. Vinci*

> The human is not now, and never was, itself.
> —**Cary Wolfe**, What Is Posthumanism?

The epigraph for Lev Grossman's 2009 fantasy *The Magicians* conjures the moment from Shakespeare's *The Tempest* when the great wizard Prospero renounces his magic: "I'll break my staff, / Bury it certain fathoms in the earth, / And deeper than did ever plummet sound / I'll drown my book" (5.1.55–58). More than abandoning his use of the magical, Shakespeare's magician relinquishes the tools that empower him to access worlds of understanding and experience that function beyond the human: his staff and his book. Considering the widely established reading of Prospero as Shakespeare's alter ego, these mystical instruments—staff and book—become metonyms for pen and paper, and those acts that have been deemed magical become aligned with acts of reading, writing, and storytelling. By conflating the world constructed between the reader and the text with the experiential world in which the novel is read, Grossman ruptures the reality/fantasy binary and contaminates it with a narrative experience in which magic never functions solely as magic: for the reader, magic operates within the internal rules of the fantasy narrative while resonating as the linguistic material that makes possible the writing and reading of the narrative itself. Magic, then, at least in relation to Grossman's novel, is something much more complicated than simple wish fulfillment or the brandishing of wands while screaming *faux* Latin phrases—it becomes a means by which one enters into a conceptual orbit that negotiates multiple levels of reality and identity without privileging any singular life or vantage point as essentialized or authentic. Fortunately, the reader is not alone when attempting to navigate these unruly realities; Grossman's characters engage in similar epistemological crises.

*The Magicians* tracks Quentin Coldwater, a hyper-intelligent and depressed teenager who fetishizes the five fictional fantasy novels in Christopher Plover's Fillory and Further series. Populated by talking animals, an assortment of mythological creatures, a family of human monarchs, and a pair of well-intentioned animal-gods who oversee the land with care and benevolence, Plover's novels bear an aggressive resemblance to C. S. Lewis's Chronicles of Narnia (a point to which I will return). For Quentin, they function as both salve for the depressing realities of his unremarkable adolescence as well as a source of hope that he, like the Chatwin children (the human rulers of Fillory), is destined for a remarkable life. Quentin's adventures begin in Brooklyn, on the day he is to interview for admittance into Princeton University. Instead of meeting the Princeton interviewer, however, he encounters the interviewer's corpse, along with an uncannily pretty paramedic who gives him a unique and unpublished manuscript titled "The Magicians," presumably the sixth book of the Fillory and Further series. When a slip of paper slides free from the manuscript and is taken by the wind, Quentin follows it until it leads him through a magic portal to another world—not Fillory, but upstate New York, to Brakebills College for Magical Pedagogy (a collegiate version of Harry Potter's Hogwarts School of Witchcraft and Wizardry).

As with everything else in his life, Quentin finds Brakebills disappointing. Studying magic proves to be an arduous and oddly banal labor, inspiring his social group to mitigate the stresses of school with the all too common practices of alcohol, drugs, and sexual promiscuity. More disappointing than Brakebills is life after graduation, a seemingly pointless wasteland filled not with magical quests and heroic purpose, but with hedonistic excess and immature social drama. His life does not take a turn for the miraculous until he cheats on his brilliant and powerful girlfriend, Alice, and learns that Fillory, the fictional land from Plover's novels, is real. To escape his shame and embarrassment, he leads his companions to Fillory and embarks on a journey to assist Ember and Umber, Fillory's animal-gods, and to defeat the fabled enemy of Fillory, the Watcher Woman. Through a series of failures, the quest, along with Quentin's understanding of himself and the world, unravels. It turns out that the pretty paramedic who instigates Quentin's adventure is in fact Jane Chatwin, the youngest of the Chatwin siblings and author of the manuscript that claims to be the sixth book of Fillory and Further. According to the book within the book, she had spent her life in Fillory as the misunderstood Watcher Woman, turning time back again and again in an effort to defeat her oldest brother, Martin, who had cheated Fillory's gods, found a way to stay in Fillory forever, and become The Beast, Fillory's actual adversary. Thus, Quentin is revealed to be little more than Jane's puppet—a tool to defeat her brother. In the end, Martin is indeed defeated and Fillory is saved, but Alice sacrifices herself in the battle. Disgraced and disenchanted, Quentin returns to Earth, takes a job at an investment firm, and wastes his days away with vacuous entertainments.

Far from merely playing a clever game of inter-, intra-, and meta-textualities, *The Magicians* engages magic and the conventions of metafiction to critique the traditional humanist ethics of young adult fantasy, which situates the human as a specialized category of being that inhabits the apex of an imaginary hierarchy of moral and social values. As pioneering critic Patricia Waugh defines it, metafiction "is writing that consistently displays its conventionality, which explicitly lays bare its conditions of artifice, and which explores thereby the problematic relationship between life and fiction" (4). Through its treatment of language and its intertextual engagements with popular fantasy texts, *The Magicians* exploits metafiction's ability to expose the co-constitutive operations of life and fiction, refashioning the humanist ideals of rationality, social-minded intelligence, civic responsibility, and ecological awareness through an imbricated set of realities, both fantastical and quotidian. For the reader, it is the force of magic that offers access to a mode of thinking that engages this system of complex realities by operating beyond the notion of an anthropocentric human world. However, in order to offer this access, magic must first be a destructive, de-creative force that unveils the fantastical nature of humanist reality and rewrites both epistemology and ontology from a posthumanist vantage point. Thus, *The Magicians* codes the deconstruction of the traditional humanist subject as a profound act of posthumanist ethics.

Cary Wolfe's refashioning of "the human" as an ideological category—a master narrative used to essentialize or naturalize anthropocentric authority—becomes useful here as a way to unpack Grossman's treatment of magic as an ethical force in *The Magicians*. Wolfe crafts an approach to humanism that rejects human exceptionalism and replaces it with a mode of inter-subjectivity that is both porous and fluid: "'we are always radically other, already in- or ahuman in our very being—not just in the fact of . . . our physical vulnerability and mortality, as we share, as animals, with animals, but also in our subjection to and constitution in the materiality and technicity of a language that is always on the scene before we are" ("Human" 571). This posthumanist subject presents a seemingly contradictory sense of ethics: in order for the human to act humanely in posthuman environments, the notion of the human must be dismantled, allowing for a vulnerable and open relationship between the human self and the unknowable Other, human and nonhuman alike.

Working from Wolfe's model of posthumanism, I argue that Grossman uses metafictional techniques to parody the well-known conventions of fantasy narrative and, by doing so, critique the reading practices of anthropocentric humanism—how we read fantasy literature, specifically, as a means by which we empower the known and the accepted—and thus resituate fantasy narrative as an entry point to posthumanist ways of seeing the multiple identities and realities we co-create. In this way, *The Magicians* exemplifies what might be termed a posthumanist approach to reading young adult fantasy. Instead of defining the human as a discrete being in a single environment, Grossman's magic reveals the human self to be always already pluralized—deeply imbricated with varied languages, animalities, and objective realities—and the real world to be a vast matrix of multiple realities, each constructed via a species-specific engagement with the planet. By rewriting the scripts of both traditional humanist subjectivity and reality and asserting a radical posthumanist ethics of anti-anthropocentric vulnerability, Grossman's posthumanist approach to the genre opens the reader to a new set of coordinates from which to consider the cultural work of young adult fantasy narrative.

## "Not the Paradise You Were Looking For": Deconstructive Magic and the Escapist Ethics of Anthropocentric Humanism

Historian Dominick LaCapra describes recent developments in posthumanist theory in terms almost magical. For him, posthumanist thought evinces a "complex understanding of a field of distinctions, differences, proximities, voids, enigmas, wonderments, uncanny twists, and possibilities that cannot be condensed into a human-[Other] divide" (*History* 174). Employing more subdued rhetoric, Cary Wolfe clarifies the premises from which such posthumanist "magic" springs: "the human is not now, and never was, itself" and "the other-than-human resides at the very core of the human" (*Animal Rites* 9). The twin goals of this anti-anthropocentric thinking are to "unleash" the nonhuman Other from the influence of anthropocentric authority by 1) fundamentally revising conceptions of what we call the human, the world, and the real; and 2) abolishing human exceptionalism by deconstructing the cultural intellectual history of the discrete human self and locating human subjectivity in an incessant and complex series of movements between multiple subjective positions.

Two of the most fundamental contributors to posthumanist thinking, Jacques Derrida and Donna J. Haraway, both work to destabilize human essentialism by invoking Freud's thesis of humanity's central traumas: Copernicus (the Earth, and thus the human, is not the center of the universe), Darwin (humanity is a biological anomaly evolved from bestial, not metaphysical, roots), and Freud (the existence of the unconscious suggests that even the human mind is beyond knowing). Derrida adds to these traumas the philosophies of Marx (the irreducible presence and power of ideology) and, more tentatively, the animal (humanity has gained the privileged position of being a separate, unique being only through an unethical project of logocentric and ideological manipulation that traps and oppresses what we call animal). Developing Derrida's thinking from a somewhat different point of origin, Haraway addresses notions of human exceptionalism by attacking "the premise that humanity alone is not a spatial and temporal web of interspecies dependencies" (11). Her syntax focuses on what humanity is not and works to undercut assumptions about the purported uniqueness of human subjectivity, but it also singles out such mythic thinking as the symptom of anxiety. We define the nonhuman as non-thinking entities enmeshed in complex overlapping systems, and these interdependencies are—perhaps because of their nonsentient, nonlinguistic autopoeic processes—coded as less than, or even subservient to, the human. Haraway locates the primary problem here to be the myth of self-reliant ontology: the human must be something separate and autonomous for it to be valuable. Haraway reads such wishful thinking as destructive, foolish, and counterintuitive, for it is our relationships with Otherness (that is really just a part of self-ness) that make humanity valuable.

Through Quentin's obsessive relationship to Christopher Plover's Fillory novels, *The Magicians* invites us to read fantasy literature through this posthumanist lens by demonstrating the limitations of reading fantasy from the privileged position of anthropocentric humanism. As parody of and homage to Lewis's Chronicles of Narnia, Plover's Fillory and Further series presents an explicitly anthropocentric narrative. In Fillory as in Narnia, the human is privileged both politically and cosmologically; it is the unquestioned reason for creation itself. Moreover, both sets of novels are coded clearly as children's fantasy. As such, they "assume a form of innocence ... on behalf of the reader" regarding the construction of reality, encouraging readers to consider the texts as either didactic parables or escapist entertainments (Moss 50). It is this oversimplified understanding of reading that Grossman replicates and critiques through his depictions of how Quentin reads the Fillory novels.

Within the inter-narrative space of Plover's novels, the process of entering Fillory replicates the process of reading itself. Echoing Linda Hutcheon's assertion that "the reading of metafictive fantasies is 'emblematic' of the reading of fiction in general" (81), when Martin Chatwin, the eldest of the Chatwin children, crawls through the aperture in the old grandfather clock and discovers a strange otherworld awaiting him, "it's like he's opening the covers of a book, but a book that did what books always promised to do and never actually quite did: get you out, really out, of where you were and into something better," a place where "[h]appiness was a real, actual, achievable possibility" that "never left you" (Grossman, *Magicians* 7). However, instead of reading fantasy "as [a] system of orientations" (Fiske 11) that antagonizes "what is generally accepted as possibility" (Irwin 4) or as an access point to another reality that highlights "material which our consciousness normally filters out" and compels us to consider "outlooks we would not otherwise take" (Hume 84), Quentin understands the act of reading fantasy as an escapist, self-gratifying gesture.

This escapist ethic of reading fantasy lends ideological authority to Quentin's privileged position as human. Such humanist reading practices enable him to code himself as an essentialized and discrete human subject who lives in a reality constructed explicitly for his use; however, they also inhibit him from coding fantasy as a revolutionary narrative force that reveals "reason and reality to be arbitrary, shifting constructs," exposing "a culture's definitions of that which can be," subverting "this unitary vision" by "introduc[ing] confusion and alternatives" (Jackson 21, 23, 35). Quentin can see the young Martin only as a metonym for himself—a bored child looking for adventure and romance—and, as in Lewis's Chronicles of Narnia, the only requirement for being deemed royal and exceptional within the pages of the Fillory and Further novels is being human. Enamored by this overly convenient mechanism for offering readers a sense of cosmological significance, Quentin reads the Fillory novels not for inspiration or intellectual engagement or civic-minded activism or even flight from a reality of oppression; he reads them to escape from his own inability to create meaning, construct purpose, or participate in a reality that refuses to bend to his desires.

Quentin falls into the trap Jack Zipes outlines in "Why Fantasy Matters Too Much." Employing Theodor Adorno's critique of the culture industry, Zipes argues that popular modes of fantastic fiction have been reified to become easily consumable entertainments. Instead of offering ways to reimagine and thus transform our realities, fantasy as categorizable commodity antagonizes the most significant work of the genre: to impel the reader to venture beyond the limits of the knowable. Paradoxically, "The culture industry realizes the potential of the fantastic by commodifying it: fantastic elements are produced and reproduced to become important ingredients in the constitution of constant spectacles that impede cognition of the operative principles of the social-economic system in which we live" (Zipes 81). Through the genre's well-trodden conventions and categories, then, fantasy readers know all too well what they will find within fantasy fiction and thus code it as a facet of the quotidian, muting its revolutionary potential. As Zipes argues forcefully, "Delusion has become the goal of fantasy, not illumination. Fantasy has become so common that it has become banal" (81).

Zipes's analysis of how fantasy-as-commodity undercuts the power of the fantasy narrative by granting, instead of upsetting, the prefabricated desires of readers, clarifies why, to Quentin and his companions, their Fillorian quests "felt like they were going on a summer-camp nature hike, or a junior high field trip" (315). Ignoring the actual stakes of their actions, Quentin and his human comrades frame their experiences in Fillory within a network of commodified allusions that conflate fantasy tropes with everyday expressions of popular culture. They make consistent references to fantasy novels, Dungeons & Dragons campaigns, video games, Oz's Yellow Brick Road, the sexual attractiveness of nonhuman Others, high school dodge ball, *Scooby-Doo*, Porky Pig—all as a means to imperialize the fantasy world, to make it bow down to their provincial imaginations, to make Fillory the literalization of the wish fulfillment that they seek. For them, even the actual Fillory cannot exist beyond the boundaries of their narrative expectations. However, as Lucy Armitt reminds us, "the fantastic concerns itself with the world of the 'beyond' (beyond the galaxy, beyond the known, beyond the accepted, beyond belief)" (3); therefore, as the literalization of the fantasy narrative, Fillory operates in a space both within and without the ideological perimeters of fantasy-as-commodity. When Quentin realizes that the fantastic creatures of Fillory, which seem harmless and uncannily cute, can indeed kill, hurt, and maim him and his friends, he thinks, "This was the opposite of magic. The world was ripping open" (322). For Quentin, the opposite of magic is not just reality but the loss of his personalized fantasy. His world rips open because the reality of Fillory does not reify commodified narrative conventions, nor does it accommodate the escapist work that Quentin expects fantasy to perform. By incorporating imaginative traces that operate beyond the parameters of known reality, Fillory's symbolic economy ruptures the commodified fantasies of anthropocentric humanism and introduces an ethic of posthumanist vulnerability.

On a metafictional valence, Quentin and his friends are simply readers who enter a text. According to Robyn McCallum, engagement with such a complicated work of metafiction might not only "teach readers specific codes and conventions and interpretive strategies with which to read and make sense of other, more closed, fictions" but "by analogy, show readers how representations of reality are similarly constructed and ascribed with meanings" (149). However, while the metafictionality of Fillory has the potential to open its semiotic, hermeneutic, and ideological borders, inviting Grossman's characters to deepen their readings of fantasy, fiction, and the realities that they co-create, they employ the "parodic appropriations of other texts, genres, and discourses" to foreclose such possibilities (McCallum 139). Disempowered by this limited practice of reading, the text of Fillory resists them and threatens to wound them by ignoring the fantasy/reality binary and constructing a blended space wherein traditional human agency is radically limited. Within such a space, the prefabricated desires sponsored by the culture industry and manifested in the banal realities of commodified fantasy exist only in appearances, compelling an alteration in reading practices that disavows the notion that fantasy realms exist primarily for the reader's pleasure. As the animal-god Ember declares to Fillory's human intruders, "I am sorry our world is not the paradise you were looking for. But it was not created for your entertainment. Fillory . . . is not a theme park, for you and your friends to play dress-up in, with swords and crowns" (351–52). Ember's lament becomes Grossman's reclamation of fantasy narrative as part of a posthumanist reality. It suggests that readers should be more vulnerable to the imaginary and invites them to recode the human itself as an imaginary creature, to realize that the human is always already a fantasy (as are its social and ontological constructions). Ultimately, Ember's critique of humanist reading practices that turn magic and fantasy alike into something unreal, silly, secondary to the real world, serves to remind us that, in fact, both realities are made of the same substance: symbol.

At Brakebills, magic is described, theorized, and practiced as a language: "As much as it was like anything, magic was like a language. . . . [I]t was complex and chaotic and organic. It obeyed rules only to the extent that it felt like it, and there were almost as many special cases and one-time variations as there were rules" (149). By aligning the rules of magic with the rules of language, Brakebills's magical pedagogy invites students to engage magic as a dialectical movement between humanist traditions and posthumanist possibilities. Dean Fogg explains at the Brakebills graduation ceremony:

> If there's a single lesson that life teaches us, it's that wishing doesn't make it so. Words and thoughts don't change anything. Language and reality are kept strictly apart—reality is tough, unyielding stuff, and it doesn't care what you think or feel or say about it. . . . The separation of word and thing is the essential fact on which our adult lives are founded. But somewhere in the heat of magic that boundary between word and thing ruptures. It cracks, and the one flows back into the other, and the two melt and fuse. Language gets tangled up with the world it describes. (217)

From a humanist point of view, magic operates as art operates, perhaps even as J. R. R. Tolkien hoped fantasy itself operates, by imaginarily rethinking the reality/fantasy binary and offering readers an experience that, at least momentarily, creates an arena in which one might escape the rules of reality. For Tolkien, fantasy narratives create magical secondary worlds so that one may experience a process of "Fantasy, Recovery, Escape, and Consolation" (46). That is, through participating in the fantastic world, a reader's perspective can be cleansed "so that the things seen clearly may be freed from the drab blur of triteness or familiarity" (57). Through escape, one may instigate praxis by arriving "at the condemnation . . . of things like factories, or the machine-guns and bombs, that appear to be their most natural and inevitable . . . products" (63). Such an ethical vision rests on the presupposition that language is a human technology that works to mediate human experience with a real world that exists objectively outside of human subjectivity. By cracking the impenetrable border between word and thing, magic (and language as art) allows human desire to influence the world.

However, from a posthumanist vantage point, the gap between word and thing, signifier and signified, is paradoxically both breachable and unbreachable. Language does indeed "get tangled up with the world it describes" because it does much more than describe the world: for the human, language *is* the world, it is what makes the very concept of *world* possible, and what we term *the human* is itself a linguistic construct. Relating this idea to magic implies that magic does not create the connection between words and things, but rather, it reveals that language is always already at the heart of our experience with reality. It frames our perceptions, prefigures our conceptions, and continuously alters our engagement with our worlds. In other words, magic reveals both the human and the world to be fantasy constructions. Early on in his Brakebills experience, Quentin learns that the language of magic must be negotiated with both the subjective and external worlds: "The same way a verb has to agree with its subject, it turned out, even the simplest spell had to be modified and tweaked and inflected to agree with the time of day, the phase of the moon, the intention and purpose and precise circumstances of the casting, and a hundred other factors" (55). Magic highlights the strange and uncanny imbrications evidenced between the human subject, language, and the worlds we create. Thus, for the magician, "there is no very clear line between what lies inside the mind and what lies outside it" (164). Especially in the extreme, isolated environments of Brakebills South, removed from anthropocentric human routines, the study and utilization of magic becomes a posthumanist becoming-with Otherness. As Professor Mayakovsky explains: "You cannot learn [magic]. You must ingest it. Digest it. You must merge *with* it. And it with you" (143). More than a simple metaphor for "becoming one with the world," Mayakovsky's tutelage suggests an active participatory engagement with Otherness; by submerging "the language of spellcasting deep into who you are" (144), the magician rejects an essentially human center of his existence and replaces there an openness to the Other. In this way, the magician's soul becomes a posthumanist soul.

Derrida finds the perfect metaphor for this trans-subjective soul from Paul DeMan. In the late 1970s, riding in a car after a jazz concert in Chicago, Derrida overhears his son speak with Paul DeMan about the construction of violins. The soul is "the small and fragile piece of wood—always very exposed, very vulnerable—that is placed within the body of these instruments to support the bridge and assure the resonant communication of the two sounding boards" (*Work* 75). Instead of the soul being some stable, central element of a single subject, Derrida positions it as a space between subjects. It supports a "bridge" that facilitates "resonant communication." Here, the center of the self exists partially outside the self, as that which assists a vibration between two subjects. Perhaps most significantly, this trans-subjective soul is "fragile" and "vulnerable," suggesting that this trans-subjectivity is not only porous and transient but subtle and endangered.

Understanding magic as a deconstructive force that reveals soul to be a fragile connection with unknowable otherness is crucial in rethinking the ethics of reading fantasy from a posthumanist vantage point. Early in the novel, when Quentin takes his Brakebills entrance examination, he expresses continued frustration at the strange nature of the questions and problems posed to him. From his anthropocentric humanist perspective that views magic, both within fantasy narrative and reality, as a source of power and entertainment, the test scenarios seem ridiculous, pointless. This is perhaps especially true of the problem in which he must respond to an excerpt from *The Tempest*:

> [T]he test gave him a passage from *The Tempest*, then asked him to make up a fake language, and then translate the Shakespeare into the made-up language. He was then asked about the grammar and orthography of his made-up language, and then—honestly, what was the point?—questions about the made-up geography and culture and society of the made-up country where his made-up language was so fluently spoken. Then he had to translate the original passage from the fake language back into English, paying particular attention to any resulting distortions in grammar, word choice, and meaning. Seriously. (23)

Despite his reluctance, Quentin must attempt to read the original passage (which might very well be the epigraph from the beginning of the novel); create a personalized, private world around a language he creates; translate the passage into this language (and subsequently, into this culture, this world); and finally translate it from this language-world back to its original language while noticing the ways in which words and meanings may become distorted via the translation. This is precisely the type of posthumanist reading practice that *The Magicians* compels its readers to perform. They must first recognize the system of language they are reading, then recreate the narrative in their own language—their own idiosyncratic version of the world—then articulate the differences, nuances, ambiguities, distortions between the three versions, thus making reading fantasy a project of living in pluralized, multivalent realities.

## "Abjectly Human": Animality and Hyperobjectivity in Posthumanist Fantasy

When lecturing on the origins of magic, Professor March invokes the apocryphal anecdote in which, after a lecture on astronomy, British philosopher Bertrand Russell engages a woman who "disproves" his theoretical assumption that the earth revolves around the sun, arguing instead that the Earth is a disc, supported on the back of a giant turtle. According to March's telling of the tale, when Russell asks, rather sarcastically, what the turtle itself stands on, the woman replies: "it's turtles all the way down" (53). The turtle metaphor does more than clarify the impossibility of rooting out the sources or origins of magic within the narrative; it aligns the study of magic with the interdisciplinary practices of critical animality studies. Rather than foregrounding the political and cultural practices of animal advocacy, as does critical animal studies, critical animality studies emerges from "theorists of the posthuman, who want to move beyond the human-animal distinction" (Dekovan 368). Led by the pioneering posthumanist thinking of Derrida, Haraway, and Giorgio Agamben, critical animality studies experiments with an evolving set of mental and social maneuvers that originate from an ethical impulse that compels an incessant rethinking of such traditional concepts as life, body, subjectivity, and world. Like the origins of magic in *The Magicians*, the concept of the animal reveals itself to be irreducible, and it is this irreducibility that seems to reside at the heart of Grossman's engagement with magic and the animal.

For Derrida, the animal Other—biological and textual, human and non-human—presents an "existence that refuses to be conceptualized" (*Animal* 9). The animal's irreducibility is particularly vexing because the endless forms of animal life that surround us and operate within us are so undeniably present, yet they struggle against being tamed under a single word or concept. Thus, what lives inside of us and in front of us gazes at us from a completely alien point of view, and "the gaze called 'animal' offers to my sight the abyssal limit of the human" (*Animal* 12). The dynamic tension between the animal gaze and the "abyssal limit" of human subjectivity compels a rethinking of both human/

animal relationships as well as the formulation of the human subject that can be explained via Grossman's treatment of the turtles. Considering the ways in which Grossman tethers magic with language, the turtle anecdote aligns animality with both biology and textuality. The endless string of turtles can be read as a symbol of posthumanist magic in that they highlight the interconnected nature of human subjectivity with multiple valences of biological and textual animalities (including the bestiaries of the fantastic). As professor March clarifies, "the farther down you go, the bigger and scalier the turtles get, with sharper and sharper beaks. Until eventually they start looking less like turtles and more like dragons" (53). The same could be said of posthumanist notions of subjectivity: the deeper down we go, searching for an imagined center, the more we find surprising modes of hybridity, suggesting that, as the animal that balances the world on its back becomes a hybridized mythological creature, the human becomes a being-with the human and nonhuman animal Other, "a hybrid, indeterminate set of interlocking relations, in constant flux" (Dekovan 367).

*The Magicians* employs the well-trodden fantasy trope of having human characters become animals. Yet, unlike many of their literary cousins who "retain a humanist perspective" in their animal states (Heise 505), Grossman's magicians do not retain their discrete human identities as they live as animals; rather, the animal Others in *The Magicians* exercise their authority in the text by remaining radically Other. When they transform, Grossman's magicians lose their fantasies of humanity and experience the world as nonhuman animals, which is to say that they do not experience *the world* at all—what they experience are the environment-worlds of nonhuman animals. As Giorgio Agamben explains via the theories of arch-ecologist Jakob von Uexküll, "a single world in which all living beings are situated . . . does not exist" (40). According to Uexküll's analysis, there is no objective space, there is no single thing called *world* or *environment*, only an infinite number of overlapping "environment-world[s]" (40). Within this model, the human is neither able to remain in nor leave its environment-world and thus seeks to locate within the subject a mode of Otherness that opens up onto other environment-worlds. In order to access this opening, Agamben argues that we must cease the articulation of ontological difference between the human and the animal: "To render inoperative the machine that governs our conception of man will therefore mean no longer to seek new—more effective or more authentic—articulations, but rather to show the central emptiness, the hiatus that—within man—separates man and animal, and to risk ourselves in this emptiness: the suspension of the suspension" (92). Agamben's anthropocentric machine refers to the philosophical history of the distinctions between the human and the animal. Such a history relies upon the essentialized nature of the human, which is to say, the fantasy that the human is what it claims others cannot be. Agamben argues, as do Derrida and Haraway, that in order to access a more accurate understanding of the human/animal dynamic, we must suspend the ideological suspension of the mythic human/animal divide and, instead, allow for biological, psychological, and textual intersectionalities to emerge. In Haraway's rather wonderful and inclusive language, we are involved in interspecies "contact zones" in which we (and our counterparts) become "material-semiotic nodes" (4). We are "knotted beings" in the process of "becoming with" our "companion species," and we "must learn to live intersectionally" (5, 16, 18).

Such posthumanist lessons are common at Brakebills South—what might be thought of as Brakebills's experientially posthumanist campus. Positioned in the icy wastes of Antarctica and run by a single faculty member who was banished from Upstate New York because of his transgression of social propriety (he had an affair with a student, which resulted in his paramour's disfiguration and another student's death), Brakebills South operates beyond the boundaries of the human. It is a site in which the practice of magic necessitates an epistemic rerouting of both ontology and human sociality. In order to locate and travel to the campus, students must first fade from their ostensibly human selves and be transformed into animals. While flying to Antarctica as a goose, Quentin's participation in the world loses its anthropocentric origins and becomes alien and refocused: "His senses now tracked only a handful of key stimuli, but it tracked those very closely.... The sky now appeared to him as a three-dimensional map of currents and eddies" (138). As a nonhuman animal that bears only the slightest trace of human consciousness, he does not simply experience the world differently, but rather, he recreates a world "from a wholly other origin" (Derrida, *Animal* 13). This first animal episode serves to destabilize his anthropocentric human identity and demonstrate the value of a world without human consciousness and civilization. As a bird, "He had no name anymore. He barely had any individual identity, and he didn't want one. What good were such human artifacts? He was an animal" (140). In a provocative move of posthumanist inclusion, Grossman allows the reader to consider Derrida's conception of the intersecting gazes of the human and the animal by narrating the inverse point of view. Instead of having the animal bring to the human an alien gaze, Grossman codes the human (Quentin's personality and identity) as an alien artifact within the environment-world of the animal.

Mayakovsky's pedagogy at Brakebills South amplifies this sense of intersectional confusion between the human and the animal. As a routine practice, he turns his group of sexually charged, overworked students into animals. One such episode, in which he turns Quentin and his companions into foxes, culminates in Quentin and Alice having sex. Or, perhaps, Quentin and Alice have sex as foxes. Or, possibly more accurately, the foxes that Quentin and Alice become, respectively, copulate. Like the goose experience, human subjectivity fades and the world itself is recreated through a nonhuman set of senses, drives, and stimuli. The episode causes an extraordinary sense of bewilderment for Quentin. Who slept with Alice? Him? A fox? Later, Quentin will reduce this experience into a reductive human lesson that translates into a condonement of hedonistic indulgence in sex, drugs, alcohol, and indiscriminate social-sexual engagement. The actual lesson, if such a thing exists, has to do with his perplexity regarding his species-being and his difficulty in understanding his human identity within intersectional or trans-subjective schemas.

To further their posthumanist educations, Mayakovsky removes his students' ability to speak. While this certainly does not abolish language or the ways it circumscribes and alters human life, it does suggest that a nonverbal experience functions as a radically alien encounter that compels the student magicians to access more fully the animalistic components of their beings, causing momentary shifts in their environment-worlds. After the afternoon as a fox, Quentin's "state of mind devolved from mesmerized to hallucinatory. Tiny random things became charged with overwhelming significance—a round pebble, a stray straw from a broom, a dark mark on a white wall—that dissipated again minutes later" (157). There is not simply a fox within him that influences his subjectivity; there is a trace of another gaze within him, another origin of the world. As human, Quentin begins to experience a mode of species vulnerability, a crack in his ideological fantasy of being human, and increasingly, becoming a magician means becoming posthuman. The lesson of the foxes, the lesson of nonhuman animality is that all human experience is fundamentally "abjectly human" (158).

The novel's engagement with the abjectly human experience of negotiating multiple environment-worlds is compounded by the novel's treatment of what Timothy Morton terms hyperobjects: entities that resist human intelligence in their scope. What we understand to be the entirety of a hyperobject is in reality a fragment of its totality. Hyperobjects are "not simply mental (or otherwise ideal) constructs, but are real entities whose primordial reality is withdrawn from humans" (Morton 15). The hyperobject compels us to rethink the concept of environment-world from the perspective of object-oriented ontology, forcing us to engage the fact that "the concept of *world* is no longer operational" (6). Like the concept of the human, *world*, Morton argues, has been utilized as an ideological placeholder—a universalizing of human perception and conception as reality—when, in reality, they are rhetorical moves. In *The Magicians*, the hyperobject comes into focus through The Beast and the Neitherworld.

When The Beast emerges at Brakebills, Quentin's perception of the world alters: "the film of reality slipped off the spokes of its projector. Everything went completely askew and then righted itself again as if nothing had happened. Except that, like a continuity error in a movie, there was now a man standing behind Professor March" (111). The film metaphor is apt in that Quentin's engagement in the world is a preformed, humanist projection with which he engages and augments. The intrusion of The Beast rewrites the script of this reality as one valence of larger and more complicated dimensions. The Beast is the perfect embodiment of the hyperobject. While it is unfathomably vast, the students experience only an excrescence of the hyperobject. As Dean Fogg explains, "what we saw would have been a small part of it, an extremity it chose to push into our sphere of being" (115). The result of the insistent and pervasive reality of the hyperobject in *The Magicians* is demonstrated through the existence of the Neitherworld, as explained by Quentin's sometimes-friend Penny: "Our world has much less substance than the [Neitherworld], and what we experience as reality is really just a footnote to what goes on there" (250). If the lesson of the foxes is that the human is an ideological trick, its unitary engagement with an environment is an ideological fantasy, then the lesson of The Beast and the reality of the Neitherworld is the lesson of the hyperobject: there is not a single world in which the human operates, and the notion of a singular world is itself the ideological trace of human exceptionalism.

Ultimately, *The Magicians* combines the reality of hyperobjects with textual animal figures that demonstrate the fragility of both the humanist and posthumanist subjects while reconfiguring magic as an openness to the vulnerable Other, even if that Other is purely textual. Together, animality and hyperobjectivity in *The Magicians* function as a call to a radical ethics of non-reciprocation, what Cary Wolfe denotes as "the *truly* ethical": an act "that is directed toward the moral patient from whom there is no expectation, and perhaps no hope, ever, of reciprocity" (*Animal Rites* 20). Susan McHugh's theory that "textual animals locate biopolitical knowledges as following from acts of reading" is also useful here in that it positions the lives of animals within texts as "contact points of aesthetic and ethical systems" (488). This line of thought is particularly important in scholarship that attempts to unpack the ethical and biopolitical implications of the fantastic in general and becomes crucial for my argument that textual constructions of animality create textual cues that invite readers to reconsider traditional frameworks of subjectivity, agency, and ethical efficacy.

The novel presents a series of small animals enlivened by magic. For both character and reader, they function as symbols, subjects, and hyperobjects that elicit an uncanny unsettlement. By impelling readers to care about beings that function primarily as objects and textual metaphors, rather than living subjects, these posthumanist magical animals allow us to feel for and with creatures that reside within us biologically and textually. Early in the novel, Quentin notices a statue of a silver bird that, imbued with an uncanny life, falls off Dean Fogg's desk: "Someone tried to change it into a real bird, but it got stuck in between. It thinks it's alive, but it's much too heavy to fly" (39). Like both characters and readers, the bird is stuck in between, not essentially real but undeniably present. The symbolic resonance of being too heavy to fly embodies perfectly the humanist subject existing in posthumanist realities, and because of this uncanny, precarious life, the bird invokes a strange sympathy for that which will never be what it conceives itself to be. The perilous nature of this life is extended with the figure that Alice creates from her marble on the first day of class at Brakebills. She forms from the delicate glass a miniature animal that she animates. However, "Forgotten, the little glass creature reached the end of the table. Alice made a grab for it, but it fell and smashed on the hard stone floor" (52). This animal life is proven to be only a momentary utterance; once it reaches the limits of its life-world (the desk, in this instance), it collapses, instigating in the reader empathic unsettlement. This feeling is perhaps invoked most strongly through the spider that Mayakovsky both kills and revivifies. Like the other magical animals in the novel, the spider's life exists only on a tabled surface—a radically limited world: "Quentin watched the poor thing creep around in circles on the tabletop, hopelessly traumatized, making little dazed rushes at nothing and then retreating to a corner, hunched up and twitching" (153). What all these magical animals share is that they are given life for clear, specific reasons. In other words, they have what Quentin has so desired: a purpose, a grand pronouncement from the powers that be that justifies his unique and special existence. These animals—alone, traumatized, afraid, broken—represent both the human selves we cling to as well as the radical ethical possibilities that become available once the human subject is revealed to be enmeshed in intersectional and trans-subjective networks of being.

Magic, then, is the means by which the human is revealed as the always already abjectly human, and this self-revolting state is precisely the mental maneuver that opens the environment-world of the human to other valences, other realities, other ethical possibilities. The human's innate imbrications with animality along with its utter inability to engage with the totality of hyperobjects deconstructs not only epistemology and ontology but the very notion of *world*. All this radical openness to Otherness positions the posthumanist subject as a radically vulnerable being, one whose borders and boundaries are always fluid and shifting and whose identities are always too multitudinous and nebulous to locate and codify. This posthumanist mesh offers a way to conceive of the posthumanist subject as able to perform, through intellectual effort and social projects of imagined empathy, the ethics that humanism purports to exist as an essential quality of the human. Grossman's posthumanist magic denotes the anthropocentric human as a fragile being enlivened only through the ideological magics of privilege and, by doing so, opens a way to operate beyond the boundaries of the human. In other words, the final lesson of the magician is to give up the illusion of the human.

## Reading Fantasy in Willing Unbelief: Posthumanist Conclusions

Despite its seeming narrative trajectory, *The Magicians* is not a posthumanist bildungsroman. It is not a becoming-human of the Pinocchio figure, as Quentin initially dreams his life with magic will make him, nor is it a narrative of a real boy who has been turned into something else, something Other. It is a narrative about a boy who cannot quite get himself to believe in a reality beyond the human. Framed by the ideological coding of the exceptional humanist subject who exists in a singular reality shared by all, Quentin's reading practices denote fantasy texts to be nothing more than escapist pleasures and magic itself to be an immature mode of wish-fulfillment that not only heals pain but removes it from the world entirely. Despite his violent and traumatic experiences in Fillory, he continues to interpret the land of Fillory, in both text and actuality, as a type of adolescent utopia: "there was conflict, and even violence, but it was always heroic and ennobling, and anybody really good and important who bought it along the way came back to life at the end of the book. Now there was a rip in the corner of his perfect world, and fear and sadness were pouring in" (118). Instead of engaging this wound in the world and attempting to work through his fear and sadness, he reads such feelings—fear, sadness, despair, alienation, loss, grief—as externalized forces that intrude into his reality of human entitlements. Even after Fogg's declaration about pain and strength—"A magician is strong because he feels pain. He feels the difference between what the world is and what he would make of it. . . . A magician is strong because he hurts more than others. His wound is his strength" (217)—Quentin remains incapable of accepting a world that pains him and, consequently, never learns to read fantasy as something that itself wounds the human and compels a rethinking of subjectivity. Quentin returns from all his adventures, textual and bodily alike, without a transformative impulse. In his post-Fillory and post-Brakebills lives, he wastes his time and his talents with "multifarious meaningless entertainments and distractions. . . . Video games; Internet porn" (395). He has become what Grossman has called elsewhere a "twixtser"—one who inhabits "a strange, transitional never-never land between adolescence and adulthood in which people stall for a few extra years, putting off the iron cage of adult responsibility that constantly threatens to crash down around them" ("Grow Up" 1). Rather than build structures in which they may create meaning and purpose, they expect the world to provide such stabilizing frameworks. They "look for something that will *add* meaning to their lives" [my emphasis], and when they do not find it, they resort to a paradoxical mode of idealistic hedonism rooted in the notion of human exceptionalism (3).

Paradoxically, it is Quentin's humanness, his belief in a secure, unitary identity, that keeps him from engaging the fantasy narrative as a means to feel and work through pain and loss. Judith Butler's now famous declaration—"We're undone by each other. And if we're not, we're missing something" (22)—becomes instructive here as a way to clarify the ethical limits of humanist reading practices of fantasy. Quentin fights wildly not to be undone and thus misses Butler's "something," which she clarifies as the transformative power of grief. For Butler, "grief contains the possibility of apprehending a mode of dispossession that is fundamental to who I am" (28). If, as Butler contends, "[t]he disorientation of grief... posits the 'I' in the mode of unknowingness" (30), then humanist "invulnerability" becomes a mode of dangerous narcissism, an unethical practice of denying the complex personhood of both self and Other. The subject's consistent reconstitution of its imagined wholeness comes at the "price of denying its own vulnerability, its dependency, its exposure, where it exploits those very features in others, thereby making those features 'other to' itself" (41). Grossman's posthumanist magic invites readers of fantasy, both within and without the text, to engage painful experiences, especially those of unknowable origins, so we may recognize "the other in me, that my own foreignness to myself is, paradoxically, the source of my ethical connection with others" (46).

I conclude by suggesting that the empathetic unsettlement instigated through a posthumanist reading of fantasy may facilitate a process by which readers can "dislocate human subjectivity" and disrupt the concept of the "secure unitary personality" (Butler 5, 6). Instead of inviting readers to consider the fantastic through a willing suspension of disbelief, as so much young adult fantasy does, Grossman's posthumanist fantasy employs textual cues that encourage readers to enter the text in what might be termed willing *un*belief: a mode of reading that allows readers to recognize the limits of their understandings while attempting to enter the world of fantasy rather than fragmenting and filtering portions of the fantasy to the quotidian. Within the posthumanist fantastic narrative, this accepted unbelief is the primary mode of understanding. We enter the fantasy and accept its rules and impossibilities not as escape but as both an analogue of our reality and as an alternative to it—a sideshadow that allows us to bring back to our lives traces of the inexplicable, the unknowable.

*The Magicians* is not merely a text that lends itself to be read in willing unbelief; rather, it constructs a posthumanist orbit of experience for the reader that might be mapped onto other fantasy texts. Bringing to other fantasy narratives an expectation of the trans-subjective, an awareness of posthuman animality and hyperobjectivity, and a self-reflexive engagement with the technicity of language might not only compel a rethinking of the genre's diacritical specificities, but it might also encourage a rethinking of the genre's cultural work, especially in regard to ethics. By reading in unbelief that which appears to be fantastic, we become vulnerable to a radical ethics of confrontation, experimentation, and speculation, rethinking narrative depictions of pain as a mode of ontological transformation, social revision, and ethical action. We enter the posthumanist fantasy as a new geography, one that invites us to sacrifice the presupposition of the human and engage the posthumanist ethics of vulnerability and radical openness to the Other, within and without. Within the imbrications of the posthumanist fantasy, wherein language, body, history, identity, environment-world, hyperobjectivity, and human/animal ontologies construct a mesh of experience, Cary Wolfe's "*truly* ethical" act of non-reciprocation becomes possible via the wounds the text instigates in us as readers.

## Works Cited

Agamben, Giorgio. *The Open: Man and Animal*. Trans. Kevin Attell. Stanford: Stanford UP, 2004. Print.

Armitt, Lucie. *Theorising the Fantastic*. London: Arnold, 1996. Print.

Butler, Judith. *Precarious Life: The Powers of Mourning and Violence*. London: Verso, 2004. Print.

Dekovan, Marianne. "Guest Column: Why Animals Now?" *PMLA* 124.2 (2009): 361–69. Print.

Derrida, Jacques. *The Animal That Therefore I Am*. Trans. David Wills. New York: Fordham UP, 2008. Print.

———. *The Work of Mourning*. Chicago: U of Chicago P, 2001. Print.

Fiske, John. *Television Culture*. London: Routledge, 1987. Print.

Grossman, Lev. "Grow Up? Not So Fast." *Time* 16 Jan. 2005. Web. 12 Dec. 2014.

———. *The Magicians*. New York: Plume, 2010. Print.

Haraway, Donna J. *When Species Meet*. Minneapolis: U of Minnesota P, 2008. Print.

Heise, Ursula K. "The Android and the Animal." *PMLA* 124.2 (2009): 503–10. Print.

Hume, Kathryn. *Fantasy and Mimesis: Responses to Reality in Western Literature*. New York: Methuen, 1984. Print.

Hutcheon, Linda. *Narcissistic Narrative: The Metafictional Paradox*. New York: Methuen, 1980. Print.

Irwin, W. R. *The Game of the Impossible: A Rhetoric of Fantasy*. Urbana: U of Illinois P, 1976. Print.

Jackson, Rosemary. *Fantasy: The Literature of Subversion*. London: Methuen, 1981.
LaCapra, Dominick. *History and Its Limits: Human, Animal, Violence*. Ithaca: Cornell UP, 2009. Print.
McCallum, Robyn. "Very Advanced Texts: Metafictions and Experimental Work." *Understanding Children's Literature*. Ed. Peter Hunt. London: Routledge, 1999. 138–50. Print.
McHugh, Susan. "Literary Animal Agents." *PMLA* 124.2 (2009): 487–95. Print.
Morton, Timothy. *Philosophy and Ecology after the End of the World*. Minneapolis: U of Minnesota P, 2013. Print.
Moss, Geoff. "Metafiction and the Poetics of Children's Literature." *Children's Literature Association Quarterly* 15.2 (1990): 50–52. Print.
Tolkien, J. R. R. "On Fairy-Stories." *Tree and Leaf*. Boston: Houghton Mifflin, 1965. 3–86. Print.
Waugh, Patricia. *Metafiction: The Theory and Practice of Self-Conscious Fiction*. London: Routledge, 1984. Print.
Wolfe, Cary. *Animal Rites: American Culture, the Discourses of Species, and Posthumanist Theory*. Chicago: U of Chicago P, 2003. Print.
———. What is Posthumanism? Minneapolis: U of Minnesota P, 2009. Print.
———. "Human, All Too Human: 'Animal Studies' and the Humanities." *PMLA* 124.2 (2009): 564–75. Print.
Zipes, Jack. "Why Fantasy Matters Too Much." *Journal of Aesthetic Education* 43.2. (2009): 79–91. Print.

# 12

# CHINA MIÉVILLE'S YOUNG ADULT NOVELS
## Posthumanist Assemblages

*Anita Tarr*

China Miéville already has had an exceptional writing career, being the recipient of the Arthur C. Clarke Award three times, the British Fantasy Award twice, the Hugo Award, the Locus Award for Best Fantasy Novel twice, plus several nominations for these same awards.[1] Miéville has described what he writes as "weird fiction," which is located "at the intersection of sf, fantasy, and horror" ("Reveling" 358).[2] However, Miéville's works are also regularly referred to as posthumanist, mainly because he dwells on hybrid creatures—animal/human, machine/human, and alien/human—and their disenfranchisement in his adult novels. He stretches the boundaries of being human and gives every creature first-class status, corresponding to Pramod K. Nayar's statement that "[i]n the posthuman vision, . . . we acknowledge that we *are* others, and therefore the human intolerance of the Other's difference—of ethnicities, life forms, species, bodies, skin colour, languages—is not simply untenable but also unethical since we have evolved *with*, and live because of, these 'others,' and share more than just the Earth with them" (47).

Miéville's own approach to posthumanism is complicated: as he has said, "I love enhancements[,] . . . tinkering with the human body. . . . [B]ut also [I love] social justice" (RSA). Here he expresses both sides of the transhumanist-bioconservative debate: pushing technology to allow humans to do more, be more, yet fearing governmental manipulation and control. Further complicating any attempt to classify Miéville's ideological framework is his devotion to Marxism.[3] Although Miéville avows that "[s]ocialism and sf are the two most fundamental influences in my life" ("Reveling" 360), he nevertheless claims he does not consciously infuse his fantasy writings with Marxist doctrine. "I quite emphatically think my writing is not activism," he argues, and insists that he writes his weird novels "as a lover of fantastic literature who wants to write the kind of fantasy novel or sf novel that I would like to read" ("Appropriate Means" 174, 171). Despite these claims that he does not utilize a Marxist worldview to present his fantasy novels, he is completely absorbed by the tension between contradictions—dialectical interrelations—and his novels involve social/political revolutions, all of which belie his public denial. Nicholas Birns writes, "Miéville champions a patchwork, hybridized, but highly material mode of resistance to constituted authority" (200). However, at his best, Miéville's fascination with ghosts, monsters, and hybrid beings propels his writings beyond entertaining socialist propaganda to present posthumanist possibilities in his characterizations, his plotlines, and even his method of storytelling.

Miéville has a reputation for repudiating genre traditions, but what he is actually doing is re-envisioning them, not just refurbishing but making them completely new by patching them together, making hybrid genres that are not one or the other but both and neither. *The City & the City* (2009), for example, follows a detective trying to solve a murder, a familiar police procedural story; the problem is that he lives in one city and the murder took place in another city. As a hybrid city, the two parts are not just imbricated but actually overlie each other, existing in the same space and time simultaneously. The citizens of each city are forced to *unsee* buildings and people of the mirror city, impossible as this might be. Miéville's hybrid characters in his celebrated Bas-Lag series are the Remade, those who have been judged as criminals and punished by having machine or animal parts grafted onto them: a dead baby's hands grafted onto her mother's forehead or a coal furnace substituting for a torso. Miéville's storytellers often express skepticism toward their craft, wanting to write the truth but knowing this is impossible, acknowledging that language cannot always convey the experience and reveling in the contradictions.

All of Miéville's novels are, to use a term often used in posthumanist writings,[4] an *assemblage* of various genres and ideologies, most conspicuously of Marxism, posthumanism, fantasy, science fiction, and Gothic horror. He understands all these aspects intimately and works them together to create kaleidoscopic novels, never unified but multifaceted. Each one is therefore irreducible and nonreplicable. However, adding the intended audience of young adults onto his assemblage seems to have been one factor too many, weighing down his flight and preventing these novels from maintaining the breathtaking views we have gotten used to. Like his adult novels, his young adult novels *Un Lun Dun* (2007) and *Railsea* (2012) have been reviewed positively, and both were awarded the Locus Award for Best Young Adult Book. *Un Lun Dun*, though, despite its brilliant wordplay, lacks the luminosity of his adult novels, and its themes seem oriented more to children than to adolescents. But because he pulls back the curtain to reveal the cranking processes of storytelling in *Railsea*, this posthumanist-Marxist-fantasy-Gothic horror-YA novel takes readers to where no one has gone before.

## *King Rat*

Prior to looking at his two officially labeled YA novels, I would like to examine *King Rat* (1998), Miéville's first novel. Although it is not marketed as young adult, it should be, for I believe it is his best, most relatable novel for young adult readers. It thus begins what I see as a loosely connected trilogy in which Miéville, with varying success, attempts to lead younger readers on adventures that encourage them to question their limitations and embrace their posthumanist possibilities. *King Rat* leads off the trilogy and makes headway, but goes only so far; *Un Lun Dun* takes a step backwards, as it rejects stereotypical characters and adventures only by offering their opposites, unsatisfactorily; *Railsea* emerges as the one that makes the necessary leap over the abyss of denial and onward to infinity.

*King Rat* begins the trilogy well enough, being the story of a young man discovering hidden animal strengths and confronting his destiny who taps into basic adolescent anxieties involving the body, father-son relations, and moral values. We also see the introduction of an important theme for Miéville: rebellion against so-called destiny, which is crucial for adolescent characters wrestling with their subjectivity. This rebellion against destiny is also emblematic of his rebelling against genre codes, especially those in children's and YA fantasies that perpetuate the idea that protagonists must discover their identity by retracing the hero's path and somehow saving the world from destruction. *King Rat*, in spite of its adult marketing label, is an example of Miéville's nonadult assemblage, being his first posthumanist-Marxist-fantasy-Gothic horror—*and*—YA novel.

*King Rat* re-envisions Robert Browning's iconic narrative poem "The Pied Piper of Hamlin" (1842). Miéville anthropomorphizes these rats, but not in a cute way; he does not use them to amplify humankind's worst traits, but they do speak in Cockney peppered with obscenities. Like the birds and spiders, the rats have always mindlessly obeyed their monarch, but anarchy has reigned for hundreds of years since the Pied Piper lured so many to their deaths; the surviving rats' descendants believe King Rat betrayed them and will no longer obey him. King Rat wants revenge and will unscrupulously employ any means necessary, including raping a human female so that she will give birth to a hybrid rat/man whom he can manipulate to return himself to the throne and to kill the Pied Piper.

This hybrid rat/man is Saul Garamond, as yet unaware of his uniqueness, a young adult slacker drifting toward oblivion. When a teenager, "he had been a living cliché, sulky and adrift in *ennui*" (27). Miéville's narrator astutely describes the turmoil of adolescence: "Saul was paralyzed in the face of a terrifying and vast future, the whole of his life, the whole of the world" (27). Although "bright" and "educated" and barely over age twenty, he continues to let "life come to him rather than wresting what he want[s] from it" (27), seeking consolation in pubs and his friends. He has also cut off all communication with his human father, who had tried to spur his son to action by having him read Lenin and bringing him along to political demonstrations. Thus Miéville identifies Marxist ideologies as a solution to adolescent anxieties, political action as the path out of helplessness and fear. Despite apathy toward his father's teachings, Saul nevertheless embraces them, even after his "father" is murdered and Saul is told that he is actually the son of King Rat (see page 183).

Once King Rat convinces Saul he is half-human and half-rat, and he starts to appreciate his ability to digest anything, along with his acute sense of smell and superhuman strength, he begins to challenge the traditional humanist boundaries separating human and inhuman, people and rats. He asks the primary questions of adolescence: "*What are the boundaries of the world?*" (54). Where are *my* boundaries? Where does my body end and the world begin? What can I do, what should I do with this newfound power? King Rat claims to have the easy answer: deny your humanity and become all-rat. The more Saul acknowledges his rat blood, the more he finds himself "shedding his humanity like an old snakeskin, scratching it off in great swathes" (83) as he keeps "busy listening to the rat in him wake up" (104). Saul believes he has found his purpose, his destiny, at last. He surrenders to it, as if it were the Pied Piper's mesmerizing tune. Gradually, however, Saul makes himself see beyond King Rat's veneer so that he can create his own sense of self; he understands that because the boundaries are permeable, he does not have to be either/or. As Stefan Herbrechter explains, "[P]osthumanism must also be understood ... as the expansion of subjectivity to include nonhuman actors ..." (198), in this case, rats.[5] Acknowledging his fragmented subjectivity, Saul rejects the destiny King Rat has laid out for him, realizing that both King Rat and the Pied Piper are equally villainous, equally dangerous to the integrity of humans. Saul brings together a loose coalition of rats and birds and spiders, and his army is victorious in defeating both the powerful lure of the Piper and King Rat (for now).

Although it is presumably the Marxist awareness that energizes Saul to action, the posthumanist elements are most interesting. Much like the adolescent who must acknowledge his/her hybridity as both child and adult, Saul has begun to appreciate his posthuman hybridity, as human/rat represents another dialectic, another contradiction, but it allows him to braid together parts from each. Because of his hybridity, he is the only one who can resist the Siren's call of the Piper's tune and thus is positioned as the only one who can resist being seduced by any one ideology:

> "One plus one equals *one*, motherfucker," he said.... "I'm not rat plus man, get it? I'm bigger than either one *and I'm bigger than the two*. I'm a new thing. *You can't make me dance*.... Well, I'm the new blood, mother*fucker*. I'm more than the sum of my parts. You can't play my fucking tune, and your flute means *nothing to me*." (*King Rat* 301)

Herbrechter states that being posthuman means "to acknowledge all those ghosts, all those human others that have been repressed during the process of humanization: animals, gods, demons, monsters of all kinds" (9), even rats. As human/rat, Saul maintains his hybridity as a new state of being, becoming posthuman, a posthuman becoming.

Miéville's novels are always set in a city, causing some critics to label him as a writer of urban fantasy. One of the hallmarks of Miéville's novels is his protagonist's attempts to "save[] the city," as Christopher Palmer explains (224). A monster is threatening the city (e.g., slake-moths, a kraken, the rats in *King Rat*, animated smog in *Un Lun Dun*), and someone has to save it. Miéville thus retains one aspect of the fantasy formula genre—the hero as savior—but interprets it in his own way and rejects the typical hero's journey. He picks up the Victorian fascination with the underbelly of the city, the slums, the sewers, and the scum of humanity, and creates tales of two cities—the rich vs. the poor, the privileged vs. the marginalized. The upper city fears pollution from the undercity and tries to not see—to purposely *unsee*—how the marginalized live. Like Charles Dickens, Miéville breaks down those boundaries between cities, forcing the two to acknowledge each other. In *King Rat*, the rats do not stay underground but ignore boundaries: as in Victorian London, rats—"the creatures of the sewers—acted as toxic intermediaries" between the two cities since they can cross over from one to the other effortlessly (Hade and Brush 125).

In *King Rat*, London is infected with garbage and refuse; angry, anxious people; deserted factories looking like "bombed-out relics," a "purgatory" (*King Rat* 71) of ruthless capitalism. Miéville makes clear that there are many ratlike humans already in London, seeming émigrés from another country, the seamy side that lives in the shadows. But those who resist the call to easy power and money, like Saul, are the only ones who continue to acknowledge their hybridity, as all human beings must do, for humans always have been and always will be hybrids. Because of co-evolution, of humans evolving along with and because of our symbiosis with animals, plants, and even bacteria, "[w]hat we understand as uniquely human," argues Nayar, "*is the consequence of hybridization and exchange of material and immaterial—data, such as in the genetic code—across species, skin and function of animals, plants and humans*" (9). Therefore, he states, "[t]he human body is a congeries, or assemblage, of multiple species, machines and organic forms" (69).

In Miéville's works, cities are also hybrids, what he refers to as abcities that are underground or doubled or mirrored. Miranda Hill focuses on these hybrid cities as Doppelgänger: "The implication of Doppelgänger places and people is not just a doubling, but also implies the idea of infinitely palimpsestic identities[,] . . . an infinitely complex version of [one's] self, one not created through negation, but acceptance of many versions" (340). Hill argues that, in spite of Miéville's frequent use of opposites and contradictions, his works are more posthumanist than Marxist, and she cautions readers to not assume that Miéville's use of dialectics, as he has claimed, is the controlling form of his structure: "[R]unning through Miéville's works is the affirmation of difference, multiplicity, and divergent flows that can never be fully explained through a dialectical framework" (4), that is, Marxism. The tension between opposites does not generate a new unified being, as would a dialectic, "but rather the creation of multiplicities" (5), as we see in Miéville's writings. Thus the dissolution of boundaries between cities—and between humans and animals and between literary genres—does not result in one unified London, but multiple Londons, as all cities are hybrid, multiple[6]—all posthumanist.

Miéville employs a straightforward omniscient narrator in *King Rat*, but the plotline is "a twisting rat-tale" (54), as we follow various characters through the labyrinthine London streets. Using either music or words, both the Pied Piper and King Rat are mesmerizing storytellers, and our own desires allow us to be tempted with good food or rotten; we do not care—our bellies "won't rebel" (51). The Piper *feeds* us illusions and dreams, promises of complete satiation we cannot resist because we are addicted to stories. But Miéville does not believe that we are "hard-wired for story," nor that stories are obviously good for us ("An Interview" 422).[7] He says, "What if it's one of the great tragedies of humankind that we're hooked on stories, and they're no better for us than junk food? Or heroin? . . . [Even though] I love storytelling, . . . I do ongoingly think the narrative drive is a suspect one—psychologically, politically, in all things" ("An Interview" 423). Here Miéville presents us with another set of contradictions: he tells stories—this is how he makes his living, after all—but he wants us to resist them. Saul shows us how: even though King Rat kills the Piper, Saul lies and takes full credit for the death, telling his rats that the king abandoned them, sold them out. The rats lick it up, as Saul knows they will, and their resentment will not let them be so easily seduced by King Rat's attempts to reestablish a monarchy after Saul leaves. Miéville says, "I am very suspicious of the notion that the presentation of the story is about *persuading* an audience of a truth—I think a lot of the time, people know very well they are being lied to" ("An Interview" 436). The rats do not know, and that is why they remain rats.

## Un Lun Dun

*Un Lun Dun* operates quite differently as an assemblage: a posthumanist, Marxist, whimsical children's fantasy. Although marketed as a YA novel, it displays few traces of adolescent anxieties, and its outward appearance marks it as a book for children, as the cover features an extremely wide-eyed young girl reading a book about umbrellas.[8] It is heavily dependent upon Lewis Carroll's *Through the Looking-Glass* (1871) and, to a lesser degree, Neil Gaiman's *Neverwhere* (1996). This dependence is not necessarily a problem, especially when we consider Zoe Jaques's assessment of the Alice books as posthumanist. Focusing on the fluid boundaries between human and nonhuman so common in classic children's fantasy, she argues that *Alice's Adventures in Wonderland* and *Through the Looking-Glass* "might be said to align with, and often predict, the agendas of posthumanism" (5–6). Not just Alice's wondering about who she is, if she has changed in the night, but also her long serpent-like neck denies her humanness, making her a human/animal hybrid that "raises particular anxieties about humanness" (47). This theme of hybridity makes the Alice books "fracturing and unsettling" for young readers (53).

*Alice*, then, is galumphing toward posthumanist ideas; but is *Un Lun Dun*? It is undeniably Marxist and would fit comfortably into Marxist Jack Zipes's classification of a "liberating fairy tale": it must reflect "*a process of struggle* against all types of suppression and authoritarianism and posit various possibilities for the concrete realization of utopia" (178). Identifying *Un Lun Dun* as an example of leftist literature—"literature that encourages children to think for themselves and argue with authority" ("Reinventing" 295)—Joe Sutliff Sanders argues that by "discourag[ing] comfortable, passive reading," it "provides a new set of unsettling subjectivities that encourage the kind of active, critical reading children's literature scholars prize" ("Reinventing" 294). Although such critical reading is a process many educators already strive to induce in young readers, Sanders identifies these skills as Marxist, since "children's literature can be another tool in the production of workers ideally and ideologically suited to fill their roles in capitalist society" and thus helps "maintain[] an oppressive status quo"

("Reinventing" 296, 297). *Un Lun Dun* definitely encourages Marxist thinking, as the characters rebel against deceitful adults who claim to be working for the good of society. *Looking-Glass* is more focused on the oppression of children as adults force upon them a master narrative, one that can override their developing awareness of posthumanist sensibilities like fragmented subjectivities and erosion of boundaries. *Alice* takes us to the brink of posthumanist possibilities, but by identifying her adventures as a dream, Carroll equivocates and draws us back. Still, he seems to be winking at his young readers, whispering to them that they, too, can go on similar adventures of their own. *Un Lun Dun*, however, wants us to believe that the adventures are all real, yet Miéville's adventures do not seem replicable by anyone at any time.

*Un Lun Dun* picks out Gaiman's one mention of London's big fog of 1952 "that they reckon killed four thousand people" (Gaiman 228) and inflates it into the ultimate villain, Smog. The rest of the novel is dependent upon the prefix *un* from *Looking-Glass*: Humpty Dumpty's un-birthday present is applied to London/UnLondon, gun/ungun, chosen/unchosen, umbrella/unbrella. Miéville's constant use of *un* grounds the novel in negation rather than in posthumanism. Also, since Miéville's protagonists are only eleven years old, the novel does not demonstrate the thrills and agonies of adolescence. The plot involves one subversive rebellion after another during the course of the mission to destroy Smog; however, these individual elements are just extensions of Carroll's subversiveness played out in *Alice Through the Looking-Glass*, itself a highly subversive book. Alice questions authority figures time after time, from the Red Queen to the Caterpillar to Humpty Dumpty, and of course she completely overturns her own trial in *Wonderland* and then, in *Looking-Glass*, the feast celebrating her rise to Queen Alice. Miéville's many fantastic creatures, too, seem derivative of Carroll's: huge ravenous giraffes, a school of sentient fish inside a deep-sea diving suit, a man with a bird enclosed within a cage instead of a head. Admittedly weird, these creatures are not as imaginative as a croquet game played with hedgehogs and flamingoes, a baby that transforms into a pig, a borogove or tove or jabberwock. Calling *Un Lun Dun* a palimpsest of *Looking Glass* would be generous, since Carroll's original shines through so vividly.

*Un Lun Dun* begins with best friends Zanna and Deeba finding themselves in UnLondon, a fantastical city beneath London. UnLondon is uncanny in its familiarity,[9] as much of it is formed from the refuse of London, including Smog, an animated humanlike figure that wants to destroy all life. Dirty laundry, trash, broken things all wind up in UnLondon; it serves as London's landfill. UnLondon desperately needs a hero, and the UnLondoners immediately recognize tall, blonde Zanna as the Schwazzy, the chosen one (French: *choisi*), because the talking book of prophecies that contains a detailed record of all her future adventures has prepared them for her arrival. Here is where Miéville performs his twist on Harry Potter and His Dark Materials and all the other stories that depend upon prophecies: the Schwazzy is defeated at her very first battle with Smog and returns to London, her mind wiped clean of any memories of UnLondon. Deeba, no longer the sidekick, calling herself the "Unchosen," decides to travel back to UnLondon to help defeat Smog. To do so, she must find and use an "ungun," since the "Kilinneract"—the Clean Air Act—that defeated the Smog after 1952 is no longer effective. Whatever the ungun is filled with—a grape seed, a grain of salt, hair—it shoots out in multitudes, so that a bullet of salt can turn an entire river into brine. Eventually, of course, Deeba and her motley crew defeat Smog by fantastical means; the ungun's chambers are empty, but by Deeba's shooting *nothing* from the ungun, Smog dissipates and becomes nothing as well.

Unlike *King Rat*, which employs a twisting tale, the omniscient narrator of *Un Lun Dun* lays out the story in a fairly straight trajectory with a fast and furious pace and frequent cliffhangers. Storytelling itself is not as suspect as it is in *King Rat*, but we see here a repeat of Miéville's contradictions regarding storytelling: Deeba can see through and does not believe in the power of authority figures, yet she is supposed to believe that what she sees in UnLondon is not a fantasy but is real. Unfortunately, there is nothing in *Un Lun Dun* that is believable; none of the fantastic creatures is half as menacing as King Rat, and even though both girls' lives are threatened, we do not take the threat very seriously. Miéville's black-and-white illustrations only add to the whimsical nature of the story: the *un*gun looks like an ordinary gun, an *un*brella looks like a broken umbrella, the written descriptions of the weird creatures ("a presence like a noseless man's face on stumpy caterpillar legs" [348]) are more vivid than the accompanying sketches. Many of Miéville's illustrations adorn the words, but they seem self-indulgent and completely unnecessary. His illustration of the ravenous giraffe—horned head, fanged teeth, slobbering mouth—simply does not compare with Tenniel's Jabberwock—whose clawed hands and feet, sharp-edged wings, and long tail poised to whip—is threatening mainly because it is ready to strike at the small boy in its path, who is not likely able enough to heft the heavy sword in time to kill the monster, itself an assemblage of several creatures. In *Un Lun Dun*, Miéville appears to misjudge his audience, assuming that young adult readers cannot deal with such heavy issues as violence or with wordy descriptions. Nor can they deal with posthumanist issues, apparently.

In *Un Lun Dun*, Miéville takes Carroll's subversive qualities and inflates them, as he does Smog, and the effect is not as powerful; Miéville's Marxist message gets in the way. The subversiveness is maintained throughout the novel when Deeba makes clear that she can easily travel between the two cities.

Sanders, though, is most impressed by the undermining of the Schwazzy's destiny as the chosen one. He sees this as a potent example of showing readers how to question the authority of the book, for it is "the book" kept sacred by the Propheseers—professors/seers—that has prophesied the Schwazzy's heroic exploits to defeat Smog. When Zanna is so quickly rendered helpless, the book must admit that its prophecies are all wrong (at the end of the story the Propheseers change their name to the Order of Suggesters).

In spite of Miéville's deliberate undermining of readers' confidence in books, and by extension the books' storytellers, undoubtedly the most brilliant aspect of *Un Lun Dun*, as in Carroll's books, is Miéville's wordplay: there is not just UnLondon, but also "Parisn't, or No York, or Helsunki, or Lost Angeles, or Sans Francisco, or Hong Gone, or Romeless" (60). Throughout the book Miéville makes a point not just to highlight the importance of words, but to give them a Humpty-Dumpty bump regarding their relationship with speakers and society as a whole. UnLondon is *below* London, but for Deeba to return to UnLondon she must climb *up* a seemingly infinite number of library bookshelves until she arrives inside the Wordhoard, the city's library, where all of UnLondon's books are held for safe-keeping against Smog, who, in its quest for omnipotence, will burn the books and inhale their smoke: "*Lovely books. Burn and learn, burn and learn*" (433). One of the most memorable scenes in *Un Lun Dun* is modeled after the one in *Looking-Glass* in which Humpty Dumpty lectures Alice on the meaning of words: "When I use a word," he says, "it means just what I choose it to mean—neither more nor less." When Alice questions "whether you *can* make words mean so many different things," Humpty Dumpty insists, "The question is . . . which is to be master—that's all" (Carroll 163).

During her journey, Deeba is impeded by Mr. Speaker, whose every word "seemed to coagulate. The word thickened and tumbled out," becoming an "animal-thing" (*Un Lun Dun* 263). Called "utterlings," they range from lizards and snakes to beakless birds and bear cubs, and none can talk; as words, ironically, they *are* speech, but the forms they take once uttered are not connected to what Mr. Speaker has just said. They are apparently a literal representation of the arbitrariness of the relationship between the signifier and the signified. Mr. Speaker will let Deeba pass only if she pays him in "CURRENCY" (265), that is, words; he has commodified words, just as Humpty Dumpty does, who says, "When I make a word do a lot of work like that . . . I always pay it extra" (Carroll 164). Mr. Speaker will not let Deeba go, even after she offers him such delightful British slang words as "bling" and "lairy." Just like Humpty Dumpty, Mr. Speaker shouts, "WORDS MEAN WHATEVER I WANT. WORDS DO WHAT I TELL THEM!" (*Un Lun Dun* 267). Since she cannot escape, a desperate Deeba informs the utterlings that they can free themselves from their oppression, and during the ensuing confusion, Deeba runs off, accompanied by a few now free utterlings.

We see a similar scene played out in *Un Lun Dun* involving London's iconic umbrellas: part of London's refuse found in UnLondon consists of broken umbrellas. Brokkenbroll, who has gained the city's trust, claims to be preparing them to be used as shields against Smog. Actually, though, the "*un*brellas" are under Brokkenbroll's thrall and are being prepared as a weapon against the people. Deeba realizes that she can patch up the unbrellas and help break Brokkenbroll's spell over them; that is, under her guidance, they free themselves, as the utterlings do. Acknowledging that they are no longer umbrellas or unbrellas, she calls them "rebrellas." Once free, each rebrella is "*something new . . . not an* um*brella, and . . . not an* un*brella. . . . Whatever it is, . . . it's its own thing, now*" (425–26). These rebrellas, like the utterlings, and like UnLondon itself, must free themselves from domination so that they can begin the unending process of becoming, no longer yoked to a classification or destiny. Deeba fights the oppressors and frees the unbrellas, but then it is their choice what they want to do, and a few join in her cause against Smog. Justyna Deszcz-Tryhubczak argues that Deeba's "role as a catalyst of resistance rather than a heroine sacrificing herself in a solitary struggle" is a positive move, for unlike Harry Potter, who is willing to martyr himself to Voldemort, Deeba's struggles "focus on ethically and biologically diversified groups of the marginalized and the oppressed who collectively struggle against concrete economic and political exploitation" (147, 140). Like Saul, she resists the call to absolute power and instead inspires the powerless to think for themselves, or at least it seems that way.

Sanders sees *Un Lun Dun* as a new kind of fantasy for children because Deeba refuses to go back to London and stay put; at the end of the novel she returns to UnLondon so that she can continue her fight to keep the two cities open to each other. "[I]n a great deal of pivotal children's fantasy published over many decades and from a variety of aesthetic and political positions, the argument is made again and again that children must leave the world of magic after the crisis has been solved," writes Sanders ("*Blatantly* Coming Back" 123). Referring to novels such as the Alice books, the Narnia series, and the His Dark Materials trilogy, Sanders posits that their "fervent policing of the line between magical, which links with child, and mundane, which links with knowing/sexual/growing adult, can be read as part of a broader cultural tradition of fetishizing the arbitrary line between childhood and adulthood" (133). The implication is that fantasy is a childish genre and must be abandoned in order for the child to enter the adult world of mimetic reading. In *Un Lun Dun*, Deeba's return again and again to UnLondon indicates that she is willing to remain open to the impossible and rejects the idea of accepting only that part of herself that lives in London. She has dual citizenship, in both London and UnLondon. Although Sanders's reading appears reasonable, I maintain that because of the many riffs from *Through the Looking-Glass*, *Un Lun Dun* seems to offer not much new in the way of rebelling against classic fantasies. It is clever, even brilliant, and is definitely an antidote to the prescribed fantasies that our culture is steeped in. We still want a hero, but just because Deeba is short and poor and black does not make *Un Lun Dun* a trailblazer. Like the Alice books, it is subversive, with cartoonish but significant adversaries. Still, although Carroll equivocates by making Alice's adventures all a dream, Carroll's creations seem more real and believable than Miéville's. And the Alice books overall seem to approach posthumanist issues more seriously, not whimsically. Miéville has created an unlikely hero in Deeba, who is able to control her fear and defeat Smog; *Un Lun Dun*, however, is so derivative of *Looking-Glass* that it is unable to drive on its own steam. Although Miéville takes a few detours, he still follows the yellow brick road to emasculate the powerful, free a subjugated people, and find a way home again, only to return again and again—something that Alice can do easily if she just closes her eyes and dreams.

## *Railsea*

Whereas *Un Lun Dun* fails to make the leap, *Railsea* is truly a posthumanist-Marxist-Gothic horror-young adult assemblage. It is not a pale palimpsest, though Miéville deliberately evokes other classic stories, including his own. Although we could not call *Railsea* a sequel to Miéville's novel *Iron Council* (2004), his most Marxist novel, it seems to be another path for *Iron Council*'s story, and the two novels share many characteristics. Foremost is that the two could be set on the same planet, although centuries apart, and both are driven by the presence of trains. In *Iron Council*, Captain of Industry Weather Wrightby is building a railroad, originating at the city of New Crobuzon, across the continent, in spite of effectually ruining the environment and exterminating any ethnic peoples who are in the way of progress. When money runs out and wages go unpaid, there is an uprising among the many workers: the male human train workers; the hybrid Remades; the xenian races of Cactacae, Khepri, Wyrmen, and Garudas; and the camp-following whores. Such an uprising would be doomed to fail if they did not come together in a kind of "vagabond socialism" (Newell 496). Chased by the government militia, the train becomes a mobile city as they try to stay ahead of their pursuers. Their tactic is unique: they lay enough track every day to move forward—whatever way that might be—and then tear up the track behind them so that no one can follow. It becomes a city on the move, a perpetual train, a train of endless becoming. After two decades of successful escape, they feel compelled to return to New Crobuzon, to join up with a citizens' uprising against a corrupt and tyrannical government. They learn that the citizens' rebellion has been put down, forcefully, but the train people refuse to turn back, even though they face total extinction from the railway controllers and government forces. To "save" them, the main character, Jonah, magically freezes the train and all its people in midmotion so that it is preserved in time, still moving.

Ironically, *Iron Council* is all about stopping railroads from traversing the continent, but Weather Wrightby says that the perpetual train has actually proven to him that he *can* build a railway across the continent. We could assume that *Railsea* shows us that he accomplished his goal and that many other railroads followed suit. Whereas *Iron Council* details the building of railroads and the consequent destruction of the environment, *Railsea* takes place on a continent that is already overlaid with multiple railroad lines, the result of "a fight between different railroad companies. . . . They were competing, all putting down new routes all over the place. . . . They burnt off years of noxious stuff—that's where the upsky comes from—& ended up chugging stuff into the ground, too, changing things. . . . We live in the aftermath of business bickering" (182–83), a clear lesson in Marxism.

*Iron Council* suggests posthumanist possibilities with its human, hybrid, and alien characters. The hybrid characters, called the Remade—renamed the fReemade after they rebel—exhibit the many ways the government thaumaturgists can think of to punish so-called criminals not by positive enhancement (say, eagle eyes) but by making their bodies grotesque reminders of their crime. In contrast, there are no alien races or Remades in *Railsea*; rather, it is a multilayered world with tenuous boundaries separating the five layers. The upsky (1) is full of dangerous flying creatures, and robotic "angels" constructed to clean and repair the railroad tracks have now gone awry; the downsky (2) is the cloudy air that the people see above; the continents (3) are raised earth, hills and valleys of tillable soil and cities; the flat earth (4) is where the railroads travel from one city-state to another; and the subterrestrial (5) is populated by huge, ravenous animals including owls, worms, rats, and moles that will eat anyone unlucky enough to fall from a train. In *Iron Council*, there are many monstrous creatures and predators, such as the huge human-caterpillar hybrid Inchmen that tear apart the workers limb by limb. *Iron Council* is filled with magical creations, most notable of which are Jonah's golems. In *Railsea*, however, there is no magic, but there is evidence of once-modern technology, such as telephones, steam or diesel train engines, electric autos, flatographs (photos), and ordinators (portable computers), which some people still use. And the giant predators all come from underground, as if the acid rain and atomic waste have altered much animal DNA. There is enough technology to create cyborgs, as there are several train captains who have artificial, enhanced limbs.

Because of all this revenant technology, Zak Bronson identifies *Railsea* as an example of salvagepunk: "In salvagepunk, the world does not end with a bang but slowly decays" (84). There are no "atomic bombs, alien invaders, natural disasters," but such apocalyptic events are "replace[d] with images of the Earth's attrition. . . . Salvagepunk . . . distinguishes itself . . . by offering apocalypse without any possibility of recuperation" of capitalist excesses that destroyed the world in the first place (84). Bronson is assuming here that the salvage dug up is put to the same use as it once was—and sometimes it is, as in the ordinators, steam engines, flatographs, and telephones. In *Railsea* there is nothing new to be had, only salvage, dug for or emerging from the underground as markers of the Heavy Metal Age, the Plastozoic, or the Computational Era. Many of the buildings in the cities consist of old appliances that simply provide heft: the Shroake family has constructed an arched entryway to their strange house out of defunct washing machines; the house itself is made of bricks and of "old ice makers called fridges, of antique ordinators, of black-rubber wheels & the hulking fish-body of a car" (157); professional salvagers wear remnants of high fashion from long ago. The planet has distinguished itself as a dumping ground, "a stopover point . . . frequented by [space] vehicles en route from one impossibly far place to another, with trash to dump" (110). In this view, it is, as Sandy Rankin states, "dystopian rather than utopian" (157). Yet Bronson insists that "[w]ith no place left to grow and no future to which to cling, salvagepunk seeks to recreate the world anew out of the wreckage that remains. . . . In fully separating itself from the past, salvagepunk envisions the utopian possibilities of recreating the world anew" (84), "radically rebuilding something new out of the debris" (85). I take issue with this aspect of salvagepunk, for Bronson's definition elides how much of the salvage is put to another use. The world of *Railsea* does not separate itself from the past, and therefore it fits the description of posthumanism better than Bronson's description of salvagepunk. Neil Badmington warns us that posthumanism "does not . . . mark or make a break from the legacy of humanism . . . [and] must not forget that it cannot simply forget the past" (121). Posthumanism always *includes* some aspects of humanism, as N. Katherine Hayles writes: "We do not leave our history but rather, like snails, carry it around with us . . ." (137).

As usual, Miéville riffs off other authors in *Railsea*, but this time he does it openly, as an homage, offering readers the opportunity to play amateur archeologist in discovering his source material. Teenage protagonist Shamus

Yes ap Soorap—Sham—goes on a journey that evokes such classic seafaring adventures as *Treasure Island*, *Robinson Crusoe*, and especially *Moby Dick*, but instead of a ship he is on a train speeding across the railsea.[13] Sent out by his uncles as an apprentice to a doctor on the *Medes*, a mole train seeking to kill giant moles as we once did whales, Sham ends his directionless journey with the onset of another journey, this time on an actual ocean, the one he finds at the end of the railsea. Like Deeba, he has attracted a motley crew to accompany him, and as he progresses, he changes from a clumsy, dopey boy into an athletic young adult whose curiosity gives him drive and purpose. Sham looks and acts like Saul in *King Rat*, but Sham does not require a background in Marxism or a realization of his human-animal hybridity to spur him to action; the catalyst appears to be the attraction he feels for Caldera Shroake, which is more in keeping with an adolescent boy's priorities. The Shroake siblings, Caldera and Dero, are continuing their dead parents' quest to find what is at the end of the railsea, and their cause parallels Sham's and eventually that of Abacat Naphi, captain of the *Medes*, who also is purposeless after her obsession with the giant tooth-colored moldywarpe she has named Mocker-Jack ends in its death. Abacat Naphi, whose name is an anagram for Captain Ahab (Bronson 86, n. 1), has a high-tech artificial arm, instead of Ahab's wooden leg, to replace the one Mocker-Jack took from her. However, her cyborgness is later revealed to be an affectation; she thought that losing a limb would give her more credibility among her colleagues. More important is the fact that, as in *King Rat*, she is a storyteller; she is not just Sham's captain but also the mentor of his storytelling, teaching him to embellish and twist, manipulate and enthrall. In *Railsea*, storytelling is a prominent manifestation of its posthumanist tendencies.

Because Miéville highlights Sham's process of becoming a storyteller, we are warned once again to be suspicious: like all stories, Sham's stories are a *sham*. Harking back to his mistrust of storytelling as an addictive drug, in *Railsea* Miéville combines storytelling with the Marxist condemnation of commodification.[11] There is even a market for stories, or rumors: a better story yields a "higher price tag," and there are buy-one-get-one-free sales (67). There are stories about the origin of the railsea ("heavenly script," the result of a "godsquabble"), and stories about Heaven and about the mythological treasure there and about gods like That Apt Ohm, the "[g]reat chimney-headed controller in dark robes," an image evoking both pollution and religion (186, 181–82). The nomadic Bajjer tell stories around their nightly campfire; the Shroake siblings tell each other stories to keep up their spirits; the train workers tell stories when they pull into port; the mole-train captains (each of whom has lost a limb) exchange stories of their philosophies in their favorite pub, where "[t]he story of the hunt [is] as much their work as the catching of meat" (102). Sham is in the audience for one of Naphi's storytelling sessions. He wonders what she can talk about when he knows they had not seen Mocker-Jack even once during their journey to the South Arctic, but she manages to live up to her reputation as both a great mole-train captain and a storyteller by saying, "[Mocker-Jack's] absence was a looming presence. The lack of him filled me with him. . . . He stayed away & came closer in one magic movement" (104). Naphi's story entrances the audience by demonstrating that although she has yet to capture Mocker-Jack, she has already captured her audience.

Miéville presents storytelling as a skilled art, needing lots of practice. Sham is aware that to become a true train worker he must learn to tell a story well, for the two activities are closely intertwined. His first attempt coincides with his mates' initiation into the world of pub-hopping, so that his story is a "garbled version" which he drunkenly attempts to control "like a train on a straight stretch" (75). He sees the many faces surrounding him, and he thinks, "*Look at me, . . . the storyteller*," unaware that he has just divulged his discovery of the Shroakes' parents' flatographs of the single rail that leads to the mythological treasure, and that is the main reason why he has commanded such an attentive audience. But his talent improves and he learns to embellish, though "there were some events he told & varnished nothing" (99). His uncles, his first true audience, are enrapt with his tales of his pet daybat, and declare him to be "a proper grown man now," as a commendation of being able to turn his small adventures into a rousing story (99). His fledgling storytelling flounders when he is in front of a new, more seasoned audience, the Shroakes: Sham "stumblingly turned an anecdote or two from his ordinary childhood into stories of an exotic land" (191), but they are not impressed. When he decides not to go with the Shroakes on their own train journey, he is dejected and tells a "scrappy version" of the story of finding the flatographs and the Shroakes, speaking "in vague terms of 'evidence,' of 'something,' of a secret," to his new friend Robalson (205–96). Sham is still naïve and lacks judgment, for Robalson tricks Sham into following him into the shadowy night, where the pirates abduct him.

Bronson extends his concept of salvaging, repurposing rather than restoring, not just to the world of *Railsea* but to the method of Miéville's storytelling. In their "UnIntroduction," Caroline Edwards and Tony Venezia claim that Miéville's "strategy of absorbing numerous other sources thus gives rich texture to the intertextual density of Miéville's works, and may be read as informed by avant-garde literary experimentation" (28). This comment is more applicable to *Railsea* than to *Un Lun Dun*, which I find quite disturbing in its downright pilfering, especially from *Through the Looking-Glass*. Miéville admits, "I still find myself riffing off books from my past constantly, sometimes without remembering what I'm basing my writing on. . . . I'm still scared of inadvertently ripping people off. . . . God knows what else I've filched" ("Reveling" 358, 369).[12] Bronson, though, declares *Railsea* to be provocatively new and unique, for Miéville *salvages* elements from *Moby Dick, Treasure Island, Robinson Crusoe, Tremors, Dune,* and many other sources, as if these classic novels and cult films are dead and buried: "Miéville reuses both his own ideas and others', offering *Railsea* as an amalgam of the past's remnants that simultaneously builds on them and transforms them into something entirely distinctive. Miéville imagines his world by plumbing a vast archive of literature, repurposing it to construct a new world out of the confines of what already exists" (92).

For example, Miéville borrows Robert Louis Stevenson's solution to the dilemma of recording events necessary to the plot when the narrator is not present to record them. In *Treasure Island,* when Jim is being held captive in the pirates' hut, he is incapable of knowing what is going on outside the hut's confines. Stevenson blithely switches narrators, from Jim to Doctor Livesay—problem solved—to tell how his friends arranged to rescue Jim. Similarly, when Sham, the focalizer but not the narrator, is unconscious, the narrator asks, "*What should the story do when the primary window through which we view it is shuttered?* we might say: *It should look through another window. That is to say, follow other rails, see through other eyes,*" thus "perform[ing] the cheeky escapology of narrative" (*Railsea* 211). Miéville also borrows J. M. Barrie's narrator from *Peter Pan,* who addresses the audience directly and plays with the various strands of stories as he pleases, sometimes just to be sp(r)iteful. Miéville's narrator instructs readers to "[i]nvestigate a map" to find the "all-around particularly problematical parts of the railsea" where "[t]he rails misbehave. Switches do not do as they are bid, ground is not so strong & stable as it appears, there are chicanes & trouble, the iron itself has been made to mess with trains" (285). Bronson refers to *Railsea* as an "amalgam," which implies that it is a combination of items that work together. I would argue instead that *Railsea* represents an *assemblage* of elements that do not work together, do not coalesce into an alloyed story, and therefore inform a posthumanist style of storytelling.

Miéville gives readers fair warning regarding the twists and turns in *Railsea*. Captain Naphi describes the journey to find Mocker-Jack as "a long trip, this one. You never know *where* we might end up, or by what route we might have to go" (122). Miéville uses the ampersand to describe his narrator's process of telling the stories of *Railsea*. The ampersand also describes the crisscrossing of the many tracks of the railsea:

> The lines of the railsea go *everywhere* but from one place straight to another. It is always switchback, junction, coils around & over our own train-trails.

> What word better could there be to symbolize the railsea that connects & separates all lands, than "&" itself? Where else does the railsea take us but to this place & that one & that one & that one, & so on? & what better embodies, in the sweep of the pen, the recurved motion of trains, than "&"? (163–64)

Miéville's use of the ampersand as a symbol of storytelling is somewhat more devious, for we never know where he is going. The narrator tries to braid together stories about Sham, the Shroakes, and the crew of the *Medes*—on three different trains—and since he cannot layer the stories, he must use "a veering route, up & backwards, overshooting & correcting" (163). The McGuffin of *Railsea* is that there are myths about there being a treasure at the end of the railsea; the Shroakes' parents were on their way there but failed to return, and Sham has seen the parents' flatographs and made sketches of them. The result is that the Shroakes and Sham are being pursued by pirates and city militia who believe the three can lead them to the treasure. Caldera Shroake and her younger brother Dero are on their own train, not to discover a forgotten treasure but to find the route their parents had taken that will show them what, if anything, is at the end of the railsea. Meanwhile, Sham has been on a mole-hunting mission on the *Medes*, but he has been kidnapped by pirates and is on another train. The narrator begins to tell about the Shroakes, but changes his mind:

> —but wait. On reflection, now is not the time for Shroakes. There is at this instant too much occurring or about to occur to Sham ap Soorap. . . .
> *This* train, our story, will not, cannot, veer now from this track on which, though not by choice, Sham is dragged.
> Later, Shroakes. (273)

So we are told of Sham's capture and his later escape to a small deserted island off the railsea, where he tries to figure out how to outwit the subterranean creatures and get back to the *Medes*. Later, the narrator intercedes again to explain why he cannot switch back to the Shroakes:

> At this point, the intention had been to say that it was such slippery western terrain as few trainsfolk ever see, such strange wrong rails, that the Shroakes, by then, had reached, & in which & on which they travelled. But the time is not right yet.
> The instant it is feasible, the Shroakes will be found. It's Caldera & Dero, after all: as if they could be ignored. . . . It would be wrong to leave them forever. But though the rails themselves are everywhere in profusion, fanned out & proliferating in all directions, we can ride only one at a time. (296)

A few pages later: "Time for the Shroakes? Not yet" (308). And later again: "It is, in fact, not time for the Shroakes. Not quite" (335). Then finally: "Now. At last. Surely. This must be the moment to return to the Shroakes & to their rail. Surely. It is, in fact, yes, Shroake O'Clock" (342), which introduces the intersection of all three stories: Sham's, the Shroakes's, and the *Medes*'s. Here, the narrator can tell all three stories at once because Caldera, Dero, and Sham are all on the *Medes*: one new story, one track that leads them to the end of the world. But this unification is only temporary, as on this one train they indirectly destroy the mechanical angel guarding the rails and the moldywarpe Mocker-Jack, both of which are chasing the *Medes*: having been lured to the *Medes*, they are entangled together and fall into a large abyss. Now there is nowhere for the *Medes* to go except across the one track that traverses the abyss, and though some characters abandon the journey at this point, the narrator sticks to this one track until they reach the end of the railsea.

This abyss is the implied goal of the *Medes* and of the narrator, who addresses readers directly to explain the *mise-en-abyme*—story of a story of a story *ad infinitum*. After Captain Napthi's storytelling session at the pub, the narrator tells us, "We have just had a story of a story. Tell it yourself, again, & story of a story in a story will be born, & you will be en route to that *abyme*. Which is an abyss" (106). Indeed, after all the tantalizing rumors and stories about the heaven or the treasure that lies at the end of the railsea, when the characters finally arrive, they find that "Heaven, the world beyond the railsea, was empty, & very long dead. . . . Everything was made at once clear & meaningless . . ." (399). There is no treasure, no heaven here, just a few descendants of the railsea's controllers. In Marxist mode again, Miéville implies that this is where capitalism leads us—to the abyss or to a dead end. These descendants, like the rats in *King Rat* who stupidly believe a new king will lead them back to dominance, still believe the story the railroads had told them so long ago, that they would be paid for their work, eventually, with interest. Over the centuries, obsessed with what they were due, they have transformed into hybrid human/animals: "Rag-clad, hulking & shaggy, creeping, sniffing, they loped out of the dust that announced them . . . , baring their teeth, coming on two limbs & four, apelike, wolflike, fatly feline" (406). Existing on their eternal greed, in thrall to "the hunger of a company presiding over ruin," they are "the remnants of this bureaucratic heaven" (406, 410). Beyond them is a vast ocean, which they have ignored.

These "remnants" attack Sham and his friends savagely, but Sham shouts, "This isn't how it ends!" and barely avoids death, as well as the end of the story. The never-ending journey continues as Sham devises a sailing boat from an upside-down railcar, and he and the Shroakes and Naphi set off to explore without a map or star-chart or photographs to guide them. They embark on a journey of endless possibilities, shed of capitalist progress, competition, and destruction. Rhys Williams sees this nonending as Sham's break with his known world, "driven to escape the closed tangle of his society, to escape the accustomed routes and arrive at a new frontier.... He does not have a preconceived idea of where he is going or what he wants—such ideas would have tied him back into what he already knows. What he does, in contrast, is reject the traditional narratives, the traditional fates available to him" (629–30). Sham is Ishmael and Jim Hawkins and Hawkeye and Robinson Crusoe, an example of what Herbrechter defines as posthumanist: "The posthuman individual as social and political actor within a deanthropocentred environment is not so much a singular identity but a collection of co-operating actors..." (205). Sham is an assemblage of all these beloved characters and more, and tied to none of them. He is journeying beyond maps, beyond destiny, beyond scripted stories.

Just as Sham is freed from traditional characterizations, so are Miéville's fetters to genre. Borrowing from *Moby Dick* does not require strict adherence to its plot or to its characters' fate. Miéville is not eschewing all genres but braiding them together as an assemblage of many. Miéville says himself, "I don't think genre is muck to be kicked off. I think it's a set of protocols you can do wonderful things with" ("An Interview" 419). He is not throwing out all of history, either, which is what Bronson argues; Sham's creation of a boat from an upside-down train car points to a posthumanist process because, as Herbrechter claims, throwing out all humanist tendencies or capitalism in an apocalyptic destruction would signal a rebirth of the same ideology (48–49). Sham does not want another railsea built on a drained ocean, but he does want to explore other possibilities and help in the creation (not the rebirth) of a better world(s). Herbrechter defines critical posthumanism as "postanthropocentric" with "the possibility of a return to some fundamental aspects of humanism" (106). We can see these "fundamental aspects" in Sham's character—his compassion and empathy, his loyalty, his curiosity, his courage. These are worth keeping.[13]

Separating from Miéville's Marxist considerations, Kristen Shaw focuses on the *mise-en-scene* design of the railsea: "From the very start the reader is treated to a highly rhizomatic landscape, an illustration of Deleuze and Guattari's 'machinic assemblage' made literal" (16). The tangle of rail lines has no beginning and seemingly no end, a network lying across the land tentatively and haphazardly. The rhizome, write Gilles Deleuze and Félix Guattari, "always has multiple entryways" (12). Shaw describes how Captain Naphi as humanist and Sham as posthumanist view the landscape differently: she sees it as ordered according to her hunting of Mocker-Jack, so that everything is hierarchized by what is either aiding or detouring her obsessive hunt; Sham, though, sees in a "nomadic, rhizomatic, or heterogeneous" way to create an opening to other possibilities. Naphi is reduced to one way; Sham has "the *multiplicitous*, the plural, the diverse" (Shaw 26–27). "Naphi relates to the railsea as though it is a grid mapped out in advance, and as such, her perception of the railsea is fixed." Everything is invisible except for Mocker-Jack; it is her "philosophy" because it is her "organizing principle" (30–31). Sham, however, rebels against such a unifying perspective and comes to admire the Bajjer nomads who rescue him after he escapes from the pirates. These wandering people on "wind-powered trains [that] hauled a zigzag way across the railsea" move on an "unending journey" (Miéville 322, 324), living naturally within the environment, neither enhancing by farming nor destroying by building. They have no maps, they need no maps, yet they show the way into the future, with Sham, to "the unknown. Off the edge of the map" (340). The fact that Naphi, no longer hunting her philosophy (Mocker-Jack), joins Sham and the Shroakes on their new journey indicates that she, too, is beginning to see nomadically. The Bajjer seem to exemplify Miéville's vision of posthumanist storytelling, leaving no traces of their movement, jumping easily from track to track, from one wind-powered train to another just as the narrator does.

In *Railsea*, by comparing storytelling to the ampersand, the narrator concedes upfront that there will be twists and turns and retracing routes. "We are slowing. We will soon be done, & at our destination," he tells readers in the last few pages (412). He even challenges any readers who would question his method that if they do not like it, they can take over his position: "Had you been in charge you would, even had you started and ended in the same places, have described a different figure. A different '&.' But nothing's done. If you tell any of this to others, you can drive, & if you wish, go elsewhere on the way. Until then, safe travels & thank you" (413). Only when Sham and Caldera and Dero and Naphi are on their upside-down train car does the narrator give up his reign, ceding the navigation to the reader. Naphi and Sham have traded roles, and he is now the captain of the ship. But as the narrator says, Sham will tell his story, and each one of us will tell ours. He is setting us free, to explore all the possibilities, all the infinite ways of a posthumanist storyteller telling a posthumanist multitude of stories.

## Conclusion

Allow me to use Miéville's ampersand as a conclusion. Look at "&." Notice how after it twists and turns it ends very near its beginning. *King Rat*, *Un Lun Dun*, and *Railsea* are all assemblages, being more or less posthumanist-Marxist-fantasy-young adult/

children's books. Miéville has created a rat's tail of three novels, moving forward with *King Rat*, backwards with *Un Lun Dun*, and finally making the leap across the abyss with *Railsea*. But *Un Lun Dun* remains a disappointment, too tethered to Marxism to be more than a cover performance of Carroll's earlier masterpiece.

Young adult readers deserve more from Miéville. They deserve to be able to consider not just his subversiveness, which is not uncommon in YA literature, but also his high-flying ideas that help us understand ourselves as fragmented beings and see a future full of posthumanist possibilities. The truth is that despite all the weird creatures and narrative play, neither *Railsea* nor *Un Lun Dun* is as engaging as any of Miéville's adult novels. His matchless ability to create pleasurable cognitive dissonance for readers of his adult science fiction is weakened so much in *Un Lun Dun* that the novel's prominent theme of resisting consumerism becomes irritatingly didactic. *Railsea* is more singularly creative and opens up more posthuman options, but Miéville declines to offer a full portrait of any character, even Sham, thus draining its power and impact on readers. *King Rat*, Miéville's most realizable young adult posthuman novel, is the real thing, but unfortunately has been mismarketed to adult readers.

From the beginning, humans evolved symbiotically with other species, and though we have been addicted to many stories that insist there are humans and then there are nonhumans, there has never been an exclusive *human*. We have always been multiple, fragmented, posthuman. Perhaps Miéville's most prominent feature of posthumanism is his self-awareness, his condition that, indeed, to be human we must acknowledge our posthumanity. If only he would share this awareness with *all* his YA audiences.

## Notes

1. *Perdido Street Station* won the 2001 Arthur C. Clarke Award and the British Fantasy Award. *The Scar* won the 2003 British Fantasy Award and the Locus Award for Best Fantasy Novel. *Iron Council* won the 2005 Arthur C. Clarke Award and the 2005 Locus Award for Best Fantasy Novel. *The City & The City* won the 2010 Arthur C. Clarke Award and the 2010 Hugo Award.

2. In an interview with David Naimon, Miéville says, "'Weird Fiction' was a term I borrowed from the tradition most obviously associated with writers like H. P. Lovecraft . . . The reason I like it is because it was a tradition that stressed the grotesque but also had a blurry line between the fantastic and the science fictional . . . [which I] think is a spurious distinction. I don't buy it. A tradition that glories in that blurriness is very attractive to me, very appealing . . ." (Miéville, "Conversation" 64). Although New Weird is a good descriptor of Miéville's overall emphasis (if not style, which changes with each book), he has since 2005 distanced himself from the term (Edwards and Venezia 33, n. 3).

3. Miéville is open about his Marxist beliefs. His dissertation at the London School of Economics was published as *Between Equal Rights: A Marxist Theory of International Law*, and in 2001 he ran for a seat in the general election for the Social Alliance. He continues to write nonfiction and edit socialist publications.

4. For example, in their "UnIntroduction," Edwards and Venezia, acknowledging Miéville's genre blending but insisting upon referring to it just as Weird, offer a suitable description of Miéville's novels as posthumanist: "the moment when disparate and wholly incompatible entities are yoked together into a bastardized assemblage which cannot be reconciled into any form of union, but jostle uneasily" (14). Nayar defines *critical posthumanism* as "seek[ing] to move beyond the traditional humanist ways of thinking about the autonomous, self-willed individual agent in order to treat the human itself as an assemblage, co-evolving with other forms of life, enmeshed with the environment and technology" (3–4).

5. Herbrechter explains that "boundaries have been constructed which are supposed to create a community of humans based on their 'humanity' ('we' as a species)," but "these boundaries are supposed to protect 'us' in our essence from more or less concrete and threatening forms of 'otherness.'" However, "these boundaries which are always portrayed as absolute, inviolable and universally valid for all times are in fact concealing a perfect permeability" (47).

6. In their efforts to explain how electrons can be both waves and particles, quantum physicists suggest that there are infinite multiple universes; every action results in one consequence that we see here on our world, but the many other possible consequences are each played out in other universes. Such a theory corresponds nicely with Miéville's concept of abcities.

7. Miéville's fear that we are addicted to story is cast in a more positive light by Brian Boyd, who argues in his *On the Origin of Stories* that "art in general and storytelling in particular are . . . adaptations in our species," an adaptation being "any trait modified by natural selection that enhances fitness, the capacity to survive and produce viable offspring" (35, 34). That is, "the chief functions of art and story lie in improving human cognition, cooperation, and creativity" (378), implying that storytelling is in fact part of our evolutionary constitution. Jonathan Gottschall adds in his *The Storytelling Animal: How Stories Make Us Human*, "the human mind was shaped *for* story, so that it could be shaped *by* story" (56).

8. I am using the 2008 Del Rey Books trade paperback edition. On the cover is a quote from Salon.com: "Endlessly inventive . . . [a] hybrid of *Alice in Wonderland*, *The Wizard of Oz* and *The Phantom Tollbooth*."

9. UnLondon is very much its own city, separate from London-above, but it is not some utopian city or children's playland. It marginalizes some of its own citizens, especially the ghosts in Wraithtown. As in J. M. Barrie's Neverland, there are real dangers such as the giant ravenous giraffes, and Deeba and Zanna are supposedly in mortal danger. Only the Propheseers have control over the city's future. And UnLondon's leaders are not immune to Smog's promise of power, even though its purpose is to destroy their city.

10. Writing *Railsea*, says Miéville, "allowed me to riff off lots of sea books: *Treasure Island*, *Robinson Crusoe*, as well as *Moby-Dick*, of course. It seems like most writers have their *Moby-Dick*

riff book in them somewhere. Plus, people have been making Melville jokes about me for many years—Melville, Miéville. So why not take it head on" ("An Interview" 428).

11. In all three novels discussed here, Miéville obviously conflates eating with listening to stories, exaggerating the Marxist implications. In *Railsea* the monsters are not just carnivores; they are *consumers*. Often blind, sometimes humanlike in form with torsos and limbs, they mindlessly devour flesh. Smog in *Un Lun Dun* devours anything or anyone in its way. In *Railsea* the hungry monsters rise up from underneath and are all teeth: "[a]lmost everything wants to eat almost everything else" (45). Their pursuit of reward or glory eats at everyone, just like Captain Naphi's obsession with Mocker-Jack eats at her (he is tooth-colored, after all). The railsea itself is a result of corporate greed, competing for dominance. To build the rails, the corporations had to first drain the ocean—consume it—before laying down any track. Rampant capitalist consumerism has destroyed Sham's home continent, and when he reaches the end of the railsea, the descendants of the railway corporations demand payment, which Sham cannot and will not pay. We could even suggest that Miéville's voracious reading habits are part of this theme, but unlike Smog's burning, which destroys the books, he enlarges them, enhances them. In children's stories, eating is analogous to desires, such as sexual urges, that need to be controlled—think of all the trouble Hansel and Gretel get into.

12. Birns recalls the same complaint at a book talk when Miéville "denied a connection" with another work that Birns suggested. "He is under no obligation to acknowledge those precursors, which would make things tighter and more convenient for the critic, but one wonders if what Harold Bloom famously called the Anxiety of Influence is going on here. Surely, his opposition to Tolkien is much like Philip Pullman's opposition to C.S. Lewis, a kind of inverse tribute. Miéville is so outstanding a writer his critics perhaps owe it to him to be slightly tougher on his claimed genealogies. To trace Miéville back to writers he does not overtly acknowledge but who, in the light of literary history, would seem to have an effect is to pay tribute to his work" (210, n. 1).

13. Rosi Braidotti argues that humanist values cannot be shunned totally, especially "individualism, autonomy, responsibility and self-determination," as well as "social justice and principles of equality," and "respect for science and culture" over "religious doctrine" (29).

## Works Cited

Badmington, Neil. *Alien Chic: Posthumanism and the Other Within.* Oxon: Routledge, 2004. Print.
Birns, Nicholas. "From Cacotopias to Railroads: Rebellion and the Shaping of the Normal in the Bas-Lag Universe." *Exploration* 50.2 (2009): 200–12. *Art and Humanities Citation Index.* Web. 7 May 2016.
Boyd, Brian. *On the Origin of Stories: Evolution, Cognition, and Fiction.* Cambridge: Belknap/Harvard UP, 2009. Print.
Braidotti, Rosi. *The Posthuman.* Cambridge: Polity, 2013. Print.

Bronson, Zak. "Reproduce, Reuse, Recycle: The End of the Future, Salvage, and China Miéville's *Railsea*." *Paradoxa* 26 (2014): 81–96. *Humanities International Complete*. Web. 6 July 2016.

Carroll, Lewis. *Alice in Wonderland: Authoritative Texts of Alice's Adventures in Wonderland, Through the Looking-Glass, The Hunting of the Snark*. Ed. Donald J. Gray. New York: Norton, 1971. Print. Norton Critical Edition.

Deleuze, Gilles, and Félix Guattari. *A Thousand Plateaus: Capitalism and Schizophrenia*. Trans. and Foreword by Brian Massumi. Minneapolis: U of Minnesota P, 1987. Print.

Deszcz-Tryhubczak, Justyna. "'Minister,' Said the Girl, 'We Need to Talk': China Miéville's *Un Lun Dun* as Radical Fantasy for Children and Young Adults." *Critical Insights: Contemporary Speculative Fiction*. Ed. M. Keith Booker. Englewood Cliffs: Salem P, 2013. 137–51. Print.

Edwards, Caroline, and Tony Venezia. "UnIntroduction: China Miéville's Weird Universe." *China Miéville: Critical Essays*. Ed. Caroline Edwards and Tony Venezia. Canterbury: Gylphi, 2015. Print.

Gaiman, Neil. *Neverwhere*. 1996. New York: HarperCollins, 2003. Print.

Gottschall, Jonathan. *The Storytelling Animal: How Stories Make Us Human*. Boston: Houghton Mifflin, 2012. Print.

Hade, Daniel D., and Heidi M. Brush. "'The Disorders of Its Own Identity': Poverty as Aesthetic Symbol in Eve Bunting's Picture Books." *Little Red Readings: Historical Materialist Perspectives in Children's Literature*. Ed. Angela E. Hubler. Jackson: U of Mississippi P, 2014. 116–32. Print.

Hayles, N. Katherine. "Afterword: The Human in the Posthuman." *Cultural Critique* 53 (2003): 134–37. *JSTOR*. Web. 17 June 2016.

Herbrechter, Stefan. *Posthumanism: A Critical Analysis*. London: Bloomsbury, 2013.

Hill, Miranda. "Minding the Gap: Connecting the Mirror Cities of London in the Novels of Neil Gaiman and China Miéville." Honors thesis. U of Tennessee at Chattanooga. *OAlster*. Web. 7 June 2016.

Jaques, Zoe. *Children's Literature and the Posthuman: Animal, Environment, Cyborg*. New York: Routledge, 2014. Print. Children's Literature and Culture 102.

Miéville, China. "Appropriate Means: An Interview with China Miéville." Interview by Mark Bould. *New Politics* 9.3 (2003): 169–76. *MasterFILE Premier*. Web. 7 May 2016.

———. *The City & The City*. New York: Del Ray/Ballantine, 2010. Print.

———. "A Conversation with China Miéville." Interview by David Naimon. *Missouri Review* 34.4 (2011): 53–66. *Project Muse*. Web. 4 June 2016.

———. "An Interview with China Miéville." Interview by Kristen Tranter. *Contemporary Literature* 53.3 (2012): 417–37. *MLA International Bibliography*. Web. 7 May 2016.

———. *Iron Council*. New York: Ballantine, 2005. Print.

———. *King Rat*. New York: Tom Doherty Associates, 1998. Print.

———. *Railsea*. New York: Ballantine, 2013. Print.

———. "Reveling in Genre: An Interview with China Miéville." Interview by Joan Gordon. *Science Fiction Studies* 30.3 (2003): 355–73. *Arts and Humanities Index*. Web. 7 May 2016.

———. *Un Lun Dun*. New York: Del Ray/Ballantine, 2008. Print.

Nayar, Pramod K. *Posthumanism*. Cambridge: Polity, 2013. Print.

Newell, Jonathan. "Abject Cyborgs: Discursive Boundaries and the Remade in China Miéville's *Iron Council*." *Science Fiction Studies* 40 (2013): 496–509. *JSTOR*. Web. 30 Mar. 2016.

Palmer, Christopher. "Saving the City in China Miéville's Bas-Lag Novels." *Extrapolation* 50.2 (2009): 224–38. *Humanities Index Complete*. Web. 2 June 2016.

Rankin, Sandy. "The Fantastic as a Marked Absence (or Not) in China Miéville's *Railsea*." *Critical Insights: Contemporary Speculative Fiction*. Ed. E. M. Keith Booker. Englewood Cliffs: Salem P, 153–68. Print.

RSA (Royal Society for the encouragement of Arts, Manufactures and Commerce). "Humanity 2.0." Online video clip. *YouTube*. YouTube, 10 Oct. 2011. 27 May 2016.

Sanders, Joe Sutliff. "'*Blatantly* Coming Back': The Arbitrary Line between Here and There, Child and Adult, Fantasy and Real, London and UnLondon." *China Miéville: Critical Essays*. Ed. Caroline Edwards and Tony Venezia. Canterbury: Gylphi, 2015. 119–38. Print.

———. "Reinventing Subjectivity: China Miéville's *Un Lun Dun* and the Child Reader." *Extrapolation* 50.2 (2009): 293–306. *Humanities Index Complete*. Web. 7 May 2016.

Shaw, Kristen. "Ruining Representation in the Novels of China Miéville: A Deleuzeian Analysis of Assemblages in *Railsea*, *The Scar*, and *Embassytown*. MA thesis. U of Western Ontario, 2012. *Electronic Thesis and Dissertation Repository* Paper 847. Web. 5 June 2016.

Stevenson, Robert Louis. *Treasure Island*. 1883. New York: Scholastic, n.d. Print.

Williams, Rhys. "Recognizing Cognition: On Suvin, Miéville, and the Utopian Impulse in Contemporary Fantastic." *Science Fiction Studies* 41.3 (2014): 617–33. *JSTOR*. Web. 30 March 2016.

Zipes, Jack. *Fairy Tales and the Art of Subversion: The Classical Genre for Children and the Process of Civilization*. New York: Routledge, 1991. Print.

# NOTES ON CONTRIBUTORS

**Torsten Caeners** studied British and American Literature and Culture in combination with Computational Linguistics at the University of Duisburg. He finished his studies in October 2004 with an M.A. thesis on the shorter poetry of the Augustan poet Dr. William King. Since then he has been teaching at the Department for Anglophone Studies at the University of Duisburg-Essen. In 2010, he was awarded his Ph.D. with a thesis investigating the application of poetic writing for psychoanalytical treatment in the context of post-structuralist literary theory. In addition to being a lecturer for Anglophone Literature and Culture, he currently holds the position of Study Program Manager for the B.A./M.A. in Anglophone Studies and the B.A./M.A. in Business Administration and Cultural Studies within the Department of Humanities. His research and teaching focus on poetry and poetics, literary and cultural theory, and popular culture.

**Phoebe Chen** is a doctoral student in the faculty of Education at the University of Cambridge. She is a member of Homerton College and the Research and Teaching Centre for Children's Literature. Her research interests include ecocriticism, speculative fiction, and young adult literature. Her doctoral thesis explores alternative historical modes of human/nonhuman interaction in young adult speculative fiction.

**Mathieu Donner** recently finished his Ph.D. in English at the University of Nottingham. His research focused on the representation of fictional contagious diseases in contemporary American speculative fiction and examined the ways in which these texts may inform our cultural response to real epidemics and those they affect. He is also currently editing a special issue of the *Journal for the Fantastic in the Arts* dedicated to embodiment in young adult speculative fiction and is working on his next project, a study on the impact of capitalism on society as portrayed by contemporary British authors from 1979 to the present.

**Shannon K. Hervey** is a lecturer in the Program in Writing and Rhetoric at Stanford University, where she teaches humanities-based courses dedicated toward developing student researched writing. She graduated from the University of California, Riverside with her Ph.D. in 2015. Her immediate research focus is Rhetoric and Composition pedagogy, especially as it relates to multimodality and the intersectionality of race and sexuality in the writing classroom. More broadly, Dr. Hervey's research interests are at the intersection of composition and American literature and popular culture from 1920 to present day; she is especially interested in the teleology of posthumanist thought and how it is promulgated in the writing we do on a daily basis, for instance, in the space of social networks.

**Angela Suzanne Insenga** received her Bachelor's degree from West Georgia College, her Master's degree from Clemson University, and her doctorate from Auburn University. She is an Associate Professor of English at the University of West Georgia. Her scholarship comprises young adult literature, adolescent literacies, and pedagogy, both collegiate and secondary. In particular, Dr. Insenga's work investigates representations of girlhood in YA literature, and she consistently advocates for curricula and teaching practices that engage students' cultural currency and increase their critical acumen via the deployment of age-appropriate literature.

**Patricia Kennon** is a lecturer in English Literature in the School of Education, Maynooth University, Ireland. She is the president of the Irish Society for the Study of Children's Literature, a former editor in chief and features editor of *Inis: The Children's Books Magazine*, and a former President of iBbY Ireland. Her research interests include young adult science fiction, gender in youth literature and popular culture, horror narratives, and visual culture and picture books.

**Maryna Matlock** is a Ph.D. student at The Ohio State University, where she studies the intersection of young adult literature with fairy tales and other neo-Victorian revenants of fantasy and horror. As an instructor of writing and literature at Ohio State and as a former secondary educator, she greatly appreciates the contribution her students, past and present, make to her work and her life.

**Ferne Merrylees** was awarded a Ph.D. in English from the University of Newcastle, Australia, in 2015. Her body of work included a creative project as well as an exegesis, which explored digital landscapes and the relationships humans have with each other and technology. She has had the pleasure of presenting papers at the 2013 SFRA Eaton Science Fiction Conference in Riverside, California, and the 2014 International Association for the Fantastic in the Arts Conference held in Orlando, Florida. Additionally, she has presented at conferences a little closer to home, such as the 2016 Australasian Children's Literature Association for Research in Wagga Wagga, Australia. Her critical focus is the revolution of social media and technology in young adult science fiction.

**Lars Schmeink**, Ph.D., is Professor of Media Studies at the Institute for Cultural and Media Management at the University for Music and Theater in Hamburg, Germany. He is the president of the Gesellschaft für Fantastikforschung and served as editor of the association's membership journal *Zeitschrift für Fantastikforschung* from 2010–16. He is the author of *Biopunk Dystopias: Genetic Engineering, Society and Science Fiction* (Liverpool UP, 2016), a study of the genetic posthuman in contemporary popular culture, and co-editor of *Cyberpunk and Visual Culture* (Routledge, 2017), which investigates the visuality of cyberpunk. His research has been featured in *Science Fiction Studies, Science Fiction Film and Television*, and *Extrapolation*.

**Anita Tarr** is a Professor of English from Illinois State University, retired, now living on Callawassie Island, South Carolina, a natural playground for alligators, copperheads, Great Blue Herons, and errant golfers. She has published on J. M. Barrie, Thomas Carlyle, Virginia Woolf, Marjorie Kinnan Rawlings, Robert Cormier, and Scott O'Dell, as well as on censorship and children's poetry. In 2006 she co-edited, with Donna White, *J. M. Barrie's* Peter Pan *In and Out of Time: A Children's Classic at 100*. Several presentations and many of the courses she taught focused on fantasy and science fiction. Her favorite young adult science fiction novel is Peter Dickinson's *Eva*.

**Tony M. Vinci** is an Assistant Professor of English at Ohio University-Chillicothe, where he teaches literature, humanities, and creative writing. He is co-editor of *Culture, Identities, and Technology in the Star Wars Films* and has published in the *Faulkner Journal, Journal of Popular Culture, Science Fiction Film and Television, Journal of the Midwest Modern Language Association*, and numerous collections of literary scholarship and cultural criticism. His research interests include twentieth-century American literature and culture, ethics, trauma studies, posthumanism, and speculative fiction and film. His current projects examine how posthumanist theories of ethics and subjectivity necessarily reframe our understanding of the traumatic, especially as narrated in the literature and film of the fantastic.

**Donna R. White** is a Professor of English at Arkansas Tech University, where she teaches courses in young adult literature, graphic novels, folklore, fantasy, and science fiction. She is the author of *Dancing with Dragons: Ursula K. LeGuin and the Critics* and *A Century of Welsh Myth in Children's Literature* and co-editor of *Diana Wynne Jones: An Exciting and Exacting Wisdom*, *J. M. Barrie's* Peter Pan *In and Out of Time*, and *Kenneth Grahame's* The Wind in the Willows: *A Children's Classic at 100*.

# INDEX

Aarne, Antii, 69n1
abjection, 124
*Absolutely True Diary of a Part-Time Indian, The* (Alexie), 27
actualization, 40, 71n10
adolescence, xvi, xvii, xviii, 4, 5, 75; and agency, 18, 27, 30, 81, 90; as alien, 68; as alienation, xvi, xvii, 87–88, 181, 182; and ambiguity, 6, 7; and ambivalence, 201; as analogous to biotechnical modification, 121, 182; as analogous to posthumanism, 201–4, 209, 210, 214, 215, 224; anxieties of, xx; and apathy, 250; and autonomy, 5, 18, 23n5, 81, 83, 76; as becoming, 168; and being human, 160; and body image, xvi, 87, 88, 90, 91, 93, 166, 186, 199, 211, 212, 249; changing paradigms of, 30, 68; and commodification, 167, 218; as danger, violence, suffering, 7, 8, 9, 14, 15, 20; and death, 204, 205, 209; as decentered, 201, 205, 212, 214, 215, 224; and dependence on father, 208, 209, 213, 218, 219, 249; dependent to independent, 5, 9; and disappointment, 228, 243; and embodiment, 179; and homelessness, 50; as hybrid, 251; as in-between-ness, 209, 212, 213, 222, 224n12; as individual to group, 7, 8, 9, 15; as liminal state, 209; and Marxism, 250; as never-never land, 243; as Other, 168; as paradox between seeking uniqueness or belonging, 8, 9, 12, 13; and peer influence, 6–8, 10, 18; as perpetual liminality, 50; perpetual state of, 206, 209, 216, 217, 220–22, 224n5, 224n11; as posthuman construct, 192; as power struggle, 83, 132,

174, 199, 204, 213, 218, 223n5, 249; and regression, 208–10, 213, 220, 224n10; and religion, 204–8, 210; and right to privacy, 83; as rupture, 6; and selfhood, 179; as space of instability, 23; and stories, xvi; traditional paradigms of, 61, 68; as transformation, 203, 209, 211, 217, 218; as transition: latent to active, 5; and violence, 121; as vulnerability, 6, 7, 9, 14, 15, 23
adolescent anxieties, xx, 27, 93
adolescent posthuman, 75
*Adoration of Jenna Fox, The* (Pearson), 30
Adorno, Theodor, 232
Agamben, Giorgio, 237, 239
*Alice's Adventures in Wonderland* (Carroll), 253, 256–58, 269n8
*Alien Chic* (Badmington), xvin2
aliens, xi, xii, xv, xxvi, xx, xxin2, 21, 64, 65, 68, 69, 93, 80, 93, 117, 119, 122, 124, 126, 130, 182, 186, 200–202, 211–13, 218, 221, 224n6, 224n10, 237, 239, 240, 247, 258, 259
Alien films, xx, xxi
Allen, Joseph P., and Jill Antonishak, 11
Ames, Mildred, 71n10
amplifier, 101–4, 108, 113. See also enhancements; prosthetics
Anderson, Benedict, 17
Anderson, Daniel Gustav, 185
Anderson, M. T., 28, 39, 45–51, 71n10
androcentrism, x, 23n4
androids, xiii, xx, xxi, 57–59, 61, 62, 64, 67, 77, 80, 199, 200, 204, 212–16, 223n2, 224n10
*Animal, The* (Derrida), 237, 239
*Animality in Children's Literature and Film* (Ratelle), xvii, 154n3

277

*Animal Rites* (Wolfe), xiv, 142, 230, 242
animals, x, xi, xiii–xv, xix, 79, 142–45, 149, 150, 153, 169–71, 175
animal studies, xiii, xvi, xvii, xviii, 237
Animorphs series (Grant), 122, 129, 130
*Anna to the Infinite Power* (Ames), 71n10
anthropocentrism, xv, xix, 104, 106, 160, 229–33, 235, 239, 242
anti-androcentricism, xviii
anti-anthropocentrism, xviii, 230, 232, 236, 243
anti-humanists, xiv–xvi, 135, 148, 149
apocalypse, xii, xx, 77, 78, 122, 128, 185, 260, 266
apocalyptic posthumanism, xii
Applegate, Katherine, 130
Armitt, Lucy, 233
ARPANET (Advanced Research Agency Network), 23n1
*Art of Place in Literature for Children and Young Adults, The* (Dewan), 179
artificial intelligence (AI), xi, 138, 199
Asher, Jay, and Carolyn Mackler, 28, 33–36, 45, 50, 51
assemblages, xx, 149, 247–49, 252, 252, 255, 258, 263, 266, 267, 269n4
audience, 42; as collective voice, 40, 41
augmentation, xiii, 56, 58, 63, 71n10, 92, 93. *See also* enhancement (augmentation)

Bacigalupi, Paolo, xix–xxii, xxiin6, 159–77
Badmington, Neil, ix, x, xii, xvi, xvii, xxi, xxin2, 113, 137–38, 260
Baggot, Julianna, xix, 76–93
Barad, Karen, 103, 107, 112
Bardugo, Leigh, xix, 97–11
Barrie, J. M., 263, 269n9
Basu, Balaka, Katherine R. Broad, and Carrie Hintz, xvii, 128, 159–61, 174
*Battlestar Galactica* (TV show), xxi
Beauvais, Clémentine, 126
becoming, x, xi, xiv, 98, 106, 107, 168, 172
Bennett, Jane, 186
Berry, Michael, 159
*Between Equal Rights: A Marxist Theory of International Law* (Miéville), 269n3
Bible, 123, 210, 223n4
Bildungsroman, 31, 33, 40, 121, 243

binaries, xv, xx, 8, 10, 12, 13, 20, 21,42, 43, 45, 46–48, 50, 51, 56, 57, 59, 60–62, 64, 68, 69, 80, 85, 97, 98, 100–114, 102, 103, 104–6, 111–13, 119, 120, 123, 124, 137–39, 142, 143, 145, 148, 149, 150, 153, 170, 172, 173, 181, 193–200, 201, 210, 212, 214, 227, 231, 234, 235
bioconservatism, 56, 57, 59, 60, 61, 62
bioconservative and transhumanist debate, 56, 68, 247
biodiversity, 66, 68
bioethical posthumanism, xiii
biological determinism, xix–xx. *See also* genetic determinism
biopolitics, 188–91, 193
biosphere, 137, 147, 149, 150
biotechnology, xi–xiv, xvii, 56, 58, 60, 68, 117, 119, 121, 138, 148
biovalue, xiii
Birns, Nicolas, 248, 270n12
Blanton, Hart, and Melissa Burkley, 8, 12
Blomkamp, Neil, xxi
Bloom, Harold, 270n12
body and boundaries, 12–14, 101, 180, 181, 187, 192
Bolton, Michael Sean, 81
Booher, Amanda, 105, 106
*Book Thief, The* (Zusak), 27
borderlines, 97–98, 107, 111, 114
border wars, 99, 103, 104, 106, 107, 114
boundaries, 98, 99, 103, 106, 107, 110, 120, 121, 123, 124, 269n5
Bostrom, Nick, 59, 120, 190
Boyd, Brian, 269n7
Boyd, Danah, 82, 83
Bradford, Claire, Kerry Mallan, John Stephens, and Robyn McCallum, 57, 120, 132, 181
Braidotti, Rosi, xii, xiii, 98, 143, 146, 147, 172, 177, 183, 270n13
Br'er Rabbit, 42
Bronson, Zak, 260–63, 266
Brooks, Peter, 102
Brothers Grimm, 57, 62
Brown, B. Bradford, Jeremy P. Brakken, Suzanne W. Ameringer, and Shelley D. Mahan, 7, 11
Browning, Robert, 60, 249

Buckingham, David, 31
Bukatman, Scott, 187
Bunch, Mary, 188
Butler, Judith, 15, 16, 103, 107–9, 113, 244
Butler, Octavia E., xviii, 3–23, 23n3, 24n7

Caeners, Torston, xx, 199–226, 273
Campbell, Norah, and Mike Saren, 123
capitalism, xiii, xviii, 46, 159, 160, 164, 166–67, 251, 253, 260, 265, 266, 269n11
Carey, Mike, 28, 30, 39–41; and Peter Gross, 28, 41
Carr, Nicholas, xiv
Carroll, Jane Suzanne, 179
Carroll, Lewis, 253–58, 268
Cart, Michael, and Christine A. Jenkins, 128
Cash, Mason, 7, 9, 11
Castree, Noel, and Catherine Nash, 192
Catts, Oron, and Ionat Zurr, 162
*Chappie* (film), xxin2
Chbosky, Stephen, 27
Chen, Phoebe, xx, 179–95, 273
Chiew, Florence, 180
childhood, 122, 140, 151; and dependence, 23n5; and innocence, 132; as posthuman, 120; as pre-human, 149
child readers, xvi, 253–54
children's literature, xii, xvii, 37, 253, 268; and posthumanism, xvii, 182; and transhumanism, xii
*Children's Literature and the Posthuman: Animality, Environment, Cyborg* (Jaques), xvi
chimera, 168–69, 172, 177
Christianity, 201, 204–7, 210, 213, 221, 224n10, 225n13
Chronicles of Narnia, 228, 231, 232, 257
*Cinder* (Meyer), xviii, xix, 55–58, 61, 64–66, 68–69, 70n2, 70n3, 70n4, 76–93
Cinderella, xix, 55, 56, 62, 64, 65, 66, 69, 70n1, 77, 79, 93
"Cinderella," xix, 56; "Aschenputtel," 62; "Cap o' Rushes," 69n1; "Cat-skin," 69n1; "Cendrillon," 55; "Donkeyskin," 55; "The Glass Mountain," 69n1; "The Little Bull Calf," 69n1; "Yeh-Hsien," 55, 69n1, 70n3, 93n1
*City & the City, The* (Miéville), 248, 268n1

Cixous, Hélène, xiv, 100
Clark, Andy, 13; and David Chalmers, 11
Clark, Bruce, 140
*Clay's Ark* (Butler), 21, 22, 23n3, 24n7
climate fiction ("cli-fi"), xix, xx, 159
clones, xv, xviii, xix, 45, 71n10, 93, 135–48, 150–53, 154n2, 218
*Close Encounters of the Third Kind* (film), xxin2
Coats, Karen, 37
co-evolution, x, xii, 76, 80, 86, 149, 161, 182, 252
collective unconscious, 40, 41, 42, 44, 45, 50
comic books, 39–40
commodification, xiii, 31–35, 46, 166, 167, 189, 218, 261
Conrad, Joseph, 124
consciousness, disembodied, xv, 119, 130, 138, 154n4, 222, 224n12
consumerism, 47–50, 70n4, 268, 270n11
*Contemporary Children's Literature and Film: Engaging with Theory* (Mallan and Bradford), xvii
*Contemporary Dystopian Fiction for Young Adults: Brave New Teenagers* (Basu, Broad, and Hintz), xvii
Cooley, Charles Horton, 88
Copernicus, Nicolaus, 231
Cox, Marian Roalfe, 62, 69n1
*Cress* (Meyer), 69, 70n2
Crew, Hillary, xxiin5, 139, 151–52, 154n2
Critchley, Simon, 7, 14, 18, 22
critical posthumanism, xvi, xv, 80, 161, 172, 177, 192, 199, 200
cultural posthumanism, xiv
Curry, Alice, 179–80, 192
cybernetics, xv, 29, 31, 51, 56, 57, 59, 63, 65–68, 70n8, 71n10
"Cyborg Manifesto, A" (Haraway), 69, 214, 215
cyborgs, x, xii–xv, xviii, xix, xxi, 55–60, 62, 64, 66, 70n4, 77–81, 83, 85, 88–90, 92, 100, 106, 138, 148, 187, 260, 261

Darwin, Charles, x, 201, 206–8, 210, 231
Davies, Helen, 103, 109, 110
Da Vinci, Leonardo, ix
deep ecology, 190

Dekovan, Marianne, 237, 238
Deleuze, Gilles, and Félix Guattari, 266
DeMan, Paul, 236
democracy, xi, xiii, 56
Derrida, Jacques, xiv, 16, 22, 148, 205–6, 208, 209, 213, 230, 231, 236, 237, 239
Descartes, René, xv, 9
Deszcz-Tryhubzak, Justyna, 257
Dewan, Pauline, 179
Dick, Philip K., 80
Dickens, Charles, 41, 251
Dickinson, Peter, xi
disabilities, xiv, xv, 90, 129–30, 131, 149, 183, 184, 186
Disney, 55, 59, 61, 62, 65, 66
*District 9* (film), xxin2
*Disturbing the Universe* (Trites), 81, 122
DNA, x, xx, 63, 136, 138–41, 153, 162, 163, 170, 174, 180, 183, 184, 200, 202, 207, 210–12, 224n13, 252, 260
"docile bodies," 102–5
domes, xix, 77, 81, 89, 117, 121, 131, 132, 186
Donner, Mathieu, xviii, 3–26, 273
doppelgänger, 113, 252
Dougherty, Carol, 223n1
Doughty, Terri, 70n3
Douglas, Mary, 6
Dracula, 4
*Drowned Cities, The* (Bacigalupi), xix, 159–61, 165–77
Duncan, Janet, xiii, xiv
*Dune* (Herbert), 124, 263
dystopia, xix, 32, 75–80, 85, 89, 92, 117, 120–22, 128, 132, 159–61, 166, 167, 174, 176, 177, 181, 184, 192, 260

*Earth Girl* (Edwards), xx, 180–81, 183–85, 188, 189, 191–93
ecocriticism, 189, 192, 193
eco-fiction, 159
ecological crisis, xx, 159, 166, 185, 188, 189, 192
ecological posthumanism, 183, 189, 190, 192
ecosystem, xv, 136, 144, 147, 150
Edwards, Caroline, and Tony Venezia, 262, 268n2, 269n4
Edwards, Janet, xx, 180
Elliott, Anthony, 5, 9

embeddedness, xv, 143, 149, 150, 185–87, 189, 190, 193, 201
embodiment, xiv–xvi, 31, 36, 46, 51, 55, 56, 58, 59, 62, 66, 68, 69, 90, 106, 127, 130, 133, 139, 140, 143, 149, 150, 154n1, 179, 187, 201, 211, 241
enhancements, xi–xiii, xviii, xix, 21, 51, 56, 59, 76, 78, 89, 93, 126, 247, 259, 260
Enlightenment, the, ix, 135
*Environmental Crisis in Young Adult Fiction* (Curry), 179–80
epigenetics, 140, 141
epistēmē, 206, 207, 221
Escher, M. C., 37
*E. T.* (film), xxi
*Ethics of Destruction, The* (Critchley), 18
eugenics, 3, 4, 183
Europeans, 69n1, 93n1, 98, 135
*Eva* (Dickinson), xi
evolution, ix, 21, 56, 76, 119, 120, 123, 133, 186, 188, 193, 201, 199, 203, 208, 211, 269
extended mind theory, 11

fairytale, xx, 55, 56, 59, 62, 64, 67–69, 70n2, 77, 79, 83, 92, 93, 103, 165, 191; posthuman fairytale, xviii, 55, 68, 253
Farmer, Nancy, xix, 135–55
fathers, 34, 40, 43, 45–47, 50, 59, 60n1, 70n8, 82, 83, 139, 146, 161, 165, 173, 175, 189, 202, 204–11, 216, 218–20, 222, 223, 224n5, 224n10, 249
*Fear* (Grant), 124, 127, 128, 130–32
*Feed* (Anderson), 28, 39, 45–51, 71n10
feedback loop, 58
female body, 11, 100, 102, 126, 212; as "docile body," 102, 105, 106; as gendered performance, 102, 103, 105–9; as one step away from being human, 106; as puppet, 103, 105; as spectacle, 101–2, 109, 113
feminism, xiv, xviii, xix, 102, 105, 106, 112, 178, 179
Ferreira, Maria Aline, 19
Fisk, John, 232
Flanagan, Victoria, xviin5, 30, 45, 46, 51, 98, 107, 126, 137, 138
Földváry, Kinga, xxiin5, 120, 185
Foucault, Michel, xiv, 102, 105, 106, 127, 148

# Index

*Frankenstein* (Shelley), 41, 42, 43, 80, 135
Freud, Sigmund, x, 12, 205, 207, 208, 211, 213, 219, 231
Fryer, David Ross, xv
Fukuyama, Francis, xii–xiii, xxin4, 58, 59, 119
Furger, Franco, xiii, xxin4
fusions, 86, 87, 88
*Future of Us, The* (Asher and Mackler), 28, 33–36, 45, 50, 51

Gaiman, Neil, 253–54
Gallagher, Shaun, 11
Gallese, Vittorio, and Alvin Goldman, 12
Garland-Thompson, Rosemary, 131
Garreau, Joel, 76, 119, 120
*Gender Trouble* (J. Butler), 109
genetic determinism, x, 160–65, 170–74, 177, 180, 183–85, 189–91
genetic engineering, xi, xii, xiv, 159, 160, 168, 169, 176
genetic enhancement, xiv, x–xiii, xviii, xix, xii, 180, 193
genetic pattern, 146
genotype, 139, 140, 162, 163
ghosts, xvi, 68, 92, 161, 248, 251, 269n9
*Giver, The* (Lowry), 78
Goebbels, Joseph, 41, 44, 45
Gomel, Elena, 122
*Gone* (Grant), 117, 122, 124, 125, 127, 129, 130
Gone series (Grant), xix, 117–34
Gooding, Richard, xxii
Google, 40, 41
Gottschall, Jonathan, 269n7
Graham, Elaine, xiii, 101–4
Grant, Michael, xix, 117–33
Grey, Chris Hables, xiii
Gross, Peter, 28, 41
Grossman, Lev, xx, 227–47
Gurtler, Janet, 27, 28, 33–38, 45, 50, 51

Haar, Michel, 185
Hade, Daniel, and Heidi Brush, 251
Hageman, Andrew, 159, 171
Halberstam, Judith, and Ira Livingston, 20, 80, 188
half-human (half-man), 169–73, 176
*Hamlet*, ix

Haney, William S., 58
Haraway, Donna, x, xiii, xiv, 69, 92, 99, 100, 103, 105, 106, 113, 114, 214, 215, 230, 230, 237, 239
Harry Potter, 40, 228, 255, 257
Hauff, Wilhelm, 44, 45
Hayles, N. Katherine, xiv–xvi, 28–31, 33, 36, 37, 39, 40, 42, 48, 51, 48, 51n1, 56, 58, 62, 65, 67, 76, 78, 82, 84, 85, 86, 98, 113, 114, 119, 131, 139, 154n1, 260
*Heart of Darkness* (Conrad), 124
Hegel, Georg Wilhelm Friedrich, 215
Heinecken, Dawn, xxiin5
Heise, Ursula K., 238
Herbert, Frank, 124
Herbrechter, Stefan, xv–xvi, 143, 161, 199, 200, 202, 215, 250, 251, 266, 269n5
Hermans, Herbert J. M., 10
*Heroes* (TV show), 122
Hervey, Shannon, xviii, 27–52, 274
Hill, Miranda, 252
Hintz, Carrie, xvii, 78, 128, 158, 160, 161, 174
*His Dark Materials* (Pullman), 255, 257
Hitler, Adolf, 147
Hix, Harvey, 76, 86
Hobbes, Thomas, and John Locke, 29
*Homo sapiens*, ix, xii
Honeyman, Susan, 120
horror, 123, 131, 190, 247–49, 258
*House of the Scorpion, The* (Farmer), xix, xxi, 71n10, 135–55
*How We Became Posthuman* (Hayles), xv, 29, 86, 139, 154n1
Howarth, Jane, 122
human, being (being human), ix, x, xi, xii, xiv, xv, xviii, xix, 117, 118, 121, 124, 135, 136; as "abjectly human," 240, 242; as adaptation, 203; as assemblage, 139, 252; and augmentation, 56; as becoming, x, xi, xiv, 22, 153; as borderless, 20, 22, 75–76; characteristics of, x, 57, 58, 79, 124; as co-evolving, x, xii, 161; as connecting with Others, xii, 187, 188, 231, 238; as cyborg, xii; and DNA, x; and ecological networks, 186; as empathy and compassion, 16, 68, 79, 124, 187; and ethical responsibility, 16, 17; as evolving,

x, xv, xvi; and flexible definition of, xiv, 133; as fluidity and mutation, 22, 93; as friendship, loyalty, courage, 132; as hybrid, 75, 76, 79, 93, 95, 238, 252–53; as informational pattern, 31; as linguistic construct, 235; as multiple subjectivities, xv, 268; as networked, 20, 21; as normativity, 120, 129; as partly Other, 211, 212; as part of nature, xv, xviii, 189; passing as, 71n10, 86, 111; as performance, 21, 22; in a post-crisis environment, 181, 192, 193; questioning of, ix–xi, 75, 98, 114, 200, 201, 203, 247, 268, 269n5; as self-sacrifice, 187; as special, 60, 61; and stories, 269n7; as superior, 76, 79; and technological prostheses, xii, 51; and symbiosis, x; under threat, 78
human and animal, ix, x, xiii, xviii, 27, 79, 86, 160, 153, 168–72, 176, 231, 237–42, 245, 247–53, 259, 261, 265
human and machine, 46, 48, 49, 58, 77, 78, 80, 82, 86, 87, 90, 105, 131, 139, 181, 214–16, 222, 247, 252, 260
human exceptionalism, ix, 103, 112–14, 142, 161, 168, 170, 171, 229, 241, 244
Human Genome Project, x
humanism, ix–xi, xiv–xvi, xix–xxi, 20, 22, 68, 118–20, 122, 147–48, 187, 188, 191–93, 210, 218; and agency, 98, 113, 146; and animals, xiv, 142–43; and anthropocentrism, 135; and autonomy, 98, 103, 146; and belief in human exceptionality, ix, x, 78, 98, 112, 114, 139, 142, 149, 171, 229–32, 238, 241, 243, 244; and binaries, xx, 104, 105, 112, 137, 143; and boundaries, x, 149, 168, 266; and classification, 22, 23; definition of, xv, 135; end of, 98, 112; as freedom from social influence, 29; and hegemony, 107, 108, 112; and language, 98; as masculinist, xiv, 98, 99, 103, 105, 106, 107, 113, 124, 146; myths of, 106, 107, 111, 112; and nationalism, 135; as opposed to animals, 170, 171; as ownership of one's self, 29; questioning of, xiv–xv, 98, 135, 250; and racism, xiv, 135; as rational, 146; and sexism, xiv, 135; and speciesism, 99. *See also* binaries

humans, xii, ix, x, xi, xiii, xiv, xv, 4, 23n2, 41, 43; as already posthuman, 200, 201; as children, adolescents, 203, 204; as commodities, 166, 167, 189; creators of, 201–7; definition of, 16; and environment, 79; and evolution, 80, 86; evolution of, 119, 120, 130; as malevolent parasites, 190; and religions, 208; search for origin of, 199–201, 221, 222
Hume, Kathryn, 232
Humpty Dumpty, 254, 256
*Hunger* (Grant), 120, 124, 125, 130, 131
Hutcheon, Linda, 231
hybridity, xviii, xix, xxi, 11, 33, 36, 38, 40–42, 45, 60, 74, 76, 77, 79, 87, 90, 93, 97–98, 106, 110, 113. 119, 123, 125, 126, 138, 165, 168, 181, 182, 187, 188, 191, 238, 247, 248, 250–53, 258, 259, 261, 265, 269n8
hyperobject, 240–42, 245

identity: as animal, 144, 145; as clone, 150; and confusion, 150, 152; as constructed, 81, 87, 93; legal claim to, 135–36, 141; search for, 159, 160, 174
identity construction, 75, 119, 161, 199, 202–3; and agency, 166; based on ecological embeddedness, 189, 190, 193; and connection with Others, 188, 193; as dialogue between self and society, 81, 82, 85, 86; and DNA, 162, 163; and ecology, 180; as fluid, 201, 203, 219; as fragmented, 92; and genetic heritage, 161, 162, 165, 166; and influence of adults in power, 83, 91; and loss of memory, 84–85; and networking, 82, 90; and peer group influence, 81, 82; and restoration of the past, 180–81, 185, 191, 193; and return to humanism, 191, 193; and self-determination, 163, 164; and separation from phallic mother, 215; and survival, 166. *See also* subjectivity
in-between-ness, xvi, 209, 212, 213, 222, 224n12, 242
*Independence Day* (film), xxi
informatics, x, 28, 39
information narratives, 39
information technology, xii, xiv, 28, 91

Insenga, Angela, xviii, 55–70, 274
internet, 27, 28, 50; addiction, xiv, 35, 36, 46; anxieties about, 27, 28, 29, 30, 31, 32, 33, 38, 46, 48; and collective unconscious, 28, 33, 38, 40; as dangerous, 35, 47; as disenfranchising users, 47; as disturbing selfhood, 31, 33, 35, 45; as extension of the mind, 85; as feed, 28, 33, 45, 46, 47, 48, 49; as inscribing identity, 36, 38, 47, 48, 51; and lack of control, 35, 37, 38; and loss or diminishment of self, 33, 35, 49, 51; and performance of self, 32, 35, 36, 37; and positive experiences, 31, 37; and self-commodification, 31, 32, 34, 35; and silencing, 39; and survival, 40; and writing, 27
intertextuality, 41, 42, 43, 50, 123, 229, 262
Iovino, Serenella, and Serpil Opperman, 190
*Invasion of the Body Snatchers* (film), xxin2
*Iron Council* (Miéville), 258, 259, 268n1
Irwin, W. R., 232

Jackson, Rosemary, 232
Jameson, R. D., 69n1
Jaques, Zoe, xvii, 182, 253
Jay, Stacey, xx, 180, 181, 185–89, 191–93
Jendrysik, Mark S., 190
Jesus Christ, 42, 144, 223n4
*jouissance*, 107, 111
Jones, Adolphe, 51
Jones, Ann Rosalind, 111
*Jud Süss* (Hauff), 44
Jung, Carl, 41, 209

Kass, Leon, 60–61
Keller, Evelyn Fox, 162
Kennan, Patricia, xix, 117–34, 274
King, A. S., 160
King, Steven, 121
*King Lear* (Shakespeare), 62
*King Rat* (Miéville), 249–53, 255, 261, 265, 267–68
Kristeva, Julia, 124, 207–8
Kroker, Arthur, 113–15
Kurzweil, Raymond, xii

Lacan, Jacques, 12, 37, 207, 208, 209, 213, 220
LaCapra, Dominick, 230

*Landscape in Children's Literature* (J. Carroll), 179
Lang, Andrew, 55
language: being deprived of, 240; commodification of, 256; deterioration of, 46, 47, 50; and failure to express, 248; "hidden," 110; as magic, 234–36, 238; and merging with reality, 234, 235; and translation, 236–37; "of women's bodies," 111; and word meanings, 256; used to dehumanize, 169–71, 183, 184, 188, 216, 218
Large, David, 44
Lauder, Hugh, 81
Lawrence of Arabia, 222, 224n7, 224n8
*Lawrence of Arabia* (film), 219–20, 222, 224n8, 224n9
Levinas, Emmanuel, 14, 15, 17, 19
Lewis, C. S., 228, 270n12
liberal humanism, ix, x, xv, 29, 55, 58, 68, 81, 82
liberal humanist subject, ix, x, xiv–xv, 135, 137, 139, 141, 148, 150, 153, 240; as authority, autonomy, and agency, 146–48; and belief in human exceptionality, ix–xi, 231, 232, 243; and binaries, xv; as constructed, xxi; definition of, 146; destruction of, 229, 244; and existing in a posthuman world, 242; as an illusion, 243; and imagined wholeness, 244; and invulnerability, 244; and language, 234; as masculinist, xiv–xv, xxi; merging with posthumanist subject, 138; and perception, 239–41; and speciesism, xxi; as unified subject, 146, 151, 153; without transformation, 243
*Lies* (Grant), 124, 127
*Light* (Grant), 118, 123, 126, 131, 131
*Lion and the Unicorn, The*, 140
"Little Red Riding Hood," 69, 70n2
*Little Women* (Alcott), 27
*Looking for Alaska* (Green), 27
*Lord of Opium, The* (Farmer), xix, 135–37, 139–51
*Lord of the Flies* (Golding), 122
*Lord of the Rings, The* (Tolkien), 123
*Lost* (TV show), 122
Lovecraft, H. P., 268n2
Lowry, Lois, Carrie Hintz, and Elaine Ostry, 78
Lyotard, Jean-François, 12, 217

MacCormack, Patricia, 20, 106
machine, x, xi, xv, 46, 50, 77, 80
Macpherson, C. B., 29
magic and magicians, xix, xx, 55, 62, 63, 65, 77, 99, 227–46, 257, 259
*Magicians, The* (Grossman), xx, 227–47
Maimon, David, 268n1
male gaze, 101–2, 108
Mallan, Kerry, xvii, 120, 57
Marx, Karl, 231
Marxism, xxi, 247–50, 252–59, 261, 265–68, 269n3
Matlock, Maryna, xix, 97–116, 274
Matrix series, The, xi
McCallum, Robyn, 7, 75, 81, 87, 179, 233–34
McCulloch, Fiona, xxii
McDonald, Matthew, and Stephen Wearing, 32
McGillis, Roderick, 123
McHugh, Susan, 241
McIntyre, Lisa, 88
McKibben, Bill, 60
McLuhan, Marshall, 51
McRuer, Robert, 130
Melville, Herman, 270n10
Melzer, Patricia, 3, 4
memory, 45, 84, 85, 146, 204
Mendlesohn, Farah, 68, 121, 181–82
Merrylees, Ferne, xix, 75–93, 274–75
*Messenger of Fear* (Grant), 122
metafiction, 229–31, 233
Meyer, Marissa, xviii–xix, 55–70, 70n2, 70n3, 70n4, 70n8, 75, 79, 80, 82–93
Miah, Andy, xi, xiii
Michelfelder, Diane P., 31, 32, 33
microchips, 136, 137, 146, 147, 152, 153, 154n5
Miéville, China, xx, xxi, 247–72
Milton, John, 43
*Mind of My Mind* (Butler), xviii, 3–26
Minh-ha, Trinh T., 106
mirror neurons, 12
mirrors and mirroring, xvi, 22, 41, 63, 83, 88, 101–2, 105, 108, 113, 162, 200, 202, 220, 248, 252
mirror stage, 220
Mitchell, Jennifer, 58, 70n5
Mixon, Veronica, 4

*Moby Dick* (Melville), 261, 263, 266, 269n10
*Mona Lisa* (da Vinci), 141
monsters, x, xi, xv, xviii, 42, 43, 44, 63, 64, 78, 79, 80, 97–104, 118, 121, 123, 125, 130, 149–51, 153, 168, 169, 186, 187, 248, 251, 255, 259, 270n11
Morley, David, 13
Morrissey, Thomas, 59
Morton, Timothy, 240
Moss, Geoff, 231
mothers, 28, 34, 50, 57, 59, 62, 77, 79, 83, 84, 87, 88, 90, 91, 93n1, 136, 138, 140, 145, 150, 161, 163–66, 175, 215–16, 219, 222, 225n13, 248
Mulvey, Laura, 102
mutations, 77, 80, 86, 90, 117–20, 122–25, 12, 140, 180

nanotechnology, xii, xiv, 77, 82
Nayar, Pramod K., x–xii, 75–76, 78, 80, 86, 93, 138–40, 142, 145, 149, 161, 182, 201, 247, 252, 269n4
Nedelsky, Jennefer, 5, 8, 11, 18
networking, xviii, xxi, 3, 5, 6, 12, 13, 17
*Neverwhere* (Gaiman), 253
Newcomb, Erin, xxin3, 68, 148, 151
Newell, Jonathan, 258
*New World Orders in Contemporary Children's Literature: Utopian Transformations* (Bradford, Mallan, Stephens, and McCallum), xvii, 57, 120
Nietzsche, Friedrich, 214
nonhuman and nonhumanity, x, xii, xvi, xviii, 13, 20, 80, 86, 104, 111, 112, 137, 142, 149, 177, 183, 191–93, 200–202, 211, 230, 231, 233, 237, 238, 239, 240, 250, 253, 268
Nussbaum, Martha, xiii–xiv

Oedipus complex, 219
*Of Beast and Beauty* (Jay), xx, 180, 181, 185–89, 191–93
O'Hara, Daniel, 104
*On the Origin of Stories* (Boyd), 269n7
*Orleans* (Smith), xx, 180, 181, 188–93
Ostry, Elaine, xxin3, xxin539, 71n10, 121, 124, 133, 138, 154n2, 159, 160, 168, 182, 202–3, 218

Other, xi, xii, xv, xviii, xxi, xxii, 12, 14, 16, 17, 18, 19, 22, 37, 58, 77, 80, 92, 98, 102, 104–6, 120, 123, 127, 141, 148–51, 153, 154n4, 160, 168, 177, 211, 212, 214–16, 220, 223n3, 224n6, 241–43
O'Toole, Peter, 219, 222, 224n8
Otto, Eric C., 159
*Our Mutual Friend* (Dickens), 41
*Our Posthuman Future* (Fukuyama), xii, 58, 59, 119
Oziewicz, Marek, Emily Midkiff, Nancy Farmer, and Harold Farmer, 140–41, 154n4

Palmer, Christopher, 251
Panou, Petros, xxii
*Paradise Lost* (Milton), 43
parents, xx, 14, 40, 75, 127, 129, 132, 199, 202–4, 208, 209, 211, 216, 218, 262, 264
Patrick, George A., 110
patriarchy, 101, 103, 111, 113
*Patternmaster* (Butler), 10, 13, 20, 21, 23n3
Pearson, Mary, 30
Pepperell, Robert, 12, 13
*Perdido Street Station* (Miéville), 268n1
*Perks of Being a Wallflower, The* (Chbosky), 27
Perrault, Charles, 55, 59
*Peter Pan* (Barrie), 263
Peter Pan and the Lost Boys, 151
*Peter Rabbit* (Potter), 143
phallocentrism, 111
*Phantom Tollbooth, The* (Juster), 269n8
phenotype, 140
Phillips, Leah, 66, 70n9, 71n9
philosophical posthumanism, xiv, xv
Pickering, Andrew, 113
Pied Piper, The, 249–52
"Pied Piper of Hamelin, The" (Browning), 249
Pinocchio, 150, 217, 220, 243
*Plague* (Grant), 123, 125
*Plutarch's Lives*, 43
popular posthumanism, xi–xii
Porky Pig, 233
postanthropocentricism, xv, 266
postapocalypse, 80, 122, 181, 183

posthuman, xi, xvi, xix, xxi, 20, 29; abilities, 121, 125, 126; agency, 117; and ambiguity, 125; anxieties, 129, 132; child, 119, 126, 225n13; as clones, 138; as cyborg, 138; as different from human, 138; and gender, 125, 126; possibilities, xix–xxi, 106, 119, 133, 169, 179, 182, 192, 201, 217, 213, 221; powers, 132; transformations, 118, 119, 122–25, 128, 131
posthuman body, xviii–xix, 40, 48, 56–60, 76, 79, 80–83, 85, 86, 87, 91, 97, 191, 106, 122, 123; as animal, 132; as battleground for adolescence, 93; as composition of organic matter, 186; as congeries, 80, 86; as cyborg, 187; fears of, 169, 171–72; as futureless, 193; as hybrid, 187; and memory, 84; as power struggle between adolescents and adults, 81–83; as subhuman, 89; as survivor, 79, 88–93, 131; as tolerance, 124; as virtual, 130
posthuman ethics, xiii, xviii, xx, 56, 63, 68, 188, 190, 229, 236; as becoming with Otherness, 235, 238, 245; as beyond boundaries of being human, 239; and invulnerability, 244; and vulnerability, 233, 236; and YA fantasy, 230, 245
posthuman identity, 214, 221; as assemblage, 215; as fragmented, 215; and in-betweenness, 202, 209, 215–19; and loss of borders, 202, 211, 212; as more than human, 216
posthumanism, x–xxi, 4, 19, 20, 23, 61, 68, 247, 248, 258, 260; as adolescent development, 71n10, 201–4, 209, 210, 214, 222, 224n5; and agency, 30, 45, 58; anxieties about, 29, 45, 48, 56, 58, 59, 60, 62, 67, 70n2, 77, 78, 119–21; apocalyptic, xii; as becoming, xvi; bioethical, xiii; and biotechnology, 138, 139, 148; and challenging humanism's binaries, xv, 137, 143; as chaos, 41; co-evolves with environment and technology, 139, 143, 149, 247, 252, 269n4; condition, 68; critical, xvi, 80, 161, 172, 177, 192, 199, 200, 266, 269n4; and critical animal studies, 237; cultural, xiv, xv, xix; and cyborgs, xii; debates about,

119; definition, 142, 143, 148; and democracy, xxi, xiii; as dialogue with nature, 112; dream of, 4, 19, 20, 21, 22; ecological, 183; and estrangement, 39; and evolution, 20, 56; as expansion of being human, 22; as homogenous, 49; and humanism, xv–xvi; and hybridity, 76, 252; as identity, community, and Otherness, xi–xii, xv, xvi, 160; and identity construction, 76; interpretations of, 20, 29; and performativity, 112, 113; as perpetual becoming, xi, 259; philosophical, xiv, xv; as plurality, 5; political, xii, xiii, xiv; popular, xi, xii; questions human exceptionalism, 142; not a replacement for humanism, 137–38, 260, 266, 270n13; as revisioning, xvi; setting, 70n2; and violence, 20; as a world view, 138

*Posthumanism* (Nayar), 138

posthumanist self, xv, 137, 138, 145; as animal and monster, 151; as assemblage, 149, 152, 153; as congeries, 139, 149; as different from human, 138; as interconnected with other organisms, 182; merging with humanist self, 138, 152–53

posthuman possibilities, xix–xxi, 59, 106, 119, 133, 169, 179, 182, 192, 201, 217, 213, 221, 248, 249, 254, 259, 267, 268

posthuman signifier, 207

posthuman subjectivity, xv, xvi, xvii, xix, 148, 180; as adapting to environment, 186, 192, 267, 269n4; as analogous to adolescence, xx, 201–14, 209; and animals, 229, 240; as assemblage, 149, 182, 187; and becoming, 172, 251, 257; as being a magician, xx, 240; as co-evolving, 149, 182; as collective, 137; as congeries, 149; as constructed, 149, 171; and family, 174–75; as a fantasy, 234; as fluid, 137, 149, 159, 152, 153, 229, 236, 242; as fragile, 181, 189, 236, 241; and hybridity, xxi; as incorporating the Other, 149; and interconnection to all life, 176, 180, 181, 186–89; and lack of dignity, 190, 191; and moral accountability, 173, 174; and multiplicity, xv, xviii, xix, 172, 230, 242, 250, 254, 260, 267; as networked, 137; and networking, xviii; as post-natural, 191;

as rejecting genetic determinism, 173; as restoration of the past, 191; as rhizomatic, 267; and social media, xviii; and survival, 191; as vulnerable, 236, 242, 245. *See also* subjectivity

posthuman vs. posthumanism, 138, 148

Potter, Beatrix, 143

*Precarious Life* (J. Butler), 244

Promethean man, 61

Prometheus, 202, 223n1

*Prometheus* (film), xx, 199–226

*Prometheus* (spaceship), 202, 202, 206, 216, 221

prosthetics, xii, 83, 86, 92, 76, 97, 103–6

Protagoras, 135

psychopharmacology, xiv

Pullman, Philip, 270n12

*Pump Six* (Bacigalupi), 159, 168

puppets, 103, 105, 109, 146, 152, 229

*Pure* (Baggott), xix, 76–93

*Question Concerning Technology, The,* (Heidigger), 50

racism, xiv, xvi, 124, 129, 135, 143

*Railsea* (Miéville), 248, 249, 258–68, 269n10, 270n11

Rankin, Sandy, 260

"Rapunzel," 69, 70n2

Ratelle, Amy, xvi

reflexivity, 37, 38, 42, 65

Remnant series (Grant), 130

Renaissance, ix

Reynolds, Kimberley, 123

Rice, Anne, 80

*Robinson Crusoe* (Defoe), 261, 263, 266, 269n10

robots, xi, 87

Rousseau, Jean-Jacques, 12

*Ruin and Rising* (Bardugo), 110–14

Russell, Bertrand, 237

Rutsky, R. L., 20, 22, 23n2

Saint Francis, 144, 145

salvagepunk, 260

Sambell, Kay, 78, 121

Sanders, Joe Sutcliff, 253–55, 257, 258

Sartre, Jean-Paul, 12, 15, 19
Sawers, Naarah, xxiin5, 151, 152
*Scar, The* (Miéville), 268n1
*Scarlet* (Meyer), 69, 70n2
Schmeink, Lars, xix, xx, xxiin6, 159–78, 275
science fiction, xxi, 4, 28, 36, 45, 68, 80, 81, 121, 135, 159, 171; and posthumanism, 199, 200, 202
*Scooby-Doo*, 233
Scott, Ridley, xx, 199
Seaman, Myra, 113, 148
*Seige and Storm* (Bardugo), 110
Sells, Laura, 111
Selye, Hans, 51
*Shadow and Bone* (Bardugo), 97–115
Shakespeare, ix, 62, 227, 236
Shaw, Kristen, 266–67
Shelley, Mary, 80, 135
*Ship Breaker* (Bacigalupi), xix, 159–74, 177
Simon, Bart, xv, xvi
Singer, Peter, xiii
singularity, xii, 104
#16thingsithoughtweretrue (Gurtler), 27, 28, 33–38, 45, 50, 51
slavery, 8, 59, 136, 154n4, 167, 170–72, 218
*Skinned* (Wasserman), 30
Smith, Sherri L., xx, 180
"Snow White," 69, 70n2
social media, xviii, 27, 34; anxieties about, 33; blogs, 28, 34, 40, 41, 45; discussion boards, 41; as disturbing selfhood, 31, 36; and exploring selfhood, 31, 36, 37; Facebook, 28, 32, 36, 37, 38, 39, 51; fan fiction sites, 28, 40, 45; questioning the purpose of, 38; and self-commodification, 33, 34; and self-image, 90; Twitter, 28, 34, 36
*Sorrows of Young Werther, The* (Goethe), 43
speciesism, xxi, 99, 104, 142, 161, 170, 171, 183, 184
Spielberg, Steven, xxin2
*Star Trek: The Next Generation* (TV show), xiii
Stephens, John, xxiin5, 151–52
Stevenson, Robert Louis, 263
story, storytelling, xvi, xvii, 41, 44, 45, 47, 48, 227, 247, 248, 252, 255, 256, 261–65, 269n7; and commodification, 261; and eating, 270n11; and evolution, 269n7; and posthumanism, 261, 263, 267
*Storytelling Animal, The* (Gottschall), 269n7
Sturgeon, Noël, 129
subhuman, xiv, 62, 71n10, 149
subjectivity, x, xix, 5, 6, 7; and agency, 19, 29, 30, 38, 50, 51, 65; as amalgam, 41, 51, 61; and autonomy, 18, 29; as awakening, 4, 17, 18; as boundless, boundaryless, 14, 29; and consumerism, 31, 47, 48, 49; as cultural composite, 29, 49; as defined by masculine traits, 23n4; as dialogue between self and the world, 9, 12, 17, 75; as distributed, 74; as emergent, 76; and environment, 183; and ethical responsibility, 4, 14, 17, 18, 19, 22; and ethics, 3, 4, 14, 15; and genetic engineering, 160; and information technologies, 28, 29, 45, 48; joined with information technologies, 40, 45, 46, 47; as multiple, xv, xix, xx, 18, 19, 22, 29, 30, 31, 56, 63, 64, 66, 67, 68; as mutation and transformation, 40, 51; as networked, xviii, 3, 18, 19, 21; for nonhumans, 171, 176; as part of a collective, 18, 19, 30; as performance, 184; posthumanist, xvii, 30, 45, 49; as self-commodification, 31, 32, 33, 49; and social media, 31; on social media, 32, 34; and violence, 24n6, 40; virtual, 30, 32, 33, 39; as vulnerability, 16, 17, 19, 22; and writing, 32; and zoe-centrism, 161. *See also* posthuman subjectivity
subjectivity, female: and agency, 103, 107, 110; and autonomy, 102, 110; as fluid, 106; as fragmented, 98; as plural, 98, 106, 113; posthuman, 98; as site of subversive performance, 108–10. *See also* posthuman subjectivity
superhuman, xiii, xviii, xix, 20, 97, 98, 117–20, 202, 214, 216, 250
superpowers, xix, xx, 120, 121, 124, 125, 132
suprahuman, 20
*Survivor* (J. Butler), 23n3
symbiosis, x, 19, 58, 103, 143, 252
Symbolic, the, 5, 207

Tarr, Anita, xx, xxi, 247–72, 275
Taylor, Charles, 14
Taylor, Matthew, 183, 192
*Technology and Identity in Young Adult Fiction: The Posthuman Subject* (Flanagan), xvii, 30, 45, 46, 51, 98, 107, 137, 138
telekinesis, 118
Telenet, 23n1
telepathy, 3, 4, 10, 11, 15, 21, 28
teleportation, 118, 125, 180, 183
teratology, 97, 99
Terminator series, The, xi
*Them!* (film), xxi
Thompson, Stith, 70n1
*Through the Looking-Glass* (Carroll), 253–55, 258, 262
Tidwell, Christy, 159, 167, 170
Tolkien, J. R. R., 234, 235, 270n12
*Tool of War* (Bacigalupi), xxiin6
Toomeos-Orglaan, Kärri, 64, 65
Totaro, Rebecca Carol Noël, 191
transhumanism, x, xii, xv, xix, 45, 51n1, 56, 58, 60, 61, 76, 78, 86, 89, 119, 130, 148, 247
*Tremors* (film), 263
*Treasure Island* (Stevenson), 261, 263, 266, 269n10
Trites, Roberta Seelinger, 81, 122, 125, 127, 128
Turner, Victor, 5, 17, 50, 209
*Types of the Folktale, The* (Aarne), 69n1, 70n1

Übermensch, 214
*Uglies* (Westerfield), xi, 116
*Under the Dome* (King), 121
*Un Lun Dun* (Miéville), 248, 249, 251, 253–58, 261, 262, 267, 268, 270n11
*Unwritten, The* (Carey and Gross), 28, 30, 39, 40–45, 50, 51
utopia, xi, xii, 4, 160, 161, 174, 177, 181, 191, 243, 253, 260, 269n9

vampires, 80, 150
ventriloquism, 103
Vermeulen, Peter, 98, 112
Vetlesen, Arne Johan, 14, 15, 18
Vinci, Tony, xx, 227–47, 275

virtual and actual, 28, 33, 35, 36, 38
Vitruvian Man, ix
Von Uexküll, Jacob, 238

Waley, Arthur, 80
Wannamaker, Annette, xxii
Wasserman, Robin, 30
Waugh, Patricia, 229
Webb, Jean, and Stephen Bigger, 192
Werner, Norbert, 65
Westerfeld, Scott, xi, 117
Westfahl, Gary, 182
Weizenbaum, Joseph, 78
*What Is Posthumanism?* (Wolfe), 20, 76, 85–86, 182, 201
*When Species Meet* (Haraway), 230, 237, 239
White, Donna, xix, 135–55, 276
white male subject, 104, 128, 129, 131
*Why Fairy Tales Stick* (Zipes), 57
*Wild Seed* (Butler), 3, 4, 8, 9, 15, 16, 19, 23n3
Williams, Rhys, 266
*Windup Girl, The* (Bacigalupi), 159, 171
*Winter* (Meyer), 62, 67, 70n2
Wittgenstein, Ludwig, 10
*Wizard of Oz, The* (Baum), 269n8
Wolfe, Cary, xii–xiv, 21, 76, 85–86, 119, 142, 170, 182, 201, 216, 227, 229, 230, 241, 245
*Work of Mourning, The* (Derrida), 236
world wide web, xiv, 31. *See also* internet
writing, act of: as an act of agency, 27; as ID, 136, 142; deterioration of, 28; private, 27; public, 27, 31, 32, 34; and technology, xiv

young adult audience, xvi, 75, 77, 80, 97, 119, 126, 181–82, 199, 202, 203, 211, 228, 229, 231, 232–34, 241, 244, 248–49, 252–53, 255, 256, 267, 268
young adult authors, xxi, 121
young adult fantasy, xx, xi, 227–30, 247–49, 251, 253, 257, 258, 267; as commodity, 232–34; as didactic, 230; as escapist, 230–32, 234–35, 243; and magical animals, 242; as posthumanist, 244–45; and posthuman reading practices, 236–37; as revolutionary, 232, 233
young adult literature, xii, xvi, xvii, xviii, xx, 27, 29–32, 37, 39, 45, 50, 51, 68, 76, 78,

79–80, 81, 89, 117, 119, 120, 122, 146, 199, 202, 267; and conservatism, 133; and death, 122, 128; and despair, 78; and didacticism, 118–24, 132, 192; and dystopias, 174; and homosexuality, 127, 128; and hope, 78, 80, 160, 161, 177, 191, 228; and horror, 122, 123; and peer influence, 10, 11; and posthumanism, xvi–xvii, 30, 32, 56, 182; and potential for change, 132; and sexual violence, 125; and subjectivity, 179; and transhumanism, xii; and violence, 122, 123

young adult science fiction, 138, 180–83, 192, 193, 202, 218

Zipes, Jack, 222, 223, 232, 253
*zoe*-centric, 161, 176
zombies, xx, 150
Zuzak, Marcus, 27

# Index

www.ingramcontent.com/pod-product-compliance
Lightning Source LLC
Chambersburg PA
CBHW030608230426
43661CB00053B/1889